Compulsory Purchase and Compensation

AUSTRALIA

The Law Book Company
Brisbane · Sydney · Melbourne · Perth

CANADA

Carswell
Ottawa · Toronto · Calgary · Montreal · Vancouver

AGENTS

Steimatzky's Agency Ltd., Tel Aviv
N.M. Tripathi (Private) Ltd., Bombay
Eastern Law House (Private) Ltd., Calcutta
M.P.P. House, Bangalore
Universal Book Traders, Delhi
Aditya Books, Delhi
MacMillan Shuppan KK, Tokyo
Pakistan Law House, Karachi, Lahore

Compulsory Purchase
and Compensation

JEREMY ROWAN-ROBINSON, M.A., LL.M., *Solicitor*
Legal Associate of the Royal Town Planning Institute,
Professor of Land Economy, Aberdeen University,
Consultant in Planning and Environmental Law,
Paull & Williamsons, Solicitors

C.M. BRAND, LL.B. *Solicitor*
Lecturer in Law at the University of Liverpool,
Editor, Encyclopedia of Compulsory Purchase
and Compensation

LONDON
SWEET & MAXWELL
1995

Published in 1995 by
Sweet & Maxwell Limited of
South Quay Plaza, 183 Marsh Wall, London E14 9FT.
Computerset by Wyvern Typesetting, Bristol.
Printed and bound in Great Britain by
Butler and Tanner Ltd, Frome and London.

No natural forests were destroyed to make this product;
only farmed timber was used and re-planted.

A CIP catalogue record for this book is available from the British Library.

ISBN 0 421 46540 9

Preface

Compulsory purchase is one of the harshest impositions by the state upon its citizens. Although in theory most people might accept that the needs of the individual should give way on occasion to the needs of the wider community, it may be difficult to accept this when faced with the prospect of compulsory purchase in practice. Expropriation often arouses strong feelings of resentment. The primary purpose of this book is to examine the procedures governing the compulsory purchase of land and the safeguards, particularly the payment of compensation, which exist to balance the interests of the state against those of the individual.

However, it is not only expropriation which may cause resentment. Major schemes of works may adversely affect not only those whose interests in land have to be acquired but also those who own land in the vicinity of the works and who will have to live with its consequences. This is well illustrated by the recent controversy over the proposed rail link from the Channel Tunnel to Kings Cross. There will also be many cases where the interests of the state may be sufficiently safeguarded simply by regulation of what happens on land rather than by its compulsory acquisition. Yet, for the landowner, the consequence of regulation will, in some cases, be almost as harsh as expropriation. A secondary purpose of this book is, therefore, to place the law of compensation relating to land in its wider context and to consider the entitlement to some form of recompense in those situations where a landowner suffers loss in the interests of the wider community.

A model for the book was provided by Jeremy Rowan-Robinson's earlier work *Compulsory Purchase and Compensation — the Law in Scotland* which was published by W. Green & Son Ltd in 1990. In August 1992 we set about the process of "translating" that book into English law. This involved rather more than the substitution of the equivalent statutory provisions applicable in England and Wales. Although the United Kingdom is a unitary state with a single legislature, the legal systems in England and Wales, Scotland and Northern Ireland remain separate. They stand, as the Royal Commission on the Constitution (Cmnd.5460, 1973) observed, "in the same juridical relationship to one another as they do individually to the system of any foreign country". Although, therefore, the process of compulsory purchase and compensation in England and Wales follows quite closely the pattern in Scotland, it operates within a separate system of land law. It is governed by a separate body of legislation, it is implemented through a separate administrative structure and it has, of course, a separate body of case law. There are also differences in practice. Inevitably substantial deletions from the original text have been necessary though these have been compensated by appropriate substitute material. While we have attempted, wherever possible, to give prominence to English authorities, we have nevertheless considered it desirable to retain much of the Scottish case law since this will permit the reader of this book to gain easy access to a wider range of illustrations of interpretation of the relevant (or equivalent) statutory provisions. We trust that this approach will be seen as a useful feature of this book.

Apart from the translation aspect of the work needed to produce this text it has of course been necessary to update the law, particularly as a result of the Planning and Compensation Act 1991 with its farrago of provisions affecting both compulsory purchase of land and its closely associated relation, town and country planning. For example, we have included the amendments to the scheme for compensation for loss of residential accommodation (home loss payments) and the introduction of provisions enabling acquiring authorities to make discretionary payments where a claimant cannot satisfy the qualifying conditions for a home loss payment. While advance payment of compensation has been a feature of the compensation scheme since 1973, improvements have been made by the 1991 Act to the advance payment arrangements which now enable additional advances to be paid; in both cases interest is also payable. Other changes to compensation rights (*e.g.* the effective revival of Part IV of the Land Compensation Act 1961) and changes of a procedural nature have all been accommodated in the text of this book.

In writing this book we have tried to bear in mind the requirements of both the practitioner and the student. While we have attempted to win the approval of both we are aware of the risk that, in doing so, neither market segment might be wholly satisfied with the resulting work. In attempting to cater for the needs of both groups of potential readers the book sets out to provide a detailed description of the law as it stands today; it also explains why it is in its present form and offers some comment on its operation. In this latter respect we have been much influenced by the work of other contributors in this field. Notable amongst these are *Cripps on Compulsory Acquisition of Land*, 11th ed. by H. Parrish, and more recently *Environmental Planning*, Vol. IV, by J.B. Cullingworth and the work of Professor Keith Davies of Reading University and of Dr Barry Denyer-Green.

We were both surprised by the magnitude of the task involved in bringing this project to fruition and are appreciative of the generous extension of time granted by our publisher. Preparation of the text involved a very substantial amount of work at the word-processing stage and we are grateful to Amanda Clare of the

Faculty of Law, University of Liverpool, for her invaluable assistance in that department. Finally, we are indebted to our respective wives and families for their uncomplaining acceptance of the inevitable reduction of what has come to be known as quality time.

We have attempted to state the law as at May 1, 1994

Jeremy Rowan-Robinson
C.M. Brand

Contents

3. CHALLENGE IN THE HIGH COURT

4. COMPULSORY PURCHASE: ACQUIRING TITLE

5. COMPENSATION: IINTRODUCTORY MATTERS

6. THE DATE FOR FIXING AND VALUING INTERESTS

7. MARKET VALUE

8. DEVELOPMENT POTENTIAL

9. DISREGARDING THE SCHEME

10. SPECIAL VALUES

11. DISTURBANCE

12. REMAINING LAND

13. COMPENSATION: OTHER MATTERS

14. THE LANDS TRIBUNAL

15. COMPENSATION FOR REGULATION

16. BLIGHT

Table of Cases

Table of Statutes

(References are to paragraph numbers)

1

Table of Statutory Instruments

(References are to paragraph numbers)

Table of Department of the Environment Circulars

(References are to paragraph numbers)

Chapter 1

Compulsory Purchase: Powers

Origins

From time to time land is required for public purposes. Land may be required, **1—01** for example, to widen a road, to build a school, to install a sewage works or achieve a statutory objective such as "regeneration" of the area in which the land is situated. Such land may be, and often is, acquired voluntarily through the normal operation of the market. However, to avoid public purposes being delayed or frustrated by the resistance of a single landowner, land may be acquired compulsorily.

The origins of the power to expropriate land probably lie in the sovereignty of the State. But the notion that the power has a proprietary core and that, as all land is held ultimately of the Crown, the Crown may resume its original grant is generally discredited,[1] so, too, is the argument that a social contract exists whereby an individual acquires property under the implied condition that it is to be surrendered at the demand of the State.[2] In his judgment in *Burmah Oil Co. (Burma Trading) Ltd v. Lord Advocate*,[3] Lord Radcliffe noted that the concept of eminent domain had been developed by the Roman-Dutch school. In litigation arising

---

[1] See Carmen F. Randolph, "The Eminent Domain" (1887) 3 L.Q.R. 314; F. Mann, "Outlines of a History of Expropriation" (1959) 75 L.Q.R. 188; and, generally, the judgments in *Burmah Oil Company (Burma Trading) Ltd v. Lord Advocate* [1965] A.C. 75.

[2] *Ibid.* Although not entering into discussion about the origins of the power of expropriation, both the Committee on the Acquisition of Land for Public Purposes (Scott Committee, Second Report, Cmnd. 9229 (1918), para. 8) and the Expert Committee on Compensation and Betterment (Uthwatt Committee, Final Report, Cmnd. 6386 (1942) para. 32) supported the notion of a social contract.

[3] [1965] A.C. 75.

from deliberate taking and destruction by the Crown of a subject's property in wartime he observed:[4]

> "If the civilian writers are consulted . . . there is not much room for dispute about their general view. The sovereign power in a state has the power of eminent domain over the property of subjects, but may exercise its power only for the public welfare or advantage or in case of necessity . . . The power covers use, acquisition and destruction. If it is exercised, compensation to the person dispossessed is manifest equity, since it is not fair that one citizen should be required against his will to make a disproportionate sacrifice to the common wealth."

Today, the power of the State to take private property for public purposes is vested, almost exclusively, in Parliament. In exercise of the sovereign powers vested in it, Parliament in turn confers conditional powers of compulsory purchase for specified purposes on various agencies of government and on others. However, the decision of the House of Lords in *Burmah Oil* indicates that there remains with the Crown a prerogative power to take or destroy a subject's property in time of war.[5]

DEVELOPMENT OF COMPULSORY PURCHASE POWERS

1—02   It was the agrarian and industrial revolutions which first led to the conferment of extensive powers of compulsory purchase. By the middle of the eighteenth century the movement of population from the towns underlined the need for improved communications. Shortcomings in the statute labour system for maintaining and improving the road network led to the advent of the turnpikes. However, for the bulk transport of raw materials for the new industries attention focused initially on the construction of canals. The railways, many of which began as canal feeders, soon established themselves as major competitors. Competition was fierce and the volume of private legislation required made considerable inroads into parliamentary time. Specific powers of compulsory purchase were also conferred on local authorities to whom responsibility for tackling the worst abuses of the Industrial Revolution was passing. More general powers were contained in the public and general legislation directed at public health, housing and planning which followed in the second half of the nineteenth century and the beginning of the twentieth century.

1—03   The acquisition of land for public purposes was envisaged on a large scale in the period of national reconstruction following the end of the First World War.

---

[4] At p. 129.
[5] But see *Attorney-General v. De Keyser's Royal Hotel Ltd* [1920] A.C. 50, H.L. where it was held that a statute providing for conditional compulsory acquisition of land by the Crown was inconsistent with the continuance of a prerogative right of unconditional compulsory acquisition.

Land would be required for housing, for the development of agriculture and forestry, for reclamation and land drainage, for the provision of an effective and co-ordinated system of transport, for access to natural and mineral resources, for the use of electricity and water power as national sources of energy, for the development of aviation for commercial purposes and for national defence and administration. The first report of the committee dealing with the *Acquisition and Valuation of Land for Public Purposes* (the Scott Committee) emphasised that:

> "Unnecessary delays or prohibitive expenses attaching to the acquisition of land essential for the purposes in question, would be liable to block the whole path of efficient reconstruction, and to stifle at their inception many valuable schemes of productive enterprise."[6]

Similar views were expressed in the final report of the *Expert Committee on Compensation and Betterment* (the Uthwatt Committee) during the Second World War.[7] The simplest and only effective method of coping with the work of post-war reconstruction of towns and cities, concluded the Committee, would be "to confer on the planning authority compulsory powers of purchase, much wider and more simple in operation than under existing legislation, over any land which may be required for planning or other public purposes."[8] Compulsory purchase powers were thus considered to be the key to positive planning. Subsequent legislation conferred on public authorities wider powers of compulsory purchase than ever before in order to cope with war damage, with the blighted areas of towns and cities, with the redistribution of population through the new town and town development programmes, with the programme of nationalisation and with the advance of the Welfare State. These powers have been widely employed to establish the new towns, to tackle town centre redevelopment and to deal with the legacy of substandard housing resulting from rapid urbanisation of the nineteenth century.

> "The rapid build up of the Nineteenth-Century city meant a rapid accumulation of obsolescent houses in the Twentieth Century. This accumulation has been acute since 1945, bringing a heavy emphasis on slum clearance and the corollaries of high-density new development or overspill beyond the city boundary."[9]

The problem was tackled through the designation of comprehensive development areas under the Town and Country Planning Act 1947, supported by a massive programme for land acquisition.

Since the Second World War, both the main political parties have acknow-   **1—04**

---

[6] Cmnd. 8998 (1918), para 4.
[7] Cmnd. 6386 (1942), paras. 6 and 7.
[8] *Ibid.* para. 144.
[9] T. Hart, *The Comprehensive Development Area* (Oliver and Boyd), University of Glasgow Social and Economic Studies Occasional Paper No. 9, 1968.

3

ledged the role of compulsory purchase powers in positive planning. The power to acquire land fundamentally performs an enabling function. However, socialist ideology, as Grant observes:

> "has viewed public ownership of development land not simply as a key to better planning, but as a desirable end in itself. This is partly a nationalisation argument, but it is also based on the clear financial and planning advantages that public ownership is capable of bringing to the community."[10]

Compulsory purchase powers were regarded as an essential component of the three comprehensive attempts by Labour administrations since the War to recover for the community increases in land values resulting from public sector actions and decisions. The financial provisions of the Town and Country Planning Act 1947, the Land Commission Act 1967 and the Community Land Act 1975 all contained compulsory purchase powers, those in the 1975 Act being particularly extensive. The three attempts ran into very considerable difficulties and were dismantled by the subsequent incoming Conservative administrations. The impact of the compulsory purchase powers was in each case limited.

During the late 1960s and the 1970s attention focused on the use of compulsory purchase powers to support the road building programme, in particular the motorways. The impact of the road programme was felt not only by those displaced from property along the line of a new road but also by those living alongside it. The environmental impact of the construction and use of a major new road, especially the urban motorways, could be very considerable. The White Paper *Development and Compensation — Putting People First*[11] acknowledged the need to strike a balance between "the overriding duty of the State to ensure that essential developments are undertaken for the benefit of the whole community and the no less compelling need to protect the interests of those whose personal rights or private property may be injured in the process." The White Paper went on to conclude that in recent years this balance in too many cases had been tipped against the interests of the individual and a better deal in the form of improved compensation was required for those who suffered from desirable community developments. This better deal was implemented in the Land Compensation Act 1973. Similar arguments about the need for a better deal were heard in connection with British Rail's proposal for a high speed rail link connecting the Channel Tunnel to London; these may have been ameliorated by the enactment of the Planning and Compensation Act 1991.

1—05   To avoid public purposes being delayed or frustrated, compulsory purchase powers have continued to be employed during the period of Conservative government dating from 1979 notwithstanding the Government's commitment to the

---

[10] M. Grant, *Urban Planning Law* (Sweet & Maxwell, 1982) Second Cumulative Supplement (1989), pp. 500–501.

[11] Cmnd. 5124 (1972), para. 1.

primacy of the market place. Broad powers were conferred on urban development corporations established under the Local Government, Planning and Land Act 1980 to acquire land for the purposes of achieving the regeneration of specified urban development areas. At a public inquiry in 1987 into objections to a compulsory purchase order made by the London Docklands Development Corporation, the Corporation's principal surveyor in his evidence on the LDDC's policy on land acquisition stated:

> "The Corporation has adopted a substantial and increasing programme of Compulsory Purchase Orders (CPOs) to complement and reinforce negotiations for acquisition by agreement with the owners. The Corporation relies on the effective and speedy resolution of its applications for CPOs to ensure regeneration on the scale and pace desired."

Similarly, Trafford Park Development Corporation have recently been given the go-ahead for a complex compulsory purchase programme as the key to the revitalisation of the Trafford Park Industrial Estate in Manchester, having concluded that normal market forces would be unable to assemble the necessary land and carry out the comprehensive treatment necessary to regenerate the area. The Urban Regeneration Agency established under Part III of the Leasehold Reform, Housing and Urban Development Act 1993 has similar powers, again with the object of regeneration of land, in particular that which is vacant or unused, situated in an urban area and under used or ineffectively used, or contaminated, derelict, neglected or unsightly. The use of such powers is strongly supported by the Royal Institution of Chartered Surveyors; in a paper to the Department of the Environment in July 1993, the RICS called for greater use of compulsory purchase of land to achieve regeneration. As Davies observes:[12] "Compulsory purchase, for all its peculiarities, will long continue to be of practical importance, just as it has been since governments began."

Streamlining procedures

The loss to the individual from the compulsory purchase of land is justified by **1—06** the gain to the wider community of which the individual is a part. The history of the development of compulsory purchase powers is one of striving to achieve a balance between retaining adequate safeguards for the interests of the individual on the one hand and the importance of not delaying schemes which are to serve a much needed public purpose on the other.

---

[12] K. Davies, *Law of Compulsory Purchase and Compensation* (Butterworths, 4th ed.), p. 1.

As already mentioned, it was the agrarian and industrial revolutions which first led to the conferment of extensive powers of compulsory purchase. The harbours, canals and railways which were so much a part of the Industrial Revolution were constructed and operated by private enterprise. These schemes were generally beyond the resources of a single individual. Promoters would therefore petition for private-Act powers from Parliament seeking the benefits of incorporation and the right to expropriate land for the purposes in question so that the schemes could not be held hostage to the whims of a single landowner. Each private Bill was self-contained. It sought compulsory purchase powers in respect of specified land, and made comprehensive provision for the machinery of acquisition and for the assessment and payment of compensation. Before granting such powers Parliament had to be satisfied that the scheme was of public utility. Furthermore, those whose property rights were to be affected by the proposal had to be given notice and accorded an opportunity of being heard. The massive output of private Acts during the railway building age required a correspondingly large input of parliamentary time.

1—07   In order to make more effective use of parliamentary time a series of Clauses Acts were passed during the middle of the nineteenth century. These Clauses Acts, in particular the Lands Clauses Consolidation Act 1845 and the Railway Clauses Consolidation Act 1845 (which concerned taking of land for undertakings of a public nature, and railway undertakings, respectively) contained numerous procedural provisions commonly to be found in each individual private Act promoting a particular type of scheme, whether it was a harbour, a water works or a railway. The appropriate Clauses Act would be incorporated into each private Act passed subsequently concerned with that type of scheme. This would avoid the need to repeat these provisions in the legislation and enable Parliament to focus more attention on the merits of the scheme proposed.

The Lands Clauses Acts were mainly concerned with procedural provisions dealing with the acquisition of land and the assessment and payment of compensation. Many of the procedural provisions are still in force, though by reason of twentieth century legislation now have very limited application. Of the Lands Clauses Acts the principal Act is the Lands Clauses Consolidation Act 1845. Section 1 of that Act (which is still in force) provides:

> "This Act shall apply to every undertaking authorised by any Act which shall hereafter be passed and which shall authorise the purchase or taking of lands for such undertaking, and this Act shall be incorporated with such Act, and all the clauses and provisions of this Act, save so far as they shall be expressly varied or excepted by any such Act, shall apply to the undertaking authorised thereby, so far as the same shall be applicable to such undertaking, and shall, as well as the clauses and provisions of every other Act which shall be incorporated with such Act, form part of such Act and be construed together therewith, as forming one Act."

1—08   The 1845 Act did not, of itself, authorise the acquisition of any land. A private Act would still be required to confer the power to acquire particular land. The

1845 Act would then be specifically incorporated into the private Act (referred to as the "special Act")[13] although certain provisions might be expressly excluded.

As originally enacted, the provisions of the 1845 Act were grouped under a number of headings including the purchase of lands by agreement, the purchase of lands otherwise than by agreement, the application of compensation, conveyances, and entry on lands. The drafting and arrangement of the provisions in the 1845 Act did not escape criticism,[14] and practical difficulties arose from the procedure for resolution of disputes relating to compensation. This proved too cumbersome, involving in many cases the assembly of a jury. The Acquisition of Land (Assessment of Compensation) Act 1919 made new provision for dealing with such disputes by conferring jurisdiction on official arbitrators, a jurisdiction which was subsequently vested in the Lands Tribunal by the Lands Tribunal Act 1949. The 1845 Act has, for the most part, since been superseded by the Compulsory Purchase Act 1965, though the 1845 Act is still relevant to some compulsory acquisitions.

Notwithstanding the Lands Clauses Act, private Bill procedure was not well-suited to the seemingly unending series of schemes of development which were coming forward in the mid-nineteenth century. As Wraith and Lamb observe:[15] "It was a mode of legislation appropriate to a simple society with poor communications, and one which had a high respect for the rights of property, but it was becoming increasingly expensive and time-consuming in the context of a developing country." A comparatively more efficient procedure, involving an application for a provisional order began to replace private Bill procedure about that time and removed from Parliament much of the time-consuming task of scrutinising proposals. Private Bill procedure is, nonetheless, still employed today on occasions as a means of acquiring compulsory purchase powers where provisional order procedure is considered inappropriate. Notable examples are the Felixstowe Dock and Railway Bill, which became the Felixstowe Dock and Railway Act 1988 and the Zetland County Council Bill which became the Zetland County Council Act 1974, which provided, amongst other things, for the compulsory acquisition of land by order for harbour purposes and for the huge Sullom Voe oil terminal in Shetland.[16] With regard to the latter, the Bill proved particularly controversial as

1—09

---

[13] "Special Act" refers to "any Act which shall be hereafter passed which shall authorise the taking of lands for the undertaking to which the same relates, and with which this Act shall be so incorporated as aforesaid" (1845 Act, s.2).

[14] For example, in *Heriots Trust Governors v. Caledonian Railway Co.*, 1915 S.C. (H.L.) 52; 1915 1 S.L.T. 347 Lord Chancellor Haldane said "The Act is badly drawn. The draftsman seems in more places than one not to have realised clearly the matter of the changes which he was seeking to effect. I think it is idle to find in the various sections a constant and harmonious purpose."

[15] R.E. Wraith and G.B. Lamb, *Public Inquiries as an Instrument of Government* (George Allen and Unwin, 1971) pp. 18–19.

[16] The passage of the Bill was described in C.M.G. Himsworth, "The Origins and Legislative History of the Zetland County Council Act 1974," unpublished paper presented to a seminar on Legal Research Related to the Social and Economic Impact of Offshore Oil and Gas, Centre for Petroleum and Mineral Law Studies, University of Dundee, 1979.

it proposed that objections to an order on the grounds that acquisition was unnecessary or inexpedient should be disregarded. Other recent examples are provided by the British Railways Act 1992 and the British Railways (No.2) Act 1992 which both detail a large number of railway engineering works and conferred powers on the British Railways Board to acquire compulsorily land required for the purpose of the authorised works. The key to the private Bill procedure is the committee stage which follows the second reading. The committee has to decide whether the need for the powers sought is established. Procedure is quasi-judicial with the promoter calling witnesses to give evidence who may be cross-examined by those opposing the Bill and with the opponents also giving evidence. The committee proceedings on the Felixstowe Dock and Railway Bill lasted 24 days; the amount of parliamentary time required for this and other private Bills was reviewed by a Joint Select Committee of both Houses which recommended that a non-parliamentary procedure involving a public local inquiry would be more desirable.[17]

1—10   Application for a provisional order pursuant to a public general Act was made, not to Parliament, but to a Minister and notice would be given to those most closely affected. The Minister, in the event of objection, would arrange for a public local inquiry to be held by commissioners to consider the proposal and any objection to it. After receiving the report of the commissioners the Minister was empowered to make a provisional order. Such an order was of no effect unless and until it was confirmed by Act of Parliament. The Minister, having made an order, would promote a Provisional Order Confirmation Bill. If, as was usually the case, the Bill was passed without opposition there would be a considerable overall saving of both time and expense. On the other hand, if as occasionally happened the Bill was opposed in Parliament, it would have to go through the equivalent of private Bill procedure and hence the whole process from petition for a provisional order to eventual enactment would be very time consuming. The Confirmation Act became the "special Act" for the purposes of the Lands Clauses Consolidation Act 1845.

Provisional order procedure is still occasionally encountered. In the context of local government, use is sometimes made of the provisions of section 240 of the Local Government Act 1972 which specifies the procedure to be followed where a statute provides for conferment of additional powers on a local authority by means of an order which is "provisional only". But examples of such "provisional only" powers are now rare.[18] Where the procedure is invoked the applicant local

---

[17] *Report of the Joint Committee on Private Bill Procedure*, session 1987–88, H.L. 97; H.C. 625; (July 1988). The Report contains a comprehensive appraisal of private Bill procedure in the twentieth century. The recommendations of that report were accepted in *Private Bills and New Procedures—A Consultation Document*, Cm. 1110 (1990) and ultimately in legislation in the form of the Transport and Works Act 1992. This Act applies to the construction or operation of railways, tramways, trolley vehicle systems, other guided transport systems and inland waterways and enables such projects to be authorised by statutory instrument made by the Secretary of State.

[18] See the Local Government Act 1972, s.262(10).

authority must advertise the purport of the order in the *London Gazette* and one or more local newspapers. This may lead to objections, in which case the Secretary of State will convene a public inquiry (unless for any special reasons he considers an inquiry is unnecessary) and after considering the objections may agree to submit the provisional order for confirmation by Parliament. Opponents to the confirmation Bill can nevertheless present a petition against the order, in which case the petitioners are entitled to be heard by the Select Committee to which the Bill is referred.

In 1918 the Scott Committee,[19] looking ahead to the period of national reconstruction which would follow the First World War, drew attention to the "indefensible complexities" of the procedures for acquiring land for public purposes. The Committee concluded that: "The need of establishing some simpler, more uniform, less costly, and more expeditious system for the compulsory acquisition of land for any purposes of national importance appears, therefore, to be imperative." The Committee's report produced no immediate response but aided the gradual transition in public and general Acts from provisional order to the modern compulsory purchase order, a transition which continued up to the end of the Second World War. The effect of the transition was that once Parliament had conferred a general power on, for example, a local authority to acquire land compulsorily for public purposes, the exercise of the power by the authority in a particular case was removed from the scrutiny of Parliament and placed wholly under the control of a Minister.[20] The public and general Act under which the purchase was authorised together with the compulsory purchase order were together treated as the "special Act" for the purposes of the Lands Clauses Consolidation Act 1845.

1—11

The Uthwatt Committee in 1942 endorsed the conclusion of the Scott Committee about the need for a "simpler, more uniform, less costly and more expeditious system for the compulsory purchase of land" for public purposes in the aftermath of the Second World War.[21] The somewhat draconian measures proposed by the Committee were not implemented, but in the Acquisition of Land (Authorisation Procedure) Act 1946 a standardised procedure for compulsory purchase was at last introduced. This procedure, which operates today, is now contained in the Acquisition of Land Act 1981. It is considered in detail in Chapters 2 and 3.

The procedure draws on the experience of earlier legislation. Its centrepiece is the compulsory purchase order. The procedure differs slightly according to whether the order is promoted by a local or other authority or by a Minister. A local authority seeking to acquire land compulsorily makes such an order which

1—12

---

[19] *First Report of the Committee on the Acquisition of Land for Public Purposes*, Cmd. 8998 (1918).
[20] Local authorities were empowered to make compulsory purchase orders by s.161 of the Local Government Act 1933, if that procedure was prescribed by any enabling Act passed after June 1, 1934.
[21] *Final Report of the Expert Committee on Compensation and Betterment*, Cmd. 6386 (1942), para. 158.

is submitted for confirmation by the Secretary of State. Notice of the making of the order must be given to those whose interests the acquiring authority seeks authority to acquire and to the public at large. In the event of an objection by a person whose interest is being acquired a public inquiry must be held. The Secretary of State's decision to confirm the order must be notified to those with an interest in the land and to the public at large. There is an opportunity to challenge the validity of the order by way of application to the High Court on specified grounds within six weeks of publication of the notice of confirmation. The compulsory acquisition of certain special categories of land (*e.g.* land forming part of a common or open space or held inalienably by the National Trust may still, however, be required to go through an additional parliamentary procedure (termed "special parliamentary procedure") under the Statutory Orders (Special Procedure) Acts 1945–65.

The 1946 Act not only introduced a standardised compulsory purchase procedure, it incorporated a provision which had appeared in earlier legislation allowing for entry onto the land following service of a notice of entry in advance of agreement or on determination of the compensation and in advance of the conveyancing formalities. However, provision for early entry on to the land was not enough in some cases. Acquiring authorities sometimes needed to be able to obtain title to the land speedily. An expedited completion procedure first appeared in the sixth Schedule to the Town and Country Planning Act 1944. The procedure was restricted in its scope and was subject to ministerial direction. These limitations were gradually removed and the expedited procedure for vesting title in the acquiring authority, which involves the making of a "general vesting declaration", was fully established by the Town and Country Planning Act 1968. The relevant legislation is now the Compulsory Purchase (Vesting Declarations) Act 1981.

1—13   The Uthwatt Committee was concerned not only with the need for simpler and more uniform acquisition procedures but also with the need for much wider compulsory purchase powers to facilitate the task of the public sector in the period of reconstruction following the Second World War. Wide enabling powers were subsequently conferred by the Town and Country Planning Act 1947 on planning authorities to secure the comprehensive development of an area. These powers are now contained in section 226 of the Town and Country Planning Act 1990 and empower planning authorities to acquire land compulsorily for development, redevelopment or improvement and for the proper planning of an area. Wide general powers to acquire land compulsorily for the purpose of discharging any of their functions are also conferred on local authorities by section 121 of the Local Government Act 1972.[22]

At the beginning of this section of this chapter it was suggested that the history of the development of compulsory purchase powers has been one of striving to

---

[22] The Community Land Act 1975, which was directed at bringing development land into public ownership, contained an almost unlimited power to acquire land compulsorily.

achieve a balance between retaining adequate safeguards for the interests of the individual on the one hand and the importance of not delaying schemes which are to serve a much needed public purpose on the other. Modern compulsory purchase procedure appears to strike a reasonable balance. On occasion, however, it would seem that the dictates of public policy have tipped the balance somewhat against the individual. The New Towns Act 1981, for example, permits the Secretary of State to disregard an objection to a compulsory purchase order if he is satisfied that the objection is made on the grounds that the acquisition is unnecessary or inexpedient.[23]

Construction of compulsory purchase powers

In the search for the appropriate balance between the interests of the individual **1—14** on the one hand and the importance of not delaying schemes which are to serve much needed public purposes on the other, the courts have tended to side with the individual. Indeed the general rule in the interpretation of statutes which interfere with property rights is that they are subject to restrictive construction.[24] Thus an acquiring authority has no rights beyond those expressly conferred;[25] it may not, where it is authorised to acquire land compulsorily for specified purposes, exercise those powers for a different purpose;[26] and it must act in good faith.[27]

In *De Rothschild v. Secretary of State for Transport*[28], however, the Court of Appeal firmly rejected the proposition that there were to be derived from case law special tests which are applicable whenever a court is considering a challenge to an exercise of compulsory purchase powers, beyond those which are normally applied by the courts in reviewing the actions and decisions of public bodies. There was no question that a higher standard falls to be applied by the courts relating to the scope of the powers conferred on an acquiring authority on the ground that the

---

[23] Sched. 4, Part 1, para. 4(3). The Community Land Act 1975 contained a similar provision (see s.15 and Sched. 4).

[24] St J. Langan, *Maxwell on the Interpretation of Statutes* (Sweet & Maxwell, 12th ed.), Chap. 11.4; S.G.G. Edgar, *Craies on Statute Law* (Sweet & Maxwell, 7th ed.), Chap. 12.3. And see *Moncrieffe v. Perth Harbour Commissioners* (1846) 5 Bell 333; *Simpson v. South Staffordshire Waterways Company* (1865) 34 L.J. Ch. 380.

[25] *Marquess of Breadalbane v. West Highland Railway Co.* (1895) 22 R. 307; *Attorney-General v. Frimley and Farnborough District Water Company* [1908] 1 Ch. 727; *Sovmots Investments Ltd v. Secretary of State for the Environment* [1977] 1 Q.B. 411.

[26] *Municipal Council of Sydney v. Campbell* [1925] A.C. 338; *Proctor and Gamble Ltd v. Secretary of State for the Environment* (1991) 63 P. & C.R. 317.

[27] *Stockton and Darlington Railway Co. v. Brown* (1860) 9 H.L. Cas. 246, *Michael v. Corporation of Edinburgh* (1895) 3 S.L.T. 109.

[28] [1989] J.P.L. 173. See, too, *Singh v. Secretary of State for the Environment* [1989] 24 E.G. 128; and, generally, Chap. 3, para. 3–04. *et seq.*

compulsory acquisition of private property takes place against the wishes of the owners and occupiers.

1—15   The powers of compulsory purchase are conferred on an acquiring authority in furtherance of a particular legislative objective and consequently an agreement in which an authority binds itself not to use those powers will be void.[29] It would appear, though, that there is nothing wrong in an acquiring authority giving an undertaking not to implement the powers conferred by a compulsory purchase order if the owner is prepared to fulfil the purpose for which the land was to be acquired in a rapid and effective manner.[30] However, in *R. v. Secretary of State for the Environment, ex p. Leicester City Council*,[31] McCullough J. held that the Secretary of State had not erred in law in refusing to confirm a compulsory purchase order where the acquiring authority had offered undertakings to individual owners of plots of the order land. The undertakings had been to the effect that the authority would not compulsorily acquire the land so long as the owners entered into agreements to make financial contributions towards the construction of roads and sewers. The Secretary of State was not satisfied that the order land was required to be compulsorily purchased for the purposes of redevelopment and improvement. Nor had the Minister erred in his conclusion that if he confirmed the order in these circumstances he would be exercising his power for an improper purpose, namely as a means of inducing the owners to make financial contributions to the development of the land.

---

[29] *Ayr Harbour Trustees v. Oswald* (1883) 8 App. Cas. 623.
[30] See, for example, *Singh v. Secretary of State for the Environment* [1989] 24 E.G. 128, in which the Court of Appeal noted that such undertakings are often given. The order will be valid notwithstanding that the resolution to make it stated that it would be withdrawn if the objectives of the order were achieved by the owners to the satisfaction of the acquiring authority: *Riddle v. Secretary of State for the Environment* [1988] 42 E.G. 120.
[31] (1988) 55 P. & C.R. 364.

Chapter 2

Compulsory Purchase: Procedures

The procedures[1] for making and, where appropriate, the confirmation of a com- **2—01**
pulsory purchase order are regulated in most cases by the Acquisition of Land Act
1981.

The 1981 Act procedures were applied to compulsory acquisitions by local
and other authorities under public and general Acts in force at the time of its
commencement and also to such acquisitions by certain Ministers under specified
Acts.[2] They are usually, but not always, incorporated with authorising Acts passed
subsequently. There are essentially two relevant procedures depending on
whether the acquiring authority is a Minister or a local or other authority.

Section 2(1) of the 1981 Act now applies so that the authorisation of any
compulsory purchase of land otherwise than by a Minister shall be conferred by
an order (a "compulsory purchase order") in accordance with the provisions of
Part II of the Act. Compulsory acquisitions by Ministers are effected pursuant to
compulsory purchase orders made in accordance with Schedule 1 to the Act.[3]

Some, though only a few, enactments are excepted from the 1981 Act proced- **2—02**
ure by virtue of the inclusion of relevant provisions regulating the procedure in
each Act. These include the Pipe-lines Act 1962, the Forestry Act 1967, the
Development of Rural Wales Act 1976 and the New Towns Act 1981. The
procedure in such cases is broadly similar to that of the 1981 Act. The Housing
Act 1985, whilst applying the 1981 Act procedure to the acquisition of land for
the provision of housing (section 578), makes a number of modifications to that
procedure. The same modifications apply to compulsory acquisition for the pur-

---

[1] See, generally, *Encyclopedia of Compulsory Purchase and Compensation* (Sweet & Maxwell). For Ministerial guidance see Department of the Environment Circular 6/85 and Welsh Office Circular 11/87.
[2] 1981 Act, s.1(1)(a).
[3] 1981 Act, s.2(3).

pose of implementing a renewal area designation pursuant to Part VII of the Local Government and Housing Act 1989.

What follows is a detailed description of the procedure set out in Part II of the 1981 Act. Reference should be made to the appropriate legislation for the position where an Act prescribes its own procedure or modifies the 1981 Act procedure. Part II of the 1981 Act applies to purchases by local and other authorities, including urban development corporations and statutory undertakers. Acquisitions by Ministers are considered below.[4]

Orders made by local and other authorities

1. INVESTIGATING OWNERSHIP

2—03   Once the decision has been made to acquire land compulsorily, a local authority, statutory undertaker or other acquiring authority, will investigate the ownership position, so that they can compile the schedule of ownership which forms part of a compulsory purchase order and so that they can serve relevant notices. Research into ownership or "referencing" requires meticulous care to identify the correct names of interested parties, the boundaries of each plot described in the schedule to the order (and shown on the plan accompanying the order) and the rights (if any) to which the land is subject, *e.g.* easements. To aid this research local authorities have a general power[5] to require the occupier or other person having an interest in the land to state the name and address of the owner, mortgagee or lessee, and some statutes may make their own specific provision in this connection.[6] Where title to the land is registered, office copies of the details entered in the district land registry can be obtained from the registrar.[7]

A tactic which has sometimes been employed to frustrate the acquiring authority has been to fragment the ownership of land needed for the project thus enormously increasing the burden of investigating ownership. Provision is made by section 6(4) of the 1981 Act for dealing with cases where reasonable inquiry has been made but it has not been practicable to ascertain the name and address of an owner, lessee or occupier of land which will allow the acquiring authority to proceed. In such cases service of documents is achieved by addressing the documents to the "owner", "lessee", or "occupier" of the land and delivering it to a person on the land, or if there is no one there, by leaving it on or near the land.

---

[4] At para. 2–30.
[5] Local Government (Miscellaneous Provisions) Act 1976, s.16.
[6] See, for example, the Town and Country Planning Act 1990, s.330.
[7] Land Registration Act 1988, s.1.

2. THE FORM OF THE ORDER

A compulsory purchase order which is made under Part II of the 1981 Act must **2—04**
be in the prescribed form and must describe by reference to a map the land to
which it applies (section 10(2)). The form which the order must take is prescribed
by regulations made by the Secretary of State. The current regulations are the
Compulsory Purchase of Land Regulations 1990.[8]

The regulations provide a style of the several forms (forms 1–11) which should
be used for, and which should be closely followed during, the compulsory purchase process. Styles of the following forms are provided:

— the form of the compulsory purchase order;[9]
— the form of the newspaper notice of the making of a compulsory purchase
  order;
— the form of notice to owners, lessees and occupiers of the making of a
  compulsory purchase order;[10]
— the form of advertisement and notice of confirmation of a compulsory purchase order;
— the form of newspaper notice of the giving of a certificate under sections
  16 or 19 of the 1981 Act.

Of these, the form of the compulsory purchase order bears close examination.
The order is headed with the title of the Act or Acts authorising compulsory
purchase. The order commences with the name of the acquiring authority, gives
the precise statutory authority for the compulsory purchase, and specifies the purpose for which the order is made. It concludes by stating the name of the order
so that it can be correctly cited – for example "The Borough of Redtown (Union
Street) Compulsory Purchase Order 1994."

The land to be acquired is described by reference to an accompanying schedule **2—05**
and map. The schedule is prepared in five columns setting out

1. the number on the map of each plot to be acquired (where more than one
   plot is being acquired);
2. the extent, description and situation of the land (notes accompanying the
   form advise that sufficient detail should be given to tell the reader approxi-
   mately where the land is situated without reference to the map);
3. the names of the owners or reputed owners;
4. the names of the lessees or reputed lessees; and

---

[8] S.I. 1990 No. 613.
[9] Six possible forms are prescribed, form 1 being the most commonly required. Forms 2–6 accommodate orders made in respect of clearance areas or in respect of the vesting of exchange land.
[10] Two possible forms are prescribed, form 8 being the more commonly required. Form 9 accommod-
   ates orders made on behalf of parish or community councils.

5. the names of the occupiers (except licensees or tenants for a month or less).[11]

The schedule will also show separately any "special category" land being acquired (see below) to which additional protection against compulsory acquisition applies. The colour coding or other method used on the map to identify the land to be acquired must be described; the map should clearly delineate the boundaries of each plot and should contain sufficient typographical detail to enable the situation of the land to be readily identified and related to the description given in the schedule. The scale of the map will normally be 1:500 or 1:1250. The map should state that it is the map referred to in the order, repeating the title of the order. The order itself should be sealed by the acquiring authority immediately after the schedule, signed by authorised officers and bear a date. It is necessary to seal the order map too. It is desirable to prepare several sealed copies of the order and map.[12]

3. THE MINING CODE

2—06 Section 3 and Schedule 2, paragraph 2 to the 1981 Act make provision for the acquiring authority, if they so wish, to incorporate with the legislation authorising the purchase what is generally referred to as the "mining code". If the code is not incorporated, the minerals lying under the land being acquired are included in the purchase and the compensation may reflect their development potential. To avoid paying such compensation, the general practice is to incorporate the mining code so that the mineral rights are not acquired by the authority.

To incorporate the mining code, a paragraph in the compulsory purchase order will specifically include section 3 of and Schedule 2, Part II to the 1981 Act and, if considered appropriate, Parts II and III of the Schedule. These provisions correspond to section 77 and sections 77–85, respectively, of the Railways Clauses Consolidation Act 1845, provisions which may occasionally be relevant when the 1981 Act does not apply. The terminology of the 1845 Act (which refers to railways and railway companies) may need to be modified in the order to refer to the land being acquired and to the acquiring authority.

If only Part II of Schedule 2 to the 1981 Act is incorporated in the order, the minerals are deemed to be excluded from the acquisition unless expressly conveyed except such as may have to be extracted or used during the construction of the works. The person entitled to the minerals may work them subject to obtaining any necessary grant of planning permission.

---

[11] A specimen schedule containing model entries appears as Appendix U to Circular 11/87.
[12] See the checklist of documents to be submitted to the Secretary of State contained in Appendix A to Circular 6/85.

The incorporation of Parts II and III of Schedule 2 into the order will, however, impose some constraint on the winning and working of the minerals. Thirty days notice will have to be given to the acquiring authority of an intention to work mines under or within 40 yards, or such other prescribed distance from the land acquired.[13] The notice is intended to give the authority an opportunity to consider whether such working might damage their interest. If they think it will, they may serve a counter-notice identifying the area which should remain unworked stating their willingness to treat with the owner and pay compensation for sterilising the minerals. If the parties are unable to agree on the amount of compensation the matter is referred to and determined by the Lands Tribunal.[14]

4. SPECIAL CATEGORY LAND

The schedule to the order, in addition to detailing the ownership position, will identify any "special category" land which is being acquired. The special categories are identified by sections 17–19 of the 1981 Act, as amended. They comprise land forming part of a common, open space, or fuel or field garden allotment,[15] land held inalienably by the National Trust, land belonging to a local authority or land acquired by statutory undertakers[16] for their purposes of the undertaking. These categories of land are subject to special procedural requirements.

2—07

In so far as an order authorises the compulsory purchase of land belonging to and held inalienably[17] by the National Trust, then in addition to the normal procedure, section 18 provides that the order is to be subject to special parliamentary procedure in any case where an objection has been made by the Trust and has not been withdrawn.

An order which includes land forming part of a common, open space or fuel or field garden allotment will also be subject to special parliamentary procedure unless the Secretary of State is satisfied that other land has been or will be given in exchange or that the land is being purchased in order to secure its preservation or improve its management[18] or (in limited cases) that an exchange is unnecessary

---

[13] 1981 Act, Sched. 2, paras. 1(3) and 3(1).

[14] 1981 Act, Sched. 2, para. 3(4).

[15] "Common" is defined as including any land subject to be enclosed under the Inclosure Acts 1845–1882 and any town or village green; "fuel or field garden allotment" means any allotment set out as a fuel allotment or field garden allotment under an Inclosure Act; "open space" is defined as any land laid out as a public garden, or used for the purposes of public recreation, or land being a disused burial ground: 1981 Act, s.18(4).

[16] "Statutory undertakers" means: (a) persons authorised by any enactment to construct, work or carry on any railway, light railway, tramway, road transport, water transport, canal, inland navigation undertaking, dock, harbour, pier or lighthouse undertaking or any undertaking for the supply of hydraulic power, or (b) the Civil Aviation Authority; or (c) the Post Office: 1981 Act, s.8(1).

[17] As to the meaning of land "held inalienably" see s.18(3) of the 1981 Act.

[18] s.19(1)(aa), inserted by s.70 of and Sched. 15, para. 12(1) to the Planning and Compensation Act 1991.

and he certifies accordingly (section 19(1)). Such other land to be given in exchange must not be less in area and must be equally advantageous to the persons, if any, entitled to rights of common or other rights, and to the public; and it must be vested in the persons in whom the order land was vested and subject to the like rights, trusts and incidents (section 19(1)(a)). The Secretary of State may only conclude that an exchange is unnecessary where the order land does not exceed 250 square yards in extent or is required for the widening or drainage of an existing road (section 19(1)(b)).

2—08   Where the Secretary of State proposes to certify that he is satisfied that land has been or will be given in exchange or that an exchange is unnecessary he must, before giving the certificate, direct the acquiring authority to publish notice of his intention to do so and afford an opportunity to all interested persons to make representations and objections (section 19(2)). If he considers it expedient to do so, he may cause a public inquiry to be held. Notice of the proposed issue of a certificate must be published by the acquiring authority in a form and manner which can be prescribed by the Secretary of State.[19] The Secretary of State has not yet exercised this power but it was held in *Wilson v. Secretary of State for the Environment*[20] that a clear and unambiguous notice which appeared once in each of two local newspapers is sufficient for this purpose. If a certificate is ultimately issued this will be the subject of further publicity by way of a newspaper notification in the prescribed form.[21]

The third class of special category land is identified by section 17(1) of the 1981 Act, namely land belonging to a local authority[22] or land acquired by a statutory undertaker for the purposes of their undertaking. The protection of the requirement of special parliamentary procedure does not apply, however, where the acquiring authority is itself a local authority or statutory undertaker or is one of the following authorities: an urban development corporation, the Land Authority for Wales, a Minister, the Peak Park Joint Planning Board or the Lake District Special Planning Board. Given these exceptions, the scope of the protection is limited but will apply *vis-à-vis* land belonging to a local authority or statutory undertaker where an objection is made by them to the compulsory purchase order and is not withdrawn.[23]

2—09   Special parliamentary procedure is an additional hurdle to which such compulsory purchase orders will be subject. The procedure is set out in the Statutory

---

[19] s.19(2A), inserted by s.70 of and Sched. 15, para. 12(1) to the Planning and Compensation Act 1991.

[20] [1973] 1 W.L.R. 1083.

[21] 1981 Act, s.22 and form 11 contained in the Schedule to the Compulsory Purchase of Land Regulations 1990 (S.I. 1990 No. 613).

[22] "Local authority" means a county or district council, a London borough council, the Common Council of the City of London and any joint authority established under Part IV of the Local Government Act 1985: 1981 Act, s.17(4). Special parliamentary procedure is not required in the case of compulsory acquisition by the Urban Regeneration Agency: s.169 of, and Sched. 20, para. 3 to the Leasehold Reform, Housing and Urban Development Act 1993.

[23] See, also, ss.16 and 31 of the 1981 Act.

Orders (Special Procedure) Acts 1945–65 and does not come into operation until the 1981 Act procedure has been completed.[24] A compulsory purchase order which is subject to special parliamentary procedure will be of no effect until it has been laid before Parliament and has been brought into operation in accordance with the provisions of the Special Procedure Acts. Petitions may be presented against the order within 21 days of the date on which it is laid.[25] The 1945 Act draws a distinction between petitions of "general objection" and petitions merely of "amendment".[26] Petitions are examined by the Lord Chairman of Committees and the Chairman of Ways and Means who will prepare a report to be laid before both Houses of Parliament. Either House may within 21 days resolve that the order be annulled. If no petitions are presented, the order comes into operation at the end of that period. Failing that, the petitions are referred to a joint committee of both Houses for consideration. The committee may report the order to both Houses for approval with or without amendments or, where there is a petition of general objection, report that the order be not approved. Where the compulsory purchase order is reported without amendment, it will generally come into operation on the date on which the report is laid before Parliament. Where the order is reported with amendments it will come into operation, as amended, on a date to be determined by the Minister. If the Minister does not accept the amendments, he may withdraw the order or, alternatively, submit the order to Parliament by means of a Bill for further consideration. Where the committee report that an order be not approved, it will not take effect unless it is confirmed by Act of Parliament. The joint committee has power to award costs.[27]

5. NOTICE OF THE MAKING OF THE ORDER

The compulsory purchase order requires confirmation from the authority speci- **2—10** fied in the authorising Act as having power to authorise the purchase (referred to as the "confirming authority"). For most purposes, the confirming authority is the Secretary of State for the Environment or the Secretary for Transport; other Ministers also have relevant powers but these are less frequently invoked. However, before submitting the order for confirmation, the body promoting the order must comply with a two-fold notice requirement.

First of all, the acquiring authority must serve on every owner, lessee and occupier (except tenants for a month or for a lesser period) of any land comprised in the order, a notice in the prescribed form[28] stating the effect of the order and

---

[24] Statutory Orders (Special Procedure) Act 1945, s.2(1).
[25] The manner in which petitions are to be presented is regulated by standing orders of the House of Commons (see Standing Order No. 240).
[26] Stautory Orders (Special Procedure) Act 1945, s.3(2).
[27] *Ibid.* s.7.
[28] See form 8 contained in the Schedule to the Compulsory Purchase of Land Regulations 1990.

that it is about to be submitted for confirmation. The notice must also specify the time, not being less than 21 days from the service of the notice, within which, and the manner in which, objections to the order may be made.[29]

In the case of parties having minor periodic tenancies some difficulties can arise in determining whether there is a duty to give personal notice of the making of the order. The 1981 Act gives some assistance by providing that statutory tenants within the meaning of the Rent Act 1977 or the Rent (Agriculture) Act 1976 and a licensee under an assured agricultural occupancy within the meaning of Part I of the Housing Act 1988 are all deemed to be tenants for less than a month (section 12(2)).

In *EON Motors Ltd v. Secretary of State for the Environment*[30] it was held that a tenancy granted on terms that the tenant would pay every quarter a rent calculated on the basis of £20 per week was a weekly tenancy so that the tenant company was not entitled to notice of the making of the order even though it had been in occupation for seven years. Sir Douglas Frank Q.C. said that the requirement to give notice "could not be for the benefit of those who had been tenants for a long time, but for the protection of those who might be entitled to remain for a long period."

2—11   The effect of the notice requirement is that there is no question of a proposal being made to expropriate a person's interest in land without their knowledge. This derives from the private legislation procedure of the nineteenth century which required that no Act which touched private property should be passed without notice being given to the landowners concerned.

Section 6(1) of the 1981 Act makes provision for various means of service of a notice; service may be effected by delivering it to the person concerned or leaving it at that person's proper address or by post provided that it is sent by registered letter or the recorded delivery service.[31] The "proper address" is a reference to the person's last known address or, where the person to be served has furnished an address for service, that address.[32] Service on an incorporated company or body is to be effected by service upon the secretary or clerk of the company or body[33] and the proper address in such a case is the registered or principal office of the company or body.

If the acquiring authority is satisfied after reasonable inquiry that it is not practicable to ascertain the name or address of an owner, lessee or occupier of land, the notice may be served by addressing it to him by the description of "owner", "lessee" or "occupier" of the land to which it relates (describing it), and by

---

[29] 1981 Act, s.12(1).
[30] [1981] J.P.L. 576. See, too, *McMillan v. Inverness County Council*, 1949 S.C. 77; 1949 S.L.T. 77 (small landholder with a right of common grazing in the order land not entitled to notice); and *Grimley v. Minister of Housing and Local Government* [1971] 2 W.L.R. 449 (person having the benefit of an easement of support over the order land not entitled to notice).
[31] Recorded Delivery Service Act 1962, s.1(1).
[32] 1981 Act, s.6(3).
[33] 1981 Act, s.6(2).

delivering it to some person on the land, or, if there is no person on the premises to whom it may be delivered, by leaving it or a copy of it on or near the land.[34]

The 1981 Act also requires notice of the making of the order to be given to   **2—12** the public at large.[35] This requirement implicitly recognises that there may be people who will be adversely affected by the public acquisition of the land who are not entitled to individual notice. These include, for example, tenants for a month or less who may, nonetheless, have occupied the property for many years. Notice must be published for two successive weeks in one or more local newspapers. The form of the notice is prescribed in the Compulsory Purchase of Land Regulations 1990.[36] The notice must state that the order has been made and is about to be submitted for confirmation; it must describe the land in question and the purpose for which it is required; it must name a place locally where the order and map may be inspected; and it must specify the time, not being less than 21 days from the first publication of the notice, within which, and the manner in which, objections to the order may be made.[37]

Having satisfied the requirement to give notice, the body promoting the compulsory purchase order will submit it to the confirming authority for confirmation.

6. OBJECTION

Objections should be sent in writing to the Secretary of State at the address given   **2—13** in the notice and within the time specified.[38] There is no special form for objections; a letter is sufficient.

There are no statutorily prescribed grounds of objection but one or more of the following grounds are commonly employed.

First of all, the objector may attempt to show that there is no need for the scheme for which the land is being acquired. Compulsory acquisition is justified by public necessity; if there is no such necessity, the case for compulsory acquisition collapses. It should be stressed, however, that public authorities do not lightly embark on expropriation. Such an objection is likely to require considerable preparation of technical evidence and will not often succeed. Nevertheless, subject to what follows, the need for the scheme should not be taken for granted.

In some cases, the need for the scheme will have already been established prior to the making of the compulsory purchase order, thus rendering such an objection

---

[34] 1981 Act, s.6(4) as amended by s.70 of and Sched. 15, para. 8 to the Planning and Compensation Act 1991.

[35] s.11(1).

[36] See form 7 contained in the Schedule to the Compulsory Purchase of Land Regulations 1990.

[37] The notes accompanying the prescribed form state that the period of 21 days excludes the date of first publication.

[38] In *Wilson v. City of Glasgow District Council* (1986), unreported (but see (1987) 21 S.P.L.P. 43) it was held by the Court of Session that it was not enough to prove dispatch of an objection; it must reach the Secretary of State. In that case a letter of objection was not received.

pointless. For example, section 245(1) of the Town and Country Planning Act 1990 permits the Secretary of State, as confirming authority, to disregard an objection to an order for the compulsory purchase of land which has been made for planning purposes under sections 226 and 228 of the 1990 Act, where the objection amounts in substance to an objection to the provisions of the development plan defining the proposed use of the land. The merits of the development plan will have been open to question at an earlier stage, and provided the plan is not out of date there would seem little point in repeating the exercise.

2—14   Similarly, there is little point in questioning the need for a scheme which is being carried forward as a part of established government policy. It will, for example, be too late to object to the government's civil nuclear power programme when land is being acquired for a nuclear power station; and it will be too late to object to the need for a bypass when the land is being purchased for its construction. The ability to question government policy is discussed further in the context of public inquiries (see below).

Secondly, an objector could seek to show that the importance of retaining the land in its existing use should override the purpose for which it is being acquired. Arguments about the importance of continuing the agricultural use of the land, for example, may carry weight and the owner is likely to be well placed to pursue such an objection.

Thirdly, an objector may seek to question the manner in which a scheme is to be implemented. For example, although an objector to a compulsory purchase order might not be able to challenge the need to redevelop the area for which his land is being acquired — the need having been established in the development plan — he might wish to object to the way in which it is proposed to be redeveloped. The objection in such a case is questioning whether the public need for which his land is being acquired will be served or best served by the proposed manner of implementation.

2—15   Fourthly, an objector may seek to show that slight adjustment to the boundary of the land to be acquired or some slight alteration to the manner in which the scheme is to be implemented would substantially reduce the impact of the order on his interest without prejudicing the scheme. An objector is likely to be better able to appreciate the impact of the order on his interest than the promoter. Such an objection can often be resolved by negotiation with the promoter leading, for example, to agreement over some slight alteration to the boundary of the scheme or to the carrying out of accommodation works designed to reduce its impact.

Fifthly, an objector may argue that public acquisition of his land is unnecessary because he is able and willing to implement the purpose for which it is proposed to acquire his land. He may, for example, be ready, perhaps in conjunction with other landowners, to bring land forward for redevelopment as proposed by the authority. Or the owner of a house in a housing renewal area may object to its compulsory acquisition on the ground that he will undertake to improve or demolish the house, as the case may be.[39]

---

[39] But see *Vassily v. Secretary of State for the Environment* [1976] J.P.L. 364.

Such an objection may be inappropriate where the acquisition is with a view to securing some public provision, for example, the building of a secondary school. And it may be contrary to the philosophy of the legislation under which the order is being promoted. For example, the Secretary of State, when considering a compulsory purchase order promoted under the New Towns Act 1981 may disregard an objection that public acquisition of the land is unnecessary or inexpedient.[40]

Finally, an objector may attempt to argue that there is a better alternative site **2—16** where the scheme could be implemented. Where such an objection is to be maintained at a subsequent public inquiry, the Secretary of State may require that sufficient details of the proposed alternative site are provided to enable it to be identified. The Secretary of State will then notify any owner of the site of the basis of the objection and allow an opportunity for representations to be made.

It would seem as regards alternative sites that "as long as the objectors can put forward a prima facie case, the onus will be on the acquiring authority to rebut that case.[41] In *R. v. Secretary of State for the Environment, ex. p. Melton Borough Council*[42] a local authority made a compulsory purchase order in respect of land required for the construction of a rear service road to the main shopping street in Melton Mowbray. Two possible routes had been considered by the local authority. The order site necessitated the taking of part of several buildings and part of a supermarket car park. The alternative route was said by the authority to raise planning and legal obstacles although the nature of these obstacles was not very fully explored by the authority's planning officer in his evidence at the subsequent public inquiry. The Secretary of State refused to confirm the order on the basis that he was not satisfied that the alternative route was not viable. The local authority applied for judicial review of the decision. Forbes J. dismissed the application observing that

> "[b]ecause it was the acquiring authority's duty to show that the acquisition was necessary it was its duty to lay before the Secretary of State the information necessary to convince him of that fact. If they failed to do so the Secretary of State was fully entitled to say 'I refuse to confirm this order'."

There was no obligation on the Secretary of State or his inspector to search around to make good the lacunae in the acquiring authority's case.

Where, however, the Secretary of State is minded to confirm a compulsory **2—17** purchase order notwithstanding an objection that there is a more suitable alternative site, it appears that the burden upon him is heavier. In *Prest v. Secretary of*

---

[40] New Towns Act 1981, s.10 and Sched. 4, para. 4(3).
[41] See the comment at [1986] J.P.L. 192 by M. Purdue on *R. v. Secretary of State for the Environment ex p. Melton Borough Council* [1986] J.P.L. 190. The Secretary of State acts unlawfully if he confirms a compulsory purchase order on the ground that the objector has failed to show that alternative schemes are superior: *de Rothschild v. Secretary of State for Transport* [1989] J.P.L. 173.
[42] [1986] J.P.L. 190.

State for Wales[43] the Welsh Water Authority made a compulsory purchase order for 30 acres of an estate for the construction of a sewage works. The owner did not agree with the site selected by the water authority and offered a choice of two others. The water authority argued at the inquiry that the construction costs on the order site would be cheaper. The owner subsequently pointed out that the cost of acquisition of the order site would be greater because of its development potential. The Secretary of State's decision confirming the order made no mention of the difference in the cost of acquisition. The Secretary of State's decision was quashed on appeal because in exercising his discretion to confirm the order the Secretary of State had failed to inquire into a vital consideration, namely the respective land values of the two sites. Watkins L.J. described the Secretary of State's role in dealing with a compulsory purchase order as:

> "if not inquisitional, surely investigatory, especially when he was given notice of a relevant matter which might affect his decision by a person likely to be affected by it. He must acquaint himself from the formidable amount of assistance available to him in his department and from public inquiry, with all the information which was indispensable to the making of a just and equitable decision in the making of which he was entrusted with a broad discretionary power. The proper use of a discretionary power was in peril if less than the information essential for its exercise was available to him. If proper use involved him in "routing around"—see *Rhodes v. Minister of Housing and Local Government* [1962] 1 W.L.R. 208 at page 213 . . . he must either cause that to be done or resolve the issue in favour of the landowner."

2—18   If an objector succeeds in persuading the confirming authority as to the merits of an alternative site, there is no question of the order being confirmed in respect of that site. All that will happen is that the order for the subject land will not be confirmed and it will be for the promoter to decide whether to bring forward a new compulsory purchase order for the alternative site.

An objection which relates exclusively to matters within the jurisdiction of the Lands Tribunal may be disregarded by the confirming authority.[44]

Where objection is made to a compulsory purchase order the confirming authority will notify the acquiring authority of the objection and will encourage negotiation with the objector with a view to resolving the matter. If no objection is made, or if all objections so made are withdrawn, the confirming authority may, if he thinks fit, confirm the order with or without modifications.[45]

7. THE RIGHT TO BE HEARD

2—19   In the nineteenth century, the standing orders of both Houses of Parliament pro-

---

[43] [1983] J.P.L. 112.

[44] 1981 Act, s.13(4). The Lands Tribunal deals not only with matters of disputed compensation but also, for example, with notices of objection to severance (see para. 4–15).

[45] 1981 Act, s.13(1).

vided that a person to whom notice of the proposed legislation dealing with the compulsory acquisition of his land had been given was entitled to be heard in support of any objection.[46] This safeguard has been carried through into the 1981 Act. If any objection which has been duly made by a "statutory objector", *i.e.* an owner, lessee or occupier (except a tenant for a month or any period less than a month) is not withdrawn, the confirming authority *must*, before reaching a decision on the order, either cause a public inquiry to be held or afford the objector an opportunity of appearing before and being heard by a person appointed for the purpose.[47] It is not altogether clear what the difference is between a public inquiry and a hearing but the implication is that the latter is less formal and less public. The use of a hearing is rare.

If the only objections to an order are from third parties (*i.e.* persons other than statutory objectors), the confirming authority is not obliged to hold a public inquiry but may do so at his discretion.

For the objector, the public inquiry will be the focal point of the decision making process. The inquiry has two related purposes. In the context of compulsory purchase, it provides those most closely affected by the order with an opportunity to be heard in defence of their property; and it enables the confirming authority to be better informed about the facts and opinions relevant to the decision he must make.[48]

Although the inquiry is convened in response to an objection, it would seem that with orders promoted by local authorities and statutory undertakers it is not simply an opportunity to hear the objection. It is not, as with orders promoted by Ministers, a departmental inquiry into objections;[49] it is an investigation conducted independently of the promoter with a view to informing the confirming authority.[50] The confirming authority must be satisfied that there is sufficient evidence regarding the need to acquire the land. "I am quite clear," said Denning M.R. in *Coleen Properties Ltd v. Minister of Housing and Local Government*,[51] "that the mere *ipse dixit* of the local council is not sufficient. There must be some evidence to support the assertion." In that case a local authority made a compulsory purchase order in respect of two rows of substandard houses in a clearance area. Included in the order land was a modern building in good condition situated on

2—20

---

[46] In *Cooper v. The Board of Works for Wandsworth Corporation* (1863) 14 C.B. (N.S.) 180 it was held to be a well established common law principle that no man could be deprived of his property without having an opportunity of being heard.

[47] 1981 Act, s.13(2) and the Compulsory Purchase by Non-Ministerial Acquiring Authorities (Inquiries Procedure) Rules 1990 (S.I. 1990 No. 512), r.2.

[48] See, generally, R.E. Wraith and G.B. Lamb. *Public Inquiries as an Instrument of Government* (George Allan and Unwin, 1971). Also the *Report of the Committee on Administrative Tribunals and Inquiries*, Cmnd. 218 (1957).

[49] See as regards orders promoted by Ministers *Re Trunk Roads Act 1936* [1939] 2 K.B. 515. Some Acts make it clear that the purpose of an inquiry is simply to hear objections; see, for example, the New Towns Act 1981 s.10 and Sched. 4, para. 4.

[50] *Magistrates of Ayr v. Lord Advocate* 1950 S.C. 102.

[51] [1971] 1 W.L.R. 433 at p. 437. But see *Migdal Investments Limited v. Secretary of State for the Environment* [1976] J.P.L. 365.

the corner where the two rows of houses met. The building was required, stated the authority, for the satisfactory development or use of the cleared area. At the local inquiry, however, the authority called no evidence as to the need to acquire the building. The inspector conducting the inquiry concluded that acquisition of the building was not reasonably necessary and recommended that in that respect the order should not be confirmed. The Minister nonetheless confirmed the order. The Court of Appeal, applying the "*Ashbridge* formula,"[52] held that since there was no evidence that the acquisition of the building was reasonably necessary for the development or use of the cleared area the Minister's decision was *ultra vires*. Sachs J. stated:

> "When seeking to deprive a subject of his property and cause him to move himself, his belongings and perhaps his business to another area, the onus lies squarely on the local authority to show by clear and unambiguous evidence that the order sought for should be granted."[53]

Similarly, in *Prest v. Secretary of State for Wales*[54] Watkins L.J., in the Court of Appeal, stated that statutory authority for the destruction of proprietary rights

> "was not to be used unless it was clear that the Secretary of State had allowed these rights to be violated by a decision based upon the right legal principles, adequate evidence and proper consideration of the factor which swayed his mind into confirmation of the order sought."

The need for the confirming authority's decision to be based on sufficient evidence is sometimes expressed in terms of an "onus" on the acquiring authority to show that the order should be confirmed.[55]

2—21   As a first step towards discharging this onus, acquiring authorities are urged by Ministerial guidance to provide statutory objectors with a written statement of their reasons for making the order.[56] This is later developed into a more detailed "statement of case" which must be served not later than 28 days before the

---

[52] The formula was spelt out by Lord Denning M.R. in *Ashbridge Investments Ltd v. Minister of Housing and Local Government* [1965] 1 W.L.R. 1320 and sets out the grounds upon which a court may interfere with a Minister's decision (see para. 3–05).

[53] [1971] 1 W.L.R. 433 at pp. 439 and 440.

[54] [1983] J.P.L. 112.

[55] See *Brown v. Secretary of State for the Environment* (1978) 40 P. & C.R. 285, *per* Forbes J; *Prest v. Secretary of State for Wales* [1983] J.P.L., 112, *per* Watkins L.J. and *R. v. Secretary of State for the Environment, ex p. Melton Borough Council* [1986] J.P.L. 190, *per* Forbes J. But see *Errington v. Metropolitan District Railway Co.* (1882) 19 Ch.D. 559, *per* Brett L.J. at p. 576; *Company Development (Property) Ltd v. Secretary of State for the Environment* [1978] J.P.L. 107; and *De Rothschild v. Secretary of State for Transport* [1989] J.P.L. 173, *per* Slade L.J. See, too, *Vassily v. Secretary of State* [1976] J.P.L. 364 for an example of a case where the onus was shifted to the objector.

[56] Department of the Environment Circular 6/85 para. 15. The statement of reasons will normally be issued to statutory objectors at the same time as service of notice of the making of the order.

inquiry.[57] Where the statement of reasons refers to a view expressed by a government department to the promoter about the proposed compulsory acquisition, a copy of the statement must be supplied by the acquiring authority.[58]

Difficulties may be encountered by objectors where the statement of case contains such a reference or otherwise indicates that the case for acquisition is founded on national policy. The order land may, for example, be required for the construction of a nuclear power station. Objectors may wish to question the necessity for this only to be told that the need to construct a programme of such stations is a matter of government policy and that the inquiry, while it may examine the reasons for selecting the site, will not inquire into the need for nuclear power stations. Although a statutory objector (or the acquiring authority) may request that a representative from any government department referred to in the statement of case as expressing a view on the proposals contained in the order should be available at the inquiry[59] and although the representative must state the reasons for this view and give evidence and be subject to cross-examination to the same extent as other witnesses, the inspector conducting the inquiry will disallow questions which in his opinion are directed to the merits of government policy.[60] The explanation for the difficulty in which objectors may find themselves is that Ministers and not civil servants are answerable for policy and they, in theory, are accountable to Parliament. In other words, the need to build nuclear power stations will, or should have been, already established at this level. In these circumstances, objectors may find themselves having to advance their objection in isolation from the thing objected to.

"Policy," as Lord Diplock observed in *Bushell v. Secretary of State for the Environment*[61] is a "protean word" and it may sometimes be difficult to distinguish between matters of fact, about which the confirming authority must satisfy himself that there is sufficient evidence, and matters of government policy, which will not be in issue at the inquiry. In *Bushell* the majority of the House of Lords held that particular methods of traffic forecasting employed to determine motorway construction priorities were an essential element of government policy and were thus unsuitable for investigation by individual objectors at individual local inquiries.[62] **2—22**

Public inquiry procedure is governed by the Compulsory Purchase by Non-Ministerial Acquiring Authorities (Inquiries Procedure) Rules 1990. The Secretary of State will appoint a person to hold the inquiry and to report to him,

---

[57] Compulsory purchase by Non-Ministerial Acquiring Authorities (Inquiries Procedure) Rules 1990, r.7(1).

[58] *Ibid.* r.7(2).

[59] *Ibid.* r.13(1).

[60] *Ibid.* r.13(2), (3). The dividing line between questions directed at clarifying government policy, (which are permitted) and questions directed to the merits of government policy (which are not permitted) will sometimes be difficult to draw.

[61] [1980] 3 W.L.R. 22.

[62] See, too, *Lithgow v. Secretary of State for Scotland*, 1973 S.C.1.

generally referred to as "the inspector". Forty-two days notice in writing of the date, time and place of the inquiry must be given to the acquiring authority and to every person who has lodged and not withdrawn an objection.[63] With the agreement of the acquiring authority and all statutory objectors a shorter period may be substituted. Notice of the inquiry arrangements is also published in a local newspaper by the acquiring authority if the Secretary of State directs them to do so.[64] A site notice is also displayed by the acquiring authority on or near the land and in other public places in the locality unless the Secretary of State waives this requirement.[65] All public notices must give at least fourteen days notice of the forthcoming inquiry.

Reference has already been made to the requirement to serve on each statutory objector a written statement of the acquiring authority's reasons for making the order (rule 7(2)).[66] A copy of the statement is also supplied to the Secretary of State. The statement of reasons must be accompanied by copies of any documents, including maps and plans which the acquiring authority intends to refer to or put in evidence at the inquiry. Other interested persons must also be given a reasonable opportunity to inspect and take copies of the statement of reasons and the other documents.[67] The statement of case may subsequently be altered or added to by the acquiring authority during the inquiry with the consent of the inspector.[68] Statutory objectors must, however, be given an adequate opportunity, if necessary by adjourning the inquiry, to consider such changes.

2—23   The acquiring authority, the statutory objectors and any other person who has notified the Secretary of State of his wish to appear are entitled to give evidence at the inquiry; any other person may appear at the discretion of the inspector conducting the inquiry.[69] The authority may appear by an officer appointed by them for the purpose or by counsel or solicitor; any other person may appear on his own behalf or be represented by counsel or solicitor or by any other person.[70]

Subject to the provisions of the 1990 Rules, the procedure at the inquiry is determined by the inspector.[71] He will state at the commencement of the inquiry the procedure which he proposes to adopt.[72] Generally, the acquiring authority will be heard first; other persons entitled or permitted to appear will be heard in such order as the inspector determines.[73] Any closing statements will be made in

---

[63] Compulsory Purchase by Non-Ministerial Acquiring Authorities (Inquiries Procedure) Rules 1990, r.11(2).

[64] *Ibid.* r.11(6).

[65] *Ibid.* r.11(5).

[66] At para. 2–21.

[67] *Ibid.* r. 7(6)

[68] *Ibid.* r.15(8).

[69] *Ibid.* r.12(2). The discretion to permit other parties to appear is normally exercised in favour of the requesting party since permission to do so must not be unreasonably withheld.

[70] *Ibid.* r.12(3).

[71] *Ibid.* r.15(1).

[72] *Ibid.* r.15(2).

[73] *Ibid.* r.15(2). The inspector may, with the consent of the acquiring authority, alter the arrangements.

the order directed by the inspector subject to a right of final reply granted to the acquiring authority by rule 15(2).

The acquiring authority and statutory objectors are entitled to make opening statements, to call evidence and to cross-examine persons giving evidence;[74] any other person appearing at the inquiry may call evidence but may cross-examine only to the extent permitted by the inspector.[75] The inspector may require evidence to be given on oath.[76]

Any evidence may be admitted at the discretion of the inspector and he may direct that documents tendered in evidence should be available for inspection by any person entitled or permitted to appear at the inquiry and that facilities be afforded for taking or obtaining copies.[77] However, the inspector may refuse to permit the giving of evidence which he considers to be irrelevant or repetitious.[78]

    2—24

Should a statutory objector or other person entitled to do so fail to appear at the inquiry, the inspector may at his discretion nonetheless proceed with the inquiry. If he does so, he must disclose to the inquiry and take account of any previous written representations of such objector.[79]

It is clearly desirable that the inspector should see the land which is the subject of the compulsory purchase order. He may make an unaccompanied inspection of the land before, or during the inquiry without giving notice of his intention to any person entitled to appear at the inquiry.[80] He may, and must if so requested by either the acquiring authority or a statutory objector, inspect the land during or after the close of the inquiry in the company of a representative of each of the acquiring authority and the statutory objectors.[81] When an inspection is to take place, he must announce the date and time of the inspection during the inquiry.[82]

8. POST INQUIRY PROCEDURE

After the close of the inquiry the inspector will prepare his report to the Secretary of State. This must include the inspector's conclusions and recommendations or the reasons for not making any recommendations.[83] No other requirements are specified in the 1990 Rules, but in order to advise the Secretary of State adequately, the report should contain a summary of the main evidence and arguments presented at the inquiry, and the matters and inferences of fact which led

    2—25

---

[74] But see para. 2–21.
[75] *Ibid.* r.15(3).
[76] 1981 Act, s.5(2), applying s.250(2) of the Local Government Act 1972.
[77] *Ibid.* r.15(6).
[78] *Ibid.* r.15(4).
[79] *Ibid.* r.15(9), (10).
[80] *Ibid.* r.16(1).
[81] *Ibid.* r.16(2).
[82] *Ibid.* r.16(3).
[83] *Ibid.* r.17(1).

to the conclusions.[84] While the standards expected of the inspector in preparing his report are undoubtedly high he is not required to deal with every point made at the inquiry. He is entitled to omit material he considers irrelevant provided the case for each party is still properly presented to the Secretary of State.[85] Moreover, the quality of drafting which is required is not the standard which is expected in a conveyancing document.[86]

Rule 17(4) of the 1990 Rules provides that where, after the close of an inquiry, the Secretary of State: (a) differs from the inspector on a matter of fact mentioned in a conclusion reached by the inspector, or appearing to him to be material to a conclusion, or (b) after the close of the inquiry takes into consideration any new evidence or new matter of fact (not being a matter of government policy) and because of this is disposed to disagree with a recommendation made by the inspector, he must not come to a decision at variance with such recommendation without first notifying the persons entitled to appear and who did appear at the inquiry of his disagreement and the reasons for it. He must then afford those who have been notified an opportunity of making representations in writing within 21 days or (if the Secretary of State has taken into consideration any new evidence or taken into consideration any new matter of fact, not being a matter of government policy) of asking within 21 days for the reopening of the inquiry. Rule 17(5) goes on to provide that, if so requested, the Secretary of State must reopen the inquiry; and he may do so in other circumstances if he thinks fit.[87]

2—26   In *Hamilton v. Roxburghshire County Council*[88], for example, the Court held that there had been a breach of an equivalent provision in previous Compulsory Purchase Inquiries Procedure Rules when the Secretary of State sought and obtained information from one party after the close of the inquiry which led him to depart from the recommendation of the inspector without notifying the other parties and giving them an opportunity to make representations.

The corresponding provision in the procedural rules applicable to town and country planning inquiries has provoked considerable litigation.[89] The reference in rule 17(4) (a) to a matter of fact replaced a provision in earlier procedural rules which referred to a "finding of fact", as the previous provision caused difficulties in drawing a distinction between fact and opinion.[90] In *Wordie Property Co. Ltd v.*

---

[84] *Hope v. Secretary of State for the Environment* (1975) 31 P. & C.R. 120.
[85] *Preston Borough Council v. Secretary of State for the Environment* [1978] J.P.L. 548; *Gibbs (W.H.) Ltd v. Secretary of State for the Environment* [1974] J.P.L. 228. See further *Bolton Metropolitan Borough Council v. Secretary of State for the Environment and Greater Manchester Waste Disposal Authority* (1990) 61 P. & C.R. 343.
[86] *London and Clydeside Properties Ltd v. City of Aberdeen District Council*, 1984 S.L.T. 50.
[87] It would seem that the principles of natural justice impose obligations upon the Secretary of State similar to those set out in the procedural rules: *Hibernian Property Company Ltd v. Secretary of State for the Environment* (1973) 27 P. & C.R. 197; *Fairmount Investments Ltd v. Secretary of State for the Environment* [1976] 1 W.L.R. 1255; *Lithgow v. Secretary of State for Scotland*, 1973 S.C. 1.
[88] 1970 S.C. 248; 1971 S.L.T. 2.
[89] See M. Purdue, E. Young and J. Rowan-Robinson, *Planning Law and Procedure*, Chap. 20.
[90] *Lord Luke of Pavenham v. Minister of Housing and Local Government* [1968] 1 Q.B. 172; *Pyreford Properties Ltd v. Secretary of State for the Environment* (1977) 36 P. & C.R. 28.

Secretary of State for Scotland[91], for example, where a difference arose as to the amount and the type of shopping space that would be required in Aberdeen in the future, the Court of Session categorised the former as a matter of fact and the latter as a matter of planning judgment. Difficulties may also arise over the meaning of "new evidence"[92] and "new matter of fact" in the second part of the rule.[93] And the reference in rule 17(4)(b) to "a matter of government policy" raises again the difficulty discussed earlier of distinguishing between matters of policy and matters of fact.[94]

The confirming authority must notify his decision, with reasons, to the acquiring authority, to the statutory objectors, to any person entitled to appear at the inquiry and actually did appear, and to any other person, who, having appeared at the inquiry, has asked to be notified of the decision (rule 18(1)).[95] If a copy of the inspector's report is not sent with the notification of the decision, the notification must be accompanied by a summary of the inspector's conclusions and recommendations.[96]

2—27

Although it would seem that the Secretary of State's decision letter should not be analysed and picked to pieces "as if each sentence were a subsection in a taxing statute,"[97] it is well established, to use the words of Megaw J. in *Re Poyser and Mills' Arbitration*,[98] "that proper, adequate reasons must be given. The reasons that are set out must be reasons which will not only be intelligible but which deal with the substantial points that have been raised."[99]

---

[91] 1984 S.L.T. 345.

[92] See, for example, *Hamilton v. Roxburghshire County Council*, 1970 S.C. 248; 1971 S.L.T. 2; *London & Clydeside Properties Ltd v. City of Aberdeen District Council*, 1984 S.L.T. 50; and *French Kier Developments Ltd v. Secretary of State for the Environment* [1977] 1 All E.R. 296.

[93] See, for example, *Vale Estates (Acton) Ltd v. Secretary of State for the Environment* (1970) 69 L.G.R. 543.

[94] See *Bushell v. Secretary of State for the Environment* [1981] A.C. 75; *Lithgow v. Secretary of State for Scotland*, 1973 S.C. 1.

[95] See, too, the Tribunals and Inquiries Act 1992, s.10(1). In *Save Britain's Heritage v. Secretary of State for the Environment* (1991) 62 P. & C.R. 105, Lord Bridge described the duty to give reasons as "the analogue in administrative law of the common law requirement that justice must not only be done, but also be seen to be done" (at p. 123).

[96] A person entitled to notification of the Secretary of State's decision who has not received a copy of the inspector's report may request a copy from the Secretary of State; the request must be made within four weeks of the date of the decision: r.18(2).

[97] *De Rothschild v. Secretary of State for Transport* [1989] J.P.L. 173, *per* Slade L.J.; *London and Clydeside Properties Ltd v. City of Aberdeen District Council*, 1984 S.L.T. 50, *per* Lord Wheatley; *Wordie Property Co. Ltd v. Secretary of State for Scotland*, 1984 S.L.T. 345, *per* Lord Grieve; *West Midlands Cooperative Society v. Secretary of State for the Environment* [1988] J.P.L. 121, *per* Graham Eyre Q.C.

[98] [1964] 2 Q.B. 467; and see *Givaudan v. Minister of Housing and Local Government* [1967] 1 W.L.R. 250, *Westminster City Council v. Great Portland Estates plc* [1985] A.C. 661, H.L., *per* Lord Scarman; *Wordie Property Co. Ltd v. Secretary of State for Scotland*, 1984 S.L.T. 345, *per* the Lord President (Lord Emslie); *Landau v. Secretary of State for the Environment and Tyne and Wear Development Corporation* [1991] E.G.C.S. 119; *Save Britain's Heritage v. Secretary of State for the Environment* (1991) 62 P. & C.R. 105.

[99] For a discussion of the considerable litigation which has arisen in connection with decision letters relating to planning appeals see M. Purdue, E. Young and J. Rowan-Robinson, *Planning Law & Procedure*, Chap. 20.

9. EXPENSES

2—28   The expenses incurred by the Secretary of State in relation to the inquiry (including such reasonable sum as the Secretary of State may determine in respect of the general staff costs and overheads of his department, and the services of the inspector) are to be paid by such of the parties to the inquiry and in such proportions as the Secretary of State may order.[1] The Secretary of State may also make orders as to the expenses incurred by the parties to the inquiry and as to the parties by whom such expenses are to be paid.[2] The normal practice, where a statutory objector attends or is represented at an inquiry and is successful in his objection so that the Secretary of State refuses to confirm the order in respect of his land, is to award him his reasonable expenses unless there are exceptional reasons for not doing so.[3] The expenses are paid by the acquiring authority and will include professional fees incurred in pursuing his objection and in attending or being represented at the inquiry. A statutory objector who is partially successful will normally get a partial award of expenses. Statutory objectors who are unsuccessful and third parties (whatever the outcome) are expected to bear their own expenses. Exceptionally, where any party to the inquiry has acted unreasonably an award of expenses may be made against him.[4]

This somewhat restrictive approach to the award of expenses appears to stem from the fear that a more generous policy would encourage objectors, delay much needed public works, and impose a heavier burden on acquiring authorities. The consequence of the approach is that statutory objectors must indulge in something of a gamble as in many cases it will not be possible to forecast at the outset what the outcome of an objection will be. As the expense can be considerable this may deter objection.

10. THE DECISION OF THE SECRETARY OF STATE

2—29   The decision of the confirming authority may be to confirm the order with or without modifications or to decline to confirm the order.[5] It is not uncommon for an order to be confirmed with modifications directed at the exclusion of identified areas of land. The order may not, however, be modified by the con-

---

[1] 1981 Act, s.5(3), applying the Local Government Act 1972 s.250(4). See, also, the Housing and Planning Act 1986, s.42 and the Fees for Inquiries (Standard Daily Amount) Regulations 1994 (S.I. 1994 No. 642).

[2] 1981 Act, s.5(3), applying the Local Government Act 1972, s.250(5).

[3] See Department of the Environment Circular 8/93 "Awards of Costs incurred in Planning and Other (Including Compulsory Purchase Order) Proceedings", Annex 6, para. 1.

[4] Ibid. para. 3. In practice, such an award is likely to arise from a procedural matter, e.g. unreasonably causing the inquiry to be adjourned.

[5] 1981 Act, s.13(1), (2), see City of Glasgow District Council v. Secretary of State for Scotland [1990] 35 E.G. 68.

firming authority so as to authorise the compulsory acquisition of additional land unless all persons interested consent.[6]

If the compulsory purchase order is confirmed, the acquiring authority must, as soon as may be, publish a notice in the prescribed form[7] in one or more local newspapers describing the land, stating that the order has been confirmed and naming a place where a copy of the order, as confirmed, and the order map may be inspected.[8] A similar notice together with a copy of the order as confirmed must be served on all persons who were required to be served with notice of the making of the order. Amongst other matters, the notice will draw attention to the opportunity for an aggrieved person to question the order by way of an application to the High Court.[9]

Subject to such an application, a compulsory purchase order will become operative on the date on which the notice is first published in the local press.[10] The acquiring authority will then be authorised to proceed to acquire title to the land, and, if desired, to enter onto the land before formal acquisition of title.

Purchases by Ministers

Separate but similar procedural arrangements apply to compulsory purchase orders promoted by Ministers. These are set out in Schedule 1 to the 1981 Act. **2—30**

Such an order is first prepared in draft in such form as the Minister may determine. While there is no prescribed form for such an order it must, however, describe by reference to a map the land to which it applies. Notice of the preparation of the order in draft must be given as for the making of an order by a local or other authority. There is the same opportunity to object and a right to be heard in support of an objection.[11] In practice, similar inquiry and post inquiry procedures operate[12] although the order is not confirmed, it is "made" by the Minister. Notice of the "making" of an order must be given in much the same way as notice of confirmation of an order must be given by a local or other authority. The validity of an order made by a Minister may also be questioned by way of application to the High Court.

---

[6] 1981 Act, s.14.
[7] Compulsory Purchase of Land Regulations 1990, reg. 2(e) and Sched. 1, form 10.
[8] 1981 Act, s.15.
[9] See Chap. 3.
[10] *Ibid.* s.26(1). But see para. 2–09 above as regards orders which are subject to special parliamentary procedure.
[11] *Ibid.* Sched. 1, para. 4.
[12] See the Compulsory Purchase by Ministers (Inquiries Procedure) Rules 1967 (S.I. 1967 No. 720). See, also, a joint consultation document issued by the Department of Transport and the Welsh Office in February 1994: *Revision of the Highways (Inquiries Procedure) Rules 1976 and the Compulsory Purchase by Ministers (Inquiries Procedure) Rules 1967.*

Compulsory acquisition of statutory undertaker's land

2—31   Where a compulsory purchase order includes land which has been acquired by statutory undertakers[13] for the purposes of their undertaking, we have already seen[14] that such an order may be required to be the subject of special parliamentary procedure. An additional hurdle for the acquiring authority to surmount arises if, within the period allowed for objection to the order, the undertakers make representations to their appropriate Minister.[15] Where such representations are made the appropriate Minister may block the acquisition of that land.[16] Unless the Minister certifies either that the land can be purchased and not replaced without serious detriment to the undertaking or that it can be replaced by other land without serious detriment to the undertaking, the order cannot be confirmed or made, as the case may be, in respect of that land.

Exceptionally, where a compulsory purchase order is promoted under the provisions of Part IX of the Town and Country Planning Act 1990, (or by an urban development corporation or the Land Authority for Wales pursuant to the Local Government, Planning and Land Act 1980), the order may be confirmed or made in respect of statutory undertakers' land in the absence of a certificate provided it is confirmed or made by the appropriate Minister jointly with the Minister having power to confirm or make it.[17]

Power to extinguish public rights of way

2—32   Where land is acquired or proposed to be acquired by a body possessing compulsory purchase powers to which the 1981 Act applies and there subsists over any part of the land a public right of way (not being a right enjoyable by vehicular traffic), the acquiring authority may take steps to extinguish that right of way by means of an order[18], known as an "acquisition extinguishment order."[19] subject to confirmation by the Secretary of State.[20] If the order is unopposed it can be

---

[13] As defined by the 1981 Act, s.8(1). See para. 2–07 above.

[14] At para. 2–07.

[15] 1981 Act, s.16(1).

[16] *Ibid.* s.16(2).

[17] *Ibid.* s.31.

[18] Pursuant to s.32(2) of the 1981 Act. This provision does not apply where ss.251 or 258 of the Town and Country Planning Act 1990 applies (extinguishment of public rights over land held for planning purposes). Nor does it have any application to land acquired or proposed to be acquired by the Civil Aviation Authority under s.42 of the Civil Aviation Act 1982: 1981 Act, s.32(7), (8).

[19] Although the words "acquisition extinguishment order" do not appear in s.32 of the 1981 Act, this term is to be found in the Public Path Orders Regulations 1993 (S.I. 1993 No. 11), which specify relevant forms of notice.

[20] The Secretary of State has concurrent powers to make orders under s.32(3) of the 1981 Act.

confirmed locally. In either case the confirming authority must be satisfied either that a suitable alternative right of way has been or will be provided or that such alternative provision is not required. The date from which the right is extinguished will be specified in the order and must not be earlier than:

(i) the date of the confirmation of the order;

(ii) where the acquiring authority take possession before the acquisition is complete, the date of possession;

(iii) where the acquiring authority do not take possession in advance of acquisition, the date of acquisition.[21]

The acquiring authority must publish a notice stating that the order has been made, the effect of the order, that a copy of the order and the map can be inspected without charge at a named place in the area of the land at all reasonable hours and allow an opportunity (not less than 28 days from the publication of the notice) for objection.[22] The publication requirements are extensive. Notice of the making of the order is to be published in the *London Gazette*, in at least one local newspaper and personal notification is to be given to all owners, occupiers and lessees (except tenants for a month or less), all other local authorities (including parish or community councils) exercising functions in the area and also by means of display of a notice or each end of the footpath or bridleway which is affected by the order. Prescribed forms are to be used in carrying out the notification requirements; these are contained in the Public Paths Orders Regulations 1993.[23] If an objection, duly made, is not withdrawn a public local inquiry must be arranged.[24]

No such order is to be made with regard to a right of way over land on, over **2—33** or under which there is any apparatus belonging to statutory undertakers unless the undertakers consent to the making of the order. Consent must not be unreasonably refused. Such consent may be conditional upon suitable safeguards being included in the order for the protection of the undertakers.[25]

---

[21] 1981 Act, s.32(4).

[22] *Ibid*. s.32(2), applying Sched. 6 to the Highways Act 1980.

[23] S.I. 1993 No. 11.

[24] Highways Act 1980, Sched. 6, para. 2(2)(a).

[25] 1981 Act, s.32(6).

Chapter 3

Challenge in the High Court

3—01　The Acquisition of Land Act 1981 enables any person aggrieved by a compulsory purchase order who desires to question its validity to do so by making an application to the High Court within six weeks of the date on which notice of its confirmation or making is first published.[1] The application may be made on one or other or both of the following grounds: (i) that the authorisation granted by the compulsory purchase order is not empowered to be granted; or (ii) that any relevant requirement has not been complied with in relation to the order.[2] If the validity of the order is successfully challenged the High Court may quash the order (1981 Act, section 24).

1. MEANING OF "PERSON AGGRIEVED"

3—02　As section 23 provides an opportunity not expressly limited to those whose land is to be taken to question the validity of a compulsory purchase order, it would seem that an acquiring authority can be a "person aggrieved".[3] This could be relevant if the acquiring authority wish to question any modification made to their order by the confirming authority. A decision by a confirming authority *not*

---

[1] 1981 Act, s.23.

[2] A certificate issued by a Minister under Part III of or Sched. 3 to the 1981 Act may also be questioned within six weeks on the ground of non-compliance with any relevant requirement. The term "relevant requirement" encompasses the requirements of the 1981 Act, the Tribunals and Inquiries Act 1992 and regulations made under either of those Acts: s.23(3).

[3] *Cook v. Southend Borough Council* [1990] 1 All E.R. 243. See, however, *Strathclyde Regional Council v. Secretary of State for Scotland* [1989] 2 P.L.R. 111.

to confirm an order would be subject, not to a statutory application to quash, but to the general supervisory jurisdiction of the High Court.[4]

The phrase a "person aggrieved" would encompass owners, lessees and occupiers (except occupiers for a month or less) who are entitled to receipt of notice of the making of the order.[5] However, it is uncertain whether and, if so, to what extent it encompasses other persons generally referred to as "third parties," who may also be concerned about the outcome of the order. The requirement to give public notice of the making of an order is an acknowledgement that such concern may exist, and as Lord Clyde observed in *Martin v. Bearsden and Milngavie District Council*,[6] an

> "Appeal against a compulsory purchase order is open to 'any person aggrieved', which, while it doubtless does not give an unlimited title for complaint, extends beyond those who had the right to have the order served upon them." But it is clear that the opportunity to question the validity of the order is not available to everyone. The courts will wish to steer a course between those who might fairly be described as having a close interest in the outcome and those who are mere "busybodies."[7]

There is, however, no recent authority in the field of compulsory purchase on the question of the scope of "person aggrieved" but analogies can be drawn from the field of town and country planning. Initially the High Court took a narrow view of the scope of "person aggrieved" so as to exclude a neighbouring landowner: *Buxton v. Minister of Housing and Local Government*.[8] In Scotland the Court of Session took a similar view in *Simpson v. Edinburgh Corporation*[9] in which a resident in a city square was held to have no title and interest to question the validity of a grant of planning permission to develop other land in the square. He could not show that some legal right conferred on him by the legislation had been contravened. On the other hand, in *Black v. Tennent*[10] neighbouring pro-

3—03

---

[4] See, for example, *R. v. Secretary of State for the Environment, ex p. Melton Borough Council* [1986] J.P.L. 190; *R. v. Secretary of State for the Environment, ex p. Leicester County Council* [1987] J.P.L. 787. See, too, *R. v. Camden London Borough Council, ex p. Comyn Ching & Co. (London) Ltd* [1984] J.P.L. 661 where Woolf J. held that a resolution by a local authority to make a compulsory purchase order was not encompassed by the statutory application to quash but could be the subject of an application for judicial review. He thought it would be different once the order had been made even though it had not at that stage been confirmed. In *R. v. Secretary of State for the Environment, ex p. Royal Borough of Kensington and Chelsea* [1987] J.P.L. 567 an application for judicial review was granted to an acquiring authority in respect of a decision by an inspector not to admit evidence at a local inquiry vital to the authority's case.

[5] See, however, *George v. Secretary of State for the Environment* (1979) 38 P. & C.R. 609 (co-owning spouse who was not served with notice of making of the compulsory purchase order held not entitled to challenge the order since she had not been substantially prejudiced by the omission).

[6] 1987 S.L.T. 300.

[7] *Attorney-General of Gambia v. N'jie* [1961] A.C. 617 *per* Lord Denning M.R.

[8] [1961] 1 Q.B. 278. It was held in that case that a "person aggrieved" was someone whose legal rights had been infringed. See, also, *Ex p. Sidebotham* (1880) 14 Ch.D. 458.

[9] 1960 S.C. 313. See, also, *Gregory v. Camden London Borough Council* [1966] 2 All E.R. 196; *Bellway Ltd v. Strathclyde Regional Council*, 1979 S.C. 92 and *Reid v. Mini-Cabs* 1966 S.C. 137.

[10] (1889) 1 F.423.

prietors who had a statutory right to object to the grant of a public house licence and who had unsuccessfully objected were held to have sufficient title to question the validity of the grant of a licence.

But in recent years a much more liberal approach has been taken to the interpretation of a "person aggrieved" in the context of a statutory application to quash planning decisions. In *Turner v. Secretary of State for the Environment*[11] Ackner J. declined to follow the earlier decision of Salmon J. in *Buxton v. Minister of Housing and Local Government* and held that a local preservation society, who had been heard at the discretion of the inspector at a local inquiry to consider an application for planning permission for residential development, were entitled to be heard in support of their application to quash the subsequent grant of planning permission by the Secretary of State. Ackner J. said:

> "I see good reason, so long as the grounds of appeal are so restricted, for ensuring that any person who, in the ordinary sense of the word, is aggrieved by the decision, and certainly any person who has attended and made representations at the inquiry, should have the right to establish in the courts that the decision is bad in law because it is *ultra vires* or for some other good reason."[12]

Although these analogies are undoubtedly helpful, in view of the current dearth of authority arising from compulsory purchase order cases, the scope of the phrase a "person aggrieved" in section 23 of the 1981 Act is uncertain.

2. The statutory grounds of challenge

3—04 The effect of section 23 is that an application may be made to the High Court on the ground that the authorisation granted by the compulsory purchase order is not within the powers of the legislation or that any requirements of the 1981 Act, the Tribunals and Inquiries Act 1992 or of any regulations made under those Acts have not been complied with.

These grounds correspond broadly to the distinction between substantive and procedural issues, though the courts have at times found difficulty in distinguishing between them. There is, said Megaw L.J. in *Gordondale Investments Ltd v. Secretary of State for the Environment*,[13] "a real difficulty in seeking to define separate spheres for, or to draw a borderline between, on the one hand, situations in which the order is 'not within the powers of this Act' and, on the other hand,

---

[11] (1973) 28 P. & C.R. 123. See, too, *Attorney-General of Gambia v. N'jie* [1961] A.C. 617; *Maurice v. L.C.C.* [1964] 2 Q.B. 362; *Bizony v. Secretary of State for the Environment* [1976] J.P.L. 306, and *Times Investments Ltd v. Secretary of State for the Environment* (1990) 61 P. & C.R. 98.

[12] (1973) 28 P. & C.R. 123 at p. 129, applied in *Times Investments Limited v. Secretary of State for the Environment* (1990) 61 P. & C.R. 98 (purchaser of land after conclusion of a planning appeal but before issue of the decision held to be a "person aggrieved").

[13] (1971) 23 P. & C.R. 334.

situations in which a 'requirement of this Act has not been complied with'." The distinction will sometimes be important because section 24(2)(b) goes on to provide that the court may quash an order because of a failure to comply with some requirement of the legislation only if the interests of the applicant have been substantially prejudiced.[14]

In *McCowan v. Secretary of State for Scotland*[15] it was argued for the appellants that a failure to give notice of the making of a compulsory purchase order as required by the legislation enabled the appellant to found his challenge to the validity of the order upon either of the grounds in section 23. Lord Cameron, whilst reserving his opinion on the point, observed that if an order which is flawed by a failure to comply with the requirements of the Act is one which is not empowered to be granted under the Act, there would seem to be no purpose in presenting a person aggrieved with alternative roads to the quashing of the order. There was, he thought, much to be said for the view that the first alternative in paragraph 15 "relates to an order which in purpose or object is *ultra vires* the statute under which the authority authorising it purports to act or is *ultra vires* the authorising authority."

In some cases it would appear that a failure to comply with a statutory require- **3—05** ment will also mean that the authorisation is not within the powers of the Act. In *Fairmount Investments Ltd v. Secretary of State for the Environment*[16] Lord Russell of Killowen concluded that where there had been a departure from the principles of natural justice "it may equally be said that the order is not within the powers of the Act and that a requirement of the Act has not been complied with." In many cases, of course, there will be no doubt that the applicant has been substantially prejudiced; in these cases the distinction will be less significant.

After some initial uncertainty[17] the courts appear to have adopted a broad approach to the scope of the statutory grounds of challenge and have not generally sought to "draw a borderline" between the two. What is generally referred to as the *Ashbridge* formula has now been widely accepted[18] as defining the circum-

---

[14] See para. 3–07.
[15] 1972 S.C. 93.
[16] [1976] 1 W.L.R. 1255 at p. 1263.
[17] In *Smith v. East Elloe R.D.C.* [1956] A.C. 736 the majority of the House of Lords (Lords Reid, Morton and Somervell) gave the first ground a narrow interpretation. Viscount Simonds and Lord Radcliffe, on the other hand, gave it a broad construction. See, too, *Hamilton v. Secretary of State for Scotland*, 1972 S.C. 72; 1972 S.L.T. 233 *per* Lord Kissen (narrow construction); and *Lithgow v. Secretary of State for Scotland*, 1973 S.C. 1; 1973 S.L.T. 81, *per* Lord Dunpark (broad construction).
[18] *Re Lamplugh* (1967) 19 P. & C.R. 125; *Coleen Properties v. Minister of Housing and Local Government* [1971] 1 W.L.R. 433; *Gordondale Investments Ltd v. Secretary of State for the Environment* (1971) 23 P. & C.R. 334; *Eckersley v. Secretary of State for the Environment* (1977) 36 P. & C.R. 28; *R.v. Secretary of State for the Environment, ex p. Ostler* [1977] Q.B. 122, *per* Lord Denning; *De Rothschild v. Secretary of State for Transport* [1989] J.P.L. 173; and *Wordie Property Co. Ltd v. Secretary of State for Scotland*, 1984 S.L.T 345, *per* the Lord President (Lord Emslie). See, too, *Seddon Properties Ltd v. Secretary of State for the Environment* (1978) 42 P. & C.R. 26, *per* Forbes J., and *Bolton Metropolitan Borough Council v. Secretary of State for the Environment and Greater Manchester Waste Disposal Authority* (1990) 61 P. & C.R. 343, *per* Glidewell J.

stances in which a court may interfere with the decision of the Secretary of State. In *Ashbridge Investments Ltd v. Minister of Housing and Local Government*[19] Lord Denning M.R. said:

"The Court can only interfere on the ground that the Minister has gone outside the powers of the Act or that any requirements of the Act have not been complied with. Under this section it seems to me that the Court can interfere with the Minister's decision if he has acted on no evidence, or if he has come to a conclusion to which on the evidence he could not reasonably come; or if he has given a wrong interpretation to the words of the statute; or if he has taken into consideration matters which he ought not to have taken into account, or *vice versa*; or has otherwise gone wrong in law. It is identical with the position where the Court has power to interfere with the decision of a lower tribunal which has erred in point of law."

If this statement of the law is correct, it would seem, as Corfield and Carnwath observe,[20] "that little, if any, effect is to be given to the actual words of the statutory provision", and one must look for guidance to the authorities on the power of the Courts to interfere with decisions of inferior tribunals or administrative bodies.

3—06   In *Associated Provincial Picture Houses Ltd v. Wednesbury Corporation*[21] Lord Greene M.R., in a much cited judgment, also sought to define the circumstances in which a court would intervene to review an exercise of discretionary power:

"the Court is entitled to investigate the action of the local authority with a view to seeing whether they have taken into account matters which they ought not to take into account, or, conversely, have refused to take into account or neglected to take into account matters which they ought to take into account. Once that question is answered in favour of the local authority it may be still possible to say that, although the local authority have kept within the four corners of the matters which they ought to consider, they have nonetheless come to a conclusion so unreasonable that no reasonable authority could ever have come to it."

In *De Rothschild v. Secretary of State for the Environment*[22] the Court of Appeal firmly rejected the argument that there were to be derived from case law special rules beyond the *Wednesbury/Ashbridge* grounds which applied (and which would have the effect of limiting the discretion of the Secretary of State) wherever the court was considering a challenge to a compulsory purchase order.

The following examples provide some indication of the scope of the first of the statutory grounds. Compulsory purchase orders have been challenged, often

---

[19] [1965] 1 W.L.R. 1320 a case concerning the statutory grounds of challenge contained in the Housing Act 1957.
[20] Sir Frederick Corfield and R.J.A. Carnwath, *Compulsory Acquisition and Compensation* (Butterworths, 1978) p. 55.
[21] [1948] 1 K.B. 223.
[22] [1989] J.P.L. 173. See, too, *Singh v. Secretary of State for the Environment* [1989] 24 E.G. 128.

successfully, on the ground that the statutory basis for an order did not exist,[23] that the substratum of fact required for the exercise of power was lacking,[24] that the confirming authority failed to have regard to a relevant consideration,[25] that the decision on the order was influenced by an irrelevant consideration,[26] and that confirmation of the order was a breach of the principles of natural justice.[27]

3. SUBSTANTIAL PREJUDICE

An applicant seeking to challenge the validity of a compulsory purchase order on **3—07** the second ground, namely that there has been a failure to comply with a relevant requirement (section 23(2)(b)), must show that he has suffered substantial prejudice as a result of the failure.[28] In *Hibernian Property Co. Ltd v. Secretary of State for the Environment*[29] Browne J. said of the corresponding provision in Schedule 3 of the Housing Act 1957:

---

[23] *Sovmots Investments Ltd v. Secretary of State for the Environment* [1977] Q.B. 411; *Webb v. Minister of Housing and Local Government* [1965] 2 All E.R. 193; *Grice v. Dudley Corporation* [1958] Ch. 329; *Meravale Builders Ltd v. Secretary of State for the Environment* (1978) 36 P. & C.R. 87, *Proctor and Gamble Ltd v. Secretary of State for the Environment* (1991) 63 P. & C.R. 317.

[24] *Coleen Properties Ltd v. Minister of Housing and Local Government* [1971] 1 W.L.R. 433; *Re Ripon (Highfield) Housing Order 1938* [1939] 2 K.B. 838; also *R. v. Secretary of State for the Environment, ex p. Leicester City Council* [1987] J.P.L. 787; *Sharkey v. Secretary of State for the Environment* [1992] 32 R.V.R. 29.

[25] *Brown v. Secretary of State for the Environment* (1978) 40 P. & C.R. 285 (the existence of an alternative site); *Brinklow and Croft Bros. Ltd v. Secretary of State for the Environment* [1976] J.P.L. 299 (relocation of displaced uses); *Prest v. Secretary of State for Wales* [1983] J.P.L. 112 (the cost of developing alternative sites); *Sovmots Investments Ltd v. Secretary of State for the Environment* [1977] Q.B. 411 (cost of conversion of premises)), R. v. Secretary of State for the Environment, ex p. Kensington and Chelsea London Borough Council, [1987] J.L.P. 567 (housing management consideration); *Bolton Metropolitan Borough Council v. Secretary of State for the Environment and Greater Manchester Waste Disposal Authority* (1990) 61 P. & C.R. 343 (revival of withdrawn objection after issue of a Green Paper undermining the reason for withdrawal).

[26] *Sydney Municipal Council v. Campbell* [1925] A.C. 338 (recovery of betterment). See, too, *Hanks v. Minister of Housing and Local Government* [1963] 1 Q.B. 999 (planning matters not irrelevant); *Leggat v. Secretary of State for the Environment* [1991] 1 P.L.R. 103 (no ulterior purpose notwithstanding potential grant of a lease at a premium of the order land).

[27] *Hibernian Property Company Ltd v. Secretary of State for the Environment* (1973) 27 P. & C.R. 197; *Fairmount Investments Ltd v. Secretary of State for the Environment* [1976] 1 W.L.R. 1255. See, too, *Errington v. Minister of Health* [1935] 1 K.B. 249, and *Bushell v. Secretary of State for the Environment* [1981] A.C. 75.

[28] 1981 Act, s.24(2)(b); for examples see *Brown v. Minister of Housing and Local Government* [1953] 2 All E.R. 1385 (failure to serve notice of the making of the order on an owner or occupier, cf., *Grimley v. Minister of Housing and Local Government* [1971] 2 Q.B. 96); *Richardson v. Minister of Housing and Local Government* (1956) 8 P. & C.R. 29 (confirmation of order which should have been subject to special parliamentary procedure); *Hamilton v. Roxburghshire County Council*, 1970 S.C. 248; 1971 S.L.T. 2 (obtaining information after an inquiry from one party without notifying the others); *Cowan v. Secretary of State for Scotland* 1972 S.C. 93 (failure to give notice of the order to a landowner); *Wilson v. Secretary of State for the Environment* [1973] 1 W.L.R. 1083 (misdescription of land in a newspaper notice).

[29] (1973) 27 P. & C.R. 197. See, too, *Miller v. Weymouth and Melcombe Regis Corporation* (1974) 27 P. & C.R. 468, *per* Kerr J.

"This of course does not mean that the applicant must prove that the decision *would* have been different if the requirement had been complied with, which would usually be quite impossible. In my view, the loss of a *chance* of being better off in relation to the proposed order would usually be enough to constitute substantial prejudice."

In that case during the course of a site inspection following an inquiry to hear objections to a compulsory purchase order made under the Housing Act 1957 the inspector questioned occupiers of the premises in the absence of a representative from the applicants. The inspector's recommendation to confirm the order was accepted by the Secretary of State. Browne J., in quashing the order, said: "In my judgment the question is not whether the information obtained by the Inspector did in fact prejudice the applicants by contributing to the decision of the Secretary of State to confirm the compulsory purchase order but whether there was a risk that it may have done so."

Thus in *Wilson v. Secretary of State for the Environment*[30] a failure to use the correct description of the land in a newspaper notice of the making of a compulsory purchase order deprived the applicant of an opportunity of lodging and maintaining an objection. This was thought by Browne L.J. to be a procedural defect amounting prima facie to substantial prejudice.[31] Other examples have arisen in applications to the High Court to quash ministerial planning decisions.[32]

3—08   If the court considers that the applicant has not been substantially prejudiced by the failure to comply with statutory requirements, it is entitled to disregard the failure.[33] It seems that it is for the applicant to establish that his interests have in fact been substantially prejudiced.[34] The onus may not, however, be particularly heavy. In *Save Britain's Heritage v. Secretary of State for the Environment*,[35] Lord Bridge said[36] that "there will be substantial prejudice to a developer whose application for planning permission has been refused or to an opponent of development when permission has been granted where the reasons for the decision are

---

[30] [1973] 1 W.L.R. 1083. See, too, *McMeechan v. Secretary of State for the Environment* [1974] J.P.L. 411 and *McCowan v. Secretary of State for Scotland* 1972 S.C. 93.

[31] See, too, *George v. Minister of Housing and Local Government* [1953] 2 All E.R. 1385; the comment of Lord Clyde in *Martin v. Bearsden and Milngavie District Council*, 1987 S.L.T. 300 at p. 304 G-H; contrast *George v. Secretary of State for the Environment* (1979) 38 P. & C.R. 609; and *McMillan v. Inverness-shire County Council*, 1949 S.C. 77; 1949 S.L.T. 77.

[32] *Gordondale Investments Ltd v. Secretary of State for the Environment* (1971) 23 P. & C.R. 386; *Greenwich London Borough Council v. Secretary of State for the Environment* [1981] J.P.L. 809; *Paterson v. Secretary of State for Scotland* 1971 S.C. 1.

[33] *Steele v. Minister of Housing and Local Government* (1956) 6 P. & C.R. 386; *Gordondale Investments Ltd v. Secretary of State for the Environment* (1971) 23 P. & C.R. 334; *Miller v. Weymouth & Melcombe Regis Corporation* (1974) 27 P. & C.R. 468; *Kent County Council v. Secretary of State for the Environment* (1977) 33 P. & C.R. 70.

[34] *Gordondale Investments Ltd v. Secretary of State for the Environment* (1971) 23 P. & C.R. 334, *per* Lord Denning; *Hibernian Property Co. Ltd. Secretary of State for the Environment* (1973) 27 P. & C.R. 197, *per* Browne J.; *George v. Minister of Housing and Local Government* [1953] 2 All E.R. 1385; *Save Britain's Heritage v. Secretary of State for the Environment* (1991) 62 P. & C.R. 105, *per* Lord Bridge.

[35] (1991) 62 P. & C.R. 105.

[36] At p. 119.

so inadequately or obscurely expressed as to raise a substantial doubt whether the decision was taken within the powers of the Act."

4. THE SIX WEEK TIME PERIOD FOR CHALLENGE

Section 23(4) of the 1981 Act provides that an application to the High Court by **3—09** a person aggrieved by a compulsory purchase order must be made within a period of six weeks from the date on which notice of the confirmation or making of the order was first published. The tight schedule which this imposes is further limited by the decision in *Griffiths v. Secretary of State for the Environment*[37] in which the House of Lords held that the date actions were taken by the Secretary of State for the purpose of challenge under section 245(1) of the Town and Country Planning Act 1971 was the date a letter conveying the decision was date stamped and that time ran from that date and not from when the decision letter was received. Section 25 of the Act 1981 goes on to provide that, subject to the provisions of the Act, a compulsory purchase order shall "not . . . be questioned in any legal proceedings whatsoever." Whether section 25 is effective to exclude the jurisdiction of the court after the six week time period has elapsed is a question which has caused considerable difficulty. While the courts have adopted a consistently robust approach in the context of compulsory purchase orders, decisions involving similar provisions in other legislation are difficult to reconcile.[38]

Underlying this question is the policy of Parliament that it is necessary to achieve certainty. A balance needs to be struck between (1) the dictates of justice that those affected by a compulsory purchase order should have an opportunity, where appropriate, to question its validity and (2) the dictates of administration that there should be finality and certainty regarding the order so that schemes of much needed public works may proceed.

In *Smith v. East Elloe Rural District Council*[39] the majority of the House of Lords held that the words used in the corresponding ouster clause in paragraph 15 of Schedule 1 to the Acquisition of Land (Authorisation Procedure) Act 1946 were wide enough to cover any kind of challenge which a person aggrieved may think fit to make. In that case the appellant brought an action against the local authority more than six weeks after notice of confirmation of a compulsory purchase order on the ground that the order had been made and confirmed wrongfully and in bad faith. Lord Radcliffe said:

"I do not see how it is possible to treat the provisions of paragraphs 15 and 16 of Part IV of Schedule 1 of the Act as containing anything less than a complete statutory

---

[37] [1983] 2 A.C. 51.
[38] For a helpful review of the authorities see E. Young, "Procedural Defects and Ouster Clauses" [1988] J.P.L. 301.
[39] [1956] A.C. 736.

code for regulating the extent to which, and the conditions under which, courts of law might be resorted to for the purpose of questioning the validity of a compulsory purchase order within the protection of the Act."[40]

3—10 Subsequently, in *Anisminic Ltd v. Foreign Compensation Commission*[41] the House of Lords held that an ouster clause which provided that a determination by the Commission should "not be called into question in any court of law" would not protect a determination made without jurisdiction and which was thus a nullity.[42]

3—11   The decisions in *Smith* and *Anisminic* were considered by the Court of Session in *Hamilton v. Secretary of State for Scotland*[43] where the applicant sought to quash a compulsory purchase order outside the six week time period as being illegal and *ultra vires* because the proceedings had been contrary to the requirements of natural justice. Lord Kissen, in holding that the jurisdiction of the court was ousted by the equivalent provision in the Acquisition of Land (Authorisation Procedure) (Scotland) Act 1947, distinguished *Anisminic* on the ground that, unlike paragraphs 15 and 16 of Schedule 1 to the 1947 Act, there was no provision of any kind in the Foreign Compensation Act 1950 for an application to the court to test questions of nullity. In the 1947 Act "there is provision for quashing at least some kinds of null orders. I cannot see how it can be said, on the basis of *Anisminic*, that, as pursuer's counsel maintained, one kind of nullity can be remedied by the application of said paragraph 15 but all other kinds can be remedied by ordinary proceedings in the Court."

The decisions in *Smith* and *Anisminic* were further considered in *R. v. Secretary of State for the Environment, ex. p. Ostler*[44] where a road scheme order and a compulsory purchase order were challenged outside the six week period on the grounds of want of natural justice and bad faith verging on fraud. The Court of Appeal, following *Smith* and distinguishing *Anisminic*, held that their jurisdiction was ousted on the expiry of the six week time period. *Anisminic* was distinguished on the ground that the relevant section in the Foreign Compensation Act 1950 provided for a complete ouster of the court's jurisdiction whereas in *Smith* (as in *Ostler*) the court had power to inquire into all matters raised provided application was made within six weeks. It was, said Lord Denning M.R., more like a limitation period than a complete ouster. *Anisminic* was further distinguished on the grounds that the decision of the Foreign Compensation Commission was that of

---

[40] At p. 768.

[41] [1969] 2 A.C. 147.

[42] Lord Reid in *Anisminic* was critical of the decision in *Smith* as there had been little consideration given to the question whether an ouster clause was effective where nullity was in issue.

[43] 1972 S.C. 72; 1972 S.L.T. 233. See, too, *Lithgow v. Secretary of State for Scotland* 1973 S.C. 1; 1973 S.L.T. 81.

[44] [1977] Q.B. 122. See, too, *Cartwright v. Minister of Housing and Local Government* (1967) 65 L.G.R. 384; *Routh v. Reading Corporation* (1970) 217 E.G. 1337; *Westminster City Council v. Secretary of State for the Environment* [1984] J.P.L. 27; and *R. v. Secretary of State for the Environment, ex p. Kent* [1988] J.P.L. 706; [1990] J.P.L. 124 C.A.; *Lewis v. Hackney London Borough Council* [1990] 27 E.G. 72; *R. v. Cornwall County Council ex p. Huntingdon* [1992] 3 All E.R. 566.

a judicial body whereas in *Ostler* the order was in the nature of an administrative decision; that in *Anisminic* the Commission had acted outside its jurisdiction whereas in *Ostler* the decisions in question had been within the jurisdiction of the Secretary of State; and that the policy of the legislature was that there should be certainty with compulsory purchase orders on the expiry of the six week period.

The possibility of a future decision based on the *Anisminic* approach was revived, though perhaps only briefly, by the decision of the Court of Session in *McDaid v. Clydebank District Council*[45] in which it was held that an ouster clause in section 85 (10) of the Town and Country Planning (Scotland) Act 1972 did *not* exclude the court's jurisdiction in respect of an enforcement notice which had not been served as required by the Act and was therefore a nullity. In that case the planning authority had failed to serve enforcement notices on the landowners, although their identities were known to the authority, with the result that the owners did not become aware of the notices until the time for lodging an appeal against them with the Secretary of State had passed.

Section 85(10) of the 1972 Act provides that the validity of an enforcement **3—12** notice is not to be questioned on certain specified grounds except by way of an appeal to the Secretary of State. There is no provision in the 1972 Act corresponding to paragraphs 15 and 16 of the first Schedule to the Acquisition of Land (Authorisation Procedure) (Scotland) Act 1947 which would allow the validity of a notice to be questioned on specified grounds and within a specified time period on application to the Court of Session. In one sense, therefore, the provision in section 85(10) is equivalent to an absolute ouster clause and thus regarded the decision in *McDaid* may be reconciled with *Smith, Hamilton* and *Ostler*, to which decisions no reference was made. The decision, however, also indicates that an enforcement notice which is not properly served is a nullity and is not as a result protected by the ouster clause. The reasoning in *McDaid* has been described as "impeccably that of *Anisminic* to which the court made approving reference".[46]

The Court of Appeal took a different view, however, of the effect of the equivalent provisions of the Town and Country Planning Act 1971 in *R. v. Greenwich London Borough Council ex p. Patel.*[47] Here the view was preferred that an application for judicial review is not available in cases where the validity of an enforcement notice can be challenged by way of defence to a prosecution. *Patel* does, however, leave open the possibility of judicial review in a very limited range of cases where the alleged defect is not a specified ground of defence, for example, where bad faith is alleged.

More significantly, the decision in *McDaid* was considered in the context of a **3—13** compulsory purchase order by the Court of Session in *Martin v. Bearsden and Milngavid District Council.*[48] In that case a local authority failed to serve notice of

---

[45] 1984 S.L.T. 162.
[46] "The Exclusion of Judicial Review" 1984 S.L.T. (News) 297.
[47] [1985] J.P.L. 851.
[48] 1987 S.L.T. 300.

the making of a compulsory purchase order on the owner of land included in the order. The land was subsequently vested in the authority. Some years later, the owners, still unaware of the order, disposed of part of the order land to the petitioners. Thereafter the petitioners learned of the existence of the order and applied for judicial review seeking its reduction and damages. The district council, as statutory successors to the order making authority, relied on the ouster clause in paragraph 15 of the first Schedule to the Acquisition of Land (Authorisation Procedure) (Scotland) Act 1947.

It was held that the provision was effective to prevent challenge in the court after the six week period had elapsed since there was "a valid and significant difference" between the provisions of the 1972 Act in issue in *McDaid* and paragraphs 15 and 16 of the first Schedule to the 1947 Act. Although both made provision for recourse to the Secretary of State against the action of the authority, the 1972 Act had no provision corresponding to paragraph 15 which allowed for an application to the Court of Session.

3—14   A similar approach is to be seen in *R v. Secretary of State for the Environment ex p. Kent*[49] in the context of an appeal to the High Court under section 242 of the Town and Country Planning Act 1971 (now section 284 of the Town and Country Planning Act 1990) following the decision of the Secretary of State on a planning appeal. The case arose out of a successful appeal to the Secretary of State from the refusal of Ealing London Borough Council to grant planning permission for a cellular radio base station and mast 30 feet high. The proposal was in respect of a site situated 15 metres from a block of flats. The local planning authority carried out a non-statutory neighbour notification exercise in respect of the proposals and notified some, but not all, of the occupants of the flats. This was repeated at the request of the Secretary of State. The effect of the failure to notify all the occupants was that many of those who were not notified (including the applicant for judicial review) did not become aware of the application for planning permission until after the six-week limitation period had expired. The applicant contended that there had been a failure of natural justice and that, accordingly, the decision of the local planning authority, the appeal and the Secretary of State's decision were all void. There was therefore nothing upon which the privative provisions of sections 242 and 245 of the 1971 Act could operate. The applicant relied upon *Anisminic Ltd v. Foreign Compensation Commission*. The Court of Appeal held, however, that the applicant's reliance on the *Anisminic* decision was misconceived. In that case the relevant statute contained a complete ouster of rights to challenge the decision and not merely a time-limit; in this instance Parliament has provided a statutory scheme for challenging planning decisions, but this is subject to a strict period of limitation which could not be exceeded.

The clear weight of the current state of the authorities, therefore, is that the six week limitation period is absolute and no challenge can be entertained after

---

[49] [1990] J.P.L. 124.

that period has expired, even if the compulsory purchase order is alleged to be a nullity. It seems unlikely that this robust view will be modified since in considering the effect of a similar provision in the Wildlife and Countryside Act 1981[50] the Divisional Court held in *R. v. Cornwall County Council ex p. Huntington*[51] that the decision of the Court of Appeal in *R. v. Secretary of State for the Environment ex p. Ostler*[52] was binding. As Mann L.J. put it "When paragraphs such as those considered in *ex p. Ostler* are used then the legislative intention is that questions as to invalidity may be raised on the specified grounds in the prescribed time and in the prescribed manner, but that otherwise the jurisdiction of the court is excluded in the interests of certainty."[53]

5. POWERS OF THE COURT

Until final determination of an application under section 23 of the 1981 Act, the **3—15** court may by interim order suspend the operation of the compulsory purchase order or of any provision contained in it, either generally or in so far as it affects any property of the applicant.[54] If satisfied that one or other or both of the statutory grounds have been made out, the court in its discretion may quash the compulsory purchase order or any provision contained in it, either generally or in so far as it affects any property of the applicant.[55]

---

[50] Sched. 15, para. 12(3).
[51] [1992] 3 All E.R. 567.
[52] [1977] Q.B. 122.
[53] It may be regarded as significant that leave to appeal was refused.
[54] 1981 Act, s.24(1).
[55] 1981 Act, s.24(2).

Chapter 4

Compulsory Purchase: Acquiring Title

4—01 When a compulsory purchase order has been made or confirmed by the Secretary of State, the acquiring authority will wish to take steps to implement the authorisation granted by the order. Implementation may not necessarily follow immediately upon confirmation, but it should be noted that the power to acquire land compulsorily conferred by an order cannot be exercised after the expiration of a period of three years from the date on which the order becomes operative.[1] The operative date of an order is the date on which notice of the making or confirmation (as appropriate) of the order is first published, although some other period may be prescribed in the order.[2]

The serving of a notice to treat (see below) is sufficient exercise of the power.[3] In *Advance Ground Rents Ltd v. Middlesbrough Borough Council*[4] the Lands Tribunal held that a failure by the acquiring authority to serve a notice to treat on a mortgagee until after the expiration of the three year period meant that the notice was invalid and the authority had lost their opportunity to rectify the omission.

The acquiring authority may, as a preliminary step towards implementation, on giving not less than three nor more than 14 days notice to the owner or occupiers, enter on the order land for the purposes of surveying and taking levels, of probing or boring to establish the nature of the soil and of setting out the line of the

---

[1] Compulsory Purchase Act 1965, s.4.
[2] Acquisition of Land Act 1981, s.26(1).
[3] *Grice v. Dudley Corporation* [1958] 1 Ch. 329. See, too, *Edinburgh & Glasgow Railway Co. v. Monklands Railway Co.* (1850) 12 D. 1304; 13 D. 145.
[4] [1986] 280 E.G. 1015. See, also, *Fagan v. Metropolitan Borough of Knowsley* (1983) 46 P. & C.R. 226 L.T., reversed (1985) 50 P. & C.R. 363, [1986] J.P.L. 355 C.A.

works (1965 Act, section 11(3)).[5] If this power is exercised the acquiring authority must compensate the owner or occupier for any resulting damage.

There are two ways in which an acquiring authority may proceed to exercise the powers conferred by the order.[6] They may serve what is commonly referred to as a "notice to treat" or they may execute a "general vesting declaration." The advantages and disadvantages of the two procedures are summarised later in this chapter.[7] As a matter of practice, the general vesting declaration is preferable to the notice to treat since the former is simpler to operate. With this point in mind, the discussion of the notice to treat in this chapter may seem disproportionate; the explanation for this is simply that the notice to treat procedure has been in existence for very much longer than the general vesting declaration technique and has been the subject of considerable judicial scrutiny. There is, therefore, a lot more to say about the law relating to the notice to treat than there is about the general vesting declaration. Furthermore, as the execution of a general vesting declaration operates as a deemed notice to treat it would seem sensible to deal with the notice to treat[8] first. The two procedures are now examined in turn.

4—02

Notice to treat

Section 5 of the 1965 Act makes provision for the service of a notice to treat where the acquiring authority wish to acquire any of the order land. It provides that the acquiring authority shall give notice[8a] of their intention to implement the order to all persons with an interest in the land so far as known to the acquiring authority after making diligent inquiry.[9] The notice will give particulars of the land to which it relates, demand particulars of each recipient's estate and interest in the land and state that the acquiring authority are willing to treat for its purchase

4—03

---

[5] This is not treated as entry on the land for the purposes of establishing the valuation date or the date from which interest on compensation is calculated (*Courage Ltd v. Kingswood District Council* (1978) 35 P. & C.R. 436).

[6] The acquiring authority may, of course, decide to hold these powers in reserve and proceed to purchase the necessary land by agreement. Acquisition by agreement is authorised by s.3 of the Compulsory Purchase Act 1965.

[7] See para. 4–26.

[8] Compulsory Purchase (Vesting Declarations) Act 1981, s.7.

[8a] The acquiring authority may serve separate notices at different times in respect of different parts of the same parcel of land provided all the notices are served within the period of three years: *Coats v. Caledonian Railway Co.* (1904) 6 F. 1042.

[9] Making "diligent inquiry" does not require the acquiring authority to become involved in a very great inquiry. In *R. v. Secretary of State for Transport ex p. Blackett* [1992] J.P.L. 1041 land was sold in small plots of one square foot each to frustrate compulsory purchase of an historic battefield site. An application for judicial review arising from alleged failure to serve a notice to treat was dismissed as an abuse of the process of the court.

and for compensation (hence "notice to treat"). Service[10] may be effected in accordance with the provisions of section 6 of the Acquisition of Land Act 1981, applied by section 30 of the 1965 Act.[11] There is no prescribed form of notice[12] but it must be sufficiently specific.[13] It is usual to annex a plan.

1. PARTIES TO BE SERVED

4—04 Section 5 requires the notice to be given "to all the persons interested in, or having power to sell and convey or release the land." In any given case there may, of course, be a number of persons with separate interests in the land. The position of the more important of them is now considered:

1. Owners in fee simple and persons with power to convey: the object of the service requirement is to ensure that all parties who are capable of conveying the legal estate in the land should be involved as the acquiring authority proceeds with the acquisition of the land. In the simplest case this will comprise the person in whom the fee simple absolute is vested within the meaning of the Law of Property Act 1925. This includes a person who has acquired title as a squatter, or is in the process of acquiring title.[14] Where land is held by trustees on an express or statutory trust for sale the trustees must be notified, but not the trustees under a strict settlement within the meaning of the Settled Land Act 1925 since the tenant for life is the person with power to convey and hence is entitled to notice to treat. Personal representatives of a deceased owner are entitled to notice to treat.

2. Lessees: Where the order land is subject to a lease the acquiring authority may simply acquire the landlord's interest and allow the lease to expire by affluxion of time or following the service of a notice to quit. Where, however, the acquiring authority are unable to wait for the lease to run its course, they will have to acquire the interest of the lessee and the lessee will be entitled to notice to treat and to compensation for the loss consequent on the expropriation of the residue of his term.

Where, however, the tenant has no greater interest in the land than as a tenant for a year or from year to year (referred to as a "short tenant") such an interest will not be acquired. For these purposes any statutory protection, *e.g.* under the

---

[10] See *Shepherd v. Corporation of Norwich* (1885) 30 Ch.D. 553; and *Fagan v. Knowsley Metropolitan Borough Council* [1986] J.P.L. 355.

[11] See para. 2–11.

[12] *Coats v. Caledonian Railway Co.* (1904) 6 F. 1042; *Renton v. North British Railway Co.* (1845) 8 D. 247.

[13] *Lewis v. Hackney London Borough Council* [1990] 27 E.G. 72.

[14] *Perry v. Clissold* [1907] A.C. 73.

Landlord and Tenant Act 1954 is disregarded.[15] The acquiring authority may simply terminate such a tenancy (by a notice of entry) and the tenant will be entitled under section 20 of the 1965 Act to compensation for any consequent loss.[16] If notice to treat is actually served this does not change the tenant's compensation rights which still fall to be assessed as if notice had been given under section 20.[17]

Where part only of land which is let is to be acquired, section 19 of the 1965 Act makes provision for apportionment of the rent. **4—05**

3. Mortgagees: a mortgagee (whether legal or equitable) is entitled to a notice to treat.[18] Section 14 of the 1965 Act makes provision for redemption of a mortgage by the acquiring authority. The authority may purchase or redeem the interest of the mortgagee and pay the mortgagee the principal and interest due on the security together with any expenses and charges and six months additional interest. Thereupon, the holder of the security is to convey his interest to the authority. Alternatively, the authority may give notice in writing to the mortgagee that they will pay off the principal and interest at the end of a period of six months. At the expiration of that period, on payment by the acquiring authority of the principal and interest together with any expenses and charges, the creditor will convey or release to the acquiring authority his interest in the land comprised in the security.

If any land subject to such a security is of less value than the principal, interest and expenses secured, the value of the land or the compensation to be paid for it is to be settled in the normal way by agreement between the parties or, failing agreement, by reference to the Lands Tribunal. The amount determined upon is then to be paid by the acquiring authority to the holder of the mortgage in satisfaction of his claim so far as it will go, and upon payment, the mortgagee will convey or release all his interest in the mortgaged land; the personal obligation to repay the balance of the loan is unaffected (1965 Act, section 15).[19]

If part only of mortgaged land is being acquired and the part being acquired is **4—06** of less value than the outstanding principal, interest and costs secured on the land as a whole, and the mortgagee does not regard the remainder of the land as a sufficient security for the sum due (or is not willing to release the part being acquired), the value of the part being acquired together with compensation for severance, if any,[20] is to be determined by agreement between the parties or, failing agreement, by reference to the Lands Tribunal. The amount so determined is then to be paid by the acquiring authority to the mortgagee in satisfaction of the debt, so far as it will go. The mortgagee must then convey or discharge to

---

[15] Such protection is, however, relevant in assessing compensation.
[16] See para. 13–01 *et seq.*
[17] *Newham London Borough Council v. Benjamin* [1968] 1 All E.R. 1195.
[18] *Martin v. London, Chatham and Dover Railway Co.* (1866) 1 Ch. App 501.
[19] Provision is made for paying the money into court and execution of a deed poll vesting the land in the acquiring authority: 1965 Act, s.15(4), (5).
[20] See Chap. 12.

the authority his interest in the land to be taken. A memorandum of what has been paid, signed by the mortgagee, will be endorsed on the mortgagee deed and a copy of the memorandum is to be furnished by the authority (if required) to the person entitled to the equity of redemption of the land comprised in the mortgage (1965 Act, section 16).[21]

In the case of a payment to a mortgagee under any of sections 14–16 of the 1965 Act, additional compensation can be claimed by the mortgagee in respect of or incidental to the reinvestment of the sum paid off and in respect of any loss due to a lower rate of interest being earned by the reinvested fund than that reserved under the mortgage (1965 Act, section 17).

4. Incorporeal hereditaments: If a servient tenement is compulsorily acquired, the proprietor of the dominant tenement is not entitled to a notice to treat.[22] The existence of an easement or restrictive covenant cannot impede the carrying out of the works for which the servient land has been authorised to be acquired[23] but interference with the right will entitle the proprietor of the dominant tenement to claim compensation for injurious affection[24] under sections 7 or 10 of the Compulsory Purchase Act 1965.[25] In some instances extinguishment is essential, e.g. of an option to purchase[26] or an estate contract arising from an exchange of contracts to purchase the land.[27]

2. INTERESTS OMITTED TO BE PURCHASED

4—07 If, after the acquiring authority have taken possession of any land which they have been authorised to acquire, it appears that through "mistake or inadvertence"[28] there is a right or interest in the land which they have failed to purchase or pay compensation for, section 22 of the 1965 Act provides that the authority may remain in undisturbed possession of the land. They must, however, within six months of receipt of notice of a claim which they do not dispute, purchase or

---

[21] Provision is likewise made for paying the money into court where it is refused on tender and for execution of a deed poll (s.16(4), (5)).

[22] *Thicknesse v. Lancaster Canal Co.* (1838) 4 M. & W. 472; *Clark v. School Board for London* (1874) 9 Ch. App. 120; *Grimley v. Minister of Housing and Local Government* [1971] 2 Q.B. 96 (easements); *Long Eaton Recreation Grounds Co. v. Midland Railway Co.* [1902] 2 K.B. 574 (restrictive covenant).

[23] Some enabling Acts make specific provision to this effect: see, for example, the Town and Country Planning Act 1990 s.236 (extinguishment of private rights of way), s.237 (power to override any easement, liberty or privilege, right or advantage, including any natural right to support).

[24] See Chaps. 12 and 16.

[25] See *Clark v. School Board for London* (1874) 9 Ch. App. 120; *School Board for Edinburgh v. Simpson* (1906) 13 S.L.T. 90.

[26] *Oppenheimer v. Minister of Transport* [1942] 1 K.B. 242.

[27] *Hillingdon Estates Co. v. Stonefield Estates Ltd* [1952] Ch. 627.

[28] *Jolly v. Wimbledon etc. Railway* (1861) 31 L.J.Q.B. 95; *Martin v. London Chatham etc. Railway* (1866) L.R. 1 Ch. 501; *Hyde v. Manchester Corporation* (1852) 5 De G. & Sm. 249; *Stretton v. Great Western and Brentford Railway* (1870) L.R. 5 Ch. 751.

pay compensation for such right of interest. If they fail to do so within the time-limit the opportunity to rectify the position is lost.[29] Where the authority dispute the claim, time runs from the date on which the claim is established by law. It makes no difference that the period of three years allowed for the exercise of the power conferred by the order has expired.[30] The compensation is to be assessed according to the value of the right or interest at the time the acquiring authority took possession and without regard to any improvements carried out by the acquiring authority;[31] but the claimant is entitled to compensation for any mesne profits or interest which would have accrued to him during the period that the authority have been in possession.[32]

Section 22 of the 1965 Act is of no avail if the authority did not, prior to the expiration of the period allowed for the exercise of power conferred by the order, intend to acquire the estate or interest which they have omitted to purchase.[33]

3. THE LAND TO BE ACQUIRED

Service of the notice to treat is the first step in the actual acquisition of the order land. It is appropriate at this stage to consider briefly what is meant by "land". Statutory definitions principally require that the enabling Act should govern this matter.[34] Thus section 1(3) of the Compulsory Purchase Act 1965 defines "land" to include "anything falling within any definition of that expression in the enactment under which the purchase is authorised". The Acquisition of Land Act 1981 is similar but is specific in part in that section 7(1) of that Act provides that " 'land' (a) includes messuages, tenements and hereditaments,[35] and (b) in relation to compulsory purchase under any enactment, includes anything falling within any definition of the expression in that enactment." The Land Compensation Act 1961, however, provides[36] that " 'land' means any corporeal hereditament, including a building and includes any interest or right in or over land and any right to water." Unless the definition (if any) of land contained in the Act

4—08

---

[29] *Advance Ground Rents Ltd v. Middlesbrough Borough Council* (1986) 280 E.G. 1015. A reference of the claim to the Lands Tribunal before the six months period has expired may have the effect of extending this limitation.

[30] See para. 4–01.

[31] 1965 Act, s.22(4).

[32] *Ibid.* s.22(5).

[33] *Davidson's Trustees v. Caledonian Railway Co.* (1894) 21 R. 1060.

[34] Neither the Land Compensation Act 1973 nor the Planning and Compensation Act 1991 contains a definition of "land". The Interpretation Act 1978, Sched. 1, defines land to include "buildings and other structures, land covered with water and any estate, interest, easement, servitude or right in or over land."

[35] In *Hill v. Midland Railway Co.* (1882) 21 Ch.D. 143, Fry J. considered an easement to be "plainly a hereditament."

[36] s.39(1). "Building" is defined *ibid.* as "any structure or erection and any part of a building as so defined, but does not include plant or machinery comprised in a building."

authorising the compulsory acquisition is to the contrary, the compulsory acquisition will include title to the land itself together with the structures, or fixtures on the land and any timber or crops which have not been cut or harvested. The owner may, however, elect to remove fixtures and cut timber or crops or to sell them to the acquiring authority.[37]

Minerals also pass to the acquiring authority on compulsory acquisition. But to avoid paying compensation reflecting, for the most part, the development potential of minerals, it is common practice, as explained in Chapter 2,[38] to incorporate the "mining code" into the legislation authorising the purchase so that mineral rights are not acquired.

4—09   As the effect of section 1(3) of the 1965 Act is that "land" in relation to compulsory purchase under any authorising Act is to include any definition of that word in that Act, attention must therefore be directed to any specific definition of the term in the authorising Act. For example, section 270 of the Local Government Act 1972 provides that " 'land' includes any interest in land and any easement or right in, to or over land."[39] The reference is to an *existing* right or easement.[40] And section 228(3) of the Town and Country Planning Act 1990 gives the Secretary of State powers to acquire compulsorily a new easement or other right; section 226 of the Act (which confers powers on local authorities) does not contain an express provision in that respect but similar rights have been conferred by section 13 of the Local Government (Miscellaneous Provisions) Act 1976.

4. EFFECT OF NOTICE TO TREAT

4—10   The nature of the relationship which subsists between an acquiring authority and an owner on whom a notice to treat has been served is not detailed by legislative provisions. Consequently this has been a matter for the courts to determine. By itself, a notice to treat does not bring the parties into a contractual relationship, nor does it create an equitable interest in the land in favour of the acquiring authority.[41] Since the purpose of a notice to treat is to give formal notice of the intended acquisition it requires the owner to give details of his claim. From this follows a right by either party to have the compensation determined unless the notice to treat is withdrawn.[42] To that extent therefore it creates a relationship analogous to that of vendor and purchaser, a relationship which develops so that

---

[37] *Gibson v. Hammersmith and City Railway Co.* (1863) 32 L.J. Ch. 337.
[38] See para. 2–06.
[39] See, too, the Town and country Planning Act 1990, s.336(1).
[40] *Sovmots Investments Ltd v. Secretary of State for the Environment* [1977] Q.B. 411.
[41] *Haynes v. Haynes* (1861) 30 L.J. Ch. 578. The owner is therefore free to dispose of his interest: *Hillingdon Estates Co. v. Stonefield Estates Ltd* [1952] Ch. 627.
[42] *Tiverton and North Devon Railway v. Loosemore* (1884) 9 App. Cas. 480; *Harding v. Metropolitan Railway Co.* (1872) L.R. 7 Ch. 154.

owner and acquiring authority become parties to a "Parliamentary contract" at the stage of agreement on or determination of the price to be paid in respect of the owner's interest.[43] In *Guest v. Poole and Bournemouth Railway Company*[44] Willes J. described service of a notice to treat as "a neutral step . . . since it may lead to an agreement to sell or to the taking of compulsory powers", but in the subsequent House of Lords case of *Ayr Harbour Trustees v. Oswald*[45] Lord Blackburn was more positive and considered that "the notice . . . had the effect of a purchase by the trustees absolutely of the piece of ground."

More recently, in *Birmingham Corporation v. West Midland Baptist (Trust) Association (Inc.)*[46] the speeches in the House of Lords appear to indicate something of a shift in attitude to the notice to treat. In the words of one commentator,[47] their Lordships "expressed the effect of a notice to treat in a much lower key" than had many of their predecessors. Lord Morris of Borth-y-Gest declared, for example:

> "A notice to treat does not establish the relation of vendor and purchaser between the acquiring authority and the owner. It does not transfer either the legal or the equitable interest to the acquiring authority. It informs the owner that the land is to be taken and informs him that the acquiring authority are ready to negotiate with him as to the price of the land . . . It makes a demand for particulars of estates and interest and of claims."

Lord Donovan also stressed that the notice to treat did not operate to transfer any **4—11** kind of equitable title to the land and pointed out that it did not even deprive the owner of power to alienate the property in question. In effect, therefore, their Lordships viewed the notice to treat as little more than notification of an intention to take the land from the owner.

While the effect of service of a notice to treat remains in some respects uncertain[48] there is little doubt that it has the following significance:

1. it determines the land to be taken (but see "counter-notice" below);
2. it enables either party to insist on having compensation determined (para. 4–24 below) and the transaction completed;
3. it enables the acquiring authority to take possession of the land after service of notice of entry (para. 4–23 below);
4. the owner cannot by altering the land or creating more interests in it increase the burden of compensation on the acquiring authority;

---

[43] *Mason v. Stokes Bay Pier and Railway Co.* (1862) 32 L.J. Ch. 110; *Re Pigott and the Great Western Railway Co.* (1881) 18 Ch.D. 146.
[44] (1870) L.R. 5 C.P. 553.
[45] (1883) 8 App. Cas. 623.
[46] [1970] A.C. 874.
[47] F.A. Mann, "The Relevant Date for the Assessment of Compensation" (1969) 85 L.Q.R. 516.
[48] See para. 6–02.

trates this last point. At the date of the notice to treat the premises were occupied by a weekly tenant. Subsequently the tenant obtained a three year lease, but it was held that the tenant did not qualify for compensation in respect of the lease as it was not in existence when the notice to treat was served.

4—12   The common law position is enlarged upon as regards compulsory acquisitions to which the 1981 Act applies by virtue of the provisions of section 4(2). This subsection provides that in assessing compensation no account is to be taken of:

> "any interest in land, or any enhancement of the value of any interest in land, by reason of any building erected, work done, or improvement or alteration made, whether on the land purchased or on any other land with which the claimant is, or was at the time of the erection, doing or making of the building, works, improvement or alteration, directly or indirectly concerned if . . . the creation of the interest, the erection of the building, the doing of the work, the making of the improvement or alteration, as the case may be, was not reasonably necessary and was undertaken with a view to obtaining compensation or increased compensation."

It should be noted that section 4(2) is not confined to interests, etc. created solely since the date of the notice to treat, but would appear to be capable of applying to anything done prior to the date if it "was not reasonably necessary and was undertaken with a view to obtaining compensation or increased compensation." This does not, however, preclude an owner from continuing to manage and even to deal in his property either before or after the date of the notice to treat, for example, by assigning his interest[50] or by granting a short tenancy to ensure continuity of income pending the taking of possession by the acquiring authority.

There is some doubt whether the service of a notice to treat fixes the relevant interests to be acquired. Although the weight of authority indicates that service of a notice to treat does have this effect, it appears that this is not an immutable rule. This issue is considered further in Chapter 6.

5. WITHDRAWAL OR ABANDONMENT OF THE NOTICE TO TREAT

4—13   One effect of the service of the notice to treat, as mentioned above, is that it enables either party to insist on having compensation determined and the transaction completed. Once served, the notice cannot be withdrawn except in the following circumstances.

Section 31(1) of the Land Compensation Act 1961 provides that the acquiring authority may, at any time within six weeks of receipt from a claimant of his

---

assignee takes over the compensation claim, including a right to amend the claim: *Cardiff Corporation v. Cook* [1923] 2 Ch. 115.
[50] *Cardiff Corporation v. Cook* [1923] 2 Ch. 115. See, too, *Landlink Two Ltd v. Sevenoaks District Council* (1986) 51 P. & C.R. 100.

notice of claim, withdraw the notice to treat.[51] Where the claimant has failed to deliver such a notice, or delivered an inadequate notice[52] so that the amount of compensation has to be referred to the Lands Tribunal for determination, the period of six weeks runs from the date when compensation has been "finally determined" (1961 Act, section 31(2)).[53] The acquiring authority is liable to pay compensation to the person served with the notice to treat for any loss[54] or expenses occasioned by the giving and withdrawal of the notice (1961 Act, section 31(3)). Where no proper claim for compensation has been delivered by the claimant, the liability does not extend to any loss or expenses incurred after the time when, in the Tribunal's opinion, such notice of claim should have been delivered. In default of agreement, the amount of any loss or expenses will be determined by the Tribunal (1961 Act, section 31(4)).

A notice to treat may also be withdrawn in response to a notice of objection to severance.[55]

When an acquiring authority evince an intention to abandon the rights given by a notice to treat, the person upon whom it has been served will be entitled to treat the rights as abandoned. An extreme example occurred in *Grice v. Dudley Corporation*[56] in which a compulsory purchase order for road widening and for the erection of a market hall was confirmed and a notice to treat was served in 1939. Negotiations over compensation lapsed on the outbreak of the Second World War. After the war several new improvement schemes were considered by the council although no final decision was made. In 1954, the council raised the question of acquiring the order land at its 1939 price when the notice to treat had been served and threatened to pay that sum into court and acquire title by execution of a deed poll. The plaintiffs, the executors of the claimant, sought a declaration that the notice to treat was no longer valid and effective as the council's plans did not include road widening or the erection of a market hall. Upjohn J. held that the fact that the council were attempting to acquire land for purposes substantially different from those set out in the compulsory purchase order amounted to abandonment of the order and thus an abandonment of the rights under the notice to treat. The council's action was not consistent with the general principle that statutory powers should be exercised for the purpose for which they were conferred.

---

[51] A further notice to treat can, however, be served: *Ashton Vale Iron Co. Ltd v. Bristol Corporation* [1901] 1 Ch. 592.

[52] See *Trustees for Methodist Church Purposes v. North Tyneside Metropolitan Borough Council* (1979) 250 E.G. 647.

[53] A claim is not "finally determined" until the time within which it may be challenged in the Court of Appeal has expired (1961) Act, s.31(6)).

[54] Compensation may include any loss arising from inability to develop the land or to let it: *London County Council v. Montague Burton* [1934] 1 K.B. 360.

[55] See para. 4–15.

[56] [1958] 1 Ch. 329. See, too, *Simpson Motor Sales (London) Ltd v. Hendon Corporation* [1964] A.C. 1088 and *R. v. Carmarthen District Council ex p. Blewin Trust* (1989) 59 P. & C.R. 379.

4—14   It would seem that unexplained delay may amount to an intention to abandon the rights given by a notice to treat. In *Grice*, Upjohn J. said:

> "the promoter exercising statutory powers must proceed to enforce his notice in what, in all the circumstances of the case, is a reasonable period. If he sleeps on his rights he will be barred if his delay is not explained."

To avoid uncertainty, where a delay occurs following service of a notice to treat, an overall period of three years is permitted before the notice to treat lapses. Section 5(2A) of the Compulsory Purchase Act 1965[57] provides that the notice will cease to have effect three years after the date of service unless (a) compensation has been agreed or awarded or paid into court, or (b) a general vesting declaration has been executed, or (c) the acquiring authority have entered and taken possession, or (d) the question of compensation has been referred to the Lands Tribunal. The three year period can be extended by agreement, but if the notice to treat does lapse (whether after three years, or any extended period) the acquiring authority must inform the recipient of the notice and are liable to compensate him for any loss or expenses occasioned by the giving of the notice and its ceasing to have effect: Planning and Compensation Act 1991 section 67(2)(c)).

Counter-notice

1. HOUSE, BUILDING OR MANUFACTORY

4—15   A notice to treat may be directed at part only of a "house, building or manufactory, or of a park or garden belonging to a house." However, no person is required to sell part only if they are willing and able to sell the whole unless the Lands Tribunal determines that, in the case of a house, building or manufactory, the part can be taken without material detriment to the remainder or that, in the case of a park or garden, it can be taken without seriously affecting the amenity or convenience of the house.[58] In determining questions of material detriment or the effect on the amenity or convenience of a house the Tribunal is to take into account not only the effect of severance but also the use to be made of the part proposed to be acquired; and where the part is to be acquired for works or other purposes extending to other land, the Tribunal is to have regard to the effect of the whole of the works and the use to be made of the other land.[59]

---

[57] Inserted by s.67 of the Planning and Compensation Act 1991.
[58] 1965 Act, s.8(1). See *Ravenseft Properties Ltd v. London Borough of Hillingdon* (1968) 20 P. & C.R. 483; *McMillan v. Strathclyde Regional Council* (1982) 265 E.G. 701.
[59] Land Compensation Act 1973, s.58(1).

When a counter-notice (a "notice of objection to severance") is served, it is open to the acquiring authority to agree to acquire the whole[60] or to abandon the purchase altogether. If the authority persist with their intention to take part only, they must satisfy the tribunal that the part may be taken without material detriment to or seriously affecting the amenity or convenience of the remainder, as the case may be. The contention that there can be no material detriment unless some severance is caused for which compensation is not an adequate remedy has been rejected;[61] if that was the case, the provision would rarely, if ever come into play.

In *Ravenseft Properties Ltd v. London Borough of Hillingdon*[62] it was held that the test for material detriment was whether, on part being taken, the remainder would be less useful or less valuable in some significant degree.[63] In *McMillan v. Strathclyde Regional Council*[64] the Lands Tribunal for Scotland, applying the test in *Ravenseft*, concluded that the remainder of the land would be no less useful or less valuable than would have been the case if the compulsory purchase order had not been promoted. The regional council compulsorily acquired part of the front garden of a bungalow for road widening, the effect of which would be to bring the heel of the footpath to be constructed alongside the road to a point some 15 feet from the nearest part of the front wall of the bungalow—the existing road being at present some 31 feet away. Notwithstanding the anticipated increase in noise and loss of privacy, the Tribunal found that under the terms of the disposition of the bungalow, the owners were required, if called upon by the local authority, to form a roadway and footpath not materially different to that constructed as a result of the compulsory purchase order.

4—16

The word "house" has been given a wide meaning. In *Ravenseft* it was held to extend to a building which was used for business purposes and was not restricted to mere dwelling-houses; and it has been held that land which is part of the curtilage is to be treated as part of the house.[65]

There is no prescribed form of counter-notice[66] and no time-limit is prescribed for its service although it seems likely that it should be served before the acquiring authority have taken steps to follow up the notice to treat. In *Glasshouse Properties*

---

[60] The counter-notice must relate to the whole of the part which is not included in the notice to treat: *Pulling v. London, Chatham and Dover Railway Co.* (1864) 33 L.J. Ch. 505.

[61] *Ravenseft Properties Ltd v. London Borough of Hillingdon* (1968) 20 P. & C.R. 483.

[62] *Ibid.*

[63] See, too, *Caledonian Railway Co. v. Turcan* [1898] A.C. 256.

[64] (1982) 265 E.G. 701.

[65] *St Thomas's Hospital (Governors) v. Charing Cross Railway Co.* (1861) 30 L.J. Ch. 395; *Caledonian Railway v. Turcan* [1898] A.C. 256; as to the meaning of "building" and "manufactory" see *Regent Canal and Dock Co. v. London County Council* [1912] 1 Ch. 583; *Greswolde-Williams v. Newcastle upon Tyne Corporation* (1927) 92 J.P. 13; *Reddin v. Metropolitan Board of Works* (1862) 31 L.J. Ch. 660; *Richards v. Swansea Improvements and Tramway Co.* (1878) 9 Ch.D. 425; *Bennington v. Metropolitan Board of Works* (1886) 54 L.T. 837.

[66] A counter-notice given orally would appear to be valid: *Binney v. Hammersmith and City Railway Co.* (1863) 8 L.T. 161.

Ltd v. Secretary of State for Transport[67] the Lands Tribunal held that the counter-notice should be served prior to entry being taken by the aquiring authority since there would otherwise be no "retreat" available to the aquiring authority in the event of the Tribunal deciding that the part could not be taken without material detriment to the whole.

2. INTERSECTED LANDS

4—17 Section 8(2) of the 1965 Act provides that if any land which is not situated in a town or built upon, is cut through and divided by the works as to leave, either on both sides of the works, or on one side, a quantity of land which is less than half an acre, and the owner has no other adjoining land with which the remaining land may be merged, the owner may require the acquiring authority to acquire the remaining land. Where the intersected land can be merged with an owner's adjoining land, the cost of effecting the merger (removing fences, levelling the sites and soiling) is to be borne by the acquiring authority. The provision is a hangover from the railway building era when intersection of land was not uncommon. Road building gives rise to the same sort of problem for landowners.

Section 8(3) of the 1965 Act deals with the situation where an owner has no adjoining land with which the severed portions may be merged and the severed portions are together less than half an acre or the cost of linking them, for example, by a bridge or underpass exceeds their value. In that case, notwithstanding the wishes of the owner, the acquiring authority may insist on acquiring the intersected land.

3. AGRICULTURAL LAND

4—18 Helpful as the provisions of section 8, subsections (2) and (3) may be, they do not assist the owner or tenant of an agricultural unit, the continuing viability of which is threatened by severance arising, for example, from a motorway being taken through the unit. This situation is dealt with in sections 53 to 56 of the Land Compensation Act 1973.

Section 53 of the 1973 Act provides that where an acquiring authority serve a notice to treat in respect of any agricultural land on a person (whether in occupation or not) having a greater interest in the land than as a tenant for a year or from year to year and that person has such an interest in other agricultural land in the same agricultural unit, that person (referred to as "the claimant") may serve a counter-notice on the authority claiming that the other land is not reasonably

---

[67] (1993) 66 P. & C.R. 285. Contrast the position where a counter-notice is to be served in response to a general vesting declaration (see para. 4–30 below).

capable of being farmed either by itself or in conjunction with other relevant land.[68] The counter-notice must be served within two months of the date of service of the notice to treat.

"Agricultural unit" is defined as land occupied as a unit for agricultural purposes, including any dwelling-house or other building occupied by the same person for the purpose of farming the land.[69] "Other relevant land" is awkwardly defined to mean land comprised in the same agricultural unit in which the claimant "does not have such an interest as is mentioned in [section 53(1)]." As the interest referred to in that provision is an "interest . . . as tenant for a year or from year to year" the effect therefore is that the claimant must not have a greater interest than as tenant for a year or from year to year; the term also includes land comprised in any other agricultural unit occupied by the claimant on the date of service of the notice to treat in which he has a greater interest than as a tenant for a year or from year to year (1973 Act, section 53(3)). A copy of the counter-notice must also be served within the same period on any other person having an interest in the land to which the counter-notice relates.

Should the acquiring authority serve a separate notice to treat in respect of the other agricultural land in the same unit in which the claimant has a greater interest than as a tenant for a year or from year to year, it is to be assumed that the other land is not available to him for the purpose of making up a viable economic farming unit. The same applies where a notice to treat is served in respect of any of the "other relevant land" (1973 Act, section 53(4)).

If the acquiring authority have not accepted the counter-notice as valid within **4—19** two months of the date of its service either party may within a further period of two months refer it to the Lands Tribunal (1973 Act, section 54(1)). The Tribunal will determine whether the counter-notice is justified and declare it to be valid or invalid accordingly. Where a counter-notice is accepted as or declared to be valid, the acquiring authority are deemed to be authorised to acquire compulsorily the claimant's interest in the land to which it relates and to have served a notice to treat on the same date as the original notice to treat (1973 Act, section 54(2)).

A counter-notice may be withdrawn at any time before the compensation which follows from the deemed notice to treat has been determined by the Lands Tribunal or within six weeks of such compensation being so determined (1973 Act, section 54(3)). Where a counter-notice is withdrawn the deemed notice to treat is also considered to be withdrawn.[70]

Where as a result of the operation of the counter-notice provision, the acquir- **4—20** ing authority become, or will become, entitled to a lease but not to the interest of the lessor, they must offer to surrender the lease to the lessor on such terms as

---

[68] A similar provision applies where a notice to treat is deemed to be served under the provisions of Part VI, Chap. I, of the Town and Country Planning Act 1990 (purchase notice) (1990 Act, s.145).

[69] 1973 Act, s.87(1), applying s.177(1) of the Town and Country Planning Act 1990.

[70] The power conferred by s.31 of the Land Compensation Act 1961 to withdraw a notice to treat is not exercisable in the case of a notice to treat deemed to have been served under s.54 of the Land Compensation Act 1973 (see s.54(4)).

the authority consider reasonable (1973 Act, section 54(6)). Failing agreement as to what terms are reasonable, the question is to be determined by the Lands Tribunal.[71] Any terms as to surrender contained in the lease are to be disregarded for the purposes of this provision.

Section 55 of the 1973 Act makes similar provision for service of a counter-notice where the acquiring authority have served *notice of entry*[72] on the person in occupation of an agricultural holding,[73] being a person having no greater interest in the holding than as tenant for a year or from year to year (referred to as "the claimant") and the notice relates to part only of the holding. The claimant may, within two months of the service of the notice of entry, serve a counter-notice on the authority claiming that the remainder of the holding is not reasonably capable of being farmed, either by itself or in conjunction with other relevant land, as a separate agricultural unit and electing to treat the notice of entry as relating to the entire holding. A copy of the counter-notice is also to be served on the landlord of the holding.

"Other relevant land" in this case refers to land comprised in the same agricultural unit[74] as the agricultural holding; and also to land comprised in any other agricultural unit occupied by the claimant on the date of service of the notice of entry, being land in respect of which the claimant has a greater interest than as a tenant for a year or from year to year (1973 Act, section 55(3)).

4—21   If the acquiring authority have served a notice to treat in respect of land in the agricultural holding, other than that to which the notice of entry relates, or in respect of the other relevant land (above), that other land is not to be considered as available for the purpose of determining whether the remainder of the holding is reasonably capable of being farmed (1973 Act, section 55(4)).

If the acquiring authority do not, within two months of the date of service of the counter-notice, accept it as valid, the question may be referred to the Lands Tribunal for determination (1973 Act, section 56(1)). Where a counter-notice is accepted or declared to be valid, then if within 12 months the claimant has given up possession of every part of the agricultural holding to the acquiring authority, the notice of entry is to be deemed to have extended to the part of the holding to which it did not relate and the authority are to be deemed to have taken possession of that part on the day before the expiration of the year of the tenancy which is current when the counter-notice is accepted or declared valid (1973 Act, section 56(2)).

4—22   Where the claimant has given up possession of an agricultural holding to the acquiring authority in such circumstances but the authority have not been authorised to acquire the landlord's interest in, or in any of, the part of the holding

---

[71] Where the lessor refuses to accept any sum payable to him resulting from such an arrangement, provision is made for payment into court (1973) Act, s.54(7)).

[72] See para. 4—23.

[73] "Agricultural holding" has the meaning given to it by s.1 of the Agricultural Holdings Act 1986 (1973 Act, s.87(1)).

[74] 1973 Act, s.87(1), applying s.177(1) of the Town and Country Planning Act 1990.

to which the notice of entry did not relate (referred to as "the land not subject to compulsory purchase"), neither the claimant nor the acquiring authority are under any liability to the landlord by reason of the claimant giving up possession or the acquiring authority taking possession (1973 Act, section 56(3)(a)), but the authority must immediately give up possession of the land to the landlord and he must take possession (1973 Act, section 56(3)(b)). The tenancy is to be treated as terminated on the date on which the acquiring authority acquired possession of the holding (1973 Act, section 56(3)(c)); and the acquiring authority take the place of the claimant as regards any rights or liabilities arising on or out of the termination of the tenancy (1973 Act, section 56(3)(d)). Any disagreement over any payment to be made in respect of any such right or liability will be determined by the Lands Tribunal.

Notice of Entry

Having served a notice to treat, the acquiring authority will, at some stage, wish to take possession of the order land. They may do this in advance of the conveyance of the land to them and even in advance of the compensation being determined.[75] Section 11 of the 1965 Act makes detailed provision for entry[76] on the land. An acquiring authority may within three years[77] after serving notice to treat and after serving on the owner, lessee and occupier of the land not less than 14 days' notice[78] take possession of the order land or so much of it as is specified in the notice of entry. If the acquiring authority do not take possession at the end of the period specified in the notice of entry they are not deemed to have done so.[79] The consent of the owner, lessee and occupier is not required. The acquiring authority must, however, in due course compensate those with an interest in the land together with interest from the date of entry to the date of payment.[80] Where

4—23

---

[75] Entry may be gained, even if no notice to treat has been served, if the purpose of entry is for the purpose of surveying, etc., the land, provided not less than three nor more than 14 days notice is given (see para. 4–01).

[76] There are two possible procedures, either (a) service of a notice of entry under s.11(1) or (b) under s.11(2) (applying Sched. 3) which requires payment into court of compensation claimed by the owner, or the sum determined by a valuer for this purpose, where the owner has not given his consent to entry by the acquiring authority. A bond must also be given to the owner equal to the sum paid into court together with interest from the date of entry to the date of payment. Two sureties to the bond are required. In view of the cumbersome nature of this procedure it is rarely employed today.

[77] Compulsory Purchase Act 1965, s.5(2A) (inserted by s.67 of the Planning and Compensation Act 1991).

[78] The provisions for the serving of notices set out in s.6 of the Acquisition of Land Act 1981 apply to service of a notice of entry: 1965 Act, s.30 (see para. 2–11).

[79] *Burson v. Wantage Rural District Council* (1974) 27 P. & C.R. 556.

[80] 1965 Act, s.11(1); the rate of interest is prescribed by regulations made under s.32 of the Land Compensation Act 1961 (see para. 13–42).

an occupant fails to give up possession on the expiry of notice of entry, the acquiring authority may issue a warrant to the sheriff for possession under section 13 of the 1965 Act.

In *Chilton v. Telford Corporation*[81] possession of the order land was taken by the acquiring authority in several stages. The question in issue was whether for valuation purposes there was a single date when possession was taken of the first parcel of land or whether there were several dates, one for each parcel. The Court of Appeal held that first entry on any part of the land described in the notice constituted entry on the whole. It would seem that if an authority wish to take entry in stages they may do so with a succession of notices of entry each limited to the particular stage.

Compensation

4—24   One effect of the service of the notice to treat is that it enables either party to insist on having the compensation determined. The notice to treat requires those with a compensatable interest to provide particulars of their claim. The provision of such particulars will be the first step towards settlement of the compensation. The particulars should give details of the compensation claimed, distinguishing the amount under separate heads and showing how the amount under each head is calculated. Failure to deliver adequate particulars to enable the acquiring authority to make a proper offer of compensation may result in a reference to the Lands Tribunal and an award of costs against the claimant (see para. 14–09).[82] At any time within six weeks after the delivery of such particulars, the acquiring authority may withdraw the notice to treat.[83]

An application to the Lands Tribunal for the determination of any question of disputed compensation may not be made before the expiration of 28 days from the date of service of the notice to treat (see para. 14–05).[84] If the question of compensation has not been referred to the Lands Tribunal (in the absence of an agreement) within three years of the date of service, the notice to treat will cease to have effect.[85]

Conveyancing

4—25   Where, following service of a notice to treat, compensation has been agreed or

---

[81] [1987] 1 W.L.R. 872.
[82] Land Compensation Act 1961, s.4(1)(b).
[83] See para. 4–13.
[84] Lands Tribunal Rules 1975 (S.I. 1975 No. 299), r.16(3).
[85] Compulsory Purchase Act 1965, s.5(2A), inserted by s.67 of the Planning and Compensation Act 1991. Contrast the position with the execution of a general vesting declaration (para. 4–32).

determined, the person able to convey the land must do so when required by the acquiring authority. The conveyance will be either in the statutory form provided for in section 23(6) and Schedule 5 to the 1965 Act or by deed in such other form as the acquiring authority think fit. Where, however, land is being taken from someone who is unable or unwilling to convey it, or who cannot be traced, title may be acquired under section 2 and Schedule 1 (owner unable to convey), section 9 (owner unwilling to convey), or section 5 and Schedule 2 (untraced owner), respectively. In these cases, compensation is assessed by surveyors and paid into court; the acquiring authority are then authorised to execute a deed poll which vests the title which is being acquired. If, as is more commonly the case, a general vesting declaration is being employed in lieu of a notice to treat,[86] title will vest in the acquiring authority not under the 1965 Act but under the provisions of the Compulsory Purchase (Vesting Declarations) Act 1981. The provisions of the 1981 Act are considered in detail in the next part of this chapter. For completeness, however, it should be added that there is nothing to prevent title being acquired by way of voluntary conveyance without resort to the statutory methods of obtaining title.

General vesting declaration

The notice to treat and notice of entry procedure just described enables an acquiring authority to gain entry to the land in the shortest possible time. Having served notice of the making or confirmation of the compulsory purchase order, as appropriate, the authority may serve a notice to treat together with a notice of entry and take *possession* after 14 days. This may be important where, for example, the authority is working to a deadline for handing over the site to a contractor for commencement of the work for which the land is being acquired. However, the *title* to the land may not follow for some considerable time; compensation must first be agreed or determined so that where the authority need to acquire title in the shortest possible time, for example, in order to grant a building lease for the carrying out of the work, the general vesting declaration procedure is to be preferred. The provisions relevant to this procedure are contained in the Compulsory Purchase (Vesting Declarations) Act 1981. Under this Act, at the end of the period specified in the declaration (generally, a minimum of three months—see below) the title to the land, together with the right of entry, vests in the acquiring authority. The general vesting declaration procedure is also administratively more convenient where there are a considerable number of interests in the order land to be acquired. For these reasons the general vesting declaration procedure is widely

4—26

---

[86] It is not necessary to agree or determine compensation in advance of the execution of a general vesting declaration.

used by acquiring authorities. It can be invoked by any Minister or local or other authority which is authorised to acquire land by means of a compulsory purchase order.

The main provisions governing the procedure are contained in sections 3–9 of the Compulsory Purchase (Vesting Declarations) Act 1981. These provisions are applicable to all interests in land except a "minor tenancy", *i.e.* a tenancy no greater than for a year or from year to year. They cannot be invoked, however, where a notice to treat has already been issued, unless that notice has been withdrawn (section 3(2)).

4—27 Before making a general vesting declaration with respect to any land[87] which is the subject to a compulsory purchase order, section 3 of the Vesting Declarations Act 1981 requires the acquiring authority to include an indication of their intention to use the vesting declaration procedure in the notice of the making or confirmation of the order required to be published or served by section 15 of the Acquisition of Land Act 1981[88] or in a notice given subsequently.[89] The notice must contain a statement of the effect of sections 3–9[90] together with an invitation to those entitled to claim compensation to give information to the acquiring authority in the prescribed form[91] with regard to their name and address, the land in question, and the nature of the interest held in the land. The service of a notice under section 3 has been held to have the effect of exercising powers of compulsory purchase within the three year limitation period prescribed by section 4 of the Compulsory Purchase Act 1965.[92]

A general vesting declaration may not be executed before the end of a period of two months, beginning with the date of the first publication[93] of the notice containing the indication of the intention to use the procedure, unless every occupier of the land specified in the declaration consents in writing to a shorter period (section 5(1)).

Having executed the declaration,[94] the acquiring authority must serve a notice in the prescribed form[95] specifying the land and stating the effect of the declaration

---

[87] It is not necessary that all the order land should be the subject of a declaration; and there may be several general vesting declarations executed at different times in respect of different parts of the order land.

[88] Or required to be published or served under other procedures.

[89] The requirements relating to publication and service of a notice of making or confirmation of a compulsory purchase order apply equally to a notice given subsequently: Compulsory Purchase (Vesting Declarations) Act 1981, s.3(1)(b). The notice is required to be the subject of an entry in the register of local land charges pursuant to s.3(4).

[90] See Form 2, Part 1 in the Schedule to the Compulsory Purchase of Land (Vesting Declarations) Regulations 1990 (S.I. 1990 No. 497).

[91] *Ibid.* Form 2, Part 2.

[92] *Westminster City Council v. Quereschi* (1990) 60 P. & C.R. 380. See, however, the decision to the contrary of Vinelott J. in *Co-operative Insurance Society Ltd v. Hastings Borough Council* (1993) 91 L.G.R. 608.

[93] It is not clear why reference is made to the "first" publication as there is no requirement for second or subsequent publication.

[94] For the form of the general vesting declaration see the Schedule to the 1990 Regulations, Form 1.

[95] *Ibid.* Form 3.

on every occupier of any of the land specified (other than land in which there subsists a short tenancy or a long tenancy which is about to expire—see below) and on every other person who has given information to the acquiring authority with respect of any of that land in response to their (the authority's) invitation to do so (section 6(1)). The declaration will state the period at the end of which it is to take effect, which must be a date not less than 28 days[96] after the date on which service of these notices has been completed.[97]

The effect of a general vesting declaration is threefold. First of all, at the end **4—28** of the period specified in the declaration the specified land, together with the right to enter on and take possession of it, vests in the acquiring authority as if the authority had executed a deed poll under the provisions of the Compulsory Purchase Act 1965 (see above).[98] The scope of the deemed deed poll includes interests in the land and operates to extinguish "any rent-service, rent charge, chief or other rent, or other payment in incumbrance."[99]

Secondly, the provisions of the Land Compensation Act 1961 and the Compulsory Purchase Act 1965 apply as if on the date on which the declaration was made a notice to treat had been served. Either party may accordingly insist on having compensation determined. However, the power conferred by section 31 of the Land Compensation Act 1961 to withdraw a notice to treat[1] is not exercisable where a general vesting declaration has been employed (section 31(3)) as the interests in respect of which a notice to treat is deemed to have been served will have already vested in the acquiring authority.

Thirdly, it fixes the date for valuing the interest acquired.[2] In *Hussain and Others v. Oldham Metropolitan Borough Council*[3] the claimants, who had been allowed to remain in possession after vesting and were still continuing to trade at the date of the eventual hearing before the Lands Tribunal to determine compensation, argued that the date of valuation was the date of the assessment by the Tribunal. The Tribunal concluded that in the light of the speeches in *Birmingham Corporation v. West Midland Baptist (Trust) Association (Inc.)*[4] the valuation date where the expedited completion procedure is employed is the date of vesting.

The general vesting declaration applies to the interest of a lessee for a term of **4—29** years unexpired but has no effect as regards any person entitled to a minor tenancy or a long tenancy which is about to expire. These terms are defined in section 2 of the 1981 Act. A "minor tenancy" means a tenancy for a year or from year to

---

[96] Compulsory Purchase (Vesting Declarations) Act 1981, s.4(1).
[97] A certificate by the acquiring authority that the service of notices required by s.6(1) was completed on a date specified in the certificate will be conclusive evidence of the fact so stated (s.4(2)).
[98] As regards possession of documents of title see the Compulsory Purchase (Vesting Declarations) Act 1981, s.14.
[99] *Ibid.* s.8(2).
[1] See para. 4–13.
[2] See Chap. 6.
[3] (1981) 259 E.G. 56. See, too, *Ware v. Edinburgh District Council*, 1976 S.L.T. 2 (Lands Tr.) 21 and *Mrs Annie R. Renfrew's Trustees v Glasgow Corporation*, 1972 S.L.T. (Lands (Tr.) 2.
[4] [1991] A.C. 874. (see Chap. 6).

year or any lesser interest; a "long tenancy which is about to expire" means a tenancy granted for an interest greater than a minor tenancy, but having at the date of the declaration a period still to run which is not longer than what is referred to as the "specified period." The "specified period" is a period, longer than one year, specified in the declaration in relation to the land in which the tenancy subsists.[5] The right to enter and take possession of the land specified in a general vesting declaration will be subject to any minor tenancies or long tenancies which are about to expire.

Where such tenancies exist, the acquiring authority may be content, having acquired the landlord's interest, to let them expire in the normal way at the end of their term or to serve relevant notices to terminate statutorily protected tenancies.[6] In practice this option leads to delays which may not be consistent with the proposals of the acquiring authority. Alternatively, if they are unable to wait before taking entry, they must first serve a notice to treat under section 9(2) of the Compulsory Purchase (Vesting Declarations) Act 1981 in respect of the tenancy followed by a notice of entry stating that at the end of such period as is specified in the notice (not being less than 14 days from the date of service) they intend to enter upon and take possession of the land. This is an exception to the general rule that a minor tenant is not entitled to a notice to treat. Service of such a notice does not, however, alter the basis of compensation.[7]

4—30   Section 12 and Schedule 1 to the 1981 Act provide for service of a counter-notice objecting to severance where a general vesting declaration comprises part only of a house, building or factory, or of a park or garden belonging to a house. The notice of objection to severance must require the acquiring authority to take the interest in the whole of the property. To be effective the notice of objection to severance must be served not later than 28 days after the acquiring authority have served notice of the making of the general vesting declaration and explaining its effect.[8] Where a counter-notice is served, the interest will not vest in the acquiring authority and the authority may not enter and take possession of the land until the notice has been disposed of under the provisions of the Schedule.

Within three months of receipt of a counter-notice, the acquiring authority must either (a) serve a notice withdrawing the deemed notice to treat in respect of the land proposed to be severed, or (b) serve notice that the general vesting declaration is to have effect as if the whole of the land had been included in the declaration, or (c) refer the counter-notice to the Lands Tribunal for determination. If the acquiring authority fail to respond to the notice of objection to severance within the three month period, the effect is that the deemed notice to treat

---

[5] Compulsory Purchase (Vesting Declarations) Act 1981, s.2(2).
[6] For example by service of a notice under s.25 of the Landlord and Tenant Act 1954 to terminate a business tenancy.
[7] *Smith and Waverley Tailoring Co. v. Edinburgh District Council (No.2)*, 1977 S.L.T. (Lands Tr.) 29.
[8] See para. 4–27. But see para. 10 of Sched. 1 (position in event of failure of service of notice of the making of the general vesting declaration).

is deemed to have been withdrawn.[9] The Tribunal's powers as regards disposal of the notice are much the same as for the disposal of a counter-notice served in response to a notice to treat.[10]

The provisions of sections 53 and 54 of the Land Compensation Act 1973 apply as regards the severance of agricultural land by a general vesting declaration (1973 Act, section 53(5)).

Where land vests in the acquiring authority following execution of a general vesting declaration the authority must pay the like compensation, together with interest, as they would have paid had they taken possession of the land following service of a notice of entry under section 11(1) of the Compulsory Purchase Act 1965.[11]

In *Hussain and Others v. Oldham Metropolitan Borough Council*[12] this provision **4—31** was taken to mean that compensation, including compensation for disturbance, is to be calculated as if steps had been taken to obtain actual physical possession at the date on which title vests in the acquiring authority, notwithstanding that possession was not actually taken until five years later. In *Park Automobile Co. Ltd. v. Strathclyde Regional Council*[13] the Lands Tribunal for Scotland in construing the corresponding provision in the Scottish legislation (paragraph 30 of Schedule 24 to the Town and Country Planning (Scotland) Act 1972) reserved its opinion on the decision in *Hussain*. Such an interpretation where the former owner was left in occupation following the vesting date would appear to undermine the principle that compensation should reflect the actual loss sustained; it would also seem to undermine the related duty to mitigate that loss. The Tribunal doubted whether paragraph 30 of Schedule 24 was really intended to effect such a fundamental alteration in the law. The concept of deemed physical entry was "more likely to have been introduced to fix the valuation date . . . and not for consequential loss or the interrelated duty to minimise that loss when occasion offers; for this can only occur subsequently".[14]

Section 10(3) of the 1981 Act imposes a time-limit of six years for referring **4—32** questions of disputed compensation to the Lands Tribunal following execution of a general vesting declaration. The six year time-limit runs from the date at which the person claiming compensation, or a person from whom he derives title, first knew or could reasonably be expected to have known of the vesting of the interest.[15] In the absence of examples of the application of this limitation rule by the

---

[9] *Ibid.* paras 4 and 5.
[10] See para. 4—15.
[11] Compulsory Purchase (Vesting Declarations) Act 1981, s.10; s.11 makes provision for the recovery of overpaid compensation in the event of non-disclosure of an incumbrance in the particulars of claim, or lack of title.
[12] (1981) 259 E.G. 56.
[13] [1983] R.V.R. 108.
[14] See Chap. 11.
[15] The notice to treat procedure is subject to a three year limit since the notice to treat ceases to have effect if disputed compensation has not been referred to the Lands Tribunal within three years of service of the notice.

Lands Tribunal, reference can usefully be made to decisions by the Lands Tribunal for Scotland. In *Apostolic Church Trustees v. Glasgow District Council (No. 2)*[16] the reference to the Tribunal was made more than 11 years after vesting. The Tribunal held that the onus was on the acquiring authority to show that an owner knew, or could reasonably be expected to have known of the vesting of his interest more than six years before the date of the reference and that in the particular circumstances of the case the onus had not been discharged. In *Lawrence Garvey v. Clydebank District Council,*[17] on the other hand, where the reference was almost 12 years after the date of vesting, the Tribunal concluded in the circumstances that the claimants had been aware of the vesting and that it had no jurisdiction to deal with the matter.

In *Apostolic Church Trustees* the Tribunal emphasised that the time bar provisions do not extinguish the actual claim for compensation but merely limit the time within which a statutory reference can be made. It is still open to the parties to agree to a voluntary reference to the Tribunal. In *Smith and Waverley Tailoring Co. v. Edinburgh District Council*[18] the Tribunal held that the corresponding time bar in Schedule 6 to the Town and Country Planning (Scotland) Act 1945 was intended to refer only to statutory references. The time bar provision was "enacted within the context of statutory references and procedures which is all the draftsman can therefore have had in mind."

In *Royal Bank of Scotland v. Clydebank District Council,*[18a] differing views were expressed as to whether the statutory right to compensation was extinguished by failure to make a reference to the Lands Tribunal within the prescribed six year period. The judges agreed, however, that the acquiring authority was still empowered to reach an agreement with the claimant, but there was nothing to require the authority to do so.

Surplus land

4—33 Where land acquired by, or under the shadow of, compulsory purchase becomes surplus to requirements, no right of reversion or resumption operates for the benefit of the original owner unless express provision to that effect exists in the enabling Act. Nonetheless, as Bingham L.J. observed in *R. v. Commission for the New Towns, ex p. Tomkins.*[19]

---

[16] 1978 S.L.T. (Lands Tr.) 17.
[17] Unreported, Lands Tribunal for Scotland, April 24, 1987.
[18] 1976 S.L.T. (Lands Tr.) 19.
[18a] 1992 S.L.T. 356.
[19] (1988) 58 P. & C.R. 57.

"When land is compulsorily purchased the coercive power of the state is used to deprive a citizen of his property against his will. He is obliged to take its assessed value whether he wants it or not. This exercise is justified by the public intention to develop the land in the wider interest of the community of which the citizen is a part. If, however, that intention is not for any reason fulfilled, and the land becomes available for disposal, common fairness demands that the former owner should have a preferential claim to buy back the land which he had been compelled to sell, provided he is able and willing to pay the full market price at the time of re-purchase."

The Lands Clauses Consolidation Act 1845 in sections 127 to 132 sets out special provisions governing the sale of superfluous lands which require that, unless the lands are situated in a town or built upon, they are to be offered first to the owner of the lands from which they were severed or, failing that, to adjoining owners. Otherwise, the lands are to be disposed of in the most advantageous manner or, in default, they will vest in the owners of adjoining land.

These procedures, however, have very limited application today because there are no equivalent provisions contained in the Compulsory Purchase Act 1965, to which the great majority of compulsory acquisitions are subject. Furthermore, it should be noted that section 122 of the Local Government Act 1972 confers wide powers on local authorities to appropriate land which is no longer needed for the purpose for which it was acquired for other local government purposes.[20]

The original owner, therefore, subject to the very limited application of the provisions in the 1845 Act, has no statutory rights in respect of surplus land. Nevertheless, following the row in the early 1950s over the unsatisfactory way in which Crichel Down (compulsorily acquired as a wartime bombing range), was subsequently disposed of by the Ministry of Agriculture when it became surplus to requirements, informal guidelines on disposal were introduced. Government departments which had acquired but now had no further use for agricultural land were to offer it first to the original owner at current market value. The guidelines did not apply to non-agricultural land. However, as a result of dissatisfaction in 1980 over the way in which the disposal of land no longer required for the extension of the British Library was handled, the guidelines were revised and extended to non-agricultural land.

4—34

The revised guidelines are entitled "Disposal of Surplus Government Land: Obligation to offer land back to the Former Owner or their Successors—The 'Crichel Down Rules' ".[21] They apply to all land and buildings surplus to requirements but originally acquired by a government department, or agency, by or under the threat of compulsory acquisition or in response to a blight notice served under Part VI of the Town and Country Planning Act 1990. The rules are commended for application by local authorities and other statutory bodies. Separate

[20] See, too, ss.229 and 232 of the Town and Country Planning Act 1990.
[21] Dated October 30, 1992 and issued jointly by the Department of the Environment and the Welsh Office.

guidelines apply to disposals by the Commission for the New Towns.[22] These were issued in August 1983 and are broadly similar in effect.

The general rule under the guidelines is that land, the character of which has not been materially changed[23] since the original acquisition by the government, and which becomes surplus to requirements within a prescribed period,[24] will be offered first to the former owner at its current market value.[25] "Former owner" includes a person to whom the land would have devolved under the original owner's will or intestacy.

4—35   There are, inevitably, a number of exceptions to the general rule. These include cases where a Minister specifically authorises disposal to another government department or agency, or in very exceptional cases, to a local authority or other public body; where the disposal is in execution of government policy transferring certain functions to the private sector; where disposal would fragment a site and substantially reduce its market value or prejudice its prospects of development; and where disposal would be inconsistent with the purpose of its original acquisition.

Compulsory "rights"

4—36   Some statutes expressly confer a right falling short of compulsory acquisition, but in the absence of an express power a power to acquire new rights such as easements is not to be inferred.[26] Local authorities are empowered by section 13(1) of the Local Government (Miscellaneous Provisions) Act 1976 to purchase new rights compulsorily, subject to authorisation by a Minister. The provision of essential infrastructure such as public sewers, water mains, electricity, gas and telephone connections to support land development would be difficult and, at times, impossible in the absence of powers to acquire compulsorily the necessary right to install the services. The power is generally subject to appropriate safeguards for the

---

[22] Surplus Land in English New Towns.

[23] "Material change" will be very much a matter of fact and degree but a useful guide will be the level of expenditure required to restore the land to its former use. It would clearly include redevelopment of land by erection of buildings or afforestation of mainly open land.

[24] The prescribed period is a reference to (i) agricultural land acquired since the beginning of 1935, (ii) agricultural land acquired on and after October 30, 1992, which becomes surplus and available for disposal within 25 years; and (iii) non-agricultural land which becomes surplus and available for disposal within 25 years of the date of acquisition.

[25] An exception to the obligation to offer back applies if the market value of the land is so uncertain that clawback provisions would be insufficient to safeguard the public purse and competitive sale is advised by the relevant department's professionally qualified appointed valuer and specifically agreed by the responsible Minister. c.f. *R. v. Commission for the New Towns, ex p. Tomkins* (1988) 58 P. & C.R. 57.

[26] *Sovmots Investments Ltd v. Secretary of State for the Environment* [1977] 2 All E.R. 385.

owner such as prior service of notice, an opportunity for objection (not in respect of a proposal to install a water main) and the payment of compensation for resulting loss and damage.

Chapter 5

Compensation: Introductory Matters

The entitlement to compensation

5—01   In many countries throughout the world the entitlement to compensation for the expropriation of land is enshrined in the constitution.[1] The Fifth Amendment to the Constitution of the United States of America, for example, provides "nor shall private property be taken for public use without just compensation." There is, however, no such constitutional guarantee of compensation in Britain. Indeed, as with compulsory purchase powers, the entitlement to compensation for the last 150 years had depended upon statutory authority.[2] "No owners of lands expropriated by statute for public purposes," said Lord Parmoor in *Sisters of Charity of Rockingham v. The King*, "is entitled to compensation, either for the value of the land taken, or for damage, on the ground that his land is injuriously affected unless he can establish a statutory right."[3]

However, although, a claimant must be able to point to statutory authority to support a claim, "there is a natural leaning in favour of compensation in the construction of a statute."[4] For example, in *Wells v. London, Tilbury and Southend Railway Co.*[5] a railway company obtained private Act powers which, *inter alia*,

---

[1] See F. Mann, "Outline of a History of Expropriation" (1959) 75 L.Q.R. 188.
[2] Note, however, that in *Burmah Oil Company (Burma Trading) Ltd v. Lord Advocate*, 1964 S.C. (H.L.) 117 the House of Lords held that compensation was payable for the taking or destruction of a subject's property by the Crown in the exercise of its prerogative power in time of war.
[3] [1922] 2 A.C. 315 at p. 322.
[4] Lord Hodson in *Burmah Oil Company (Burma Trading) Ltd v. Lord Advocate*, 1964 S.C. (H.L.) 117 at p. 154.
[5] [1877] 5 Ch. 126.

extinguished certain footways across their railway. In the course of his judgment
Bramwell L.J. said on the issue of compensation:

> "The legislature, in an Act providing for the execution of public works, never takes
> away the slightest private right without providing compensation for it, and the general
> recital that it is expedient that the works should be done is never supposed to mean
> that in order to carry them out a man is to be deprived of his private rights without
> compensation."[6]

Again, in *Attorney-General v. Horner*[7] where the point in issue was whether Paving   **5—02**
Acts took away the rights of an owner of a market franchise, Brett M.R. said on
the question whether the Act provided for expropriation without compensation
"it is a proper rule of construction not to construe an Act of Parliament as interfer-
ing with or injuring persons' rights without compensation, unless one is obliged
so to construe it."[8] And Salter J. in *Newcastle Breweries Ltd. v. The King*[9] referred
to "an established rule that a statute will not be read as authorising the taking of
a subject's goods without payment unless an intention to do so be clearly
expressed."[10] There is now a line of cases which supports the judicial presumption
that an intention to take away the property of a subject without giving him a
legal right to compensation for the loss of it is not to be imputed to the legislature
unless that intention is expressed in unequivocal terms.[11] In other words, the
courts have developed what has been described as a "liability rule" to protect
private property rights in land;[12] the state may destroy the initial entitlement to
the property but only on the payment of an objectively determined value; the
loss resulting from expropriation does not lie where it falls but is shared amongst
all the citizens of the state. It is, of course, open to the legislature to make
explicit provision in an Act of Parliament for the taking of property without
compensation. For example, in *Re a Petition of Right*[13] the Court of Appeal
decided, *inter alia*, that the effect of certain regulations made under the Defence
of the Realm Act 1914 was to enable the Crown to take land without paying
compensation.[14]

---

[6] *Ibid.* at p. 130.
[7] (1884) 14 Q.B.D. 245.
[8] *Ibid.* at p. 257.
[9] [1920] 1 K.B. 854.
[10] *Ibid.* at p. 866.
[11] *Burmah Oil Company (Burma Trading) Ltd v. Lord Advocate, supra; Tiverton and North Devon Railway
Co. v. Loosemore* (1884) App. Cas. 480; *Colonial Sugar Refining Co. Ltd v. Melbourne Harbour Trust
Commissioners* [1927] A.C. 343; *Bond v. Nottingham Corporation* [1960] Ch. 429; *Belfast Corporation
v. O.D. Cars Ltd* [1960] A.C. 490; and *Westminster Bank Ltd v. Minister of Housing and Local Government* [1971] A.C. 508.
[12] G. Calabresi and P. Melamed, "Property Rules, Liability Rules, and Inalienability: One View of
the Cathedral," 85 Harv. L.R. 1089.
[13] [1915] 3 K.B. 649. See, too, *Musselburgh Real Estate Co. v. Magistrates of Musselburgh* (1905) 7 F.
113 H.L. and *The Moffat Hydropathic Co. Ltd v. Lord Advocate* (1919) 1 SLT 82.
[14] See, too, *Sheffield City Council v. Yorkshire Water Services Ltd*, Independent Law Reports, May 18,
1990.

A more explicit example of the legislature providing other than for a "full equivalent" for the compulsory acquisition of land is to be found in section 50 of the Planning (Listed Buildings and Conservation Areas) Act 1990. The section provides that where a planning authority propose to acquire compulsorily a listed building, they may, if they are satisfied that the building has deliberately been allowed to fall into disrepair, include in the compulsory purchase order as submitted to the Secretary of State a direction that only minimum compensation be paid. If the order is confirmed with the direction, any development potential which the land may have is disregarded in assessing compensation and the landowner in such a case will receive considerably less than a "full equivalent." A further example was to be found in section 10 and Schedule 2 to the Land Compensation Act 1961 as substituted by the Housing (Consequential Provisions) Act 1985[15] (see Chapter 10). This provided that, where property being compulsorily acquired under specified powers comprised a house below a prescribed standard of fitness, compensation was not to exceed the value of the site of the house as a cleared site available for development. In many cases, this, too, would result in a claimant receiving less than a "full equivalent" of the loss.

5—03   So far in this discussion we have addressed ourselves to the question of the entitlement to compensation in the circumstances of the expropriation of property rights by the state; and it is with the consequences of the expropriation of property rights in land that this book is very largely concerned. However, private property rights in land may have to give way to the demands of "public necessity or utility" in circumstances which fall short of a physical taking of the land. For example, a landowner may, as a result of a refusal of planning permission, be denied the opportunity to develop his land because it is in the wider public interest to preserve the continuation of the existing use; or the value of the land may be very substantially diminished by the construction and use on neighbouring land of much needed public works such as a motorway or airport. To determine the entitlement to compensation simply on the question whether or not there has been a taking of the land is to ignore the consequences of other forms of state intervention. Michelman[16] poses the question of "when to compensate" in broader terms:

> "When a social decision to redirect economic resources entails painfully obvious opportunity costs, how shall these costs ultimately be distributed among all the members of society? Shall they be permitted to remain where they fall initially or shall the government, by paying compensation, make explicit attempts to distribute these in accordance with decisions made by whatever process fashions the tax structure, or perhaps according to some other principle? Shall the losses be left with the individuals on whom they happen first to fall, or shall they be socialised?"

---

[15] Repealed by the Local Government and Housing Act 1989.
[16] F. Michelman, "Property, Utility and Fairness: Comments on the Ethical Foundations of 'Just Compensation' Law," 80 Harv. L. Rev. 1165.

He goes on to argue that a clear statement of the purposes of compensation practice is desirable in a form which shows how to state with precision the variables which ought to determine entitlements to compensation. However, as Farrier and McAuslan observe,[17] there has not been in the United Kingdom "a questioning of the basic assumptions or philosophy of compensation law nor any real consideration given to the relationship between compensation and development and attitudes thereto." The legislative development of compensation practice has been piecemeal; for the rest, it has been left to the courts to work out compensation entitlements in this broader area with little assistance from Parliament.

Having dealt in general terms with the entitlement to compensation for the **5—04** expropriation of private property rights in land, it is appropriate now to consider the specific entitlement upon which, for the most part claims for compensation are founded. Compulsory purchase today is carried on very largely by public bodies acting under the authority of powers conferred by public and general Acts.[18] These Acts do not themselves make specific provision regarding the entitlement to compensation.[19] Instead, reliance is placed upon the provisions of the Compulsory Purchase Act 1965, as amended. Section 1 of that Act provides that:

"This Act shall apply in relation to any compulsory purchase to which Part II of the Acquisition of Land Act 1981,[20] or Schedule 1 to that Act[21], applies . . ."

Curiously, the Compulsory Purchase Act 1965 follows The Lands Clauses Acts in conferring no specific entitlement to compensation except for tenants at will; but it is clearly phrased on the assumption that compensation will be paid. Section 5, for example, requires the acquiring authority to serve a notice to treat on all persons having an interest in the land to be acquired otherwise than by agreement stating that they are willing to treat for the purchase thereof and for compensation for any damage caused by the execution of the works; and section 6 provides that disputes over the amount of compensation to be paid may be referred to the Lands Tribunal. The closest the 1965 Act comes to conferring a specific entitlement to compensation is section 7 and this is the provision upon which most claims are founded. Section 7 provides that in assessing the compensation to be paid by the acquiring authority:

---

[17] D. Farrier and P. McAuslan, "Compensation, Participation and Compulsory Acquisition of Homes" in *Compensation for Compulsory Purchase: A Comparative Study*, J. F. Garner (ed.), (United Kingdom National Committee of Comparative Law, London, 1975).

[18] Compulsory purchase powers are occasionally conferred by private and local Acts. For a notable example see the Zetland County Council Act 1974, s.24.

[19] They may, however, make provision dealing with specific aspects of compensation. See, for example, the Highways Act 1980, ss.261 & 262, as amended by the Planning (Consequential Provisions) Act 1990, Sched. 2.

[20] Purchases by local and other authorities.

[21] Purchases by Ministers.

"regard shall be had not only to the value of the land to be purchased by the acquiring authority, but also to the damage, if any, to be sustained by the owner of the land by reason of the severing of the land purchased from the other land of the owner, or otherwise injuriously affecting that other land by the exercise of the powers conferred by this or the special Act."

In view of the judicial presumption to which we referred earlier that a statute will not be read as authorising the taking of property without compensation unless that intention is clearly expressed, the provisions of the Lands Clauses Acts and now the provisions of the 1965 Act, and in particular section 7, have been accepted by the courts as conferring an entitlement to compensation.[22] In *Horn v. Sunderland Corporation*[23], for example, Scott L.J. said of the Lands Clauses Consolidation Act 1845 that one of its leading features is that it gives to the owner compelled to sell compensation: "the right to be put, so far as money can do it, in the same position as if his land had not been taken from him."   And in *Commissioners of Inland Revenue v. Glasgow and South Western Rail Co.*[24], Lord Watson in the House of Lords said of the corresponding Scottish Act of 1845, "[a]s I read these provisions, the statute authorises, in the first place, compensation for land or an interest in land."

The measure of compensation for compulsory purchase

1. THE CONCEPT OF COMPENSATION

5—05 As mentioned above, section 7 of the 1965 Act provides that in assessing the compensation to be paid regard is to be had to the value of the land to be acquired and to any damage sustained by severance or other injurious affection. It replaces, in substantially the same form, section 63 of the Lands Clauses Consolidation Act of 1845. "Severance" occurs when the physical taking of part of a parcel of land depreciates the value of the remaining land. "Other injurious affection" is a reference to depreciation in the value of the remaining land caused by the construction and use of the works for which the part was taken. Section 7, therefore, specifies the two heads under which compensation may be claimed,[25] but it says nothing about the measure or yardstick to be applied in assessing the compensation. The

---

[22] See H. Parish, *Cripps on Compulsory Acquisition of Land* (Stevens & Sons Ltd, London, 11th ed.) para. 4–002. The entitlement to compensation for a tenant having no greater interest in land than as a tenant for a year or from year to year rests upon s.20 of the 1965 Act (see para. 13–01 below).

[23] [1941] 2 K.B. 26.

[24] (1887) 14 R.(H.L.) 33.

[25] See, also, s.20 of the 1965 Act as regards the heads of claim for a tenant having no greater interest in the land than as a tenant for a year or from year to year.

result of the "unusually open texture"[26] of the legislation from which the 1965 Act is derived was that, until 1919 (see below), the measure of compensation was left to the arbitrators or juries to determine "with a freedom which might have amazed even the compiler of a continental code."

The question "what should be the measure of compensation" depends upon the objective which compensating a claimant is intended to achieve. Objectives vary. Michelman, in a wide ranging article,[27] develops two models of compensation designed to achieve different objectives, one derived from classical utilitarianism and the other, the fairness model derived from the "justice as fairness" approach of John Rawls.[28] Michelman's main concern was with the question "when to compensate." However, Bell, in an article based on research into the compensation implications of a number of major road schemes for agricultural interests,[29] considers how the objectives of these two models might be reflected in the measure of compensation. Bell suggests that the objective of the utilitarian approach would be to maximise social welfare. His research indicates that in view of the time, trouble and expense being invested in lengthy negotiations with landowners, the greater net benefit would be likely to be achieved by a measure of compensation which provides claimants with a small balance of advantage thus encouraging less objection and speedier settlements.

An interesting example of a utilitarian approach to compensation is provided by Cullingworth who cites the Minister of Transport in a memorandum in 1958 to the Minister of Housing and Local Government as stating that his department "could not be more strongly in favour" of a Bill providing for an increase in the measure of compensation for compulsory acquisition because of the difficulties faced by his department in time-consuming procedures for compulsory acquisition at unattractive rates of compensation.[30]

Bell suggests that this small balance of advantage might be assessed by reference **5—06** to the optimum point on a claimant's satisfaction curve. On the data available he estimated that this would point to an addition of some 30 per cent to the market value of a holding.

A "Rawlsian" approach to compensation would view matters from a different perspective. Rawls suggested that the principles of justice for the basic structure of society should be those principles "that free and rational persons concerned to further their own interests would accept in an initial position of equality as defining the fundamental terms of their association."[31] Bell hypothesised that Rawls'

---

[26] See W.A. Elliott, "The Scope for 'General Principle' Legislation," in *Proceedings of the 5th Commonwealth Law Conference* (1977).
[27] F. Michelman, "Property, Utility, and Fairness: Comments on the Ethical Foundations of 'Just Compensation' Law", 80 Harv. L. R. 1165.
[28] J. Rawls, "Justice as Fairness," 67 Phil. Rev. 164 (1958).
[29] M. Bell, "Taking Justice Seriously: Rawls', Utilitarianism and Land Compensation" (1980) 3 Urban Law and Policy 23.
[30] J.B. Cullingworth, *Environmental Planning*, Vol. IV, (HMSO, 1980) p. 185. See, too, P. McAuslan, *Ideologies of Planning Law* (Pergamon Press, 1980), Chap. 4.
[31] J. Rawls, *A Theory of Justice* (Harvard University Press, 1971), p. 22.

rational men, who had no idea whether they would be faced with the prospect of the expropriation of their land, would select a measure of fairness which would ensure that the worst affected group would end up marginally better off. He considered that the compensation decisions of the lay juries prior to 1919 (see below) exhibited some of the characteristics of a Rawlsian approach to compensation and on this basis concluded that such a measure might add at least 10 per cent. to the market price.

Atiyah makes a distinction in the context of compensation for accidents between that which is intended to provide a financial equivalent for what has been lost and that which is intended as a substitute or solace for what has been lost.[32] The former is generally taken to refer to the lump sum required to leave the claimant as well off but no better off than he or she would be without the change in their expectations. This would seem to be another way of expressing the basic measure of damages for breach of contract and tort which is "that sum of money which will put the party who has been injured, or who has suffered, in the same position as he would have been if he had not sustained the wrong for which he is now getting his compensation or reparation".[33] Compensation for compulsory purchase based on equivalence might typically reflect the price which the claimant could have expected to have obtained for the property on a sale in the open market together with other consequential loss.

5—07   Compensation which is granted as a substitute or solace for what has been lost would seem to comprehend rather more intangible loss, something that cannot be replaced, something other than patrimonial loss.[34] Such an element in an award of compensation for compulsory purchase might provide recompense for the individual value which people commonly ascribe to heritable property in excess of its market value.[35] This is sometimes referred to as "householder's surplus" and reflects loss of ties with the area, friendships made, and so on — items which are difficult to value. Both the utilitarian and fairness models of compensation would be likely to make some allowance, although for different reasons, for the subjective expectations of the claimants. Some support for the provision of an allowance for loss of householder's surplus in compulsory purchase compensation was given in the report of the commission on the third London airport[36] and in the report of the Urban Motorways Committee.[37] The latter commented that:

---

[32] P. Cane, *Atiyah's Accidents, Compensation and the Law* (Weidenfeld and Nicolson, London, 5th ed.) Chap. 22.

[33] *Livingstone v. Rawyards Coal Co.* (1880) 5 App. Cas. 25, *per* Lord Blackburn at p. 39; and see, generally, Harvey McGregor, *McGregor on Damages* (15th ed., 1988, Sweet & Maxwell).

[34] See *McGregor on Damages, supra*, Chap. 3.

[35] See D. Farrier and P. McAuslan, *supra*; also J.L. Knetsch, *Property Rights and Compensation* (Butterworths & Co. (Canada) Ltd, 1983), Chap. 4, and P. McAuslan, *Ideologies of Planning Law* (Pergamon Press, 1980), Chap. 4.

[36] HMSO, 1971.

[37] DoE, HMSO, 1972.

"it will not be sufficient to assume that in the case of those who have to move the cost of compensation or rehousing fully reflects the burden that is put upon them. Many individuals are attached to their particular house or their particular neighbour-hood and would not freely move simply for the market value of their property. They suffer an additional loss—sometimes called loss of householder's surplus—which is real for them but for practical purposes very difficult to value in specific cases."[38]

The consequence of the Committee's report for the measure of compensation for compulsory purchase is discussed below.

Knetsch goes somewhat further and questions whether there might not be some **5—08** advantage in terms of both efficiency and equity in a measure of compensation the objective of which would be to enable a claimant to participate in the social worth of the scheme for which the land is acquired.[39] Such an approach would be concerned not so much with measurement of loss but with redistribution of profit but then, as one commentator has argued,[40] why should a landowner be expected to sell at a price less than that which represents the true value of the land to the purchaser and the community? The Sheaf Committee considered the possibility of encouraging the voluntary sale of land to local authorities by allowing payment of a price which gave the landowner part of the equity estim-ated to arise on its subsequent development.[41] This could be achieved by basing the price on a residual valuation, the method commonly employed by developers to determine the offer price for development land. A developer begins his calcula-tions by estimating the selling price of the development, for example, houses. From this is deducted the anticipated development costs, cost of finance, market-ing expenses, overheads, any contingency allowance and the developer's profit margin.[42] The residue is the maximum price which may be offered for the land in question. The Sheaf Committee rejected this as a measure of compensation. "Payments on such a basis," concluded the committee, "would be bound in themselves, if made on an extensive scale, to inflate the market value of the land." Furthermore, the committee recognised that there would be cases where local authorities would have to continue to acquire land at a price which excluded any element of value due to the scheme underlying the acquisition so that "a dual valuation standard would emerge." This, they felt, would be inequitable as between one landowner and another.

---

[38] *Ibid.* paras. 12, 18–19.

[39] J.L. Knetsch, *supra*, Chap. 5.

[40] W.D. Jones, "The Impact of Public Works on Farming: A Case Study Relating to a Reservoir and Power Station in North Wales," *Journal of Agricultural Economics* 23, 12 (1972).

[41] *Report of the Working Party on Local Authority/Private Enterprise Partnership Schemes* (HMSO, 1972), paras. 94–96 and Annex K.

[42] See J. Rowan-Robinson and M.G. Lloyd, *Land Development and the Infrastructure Lottery* (T. & T. Clark, 1988), Chap. 6.

2. THE MEASURE OF COMPENSATION PRE-1919

5—09   In considering the measure or yardstick to be applied in assessing compensation, reference should be made in interpreting the 1965 Act to the interpretation applied by the courts to the provisions of the Land Clauses Consolidation Act 1845, much of which was consolidated and re-enacted by the 1965 Act. Like the 1965 Act, the 1845 Act said nothing about the measure to be applied. In the absence of any guidance in the 1845 Act as to the objectives of the legislation or the measure to be adopted, it was inevitable that the courts should be called upon to interpret the intention of the legislature. Perhaps not surprisingly their decisions appear to have been influenced by principles derived from the measurement of damages at common law.[43] In *Stebbing v. The Metropolitan Board of Works*,[44] an early decision which turned on the construction of the Lands Clauses Act, Lush J. observed that:

> "The Act did not intend to put the owner of the land in a better position than he would have been in if the land had not been taken from him. What the legislature intended to give is full compensation and indemnity to the persons from whom land is taken for the loss of the land."[45]

In that case, the claimant based his claim, not on the existing use value of the three parcels of land in question as burial grounds — which to all intents and purposes was nil — but on their social worth to the purchaser and to the community for the laying out of a street and for the erection of buildings. The Court of Queen's Bench rejected this basis of assessment. Cockburn C.J. said:

> "When Parliament gives compulsory powers, and provides that compensation shall be made to the person from whom property is taken, for the loss that he sustains, it is intended that he shall be compensated to the extent of his loss; and that his loss shall be tested by what was the value of the thing to him, not by what will be its value to the persons acquiring it."[46]

5—10   In other words, the courts rejected the social worth of the scheme as the basis of assessment and opted for the measure of equivalence. The measure of compensation, said Lord Watson in the Scottish case *Commissioners of Inland Revenue v. Glasgow and South Western Rail Co.*[47] is "an equivalent for that which the railway company take and acquire and which the proprietor gives up to them." "Value

---

[43] See, for example, *Ricket v. Metropolitan Railway Co.* (1865) 34 L.J.Q.B. 257, *per* Erle C.J.; and *Palatine Graphic Arts Co. Ltd v. Liverpool City Council* [1986] 2 W.L.R. 285, *per* Glidewell L.J.
[44] (1870) L.R. 6 Q.B. 37.
[45] *Ibid.* p. 46.
[46] *Ibid.* p. 42.
[47] (1887) 14 R. (H.L.) 33 at p. 35.

to the owner" was affirmed as the measure of compensation for compulsory purchase in numerous subsequent cases.[48]

The "open-texture" of the 1845 legislation, nonetheless, enabled the courts with some ingenuity to ensure that within the constraints of "value to the owner" a claimant was fully compensated for all loss consequent on the compulsory acquisition of the land. For example, section 63 of the 1845 Act provided that, in assessing compensation, regard was to be had to two heads of compensation: the value of the land; and severance and other injurious affection. The first head of claim under section 63 of the 1845 Act was held to encompass not only the value of the land itself, but all consequential loss commonly referred to as "disturbance." As the Lord Chancellor, Lord Halisbury, said of the corresponding Scottish legislation in *Glasgow and South Western Rail Co.*[49]

> "what the jury have to ascertain is the value of the land. In treating of that value, the value under the circumstances to the person who is compelled to sell (because the statute compels him to do so) may be naturally and properly and justly taken into account, and when such phrases as 'damages for loss of business' or 'compensation for the goodwill' taken from the person, are used in a loose and general sense, they are not inaccurate for the purpose of giving verbal expression to what everybody understands as a matter of business, but in strictness the thing which is to be ascertained is the price to be paid for the land — the land with all the potentialities of it, with all the actual use of it by the person who holds it, is to be considered by those who have to assess the compensation."

The decision in *A and B Taxis Ltd v. Secretary of State for Air*[50] also illustrates that, as with the assessment of damages at common law,[51] the courts did not adopt rigid rules in valuing land but were prepared to consider in the circumstances of each case what would best achieve, if not restitution, then a financial equivalent which was the next best thing. In *A and B Taxis Ltd* compensation was assessed on the basis of the cost of equivalent reinstatement, an approach which Lord President Clyde described in the Scottish case *McEwing & Sons Ltd v. The County Council of the County of Renfrew*[52] as "indeed a typical case of a common practice under the 1845 Act of using reinstatement value, instead of market value, to fix the compensation."

Early decisions by the courts on the measure of compensation for injurious affection, the second head of claim under section 63 of the 1845 Act where land

---

[48] See, for example, *Corrie v. McDermott* [1914] A.C. 1056; *Cedar Rapids Manufacturing and Power Co. v. Lacoste* [1914] A.C. 569; *Re Lucas and Chesterfield Gas and Water Board* [1909] 1 K.B. 16; *Fraser v. City of Fraserville* [1917] A.C. 187. See, too, H. Parrish, *Cripps on Compulsory Acquisition of Land* (Stevens & Sons Ltd, London, 11th ed.) para. 4–002.

[49] (1887) 14 R. (H.L.) 33 at p. 34. See, too, *Jubb v. Hull Dock Co.* (1846), L.R. 9 Q.B. 443.

[50] [1922] 2 K.B. 328.

[51] See Harvey McGregor, *McGregor on Damages*, (15th ed., 1988, Sweet & Maxwell), Chap. 32.

[52] 1960 S.C. 53, p. 63. See, too, *Ex p. The Streatham and General Estates Company Limited* (1888) 4 T.L.R. 766, and H. Parrish, *Cripps on Compulsory Acquisition of Land* (Stevens & Sons Ltd, London, 11th ed.) para, 4–047.

was compulsorily acquired, suggest that here, too, they were concerned with a financial equivalent. However, it would seem that the measure of compensation was the whole of the depreciation in the value of the remaining land resulting from the taking of land and from the construction and use of the works. It was immaterial that the loss would not have been actionable in the absence of statutory authority. In *Cowper Essex v. Acton Local Board*,[53] for example, the House of Lords held that the injurious effects on the remaining land of the construction and use of a sewage works on the land taken were not too remote even though no nuisance might be caused. In other words, the measure of compensation in this respect was somewhat more generous than the measure of damages for nuisance (see Chapter 12).

5—11   However, while the courts, in the relatively few cases that came before them, were asserting the principle of equivalence, it would seem that the great majority of disputed claims were being settled at first instance according to a yardstick which has been described as more akin to a "Rawlsian" measure of compensation.[54] Under the Lands Clauses Consolidation Act 1845, claims not exceeding £50 were to be settled by two Justices. Claims exceeding £50 could be dealt with either by arbitration or before two Justices and in the latter case the question of compensation would be settled by verdict of a jury.[55] The universal practice of juries and arbitrators was to award an additional sum over and above the price for the land as an acknowledgement of the compulsory nature of the acquisition.[56] In England and Wales this additional sum was usually of the order of 10 per cent. of the price for the land; but in Scotland in some cases of agricultural land it seems that this allowance approached 100 per cent. The Wharncliffe Committee, appointed by the House of Lords in 1845 to consider and report on the expediency of establishing some principle of compensation for lands compulsorily acquired for the construction of railways, was of the opinion that "a very high percentage, amounting to not less than 50 per cent. upon the original value, ought to be given in compensation for the compulsion only to which the seller is bound to submit."[57]

A further example of a "Rawlsian" measure of compensation pre 1919 was referred to in the report of the Scott Committee (below) who found that in assessing the prospective value of the land "merely hypothetical and often highly speculative elements of value which had no real existence have crept into awards as if they were actual; while elements of remote future value have too often been

---

[53] (1889) 14 App. Cas. 153. See, too, *Re Stockport, Timperley and Altringham Railway Co.* (1864) 33 L.J.Q.B. 251; and *Buccleuch (Duke) v. Metropolitan Board of Works* (1872) L.R. 5 H.L. 418.

[54] M. Bell, "Taking Justice Seriously: Rawls' Utilitarianism and Land Compensation" (1980) 3 Urban Law and Policy 23.

[55] See ss.22 and 23.

[56] See the *Second Report of the Committee Dealing with the Law and Practice relating to the Acquisition and Valuation of Land for Public Purposes* (the Scott Committee), Cd. 9229, (1918), para. 9. For a discussion of this practice see F. Deas, *The Law of Railways Applicable to Scotland*, revised edition by J. Ferguson (W. Green & Sons, Edinburgh, 1897), pp. 292–299.

[57] Cited in F. Deas, *The Law of Railways Applicable to Scotland, supra*, p. 297n(a).

inadequately discounted, and valued as if there were a readily available market."[58] It would seem that awards by arbitrators and juries were much influenced by the fact that the promoters were often railway companies where profit rather than the direct interest of the state was the motivation.

3. THE ACQUISITION OF LAND (ASSESSMENT OF COMPENSATION) ACT 1919

Anticipating a major programme of public works in the aftermath of the First World War, a committee (the Scott Committee) was appointed in 1917 "To consider and report upon the defects in the existing system of law and practice involved in the acquisition and valuation of land for public purposes, and to recommend any changes that may be desirable in the public interest." In their second report, the committee reflected the changing climate of opinion on the measure of compensation:

5—12

> "In our opinion, no landowner can, having regard to the fact that he holds his property subject to the right of the state to expropriate his interest for public purposes, be entitled to a higher price when in the public interest such expropriation takes place, than the fair market value apart from compensation for injurious affection, *etc.*"[59]

Many of the recommendations of the report were given effect in the Acquisition of Land (Assessment of Compensation) Act 1919. The object of the Act was to dispense with the "extravagant, dilatory, and cumbrous" procedures of the 1845 Act and "to provide machinery by which in case of dispute, a price that is fair and reasonable may be fixed, and fixed without unnecessary expense or avoidable delay."[60] In order to introduce realism into awards and to curb excesses, the Act did away with recourse to juries and arbitrators and substituted a panel of official arbitrators having special knowledge in the valuation of land to settle disputes over compensation.[61]

The central provision, however, was a set of six "rules" to be observed by the official arbitrators in assessing compensation for the value of land compulsorily acquired. The position regarding compensation for injurious affection was left unchanged. Rule (1) abolished the payment of the additional 10 per cent. by providing that "No allowance shall be made on account of the acquisition being compulsory." Rule (2) provided that the basic measure of compensation was to be "the amount which the land if sold in the open market by a willing seller might be expected to realise." The overall purpose was still to assess the owner's loss but that part of it reflected in the value of the land was now to be assessed

5—13

---

[58] The Scott Committee, *supra*, para. 8.
[59] *Ibid.*
[60] H.C. Deb., Vol. 114, cols. 2275 & 2276 (April 10, 1919), Sir Gordon Hewart.
[61] Acquisition of Land (Assessment of Compensation) Act 1919, s.1.

under rule (2). In other words, so that there should be no doubt, the measure was now expressly defined as the objective "value to *a* willing seller" rather than the more subjective "value to *the* owner," a definition which, in the view of Scott L.J. in *Horn v. Sunderland Corporation* was, more than any other provision, "likely to check exaggerated prices for the land sold."[62] The assessment was to be made from the point of view of a hypothetical willing seller on the open market criterion rather than that of the unwilling actual owner. Rules (3) and (4) imposed some qualification on the factors which could be taken into account in assessing the value which a willing seller might be expected to realise for his land in the open market. Rule (5) reaffirmed the use of equivalent reinstatement as the measure of compensation in cases where there was no general demand or market for the land. Rule (6) safeguarded the right to compensation for disturbance (see Chapter 11).

The 1919 Act rules gave statutory expression to equivalence as the measure of compensation for the value of land compulsorily acquired. The principle underlying this statutory measure is best expressed in what is generally regarded as the leading case — *Horn v. Sunderland Corporation*.[63] In that case agricultural land was compulsorily acquired and the claimant argued, successfully, that the land had development potential and it was so valued. He further claimed compensation for disturbance to his agricultural operation. This was disallowed by the court on the ground that valuation of the land for building purposes implied a willingness to bear the agricultural disturbance. Scott L.J. outlining the purpose of compensation said:

> "what it gives to the owner compelled to sell is compensation—the right to be put, so far as money can do it, in the same position as if his land had not been taken from him. In other words, he gains the right to receive a money payment not less than the loss imposed on him in the public interest, but on the other hand no greater."[64]

and later:

> "The statutory compensation cannot and must not exceed the owner's total loss, for, if it does, it will put an unfair burden upon the public authority or other promoters, who on public grounds have been given the power of compulsory acquisition, and it will transgress the principle of equivalence which is at the root of statutory compensation, which lays it down that the owner shall be paid neither less nor more than his loss."[65]

4. POST-WAR RECONSTRUCTION

5—14 The prospect of the massive programme of reconstruction to be carried out at the end of the Second World War placed the measure of compensation for compul-

---

[62] [1941] 2 K.B. 26, p. 40.
[63] *Ibid.*
[64] *Ibid.* p. 42.
[65] *Ibid.* p. 49.

sory purchase under scrutiny again. A committee (the Uthwatt Committee) was appointed to look at the whole question of the payment of compensation and the recovery of betterment (the appreciation in land values resulting from public policies and proposals) in respect of the public control of the use of land and to advise, as a matter of urgency, what steps should be taken to prevent the work of reconstruction being prejudiced.[66] The committee made an interim recommendation that because of the effect of the war on land values, compensation on the public acquisition of land should, for a temporary period, be based on the values prevailing at the last date when there was an undisturbed market in land. This recommendation was given effect in the Town and Country Planning Act 1944,[67] which provided that in assessing compensation under the 1919 Act rules, the value of any interest in land was to be ascertained by reference to the prices current at March 31, 1939. Provision was made for the payment in certain cases of an owner-occupier supplement.

This provision was subsequently repealed by the Town and Country Planning Act 1947 which introduced comprehensive planning control and which gave effect to the decision of the post-war Labour government to appropriate development value in land to the state. The intention was that land should change hands at the value attributable to its existing use. The 1919 Act rules were accordingly modified so that only planning permission for those limited categories of development listed in the third Schedule to the Act could be taken into account in the assessment of compensation on compulsory acquisition.[68]

The incoming Conservative Government in 1951 was committed to repealing   **5—15** the financial provisions of the 1947 legislation and restoring development value in land to the landowner. The difficult question was whether development value should also be reflected in the measure of compensation for compulsory purchase. Whilst considerations of equity suggested that it should, the government were concerned that, with the advent of comprehensive planning control, public authorities would now be faced, if the measure of compensation reflected development value, with paying a price inflated by their own policies, decisions and proposals. In the event, it was decided that compensation on the public acquisition of land should be restricted to existing use value plus any "unexpended balance of established development value" together with interest.[69]

This dual price system was a clear departure from the principle of equivalence and, not surprisingly, it was short-lived. The passage of time merely served to

---

[66] *The Expert Committee on Compensation and Betterment Final Report*, Cmd. 6386, (1942).

[67] s.57. In *Powner and Powner v. Leeds Corporation* [1953] E.G.D. 99, the Lands Tribunal observed of the operation of the provision in that case "Put bluntly and with some reluctance, the claimants, by virtue of subsection (3) are denied compensation for the factual loss and can only be awarded something much less."

[68] ss. 50 and 51.

[69] Town and Country Planning Act 1954, s.31; and see generally on this J.B. Cullingworth, *Environmental Planning, Volume 10; Land Values, Compensation and Betterment* (HMSO, 1980). For an explanation of the "unexpended balance of established development value" see Chap. 15.

emphasise the discrimination between those who sold land in the open market and those who sold under compulsion to public authorities. The Franks Committee in its report in 1957 commented:

> "One final point of great importance needs to be made. The evidence which we have received shows that much of the dissatisfaction with the procedures relating to land arises from the basis of compensation. It is claimed that objections to compulsory purchase would be far fewer if compensation were always assessed at not less than market value. It is not part of our terms of reference to consider and make recommendations upon the basis of compensation. But we cannot emphasise too strongly the extent to which the financial considerations affect the matters with which we have to deal. Whatever changes in procedure are made, dissatisfaction is, because of this, bound to remain."[70]

As a result of increasing discontent, development value was restored as an element in the assessment of compensation by the Town and Country Planning Act 1959.[71]

However, the introduction of detailed planning control meant that development value was no longer "the simple function of the forces of undisturbed demand and supply which it was in a less complicated age."[72] The 1959 Act accordingly set out a complex framework for determining what planning permission(s) could be taken into account or assumed in assessing the prospective value of the land acquired.[73] The purpose of the framework of permissions and assumptions is to place the claimant as nearly as possible in the position he or she would have been on a sale of the property in the open market (see Chapter 8). In other words, it strives to maintain the analogy which is central to rule (2) of the 1919 Act.

5—16 The 1959 Act also introduced additional provisions to be taken into account by those responsible for resolving disputed claims. To counteract criticism that the return of development value to the landowner would impede much needed schemes by imposing an unduly heavy burden of compensation on public authorities, provision was made in the 1959 Act for the recoupment by public authorities of some of the betterment generated by their schemes.[74] Any increase in the value of the land acquired due to the scheme underlying the acquisition was to be ignored in the assessment of compensation. And any increase as a result of the scheme in the value of contiguous or adjacent land held by the same landowner was to be set off against the compensation for the land taken. As betterment is

---

[70] *The Report of the Committee on Tribunals and Inquiries*, Cmnd. 218, (1957), para. 278.

[71] s.1.

[72] See *Compensation for Compulsory Acquisition and Planning Restrictions*, Chartered Land Societies Committee, 1968, para. 17.

[73] Part 1.

[74] s.9; and see on this J. B. Cullingworth, *Environmental Planning, Volume 10: Land Values, Compensation and Betterment, supra*. The legislation also made provision for compensating "worsenment" generated by such schemes — see Chap. 9.

treated somewhat differently on the sale of land in the open market, those provisions would seem to depart from the analogy created by rule (2) of the 1919 Act and to have implications for the principle of equivalence. This is discussed more fully in Chapter 9.

The statutory provisions governing the assessment of compensation for compulsory purchase were subsequently re-enacted in slightly modified form in the Land Compensation Act 1961.

5. "PUTTING PEOPLE FIRST"

During the late 1960s there were clear indications that the pendulum of public **5—17** opinion, which in time of national emergency had supported a restrictive approach to the assessment of compensation, was now swinging back again. "The complaint made about the present basis [of compensation]," said the Chartered Land Societies Committee in a memorandum in 1968, "is that it produces compensation which is in some cases inadequate. This is precisely the reverse of the complaint made against the interpretation of the Lands Clauses Acts before the 1919 amendments, namely, that the compensation awarded was in many cases excessive."[75] This groundswell of "complaint" would seem to have been generated by the increasing use of compulsory powers to support major schemes of public works such as the programme of urban motorways.

A series of influential reports[76] focussed attention on perceived inadequacies in the compensation code. The Commission on the Third London Airport[77] and the Urban Motorways Committee,[78] for example, both recognised that when people's homes are acquired for public developments, the occupiers who are obliged to uproot themselves suffer a loss over and above that represented by the market value of the property plus disturbance. This loss, which was referred to earlier as "householder's surplus," reflects personal upset and inconvenience, loss of social ties with the area and so on. The Urban Motorways Committee recommended that some extra payment should be made "in recognition of the real personal disturbance that is inflicted on [residential occupiers] when they are required to move."[79] Other reports, such as those from the Chartered Land Societies Committee and from JUSTICE highlighted amongst other matters, some of the illogic-

---

[75] *Compensation for Compulsory Acquisition and Planning Restrictions*, para. 16.
[76] See *Compensation for Compulsory Acquisition and Planning Restrictions, supra; Compensation for Compulsory Acquisition and Remedies for Planning Restrictions together with a Supplemental Report*, JUSTICE (Stevens, 1973); the *Report of the Commission on the Third London Airport* (HMSO, 1971); *Report of the Urban Motorways Committee: New Roads in Towns*, Department of the Environment (HMSO, 1972).
[77] HMSO, 1971.
[78] HMSO, 1972.
[79] *Ibid.* paras. 12, 18–19.

alities in the provision of compensation for injurious affection. These are discussed in detail in Chapter 16.

The government's response to this growing concern about inadequacies in the compensation code was contained in a White Paper, *Development and Compensation — Putting People First.*[80] This stated that:

> "The Government believe the time has come when all concerned with development must aim to achieve a better balance between provision for the community as a whole and the mitigation of harmful effects on the individual citizen. In recent years this balance in too many cases has been tipped against the interests of the individual. A better deal is now required for those who suffer from desirable community developments.
>
> The Government is determined to provide this better deal."[81]

5—18 Whilst reaffirming their intention to retain market value as the basis of compensation, the government announced that they were adopting the recommendation of the Urban Motorways Committee to make a lump sum payment to residential occupiers to reflect the special hardship caused by the loss of a home. Provision for "home loss" payments was subsequently made by sections 29, 30 and 32 of the Land Compensation Act 1973 (see Chapter 13).

Farrier and McAuslan suggested that the objective of the home loss payment was "to provide for solace compensation in addition to the equivalency compensation based on the market value of the property." They went on to conclude, however, that, as the payment bore no relationship at all to the value placed by an occupier on his or her home, it bore some of the hallmarks of a utilitarian approach to compensation. "The conclusion may reasonably be that this payment is being held as a sugar-plum to tempt people to give up their homes quickly and without dispute, thus helping to save on administrative costs."[82] It nonetheless marked some slight shift in the measure of compensation back towards the pre-1919 position.

5—19 In a report published in 1989 entitled *Compensation for Compulsory Acquisition* the Royal Institution of Chartered Surveyors concluded that the time had come to pay an additional allowance in all cases of compulsory acquisition in recognition that the claimant is an unwilling seller and that, if he is an occupier, he suffers social and psychological upset for which financial equivalence makes no allowance.[83] The payment, said the Institution, should not be limited to occupiers. Publication of the report coincided with massive and strident opposition to a proposal by British Rail to build a high speed rail link through Kent from the

---

[80] Cmnd. 5124, (1972).

[81] *Ibid.* para. 5.

[82] D. Farrier and P. McAuslan, "Compensation, Participation and the Compulsory Acquisition of 'Homes'" in *Compensation for Compulsory Purchase: A Comparative Study, supra.* See, too, P. McAuslan, *The Ideologies of Planning Law, supra,* Chap. 4.

[83] Paras. 2.12–2.13.

Channel Tunnel to Kings Cross. The government's response was to produce a consultation paper seeking views on proposals to amend the law on land compensation.[84] The paper proposed no change in the fundamental principle that compensation for the compulsory purchase of land should be based on the open market value of the land disregarding any effect on that value of the proposal giving rise to the compulsory purchase. It did, however, invite comments on whether some further provision, apart from the home loss payment, would be appropriate for owner-occupiers who are displaced as a result of compulsory purchase. Given that a number of nationalised industries have been or are now being privatised and will be concerned very much with the pursuit of profit, the time seemed ripe for a move back to the payment of something akin to the pre-1919 supplement. In the event the Government decided not to enlarge the scope of the payment but simply to increase its amount and its availability for certain persons displaced from dwellings.[85]

Notwithstanding the provision of home loss payments, the present situation as regards the measure of compensation is generally said to be governed by the principle of equivalence. It would seem from what is said above that equivalence was initially a very generalised concept which gave the courts flexibility to respond in whatever way seemed best in the circumstances for ensuring that a claimant was compensated for all loss. With the passage of time flexibility has increasingly been replaced by detailed statutory provisions which prescribe how certain important elements in a claim for compensation are to be assessed. These have reflected changing perceptions in the distributive goals of society. The ability to apply general principles to the circumstances of a claim has been reduced.[86] The principle of equivalence is now largely, although not wholly, enshrined in statutory rules, the central provision of which is that the value of land shall be taken to be the amount which the land if sold by a willing seller in the open market might be expected to realise. Subsequent chapters examine these provisions and the extent to which they are capable of providing claimants with a financial equivalent of their loss.

---

[84] *Land Compensation and Compulsory Purchase Legislation*, 1989.

[85] Planning & Compensation Act 1991, ss.68 & 69 amending the provisions of ss.29, 30 & 32 and adding a new s.29A to the Land Compensation Act 1973 (see Chap. 13).

[86] It has not, however, been entirely eliminated. See, for example, the decision of the House of Lords in *Birmingham Corporation v. West Midland Baptist (Trust) Association (Incorporated)* [1969] 3 All E.R. 172; and that of the Lands Tribunal for Scotland in *Smith v. Strathclyde Regional Council*, 1982 S.L.T. (Lands Tr.) 2. See also E. Young and J. Rowan-Robinson, "Disturbance Compensation: Flexibility and the Principle of Equivalence," 1984 J.R. 133. The Chartered Land Societies Committee in their Report in 1968 commented "it may perhaps be considered in retrospect that if the 1919 reforms had been confined to the appointment of the panel of official arbitrators, the precursors of the Lands Tribunal, many of the difficulties examined in this memorandum would have been avoided." In rather similar vein see the conclusion of B. Denyer-Green in "Agricultural Compensation: The Injustice of Market Value in Severance Cases" [1980] J.P.L. 505.

Chapter 6

The Date for Fixing and Valuing Interests[1]

6—01 Compulsory purchase procedures and the settlement of compensation for the interests in land that are being acquired in response to a notice to treat or deemed notice to treat may be spread over a considerable period of time. During that period the nature and extent of those interests and the value of those interests may change. It will not be possible to assess compensation until the point in time at which the interests are to be taken as fixed and the date at which they are to be valued may have been determined. The choice of one date rather than another may decide who is to be compensated and for what and may have important consequences for the level of compensation.

Until the decision in *Birmingham Corporation v. West Midland Baptist (Trust) Association (Inc.)*[2] the position appeared to be that the date of service of the notice to treat was the key date for fixing both interests and values in land. However, in *Birmingham Corporation* the House of Lords rejected that date as the appropriate point in time for valuing interests. As a result of that decision the date at which interests are to be valued, generally referred to as the "valuation date," is now clear. Unfortunately, however, the position regarding the date at which interests in land are to be taken as fixed is now somewhat confused. The relevant dates are considered in more detail below.

---

[1] See, generally, E. Young and J. Rowan-Robinson, "Compensation for Compulsory Purchase: Equivalence and the Date for Fixing Interests" [1986] J.P.L. 727.
[2] [1970] A.C. 874.

The valuation date[3]

In *Penny v. Penny*[4] Sir William Page Wood V.C. said: "[t]he scheme of the Act   **6—02**
[*i.e.* the Lands Clauses Consolidation Act 1845] I take to be this: that every man's
interest shall be valued, *rebus sic stantibus*, just as it occurs at the very moment
when the notice to treat was given." That sentence, as Salmon L.J. remarked in
Birmingham Corporation, was accepted for a hundred years as "holy writ."[5] It was
endorsed by the courts,[6] adopted by the textbook writers[7] and consistently acted
upon in practice.

Its application during a time of inflation in land values and in other costs such
as has existed since the Second World War gave rise to very considerable injustice.
Matters eventually came to a head in the *Birmingham Corporation* case. The corporation compulsorily acquired 981 acres of the City of Birmingham, including
the chapel owned by the claimants, for a major scheme of redevelopment. It was
accepted that the compensation for the chapel was to be based on the reasonable
cost of equivalent reinstatement (see Chapter 10). At the date of the deemed
notice to treat in August 1947 the cost of reinstatement would have been
£50,025. However, the corporation were not in a position to allocate a new site
for the chapel until an advanced stage in the scheme of redevelopment and it was
agreed that the earliest date at which building on the new site might reasonably
have begun was the end of April 1961. By that time the cost of equivalent reinstatement had risen to £89,575.

The corporation contended that the general rule of law, supported by authority,
was that interests were to be valued as at the date of the notice to treat, a contention that was accepted by the Lands Tribunal. The contention was subsequently
rejected by the Court of Appeal and by the House of Lords.

Lord Reid and Lord Morris of Borth-y-Gest in the House of Lords both con-   **6—03**
cluded that the decision in *Penny v. Penny* did not support the proposition
advanced by the corporation. In *Penny* an executor held a house on trust to permit
the testator's sons to have the house at a low rent so long as they carried on the
family business there. At the date of the notice to treat the sons were still carrying
on the business. The executor argued that the effect of the notice to treat, followed by the taking of possession, would be to terminate the carrying on of the
business, thus giving him the right to sell the leasehold interests, and that his
interest as executor should be compensated accordingly. That argument was

---

[3] See, generally, E. Young and J. Rowan-Robinson, "Compulsory Purchase and the Valuation
Date," 1985 S.L.T. 205.
[4] (1868) L.R. 5 Eq. 227.
[5] [1968] 2 Q.B. 188 at p. 213.
[6] See, for example, *Horn v. Sunderland Corporation* [1941] 2 K.B. 26; *Hull and Humber Investment Co.
Ltd v. Hull Corporation* [1965] 2 Q.B. 145; *Newham London Borough Council v. Benjamin* [1968] 1
W.L.R 694.
[7] H. Parrish, *Cripps on Compulsory Acquisition of Land* (Stevens and Sons Ltd, 11th ed.), para. 2–058.

rejected. The essence of the decision was that compensation should be awarded having regard to the interests of the claimants as they existed at the date of the notice to treat and the remarks of Page Wood V.C. in *Penny* were, said their Lordships, to be construed in that context. They were not authority for the proposition that interests were to be valued at the date of the notice to treat. As Lord Morris observed: "what justification can there be for making an out-of-date valuation?"[8]

Having disposed of the date of the notice to treat their Lordships had then, of necessity, to select an alternative valuation date. It was clear that some flexibility was required as no one date would secure equivalence for the claimant on all occasions. In the words of Lord Reid:

> "No stage can be singled out as the date of expropriation in every case. Sometimes possession is taken before compensation is assessed. Then it would seem logical to fix the market value of the land as at that date and to take actual or consequential losses as they occurred then or thereafter, provided that the dispossessed owner acted reasonably. But if compensation is assessed before possession is taken, taking the date of assessment can I think be justified because then either party can sue for specific performance and the promoters obtain a right to the land, as if there had been a contract of sale at that date. In cases under rule 5 I have already said that that rule appears to point to assessment of the cost of reinstatement at the date when that became reasonably practicable."[9]

Thus, where compensation is assessed on the basis of equivalent reinstatement, the valuation date is the date when reinstatement might reasonably have begun. Although the observations of their Lordships on the position where compensation is assessed on the open market value of the land being acquired might be regarded as *obiter*, they provide, as Slade L.J. said in *Washington Development Corporation v. Bamlings (Washington) Ltd*,[10] "authoritative guidance" on the position and have been followed in practice. The valuation date in such a case is either the date when the acquiring authority take possession of the property or, if earlier, the date on which compensation is agreed by the parties or determined by the appropriate tribunal.[11]

6—04   In *Birmingham Corporation* it was not necessary for the House of Lords to consider precisely when possession is taken or when compensation is "assessed"; nor

---

[8] [1970] A.C. 874 at p. 903.

[9] *Ibid.* p. 899. Lord Wilberforce agreed with the speech of Lord Reid and Lord Morris stated the relevant principle in very similar terms. Lord Donovan in his speech appeared to suggest a slightly different approach, but see the construction put upon this by Slade L.J. in *Washington Development Corporation v. Bamlings (Washington) Ltd* (1985) 273 E.G. 980. Lord Upjohn agreed with the speeches of Lords Reid, Morris and Donovan.

[10] (1985) 273 E.G. 980. But see *Miller and Partners Ltd v. Edinburgh Corporation*, 1978 S.C. 1, *per* the Lord Justice-Clerk (Lord Wheatley) at p. 7.

[11] See, too, *W. & S. (Long Eaton) Ltd v. Derbyshire County Council* (1975) 31 P. & C.R. 99; and *Miller and Partners Ltd v. Edinburgh Corporation*, 1978 S.C.1.

did their Lordships have to consider the position where, instead of proceeding by way of notice to treat, an acquiring authority conclude a sale by agreement thus displacing the need to use a notice to treat or choose to employ the alternative procedure of making a general vesting declaration in respect of the land. These matters are now considered in turn.

1. WHEN IS POSSESSION TAKEN?

After service of a notice to treat, an acquiring authority may serve a notice of entry (see para. 4–23) on the owner, lessee and occupier and after fourteen days enter on and take possession of the land.[12] The notice of entry is, however, merely permissive. Possession does not automatically follow upon expiry of the period of notice. In *Friendly Bar Ltd v. Glasgow Corporation*[13] the claimants' public house was compulsorily acquired by the corporation and a notice to treat was served on June 19, 1969. The notice was accompanied by a notice of entry, served under the corresponding provision in the Scottish Legislation, which stated that the corporation intended to take entry on August 1, 1969. In fact, possession of the public house was not taken until March 8, 1971. The hands Tribunal for Scotland concluded that a notice containing a date of intended entry could not be equated to the taking of possession. The legal effect of giving notice was merely to give a *jus possidendi*. Possession, observed the tribunal,[14] "requires actual holding or detention coupled with the animus to possess in order to clothe the physical fact of possession with its legal consequences." The valuation date was not August 1, 1969, as contended by the landowners, but the date of actual dispossession, *i.e.* March 8, 1971.[15]

6—05

A further illustration is provided by the decision in *Courage Ltd v. Kingswood District Council*.[16] An acquiring authority served a notice to treat and a notice of entry on April 28, 1972 in respect of about 0.9 of an acre of vacant land, formerly an orchard. In July 1972, two workmen from the council under the supervision of a works superintendent entered the land, cleared a large area of overgrown grass and weeds, grubbed up a hedge and dug five trial bores. Subsequently a survey was concluded to establish levels and further site clearance work was carried out. A shed to provide shelter and storage was also placed on the land. In February, the owner attached a padlock to the gate to the land, a key to the padlock being passed to the council on February 21. The question in issue was

---

[12] Compulsory Purchase Act 1965, s.11.
[13] 1975 S.L.T. (Lands Tr.) 18.
[14] Citing J. Rankine, *The Law of Land-Ownership in Scotland* (W. Green & Son, 4th ed.), p. 3.
[15] See, too, *Buckingham Street Investments Ltd v. Greater London Council* (1975) 31 P. & C.R. 453 in which the Lands Tribunal said there must be "some overt act on the part of the acquiring authority." *Cf., Harris v. Birkenhead Corporation* [1976] 1 W.L.R. 279.
[16] (1978) 35 P. & C.R. 436. See, too, *Pandit v. Leicester City Council* [1989] J.P.L. 621.

whether possession had been taken in July 1972, in which case the compensation would be £22,500, or February 1973, in which case it would be £33,500. The tribunal held that July 1972 was the appropriate date. What had been done by the council was all part and parcel of the works for which the council required the land and was consistent with having taken possession.[17] Taking possession, said Douglas Frank Q.C. "must mean or include the doing of acts only consistent with ownership or the right to ownership unless done under some other power." Section 11 (3) of the Compulsory Purchase Act 1965, which permits access on notice for the purpose of taking levels and making test bores, was not a sufficient warrant for what had been done in this case.

6—06   In *Chilton v. Telford Development Corporation*[18] the acquiring authority took possession of some 67.87 acres of farmland, following service of a notice to treat and notice of entry under the New Towns Act 1965 and the Compulsory Purchase Act 1965, in eight separate parcels between June 1978 and October 1980. The question in issue was whether possession was taken on a single date, namely the date on which possession of the first parcel was taken, or on several dates, namely the dates on which possession was taken of the several parcels. The Court of Appeal held that where notice of entry has been given in respect of the whole land, taking possession of part in pursuance of the notice is to be treated as taking possession of the whole. The valuation date for the whole land was accordingly the date of entry on the first parcel of the land. It would appear that the acquiring authority could avoid this outcome by simply serving a notice of entry in respect of each separate parcel as and when possession is required.

It would seem that the onus, in the event of a dispute as to whether possession has been taken, rests with the acquiring authority to establish that their actions amount to taking possession.[19]

The ability to take possession following service of a notice of entry means that acquiring authorities are well-placed to choose a valuation date advantageous to them. As the Lord Justice-Clerk (Lord Wheatley) pointed out in *Miller and Partners Ltd v. Edinburgh Corporation*[20] "In a period of rising values the acquiring authority can at any time before the final award bring forward the date of assessment by taking possession of the land." Apart from seeking to expedite the making of an award by the Lands Tribunal, a claimant, however, has little unilateral control over the valuation date and could not, for example, act to anticipate a reduced award of compensation in a time of declining values. Lord Wheatley expressed the view that this inequality might "call for consideration in future legislation."

---

[17] Entry on property for some purpose unrelated to the acquiring authority's purchase of the land will not be treated as taking possession for compensation purposes (*West v. Exeter City Council* (1974) 230 E.G. 1447; *Otterspool Investments Ltd v. Merseyside County Council* (1984) 270 E.G. 46).

[18] [1988] J.P.L. 37.

[19] *Burson v. Wantage Rural District Council* (1973) 27 P. & C.R. 556.

[20] 1978 S.C. 1.

2. DATE OF ASSESSMENT

Where the acquiring authority have not taken possession of the land then, in the **6—07** absence of agreement on compensation, the valuation date is the "date of assessment" of compensation.[21] In *Corporation of Hull Trinity House v. County Council of Humberside*[22] the Lands Tribunal observed that the date of assessment could be one of three dates, namely, the date of the reference to the tribunal, the date or dates of the hearing, or the date of the decision. The tribunal concluded that the date of decision was inappropriate because, in practice, it would be impossible to assess values at the date of the decision unless the decision was given on the day of, or within a few days of, the hearing. There were also disadvantages in adopting the date of the hearing (although, as the parties were agreed, that date was taken as the date of assessment) because at the time of the hearing values might have changed and changed quite substantially between the lodging of documents under the Lands Tribunal rules and that date. On grounds of both justice and convenience, the tribunal considered there was much to be said for the date of reference. It would enable either party to fix the date of assessment thus going some way towards meeting the inequality referred to in *Miller* (above). Furthermore, valuations and comparables would not have to be altered right up to the time of, or during the course of, the hearing.

In *W. & S. (Long Eaton) Ltd v. Derbyshire County Council*[23] Buckley L.J., giving **6—08** judgment for the Court of Appeal, acknowledged the convenience of adopting the date of reference as the date of assessment but concluded that it was inconsistent with the decision in *Birmingham Corporation* that the time for measuring the compensation does not arrive until the owner is physically dispossessed of his property or the title to it passes in law or equity to the acquiring authority. Notwithstanding possible anomalies, the court held that the date of assessment was the date of the award which in practical terms meant the last day of the hearing before the Lands Tribunal.[24] The court added, however, that: "If in a particular case the tribunal were to think it likely that values had changed materially since the hearing and before the award was promulgated, further evidence could be heard and, if thought desirable, arrangements could be made for the award to follow almost immediately after the further hearing." In *Miller & Partners Ltd v. Edinburgh Corporation*,[25] the Second Division had to consider the position when considerable time elapsed between the hearing of evidence as to values and the date of the final award, time during which values might vary substantially one

---

[21] *Birmingham Corporation v. West Midlands Baptist (Trust) Association (Inc.)* [1970] A.C. 874.
[22] (1975) 29 P. & C.R. 243
[23] (1976) 31 P. & C.R. 99.
[24] See, too, *C. & J. Seymour (Investments) Ltd v. Lewes District Council* [1992] 11 E.G. 127
[25] 1978 S.C.I. It should be noted that the case was decided by the Second Division in November 1973.

way or another. The Lord Justice-Clerk (Lord Wheatley) concluded that a full reading of the speeches in *Birmingham Corporation* disclosed that where, as in this case, possession had not been taken, the valuation date "is the date at which according to law either party can sue for specific performance as if there had been a contract of sale at that date." In a case like the one under consideration in which the issue of compensation had been remitted to arbitration that date is the date of the arbiter's final award. Assessment at that date was not impracticable. Should a material change in values occur between the date of the hearing and the date of the arbiter's final award, arbitration proceedings are sufficiently flexible to allow a proper assessment as at the date of the final award. In Lord Milligan's view it was only at the date of the final award that the claimant's real loss could be quantified and the principle of equivalence satisfied.

6—09   In *Hoveringham Gravels Ltd v. Chiltern District Council*,[26] where a case was referred back to the Lands Tribunal by the Court of Appeal to determine the amount of compensation to which the court had held the claimants entitled, the claimants argued that in assessing values regard should be had not to the values prevailing at the previous hearing but to those prevailing at the time of the determination of the matters remitted. The Lands Tribunal held that it would be wrong to extend the appropriate date merely because of an appeal. Such a course would produce anomalies; in particular, it might affect a decision whether or not to appeal. A claimant, for example, might be deterred in a falling market, because he would run the risk of the payment of a penalty arising from reduced values. The decision in *W. S. (Long Eaton) Ltd* on which the claimants relied could be distinguished as the effect of an appeal to the Court of Appeal did not arise in that case.

3. SALE BY AGREEMENT IN THE ABSENCE OF A NOTICE TO TREAT

6—10   In *Washington Development Corporation v. Bamling (Washington) Ltd*[27] the claimants and the corporation, as is not uncommon, entered into a written agreement for the sale and purchase of the claimants' property comprised in a confirmed compulsory purchase order. The agreement provided that the price was to be agreed with the district valuer or, failing agreement, to be settled by the Lands Tribunal as if the necessary steps for acquiring such interest compulsorily had been taken under the New Towns Act 1965 and a notice to treat had been served on the date of the written agreement. No notice to treat had been or was subsequently served in respect of the claimants' interest. Possession of the property was taken piecemeal by the corporation in six parcels spread over a period from June 1975 to April 1980. The corporation contended that the valuation date was, in respect

---

[26] (1978) 39 P. & C.R. 414.
[27] [1985] 273 E.G. 980.

of the entirety of the land, the date of the agreement. The claimants argued that the proper date was, in respect of each of the several parcels of land, the date on which the corporation took possession.

Slade L.J., giving judgment for the Court of Appeal, stated that in view of the wording of the agreement the proper approach was to ask what would have been the valuation date if the necessary steps to acquire the interest compulsorily had been taken under the legislation and a notice to treat had been served on the date of the agreement. In the light of that approach it was clear from the decision in *Birmingham Corporation* that the date of the agreement (the date of the notional notice to treat) was not the proper date for ascertaining values. The proper date would be the date when the price was agreed between the parties or, in default, assessed by the tribunal or, if earlier, the date when possession was taken. In the circumstances of the case, the valuation date was the date when the corporation took possession of the several parcels of land.

4. GENERAL VESTING DECLARATION

An acquiring authority may, instead of proceeding by way of notice to treat, make   **6—11** use of the general vesting declaration procedure (see para. 4–26). The procedure is set out in the Compulsory Purchase (Vesting Declaration) Act 1981. The effect is that "[on] the vesting date the land specified in the general vesting declaration, together with the right to enter upon and take possession of it, shall . . . vest in the acquiring authority . . ."[28] Once the acquiring authority are vested in the land they cannot withdraw and, on the other hand, it is open to the claimant to adjust and settle compensation at that stage.

The question of the appropriate valuation date where the procedure for expedited completion is employed arose in *Mrs Annie R. Renfrew's Trustees v. Glasgow Corporation*.[29] In that case a public house and three tenement houses in Glasgow were included in an area the subject of a confirmed compulsory purchase order. The order provided for expedited completion of title and, following execution of a declaration of vesting under paragraph 3 of the sixth Schedule to the Town and Country Planning (Scotland) Act 1945,[30] a notice of title was recorded on January 12, 1966. The claimants were allowed to remain in possession of the public house and were continuing to trade at the date of the hearing before the Lands Tribunal for Scotland. The claimants argued that the valuation date should be the date of the assessment of the compensation by the tribunal. The corporation contended that the appropriate date was January 12, 1966 when the title vested in them. The

---

[28] Compulsory Purchase (Vesting Declarations) Act 1981, s.8(1).
[29] 1972 S.L.T. (Lands Tr.) 2. See, too, *Khan v. Glasgow District Council*, 1977 S.L.T. (Lands Tr.) 35. Also *Hussain v. Oldham Metropolitan Borough Council* (1981) 259 E.G. 56; *Birrell Ltd v. City of Edinburgh District Council*, 1982 S.C. (H.L.) 75; 1982 S.L.T. 363 H.L.
[30] As incorporated in the eleventh Schedule to the Town and Country Planning (Scotland) Act 1947.

tribunal concluded that, read in conjunction with the speeches in *Birmingham Corporation* the valuation date, where the expedited completion procedure is employed, is the date of vesting — in that case January 12, 1966.[31]

6—12   In a period of rising property values use of the general vesting declaration procedure has the advantage to the acquiring authority that prices are fixed at the date of vesting and any subsequent increase in property values is ignored. Having vested the property in themselves, the authority may then lease it back to the former owner until such time as it is actually required. Of course, operation of the procedure may work to the disadvantage of the acquiring authority in a period of falling property values. The claimant may face other hardship where a general vesting declaration is employed.[32] In particular, as was argued in *Renfrew's Trustees*, in a period of rapid inflation of property values, compensation measured at the date of vesting rather than at the date of assessment or possession which may follow sometime later is unlikely to be a realistic measure of the claimant's loss at the time he is required to move. Because of such difficulties the Royal Institution of Chartered Surveyors have recommended that where the vesting declaration procedure is used, the valuation date should be the date on which possession is taken by the acquiring authority.[33] However, whilst acknowledging the hardship, the Lands Tribunal for Scotland in *Renfrew's Trustees* pointed out that in such cases a claimant is in a position to compel the acquiring authority to settle the compensation at the time of vesting and if claimants choose to continue in occupation it may be assumed that this is because it suits their purpose to do so.

The date for fixing interests

6—13   Interests in land are not static. The nature and extent of an interest may change over time, existing interests may be transferred or extinguished, and new interests may be created. It is sometimes important for the purposes of assessing compensation to determine the point in time at which interests are to be taken as fixed.

1. THE TRADITIONAL APPROACH

6—14   As indicated earlier, the traditional, although not invariable (see below), approach

---

[31] In the unlikely event that compensation is agreed or determined prior to the date of vesting, the earlier date would be the valuation date.

[32] See B. Denyer-Green, "Compensation: Date of Assessment under a General Vesting Declaration" (1982) 132 N.L.J. 697; also a letter by T. J. Templeman, published at (1982) 261 E.G. 107.

[33] *Compensation for Compulsory Acquisition*, 1989, para. 6.38.

has been that the notice to treat fixes the interests to be compensated.[34] As Lord Pearson observed in *Rugby Joint Water Board v. Shaw Fox*,[35] there could be drawn from the decisions in *Penny v. Penny* (above) and *Re Morgan and London and North-Western Railway Co.*[36] "the principle that the nature of the claimant's interest is to be ascertained at the time of (or immediately before or immediately after) the service of the notice to treat." The traditional approach would appear to derive from the view taken in early decisions of the general effect of the notice to treat (see Chapter 4).

The consequence of adopting the traditional approach may be illustrated by reference to the decision of Danckwerts L.J. in *Square Grip Reinforcement Co. (London) Ltd v. Rowton Houses Ltd*[37] involving the valuation of freehold and leasehold interests. At the date of the notice to treat (January 17, 1963) it was possible that the two leases might be cut short by the exercise of a break clause the following September. By the date on which possession was taken in late 1964 it was apparent that the terms had not been cut short and would normally have continued until at least 1970. It was held that the normal rule requiring compensation to be assessed by reference to the situation existing at the date of the notice to treat should apply.

A further illustration is provided by reference to the decision of an official arbiter in *Jennings v. Edinburgh Corporation*.[38] The claimant was the owner of a shop let on a 21 year lease. The lease made provision for rent reviews at seven and 14 years. At the date of the deemed notice to treat, the first review was still a year away. However, when the owner's interest subsequently vested in the corporation, the date for the first review had passed and the right of review had not been exercised. The owner argued, nonetheless, that compensation should be assessed on the basis that her interest and that of the tenant were fixed at the date of the notice to treat and that their respective interests should be valued reflecting the possibility of a rent review occurring in a year's time. The arbiter accepted this argument.

In *Birmingham Corporation* their Lordships, as one commentator said,[39] "expressed the effect of a notice to treat in a much lower key" than had many of their predecessors (see Chapter 4). They appeared to view the notice to treat as little more than notification of an intention to take land from the owner.[40] As Lord Morris of Borth-y-Gest declared:

---

[34] H. Parrish, *Cripps on Compulsory Acquisition of Land, supra*, para. 2–059.

[35] [1973] A.C. 202. See, too, the view expressed by Lord Hodson.

[36] [1896] 2 Q.B. 469.

[37] [1967] Ch. 877

[38] Ref. No. 2/1967.

[39] F.A. Mann, "The Relevant Date for the Assessment of Compensation" (1969) 85 L.Q.R. 516.

[40] It, nonetheless, still determines the land to be taken and it generally entitles either party to insist on completion of the transaction. Furthermore, the owner cannot increase the burden of comepnsation on the acquiring authority by creating new interests (see Chap. 4).

> "A notice to treat does not establish the relation of vendor and purchaser between the acquiring authority and the owner. It does not transfer either the legal or the equitable interest to the acquiring authority. It informs the owner that the land is to be taken and informs him that the acquiring authority are ready to negotiate with him as to the price of the land. . . . It makes a demand for particulars of estates and interest and of claims."

Influenced by dicta in *Birmingham Corporation*, the Lands Tribunal has in several cases held that interests are to be considered as they stand, not at the date of the notice to treat, but at the valuation date. It is not clear, therefore, whether the traditional approach that the notice to treat fixes the interests for the purpose of assessing compensation has survived. It is not possible to reconcile the various decisions and dicta on this point and the position remains uncertain. These decisions and dicta are explored in more detail below.

2. NON-TRADITIONAL APPROACHES

6—15   Even before the decision in *Birmingham Corporation*, there are several cases which suggest that interests in land were not invariably taken as fixed by the notice to treat. In *R. v. Kennedy*[41] a lease had 25 years to run at the date of service of the notice to treat. Under the terms of the lease the landlord was entitled to regain possession on giving three months' notice. Following receipt of the notice to treat the landlord terminated the lease on giving the appropriate notice. The tenant claimed the value of the residue of the lease as at the date of the notice to treat. This was rejected by the court on the ground that no claim had been submitted prior to the notice to quit. The lessee's claim was limited to the balance of the three months' period of notice remaining at the time of actual expropriation. As Davies points out,[42] by determining the case on this basis the court evaded the issue of whether the notice to treat fixed the claimant's interest. However, in *Banham v. London Borough of Hackney*[43] (below) the President of the Lands Tribunal regarded the decision in *Kennedy* as being inconsistent with the view that interests are fixed as at the date of the notice to treat. "It is true," he said, "that the court did not go on to say 'The owner's interest too must be valued as it was at the date of entry' but I find it difficult to understand why this should not follow."

In *Holloway v. Dover Corporation*[44] a leasehold interest still had five and a half years to run at the date of the deemed notice to treat. No further procedural steps were taken by the acquiring authority and the lease expired before possession was

---

[41] (1893) 1 Q.B. 533.
[42] K. Davies, *Law of Compulsory Purchase and Compensation* (Butterworths, 4th ed., 1984), p. 120.
[43] (1970) 22 P. & C.R. 922.
[44] [1960] 1 W.L.R. 604.

taken. It was held in the Court of Appeal that it would have been open to the lessees to invoke the statutory procedures and claim compensation at any time after the date of the notice to treat; they had not done so but had continued instead in full enjoyment of the premises; no interest had in fact been compulsorily acquired from them and they were not entitled to compulsory purchase compensation. Lord Evershed M.R. commented. "I am at any rate comforted that this conclusion, I think, accords with plain common sense." Again, as Davies points out,[45] the court avoided direct consideration of the question whether the claimants' interest should be treated as fixed at the date of the notice to treat.

In *Soper and Soper v. Doncaster Corporation*[46] the claimants were the lessees under   **6—16** a five year lease due to expire in January 1963. Notice to treat was served in August 1962 and notice of entry in September 1963. Since the claimants had enjoyed the full benefit of their lease, the Lands Tribunal awarded a nominal sum of £1 on account of the acquisition of their interest plus disturbance. *Holloway* was distinguished on the ground that in *Soper* the claimants had responded to the notice to treat by submitting a claim before the expiry of the lease.

The decisions in *Kennedy, Holloway* and *Soper* all predate that of the House of Lords in *Birmingham Corporation*. However, in a number of cases since *Birmingham Corporation* the Lands Tribunal, influenced by dicta in that case, have moved away from the traditional approach that the date of the notice to treat fixes the interests to be valued. In *Banham v. London Borough of Hackney*[47] an acquiring authority rehoused a tenant between the date of the notice to treat and the date of valuation. The owner claimed compensation based on vacant possession. The President of the Lands Tribunal (Sir Michael Rowe Q.C.) concluded that in the light of the decision in *Kennedy* and of the speeches of Lords Reid, Donovan and Morris of Borth-y-Gest in *Birmingham Corporation* it seemed "impossible to say that the interests in land compulsorily acquired are immutably fixed by the service of the notice to treat." The true view, he continued, "would seem to be that interests as well as values must be taken as at the date of valuation or entry unless the owner has done something which so altered the interests as to increase the burden of compensation on the acquiring authority." The interests were accordingly valued as at the date of entry.

In *Bradford Property Trust Ltd v. Hertfordshire County Council*[48] the tribunal   **6—17** (Douglas Frank Q.C.), while expressing agreement with what had been said by Sir Michael Rowe in *Banham*, reached a slightly different conclusion. The tenants of two houses being compulsorily acquired by the county council were rehoused by the local housing authority between the date of the notice to treat and the date of the notice of entry. The tribunal held that interests subsisting at the date of the notice to treat should be valued as they stood at the date of the notice of

---

[45] K. Davies, *Law of Compulsory Purchase and Compensation, supra*, p. 121.
[46] (1964) 16 P. & C.R. 53.
[47] (1970) 22 P. & C.R. 922.
[48] (1973) 27 P. & C.R. 228.

entry (*i.e.* no longer encumbered by tenancies), a conclusion which resembles that reached in *Soper*.[49] In *Midland's Bank Trust Co. Ltd (Executors) v. London Borough of Lewisham*,[50] on the other hand, the tribunal found it impossible to accept that what had to be valued were the interests subsisting at the date of the notice to treat by reference to prices prevailing at the date of entry. "Our conclusion is that valuation at the time of entry can only be a sensible exercise or principle if the interests are to be taken as they exist on that date."

Acquiring authorities who had incurred the expense of rehousing tenants between the date of the notice to treat and the date of entry were, not surprisingly, aggrieved at being faced with claims for compensation from owners based on vacant possession value. This anomaly has been resolved by section 50 of the Land Compensation Act 1973 which broadly provides that in assessing compensation no account is to be taken of any change in the value of an interest caused by the rehousing of a tenant.

6—18 Support for the traditional approach that the notice to treat fixes the interests to be valued still, however, persists. In *Lyle v. Bexley London Borough Council*,[51] for example, where the tenants of two houses were rehoused by the acquiring authority between the date of the notice to treat and the date of entry, the Lands Tribunal held that the owner was "deemed to be selling the actual interest he enjoyed at the date of the notice to treat, for which he receives the value attaching to that interest at the date the acquiring authority took possession." In other words, compensation was assessed on the basis of tenanted occupation. And in *Runcorn Association Football Club v. Runcorn and Warrington Development Corporation*[52] the Lands Tribunal also took the view that the material date for determining the extent of the tenants' interest was the date of the notice to treat. In that case notice to treat was served in respect of a leasehold interest with more than two years to run. When the acquiring authority served notice of entry less than a year of the lease remained unexpired. The acquiring authority argued that compensation fell to be assessed under section 20 of the Compulsory Purchase Act 1965 which makes special provision with regard to compensation for tenancies for a year or less or from year to year. Given their finding on the material date, the tribunal concluded that section 20 had no application in this case.

In the light of the decisions considered above, one may readily sympathise with the Lands Tribunal member in *Metcalfe* who commented somewhat plaintively: "Having heard the arguments I find it is very difficult now to reconcile all the recent cases dealing with the alteration of interests between the date of the notice to treat and the date of entry." The difficulty remains unresolved but it may be suggested that the approach which appears to accord best with the principle of equivalence will normally result from a rule that interests subsisting at the date of

---

[49] See, too, *Metcalfe v. Basildon Development Corporation* (1974) 28 P. & C.R. 307.
[50] (1975) 30 P. & C.R. 268.
[51] [1972] R.V.R. 318; 223 E.G. 687.
[52] (1982) 54 P. & C.R. 183.

the notice to treat should be valued according to their nature or extent at the valuation date.

Interests in land and "the scheme"

There is a well-established rule that any increase or decrease in the value of an **6—19** interest which is due to the scheme underlying the acquisition is to be ignored in assessing compensation (see Chapter 9).[53] It is important, therefore, to distinguish between a change in the nature of an interest and a change in its value. For example, if, as in *Banham* (above), the acquiring authority rehouse a tenant between the date of the notice to treat and the date of valuation so that the owner gives vacant possession on entry, does this result in a change in the nature of the owner's interest or in a change in its value? If it is the latter, the effect on value is to be ignored in assessing compensation.

The distinction is not always easy to see. In *J. & D. Littlejohn v. City of Glasgow*[54] a flat was vacated by the tenant after the date of the notice to treat but before possession was taken by the acquiring authority. The evidence before the official arbiter was to the effect that the tenant had moved out because of the impending acquisition; had it not been for that she would have remained. The arbiter decided that as vacant possession was the direct consequence of the scheme of acquisition, the effect of the scheme should be ignored and the interest in the property should be valued as though the tenant had remained in occupation. In other words, the arbiter appeared to treat the change as a change in the value of the interest and one which, therefore, fell to be ignored under the rule in *Pointe Gourde Quarrying and Transport Co. v. Sub-Intendent of Crown Lands* (see Chapter 9 for a discussion of this rule).

However, in *Rugby Joint Water Board v. Shaw-Fox*[55] the House of Lords treated a similar change as a change in the nature of the interest. The water board had obtained planning permission in respect of a large part of a farm for use as a reservoir. As a result of the permission the tenant lost his security of tenure because the owner was placed in a position whereby he could serve a notice to quit which could not be contested. A notice to treat was subsequently served on the landlord who claimed compensation on the basis that his interest was subject to an unprotected tenancy. The water board contested this on the ground that their scheme had altered the landlord's interest and increased its value. In other words, this was

---

[53] Land Compensation Act 1961, s.6; *Pointe Gourde Quarrying and Transport Co. v. Sub-Intendent of Crown Lands* [1947] A.C. 565.

[54] Decision of an Official Arbiter ref. No. 6/1969.

[55] [1973] A.C. 202 approving the decision of the Court of Appeal in *Minister of Transport v. Pettitt* (1969) 67 L.G.R. 449.

an increase in value due to the scheme underlying the acquisition which falls to be ignored under the rule in *Pointe Gourde*. The House of Lords (Lord Simon dissenting) disagreed with the water board, holding that the rule in *Pointe Gourde* applied not to the ascertainment of the interests to be valued but to the value of the interests when ascertained. The change in this case had been to the interest to be ascertained. "[The] reversion to an unprotected tenancy," said Lord Pearson, "is a different interest from a reversion to a protected tenancy."[56] The landlord's interest was accordingly valued as subject to an unprotected tenancy.

6—20   Section 48 of the Land Compensation Act 1973 has been introduced to overcome the sort of hardship experienced by the agricultural tenant in *Shaw-Fox*. It applies where an authority, acting under legislation providing for the acquisition or taking of possession of land compulsorily, acquire the interest of the landlord or the tenant in, or take possession of, all or part of an agricultural holding. In assessing the compensation payable for the acquisition of the interest of the tenant of an agricultural holding, protected under the Agricultural Holdings Act 1986, or of the landlord of such a holding, the statutory security of tenure of the tenant is to be taken into account. There is also to be disregarded any entitlement of the landlord to resume land in the holding by virtue of a stipulation in the lease and any notice already given as a result of a stipulation in the lease which would not be or would not have been effective but for the power to resume the land because it is required by the acquiring authority.[57] Should the tenant have quitted all or part of the holding by reason of such a notice to quit or should land in the holding have been resumed by virtue of such a stipulation, it is to be assumed that that has not happened.

The tenant's compensation, assessed under section 48 of the 1973 Act, is to be reduced by an amount equal to any reorganisation payment which the acquiring authority are liable to make under section 12 of the Agriculture (Miscellaneous Provisions) Act 1968; but if the resulting compensation is less than it would otherwise have been, it is to be increased by the amount of the deficiency (see para. 13–37).

6—21   Similar provision is made in section 47 of the 1973 Act as regards land which is the subject of a business tenancy. It applies where an authority, acting under legislation providing for the acquisition or taking of possession of land compulsorily, acquire the interest of the landlord in or the tenant in, or take possession of, any land subject to which Part II of the Landlord and Tenant Act 1954 applies. In assessing the compensation payable for the acquisition of the interest of the tenant under such a tenancy or of the interest of the landlord, the statutory security of tenure of the tenant is to be taken into account. In assessing the compensation, it is to be assumed that the acquiring authority have not acquired and do not propose to acquire any interest in the land. Section 47 repeals section 39(1)

---

[56] *Ibid.* at p. 216.
[57] See, for example, *Anderson v. Moray District Council*, 1978 S.L.T. (Lands Tr.) 37; *Dawson v. Norwich City Council* (1979) 250 E.G. 1297.

of the Landlord and Tenant Act 1954, under which the contrary rule applied in respect of short-term business tenancies.

The decision in *Shaw-Fox* was subsequently applied by the Lands Tribunal in *Metcalfe v. Basildon Corporation.*[58] A statutory tenant in occupation of residential premises at the date of the notice to treat was rehoused by the acquiring authority five days before possession. The first question in issue was whether the owner's interest should be valued on the basis of vacant possession or subject to the statutory tenancy. The tribunal, following the guide given in *Banham* and *Bradford Property Trust Ltd* (above), concluded that interests as well as values must be taken as at the date of valuation so that the owner's interest was valued on the basis of vacant possession. The question then arose whether the resulting difference in the level of compensation for the owner's interest was an increase in value due to the acquiring authority's scheme which fell to be disregarded under the rule in *Pointe Gourde.* The tribunal concluded that, although the increment was entirely due to the scheme, the rule in *Pointe Gourde* had no application since it related to the value of an interest when ascertained rather than to the ascertainment of what is the interest to be valued. The effect of the decision in *Shaw-Fox*, said the tribunal, had been "to remove from the ambit of the *Pointe Gourde* principle any increment stemming from the event, or even the possibility of the enlargement of an interest or the removal of an encumbrance." The right to receive this sort of "windfall" profit was subsequently removed by section 50 of the Land Compensation Act 1973 (above).

In *Murray Bookmakers Ltd v. Glasgow District Council*[59] a lease provided that upon compulsory acquisition of the premises it would automatically terminate. A claim for compensation by the tenant following the compulsory acquisition of the premises was rejected by the Lands Tribunal for Scotland. The effective cause of the elimination of the tenant's interest at the date of the general vesting declaration was not the declaration, said the tribunal, but the private agreement between the parties to the lease without which the reversion would not have occurred. The landlords were entitled to full vacant possession value.

Increasing the burden of compensation

There may be an appreciable delay, perhaps a matter of years, between the date of service of a notice to treat and eventual taking of possession by the acquiring authority. In the meantime, the owner may wish to deal with existing interests in the ordinary course of the management of the land. The service of the notice

6—22

---

[58] (1974) 28 P. & C.R. 307. See, too, *Midland Bank Trust Co. Ltd (Executors) v. London Borough of Lewisham* (1975) 30 P. & C.R. 268.
[59] 1979 S.L.T. (Lands Tr.) 8.

to treat does not prevent this.[60] However, it appears to be the case that, whatever may be the appropriate date for fixing the interests to be compensated, interests created or works carried out after service of the notice to treat will, if they go beyond what is necessary for the owner's continued enjoyment of the land and will add to the burden of compensation on the acquiring authority, be disregarded in the assessment of compensation.[61] In *City of Glasgow Union Railway Co. v. James McEwen & Co.*[62] the railway company gave notice to McEwen & Co. of its intention to take their land under statutory powers. At the date of the notice, McEwen & Co., who had been tenants of the land under a three year lease which had expired earlier that year, were in occupation of the land without any written title of possession. Shortly after service of the notice, the owner of the land granted a further lease to McEwen & Co. for a term of three years. A claim for compensation by McEwen & Co. in respect of their three year term was rejected by the court: "When the respondents obtained the only lease they have, they did so with such knowledge of what was going on as to preclude them from altering the state of matters, to the prejudice of the suspenders."

Risk of damage to property[63]

6—23 In *Phoenix Assurance Co. v. Spooner*[64] buildings were destroyed by fire after the date of the notice to treat but before the acquiring authority had taken possession of the property. The court held that the authority were bound to pay the value of the subjects as at the date of the notice to treat, that being the date of valuation. The loss resulting from the fire accordingly fell on the acquiring authority.

In *Birmingham Corporation* the House of Lords held that *Phoenix* had been wrongly decided. Lord Reid said:

> "It seems to me to be wrong that the risk should pass as at the notice to treat although the promoters or acquiring authority then acquire no right or interest in the property: it would mean that the owner though still in full control would cease to have any duty to preserve the property or any incentive to insure it. It does not at all follow from the fact that [after service of a notice to treat] the owner cannot act so as to increase the burden on the promoters, that the burden on the promoters may not be diminished by events later than the notice to treat."

---

[60] *Cardiff Corporation v. Cook* [1923] 2 Ch. 115.
[61] *Mercer v. Liverpool, St Helens and South Lancashire Rly Co.* [1903] 1 K.B. 652 per Matthew L.J. at p. 667; affirmed [1904] A.C. 461 H.L.
[62] (1870) 8 M. 747.
[63] See, generally, J. Rowan-Robinson & E. Young, "Compulsory Acquisition, Compensation and Risk of Damage to Property" (1985) 30 J.L.S. 312.
[64] [1905] 2 K.B. 753.

The position now is that the risk of damage or destruction of property which is the subject of a compulsory purchase order, and the responsibility for insurance, remains with the owner until entry or determination of compensation, whichever is the earlier.[65] Where a general vesting declaration is employed, the relevant date at which the risk passes will be the date of vesting unless, which is unlikely, compensation is agreed or determined prior to vesting.

This may be illustrated by the decision in *Otterspool Investments Ltd v. Merseyside County Council.*[66] A notice to treat together with a notice of entry was served in 1973 in respect of a property comprising three flats. The acquiring authority did not, in the event, take possession until October 1982. In the meantime, the condition of the premises deteriorated. In July 1981 they were occupied by squatters. They were subsequently damaged severely in the "Toxteth riots" and, as a result, the building authority had them demolished in August 1981 because of their dangerous condition. The Lands Tribunal observed that until the claimants relinquished possession it was in their own interests to continue to maintain the premises and to insure against damage. They could, if they had so wished, have had compensation settled at an earlier date by referring the matter to the tribunal. As it was, at the date of entry the owners were entitled to compensation of £300, being the value of the property as a cleared site.

Where, however, damage to property is found to be caused by the scheme **6—24** underlying the acquisition any decrease in value falls to be ignored under section 6 of the Land Compensation Act 1961 and the rule in *Pointe Gourde* (see Chapter 9). Thus in *Macdonald v. Midlothian County Council,*[67] where the value of the subject property was depressed by some £300 because of the derelict condition of property on either side which had been acquired under the scheme and left vacant, the Lands Tribunal for Scotland held that the depreciation was to be ignored in valuing the subject property because it was depreciation resulting from the scheme underlying the acquisition.

In *Gately v. Central Lancashire New Town Development Corporation*[68] compensation was claimed in respect of a house and garage which had been left "standing alone amidst rubble and desolation" in an area cleared by the acquiring authority. While still occupied, the property suffered damage from vandalism. The Lands Tribunal held the acquiring authority responsible for 50 per cent. of the diminution in value resulting from the vandalism, this being the reduction in value entirely due to the scheme underlying the acquisition. The authority, said the tribunal, were not entitled, because of the manner in which the scheme was implemented, to increase the risk of vandalism borne by the owner. In the same

---

[65] *Socratous v. Camden London Borough* (1974) 233 E.G. 161; and *Lewars v. Greater London Council* (1981) 43 P. & C.R. 129.

[66] (1984) 270 E.G. 46. See *Simpson v. Stoke-on-Trent City Council* (1982) 44 P. & C.R. 226 for an illustration of the difficult position in which an owner may now find himself.

[67] 1975 S.L.T. (Lands Tr.) 24. See, too, *Kirby and Shaw v. Bury County Borough Council* (1973) 228 E.G. 537.

[68] (1984) 48 P. & C.R. 339.

case it was held that damage to the claimant's garage during the course of the demolition by the acquiring authority of adjoining property was a loss which was entirely attributable to the scheme and one which should, therefore, be borne by the authority.[69] It does not, however, automatically follow that the *Pointe Gourde* principle will operate merely because property being compulsorily acquired has been left empty and has been vandalised. The vandalism may be due to a claimant's failure to take reasonable steps for the protection of this property.[70]

The date for determining the planning status of the land

6—25   The value of land in the open market will depend in many cases upon its planning status. This status may alter over the period of the compulsory acquisition. In valuing land for compensation purposes it may, therefore, be important to know at what date its planning status is to be determined. Subject to what is said below, it would appear to follow from the decision in *Birmingham Corporation* that compensation is to be assessed having regard to all matters affecting the subject land and its surroundings to which a purchaser would have regard at the valuation date.[71]

Sections 14 to 16 of the Land Compensation Act 1961 provide that certain assumptions may be made about the planning status of land being valued for the purposes of compensation and give some indication of the relevant date for the purposes of the assumptions (see Chapter 8. These assumptions are stated to be in addition to any planning permissions in existence at the date of the notice to treat which have not yet been implemented (1961 Act, section 14(2)).

Section 15 (1) of the 1961 Act states that, if on the date of service of the notice to treat there is not in force planning permission for the purpose for which the land is being acquired, it is to be assumed that planning permission would be granted such as would permit development of the land for those purposes. And section 16 broadly provides that planning permission may be assumed for development which accords with the provisions of the "current development plan." The "current development plan" refers to the development plan in the form in which that plan is in force on the date of service of the notice to treat.[72]

---

[69] In the alternative, the tribunal held that the acquiring authority could not take advantage of a state of affairs they had themselves produced (*New Zealand Shipping Co. Ltd v. Société des Ateliers et Chantiers de France* [1919] A.C. 1 per Lord Finlay; also *Robinson v. Stoke-on-Trent City Council* (1980) 256 E.G. 393).

[70] See *Arrow v. London Borough of Bexley* (1977) 35 P. & C.R. 237; and *Lewars v. Greater London Council* (1981) 43 P. & C.R. 129. See, too, R. Carnwath, "Vandalism and 'The Scheme'" [1974] R.V.R. 562. For an illustration of the difficult position in which a claimant may find himself see *Simpson v. Stoke-on-Trent City Council* (1982) 44 P. & C.R. 226.

[71] See *Cupar Trading Estate v. Fife Regional Council*, 1979 S.L.T. (Lands Tr.) 2.

[72] 1961 Act, s.39 (1).

Although these assumptions relate to circumstances existing at the date of the notice to treat, section 14(3) of the 1961 Act makes it clear that nothing in sections 15 and 16 of that Act is to be construed as requiring it to be assumed that planning permission would necessarily be refused for development other than that for which permission is to be assumed. In other words, if circumstances change between the date of the notice to treat and the valuation date so that, in the absence of the acquisition of the land by the acquiring authority, there would have been some prospect of a grant of planning permission for some other development, the benefit of that prospect may form the basis of a claim for development value.

Inevitably, however, such a prospect is likely to be subject to some discount for uncertainty. The 1961 Act accordingly provides a mechanism whereby a claimant may seek to upgrade that "hope value" to a certainty. In specified circumstances a claimant (or the acquiring authority) may apply to the planning authority for a certificate of appropriate alternative development (see Chapter 8) stating the classes of development which in the applicant's opinion would be appropriate for the land in question if it were not being purchased by the acquiring authority.

In establishing the relevant date for determining what, if any, alternative devel-   **6—26**
opment would have been appropriate it would appear from the decision in *Robert Hitchins Builders Ltd v. Secretary of State for the Environment*[73] that a distinction must be made between the relevant date for applying planning policies and the relevant date for considering physical factors. In that case Sir Douglas Frank Q.C. held[74] that, having regard to the scheme of the Act, "the application of planning policies should as nearly as possible coincide with the date of the assessment of compensation." He accordingly quashed two decisions made by the Secretary of State on appeals against certificates of appropriate alternative development on the ground that he should have regard to the planning policies at the time of his decisions and not at some antecedent date. In effect, the relevant date for applying planning policies would be the date of entry[75] or the date of decision on the application for a certificate (or an appeal), whichever occurs first.[76]

However, in *Fox v. Secretary of State for the Environment*[77] Roch J. declined to follow the decision in *Hitchens* and concluded that both the physical condition of the land and planning policies should be looked at at the same time. In his judgment section 17(3)–(4) of the 1961 Act requires the local planning authority, and the Secretary of State on appeal, to determine whether or not planning permission

---

[73] (1979) 37 P. & C.R. 140. Applying the dictum of Lord Macnaghton in *Bwllfa & Merthyr Dare Steam Collieries (1891) Ltd v. Pontypridd Waterworks Co.* [1903] A.C. 426 at p. 431. See, too, an appeal decision by the Secretary of State for the Environment under reference APP/5193/D83/13 and PLUP 2/5193/B/1862 reported at (1984) 272 E.G. 659.

[74] Distinguishing *Jelson Ltd v. Minister of Housing and Local Government* [1970] 1 Q.B. 243.

[75] See appeal decision noted at [1987] J.P.L. 659.

[76] See appeal decisions noted at [1987] J.P.L. 660 and [1988] J.P.L. 47.

[77] [1991] 40 E.G. 116

would have been granted for development for one or more of the specified classes "immediately". "Immediately" in this context means "immediately after the proposal to acquire". This in turn is a reference to whichever of the three different circumstances referred to in section 22(2) (in which a proposal to acquire an interest can arise for the purposes of sections 17 and 18 (see below) applies. The reference in section 17(3) and (5) to a "future time" means, he said, no more than a future time as seen at the relevant date. His conclusion was in line with that of the Court of Appeal in *Jelson v. Minister of Housing and Local Government*[78] with Lords Dunpark and McDonald in *Grampian Regional Council v. Secretary of State for Scotland*[79] and with Lord Bridge in the same case before the House of Lords.[80]

6—27   The relevant date for considering physical factors seems not to be in doubt and is to be determined by reference to section 22(2) of the 1961 Act. Regard must be had to the state of the subject land and the area in which it is situated at whichever of the three following dates is appropriate: (1) Where an interest in land is being compulsorily acquired, the date of the publication of notice of the making of the compulsory purchase order; [81] or (2) Where an interest in land is being acquired as a result of the service of a purchase notice[82] or a blight notice,[83] the date on which the notice to treat is deemed to have been served; or (3) Where an interest in land is being acquired as a result of a written offer to negotiate, the date of that offer.[84]

---

[78] [1970] 1 Q.B. 243.
[79] 1984 S.C. 1; 1984 S.L.T. 212.
[80] [1983] 1 W.L.R. 1340.
[81] See appeal decision noted at [1987] J.P.L. 659.
[82] See para. 15–16. See, too, the appeal decision noted at [1987] J.P.L. 660.
[83] See para. 16–07.
[84] See *Jelson Ltd v. Minister of Housing and Local Government* [1970] 1 Q.B. 243. Also *Grampian Regional Council v. Secretary of State for Scotland*, 1984 S.L.T. 1212.

Chapter 7

Market Value

As mentioned in Chapter 5, most claims for compensation for compulsory pur- **7—01**
chase are founded upon section 7 of the 1965 Act. This provides that in estimating
the purchase money or compensation regard is to be had both to the value of the
land being acquired and to any damage to retained land caused by severance or
other injurious affection. In Chapters 7 to 11 aspects of the first head of claim—
the purchase price for the land—are examined; severance and other injurious
affection are considered in Chapter 12.

Except in cases where land is devoted to a purpose for which there is no general
demand or market (see Chapter 10), the measure of the purchase price for the
land is its market value[1] together with compensation for other consequential loss.
This measure derives from a recommendation of the Scott Committee in 1918.[2]
The Committee considered that the absence of a statutorily prescribed standard
of value was allowing what they regarded as excessively high settlements of compensation. They recommended that the standard should be "the market value as
between a willing seller and a willing buyer."

Although "market value" may appear to be a self-explanatory expression, it has
had to be statutorily defined because, as the Sheaf Committee commented,[3] "it
has to be ascertained in circumstances where there is in fact no market (because
the acquiring authority has stepped in with compulsory powers). There must be
rules for ensuring that 'market value' in the technical sense assigned to it in the

---

[1] Land Compensation Act 1961, s.5 (2). But see the discussion in Chap. 10 of "cleared site value"
as the measure of compensation for residential property below the tolerable standard.
[2] Cmnd. 9229, para. 8.
[3] *Report of Working Party on Local Authority/Private Enterprise Partnership Schemes* (HMSO, 1972),
Annex K.

compensation code is aligned with what the market would have paid in a normal transaction."

The theory underlying the standard, as the Chartered Land Societies Committee observed is that:

> "the dispossessed owner could go out into the market and purchase with his compensation money a property roughly similar to that which had been acquired, any incidental loss or expense being met from the proceeds of the disturbance claim."[4]

7—02 It must be doubtful, however, as the committee also observed, whether the Scott Committee anticipated that the concept of market value in the post-Second World War planned economy would prove to be "something very different from the simple function of the forces of undisturbed demand and supply which it was in a less complicated age." In particular, the introduction of a comprehensive system of planning control has introduced considerable complexity into the assessment of the purchase price for the land. This has been further aggravated by the ability of public authorities to recoup from a claimant some of the increase in land values resulting from their schemes. Both factors reflect on the ability of a dispossessed owner to purchase with his compensation money "a property roughly similar to that which had been acquired". Because of this complexity it would seem appropriate to divide the discussion of the purchase price for the land into five separate headings:

1. market value;
2. development potential;
3. disregarding the scheme;
4. special values;
5. disturbance.

This chapter is concerned with the first of these headings—market value.

Rule (2)[5]

7—03 The statutorily prescribed standard of value recommended by the Scott Committee is now contained in section 5(2) of the Land Compensation (Scotland) Act 1961 (the 1961 Act). This provides that:

---

[4] *Compensation for Compulsory Acquisition and Planning Restrictions*, 1968, para. 18.
[5] See generally on rule (2) W. A. Leach, "Market Value Under Rule (2): A Fresh Appraisal I–VII" (1975) 231 E.G. 459, 1003, 1095, 1237, and 1547; also *Compensation for Compulsory Acquisition*, published by the Royal Institution of Chartered Surveyors in 1989.

"The value of land shall, subject as hereinafter provided, be taken to be the amount which the land if sold in the open market by a willing seller might be expected to realise."

In *Oswald v. Ayr Harbour Trust* in 1883,[6] Lord Young observed that "In the case of land compulsorily taken, the compulsion is an element of price." However, a price to be ascertained by reference to the amount which the land might be expected to realise on a sale in the open market would now seem to exclude any recognition of compulsion (see Chapter 5). To be doubly sure, section 5 (1) specifically provides that in assessing compensation: "No allowance shall be made on account of the acquisition being compulsory."[7]

The term "open market" is not defined in the Act. However, in *Inland Revenue Commissioners v. Clay* and *Inland Revenue Commissioners v. Buchanan*, an estate duty case turning on a similarly worded provision, Swinfen-Eady L.J. stated that:

"A value, ascertained by reference to the amount obtainable in an open market shows an intention to include every possible purchaser . . . the section means such amount as the land might be expected to realise if offered under conditions enabling every person desirous of purchasing to come in and make an offer."[8]

This does not necessarily imply a sale by auction or roup. "A sale takes place in open market," said Lord Johnson in *Glass v. Inland Revenue Commissioners*, "if the subject is put on the market and the best offer taken, however made."[9] What is envisaged is the price which might be amicably negotiated at arm's length between willing parties with no necessity or anxiety on either side.[10] Subject to what is said below about rules (3) and (4) the proper basis of compensation under rule (2) is that which yields the greatest price for the land. In the Scottish case *Robertson's Trustees v. Glasgow Corporation*,[11] for example, which turned on the

7—04

---

[6] (1883) 10 R. 472.

[7] In *Compensation for Compulsory Acquisition, supra*, the Royal Institution of Chartered Surveyors conclude that the time has come to pay an additional allowance in all cases of compulsory acquisition in recognition that the claimant is an unwilling seller and that, if he is an occupier, he suffers social and psychological upset for which financial equivalence makes no allowance. And see para. 13–06.

[8] [1914] 3 K.B. 466 at p. 475. In *Priestman Colliers Ltd v. Northern District Valuation Board* [1950] 2 K.B. 395 it was held that "open market" does not contemplate a purely hypothetical market to be regarded as exempt from restrictions imposed by law. Valuation of this "expectation" will be according to the methods normally employed by valuers. See W. Britton, K. Davies and T. Johnson, *Modern Methods of Valuation* (Estates Gazette Ltd 8th ed., 1989); A. Baum and G. Sams, *Statutory Valuation*, (Routledge and Kegan Paul, 2nd. ed., 1990); and W.H. Rees (ed.), *Valuation: Principles into Practice* (Estates Gazette Ltd. 4th. ed., 1993) A. Bawm and D. Mackmin, *The Income Approach to Property Valuation*, (Routledge, 3rd. ed., 1989). See, also, *Encyclopaedia of Compulsory Purchase and Compensation* (Sweet and Maxwell), para. 2–1061.

[9] 1915 S.C. 449; 1915 S.L.T. 297.

[10] *Edmonstone v. Central Regional Council*, 1985 S.L.T. (Lands Tr.) 57; *Glass, supra*.

[11] 1967 S.C 124; 1967 S.L.T. 240. See, too, *Mrs Fulton's Trustees v. Glasgow Corporation*, 1976 S.L.T. (Lands Tr.) 14; and *Carter v. Windsor and Maidenhead Royal Borough Council*, unreported, but see (1988) E.G.C.S. 84.

interpretation of the corresponding provision in section 12(2) of the Land Compensation (Scotland) Act 1963, a local authority proposed to acquire a block of tenement property owned by trustees comprising a public house, shops, a store, and a number of dwelling-houses, some of which were subject to controlled tenancies. The trustees argued that each unit in the tenement, with the exception of the controlled dwellings should be valued separately. The local authority maintained that the property should be valued as a whole. The trustees' basis of valuation produced the higher figure. The court held that the trustees' approach was the correct one:

> "where compensation is being assessed under section 12(2), then, if on a sale in the open market the land or property might be expected to realise a greater cumulo price if sold in reasonable and natural lots or sub units than if it were sold as *a unum quid*, it is that greater price that is the basis of compensation."

Rule (2) introduces a hypothetical "willing seller" into the valuation exercise.[12] In other words, any disinclination by the claimant to part with the land is not to influence the assessment of compensation; neither is it to be assumed that the claimant is compelled by circumstances to sell his land for anything he can get. A willing seller, said Pickford L.J. in *Clay*:

> "means one who is prepared to sell, provided a fair price is obtained under all the circumstances of the case. I do not think it means only a seller who is prepared to sell at any price and on any terms, and who is actually at the time wishing to sell. In other words, I do not think it means an anxious seller."[13]

And in *Robertson's Trustees* Lord Justice-Clerk Grant said "We have to assume a *hypothetical* sale by a willing seller . . . in the open market. One cannot assume that in such a sale the seller will act without due regard to his own interests."[14]

7—05   The reference in rule (2) to the amount which land might be "expected" to realise refers to "the expectations of properly qualified persons who have taken pains to inform themselves of all the particulars ascertainable about the property and its capabilities, the demand for it, and the likely buyers."[15] Market value is not, of course, a precise measure. It is an approximation. As Ungoed-Thomas J.

---

[12] One consequence of assuming a hypothetical owner would seem to be that in assessing the value of the land the actual owner may be included as a possible bidder. Although no mention is made of a "willing buyer" in rule (2) (*i.e.* one not acting under compulsion), this would seem to be implied; see the *Expert Committee on Compensation and Betterment: Final Report*, Cmd. 6386, (1942), para. 185; see also the RICS paper, *supra*.

[13] [1914] 3 K.B. 466 at p. 478. And see *Glass v. Commissioners of Inland Revenue*, 1915 S.C. 449; 1915 S.L.T. 297.

[14] 1967 S.C. 124; 1967 S.L.T. 240.

[15] *Inland Revenue Commissioners v. Clay; Inland Revenue Commissioners v. Buchanan* [1914] 3 K.B. 466, *per* Swinfen-Eady L.J. at p. 475 commenting on a similar provision in the Finance (1909–1910) Act 1910, s.25.

aptly observed: "It has been established time and again in these courts, as it was in our case, that there is range of price, in some circumstances wide, which competent valuers would recognise as the price which 'property would fetch if sold in the open market'."[16]

Restrictions

From what has been said so far, it will be clear that statutory valuation involves "something of the hypothetical and unreal."[17] The valuer is to assume a sale in the open market by a willing seller. The land which is notionally being sold is, however, to be valued subject to all its restrictions. As Lord Dunedin stated in *Corrie v. MacDermott*:

> "The value which has to be assessed is the value to the old owner who parts with his property, not the value to the new owner who takes it over. If, therefore, the old owner holds the property subject to restrictions, it is a necessary point of inquiry how far these restrictions affect the value."[18]

Thus, in *Abbey Homesteads (Developments) Ltd v. Northamptonshire County Council*[19] it was held that compensation should be assessed having regard to restrictions on use imposed by an agreement under section 52 of the Town and Country Planning Act 1971; and in *Stokes v. Cambridge Corporation*[20] the compensation for land with development potential reflected the price a purchaser would have expected to pay to secure a satisfactory access to the land. In *Odeon Associated Theatres Ltd v. Glasgow Corporation*[21] a derelict cinema was compulsorily acquired by Glasgow Corporation. The claimants, who were the landlords of the premises, claimed that in assessing compensation account should be taken of the rent of £3,500 which they received from a lease of the property. The local authority contended that the lease should be disregarded on the ground that it was in favour of a holding company. The holding company would have ensured that the claimants, as a wholly owned subsidiary company, would not have been permitted to sell the property to a third party subject to the lease. The claimants' interest in the lease was not, therefore, marketable and should be disregarded in assessing compensa-

7—06

---

[16] In *re Hayes' Will Trusts* [1971] 1 W.L.R. 758 at p. 768. See, also, *Inland Revenue Commissioners v. Clay* [1914] 3 K.B. 466, *per* Swinfen Eady L.J. at p. 475; *Church Cottage Investments Ltd v. Hillingdon London Borough Council,* [1990] 15 E.G. 51.
[17] Lord Johnston in *Glass, supra*
[18] [1914] A.C. 1056 at p. 1062.
[19] (1986) 278 E.G. 1249.
[20] (1961) 13 P. & C.R. 77.
[21] 1974 S.C. 81; 1974 S.L.T. 109.

tion. The claimants contended that for the purposes of rule (2) in the corresponding Scottish legislation, the attitude of the holding company to the claimants' interest passing to a third party had to be ignored. The statutory hypothesis of a "willing seller" and an "open market" meant that the fact that the landlords were likely to be restricted by the attitude of the holding company was irrelevant to the valuation exercise.

The Second Division of the Court of Session disagreed with the claimants. The correct approach was to estimate the value of the claimants' interest on the open market subject to the existing lease to the holding company but on the basis that the rent and the tenants' other obligations would be exigible only if the purchaser were a subsidiary of the holding company and that they would cease to be exigible if the purchaser were an outside third party. Assessment on that basis would, it seemed to Lord Fraser "give effect to the realities of the situation so far as one can give effect to them in relation to a hypothetical sale on the open market."[22] As Lord Kissen observed "if the appellants' argument is correct they would be entitled to payment of a sum as compensation which they could not have obtained if they had tried to sell the subject voluntarily in the open market."[23]

Potentialities and rule (3)

7—07 The analogy which rule (2) seeks to create with a sale by a willing seller in the open market means that not only is the land to be valued subject to any restrictions but also with the benefit of all its potentialities. "So far as rule (2) is concerned," said Lord President Clyde *in McEwing and Sons Ltd v. Renfrewshire County Council*, "the value of land is not restricted to its actual use at the time it is taken. Its potentialities must be taken into account, for these would obviously enter into the market price."[24] The extent to which they will enter into the market price will depend very largely upon what assumptions may be made about the planning status of the land (see Chapter 8) and upon the extent to which the potentialities arise from the scheme underlying the acquisition (see Chapter 9).

Under the Lands Clauses Act such potentialities could encompass any special suitability or adaptability which the land might have for a particular purpose by reason of its location, its configuration or its surroundings. This could include any special suitability or adaptability which the land might have for the purposes of

---

[22] *Ibid.*

[23] *Ibid.*

[24] 1960 S.C. 53; 1960 S.L.T. 140. See, too, *Commissioners of Inland Revenue v. Glasgow & South-Western Rail Co.* (1887) 14 R. (H.L.) 33, *per* Lord Chancellor Halsbury at p. 34; *Sri Raja v. Revenue Divisional Officer, Vizagapatam* [1939] 2 All E.R. 317, *per* Lord Romer at pp. 321–322.

the acquiring authority although such potential could be taken into account only as a possibility and not as realised.[25]

However, the ability to take into account such potentialities has been somewhat curtailed by section 5(3) of the 1961 Act, as amended by the Planning and Compensation Act 1991.[26] This provides that in assessing compensation: **7—08**

> "The special suitability or adaptability of the land for any purpose shall not be taken into account if that purpose is a purpose to which it could be applied only in pursuance of statutory powers, or for which there is no market apart from the requirements of any authority possessing compulsory purchase powers.

The effect of the 1991 Act amendment was to narrow the scope of the rule. It is directed at two situations:

— First of all, it provides that, in assessing compensation, no account is to be taken of any value due to the special suiatbility or adaptability of the land for any purpose to which it could be applied only in pursuance of statutory powers.
— Secondly, it also directs that no account is to be taken of any value arising from the special suitability or adaptability of the land for any purpose for which there is no market apart from the requirements of any authority possessing compulsory purchase powers.

These situations are considered in turn below.

The 1991 Act amendment removed a third situation in which the rule operated. As much of the interest in rule (3) in recent years focussed on the operation of this third limb, we think it deserves mention. The third limb of the rule provided that no account was to be taken of any value which the land might have because of its special suitability or adaptability for a purpose for which there was no market apart from the special needs of a particular purchaser. That part of the rule was aptly described as "the unsure progeny of a footnote in the report of the Scott Committee".[27] The Committee expressed some concern about the effect of the decision of the English Court of Appeal in *Inland Revenue Commissioners v. Clay* and *Inland Revenue Commissioners v. Buchanan*[28] which involved the valuation of land for estate duty purposes. The facts were that a house in Plymouth was worth not more than £750 as a private residence. The house, however, adjoined a nurses home, the trustees of which wanted to extend their premises. The value

---

[25] See *Gough v. The Aspatria, Silloth and District Joint Water Board* [1904] 1 K.B. 417; *In re Lucas and Chesterfield Gas and Water Board* [1909] 1 K.B. 16; *Glass v. Commissioners of Inland Revenue*, 1915 S.C. 449; *Sri Raja v. Revenue Divisional Officer, Vizagapatam* [1939] 2 All E.R. 317. See, also, *Countess Ossalinsky v. Manchester Corporation*, unreported but referred to in *Gough supra*.
[26] s.70 and Sched. 15, para. 1.
[27] J. Kekwick, "On Rule (3)", the Chartered Surveyor, July 1955, at p. 15.
[28] [1914] 3 K.B. 466.

of the house to them because of its advantageous location was at least £1,000. The Court of Appeal held that "a value to be ascertained by reference to the amount obtainable in an open market shows an intention to include every possible purchaser" including the trustees of the adjoining nurses home. The Scott Committee expressed the view that the price realised in that case was not the market value as between a willing buyer and a willing seller but was solely due to the necessities of the adjoining owner.[29] The intention of that part of rule (3) would seem to have been to eliminate any value arising from such potentiality where there was only one person in the market: "if one of the potentialities of the land is such that there is only one purchaser of the land interested in that potentiality the added amount which he would pay is to be ignored".[30]

This third situation in which the rule operated typically arose where the land acquired was the key to the development of other land. However, acquiring authorities encountered considerable difficulty because the courts and the Lands Tribunal appeared reluctant to accept that the facts disclosed in any given case constituted a "no market situation".[31] They seemed to be, as one commentator observed, "motivated by the view that the rule is a restriction placed upon the generally accepted 'fair' measure of compensation afforded by rule (2). They therefore seem to perceive their duty to be the circumnavigation of the rule whenever possible".[32]

7—09
That part of rule (3), in the limited number of cases in which it applied, departed in a significant way from the analogy which rule (2) seeks to create with a sale in the open market. Not surprisingly, there was pressure for change and in a consultative document published in 1979, the Department of the Environment indicated an intention to repeal this limb of rule (3).[33] It was eventually repealed in the 1991 Act.

The two situations in which rule (3) still applies come into operation where land has a quality which makes it specially suitable or adaptable for any purpose.[34] In *Batchelor v. Kent County Council*[35] the land comprised in the compulsory purchase order provided the most suitable access to other development land but it was not the only land across which access could be taken. Rule (3) was held not to apply. In the Court of Appeal, Mann L.J. concluded that, although a special

---

[29] Cd. 9229, (1918), footnote to para. 10.

[30] *Lambe v. Secretary of State for War* [1955] 2 Q.B. 612, *per* Parker L.J. at p. 619.

[31] See, for example, *Barstow v. Rothwell Urban District Council* [1970] R.V.R. 271; *Rathgar Property Co. Ltd v. Haringay London Borough* (1978) 248 E.G. 693; *Chapman, Lowry and Puttick v. Chichester District Council* (1984) 269 E.G. 955; *Corrie v. Central Land Board* (1954) 4 P. & C.R. 276; *Dicconson Holdings Ltd v. St. Helen's Metropolitan Borough Council* (1978) 249 E.G. 1075, 1178.

[32] T.J. Templeman, (1981) 260 E.G. 1171. In both *Dicconson Holdings* and in *Chapman, supra*, the Lands Tribunal were concerned that the application of rule (3) would deny the claimants equivalence.

[33] "Land Compensation—Minor and Miscellaneous Legislative Changes", 1979.

[34] *Batchelor v. Kent County Council* [1990] 14 E.G. 129. See, too, *Blandrent Investment Development Ltd v. British Gas Corporation* (1979) 252 E.G. 267.

[35] *Ibid.*

suitability could be found where land has a positional advantage for the purpose in hand, "most suitable does not correspond with specially suitable".

The two parts or limbs of rule (3) are now considered in turn.

(i) Land has special suitability or adaptability for any purpose to which it could be applied only in pursuance of statutory powers: This part of rule (3) would seem to be directed at eliminating the basis of value permitted by the Privy Council in *Cedar Rapids Manufacturing and Power Co. v. Lacoste.*[36] In that case the purpose for which the land was specially suited, in the absence of the actual acquisition, was as part of a water power development, a purpose which could only be achieved if appropriate statutory powers were granted. The Privy Council concluded that if the land was put up for auction, "there was a probability of a purchaser who was looking out for special advantages being content to give this enhanced value in the hope that he would get the other powers and acquire the other rights which were necessary for a realised scheme". The compensation should accordingly reflect this enhanced value.

This part of rule (3) is designed to eliminate this enhanced value when assessing compensation. For example, in *Livesey v. Central Electricity Generating Board*[37] agricultural land was acquired as the site of a power sation. The claimant based his claim on the special suitability of the land as a site for a power station. The Lands Tribunal held that as statutory powers were required to use the land as a power station, rule (3) applied to eliminate that potentiality.

However, the decision of the House of Lords in *Hertfordshire County Council v. Ozanne*[38] makes it clear that the use of the word "only" means that this part of the rule only applies where statutory powers are a legal requirement for the purpose in question. Lord Mackay of Clashfern giving judgment for the House said "the statutory powers in question must be powers enabling a person entitled to use the land to apply it to the purpose in question and since the purpose in question is one to which the land could be applied *only* in pursuance of the statutory powers the statutory powers must be necessary to enable such person to use the land for that purpose. I do not see how statutory powers not related to the use of the land acquired could form a basis for the application of this part of the rule".

In that case, the acquiring authority argued that the land in question had an **7—10** enhanced value over the agricultural value only in respect of its special suitability or adaptability for the purpose of providing a road realignment which would enable development to proceed. To use the land for the realignment, it was necessary to stop up part of the existing road and as the road was a public road, such stopping-up required the exercise of statutory powers. The House concluded that statutory powers conferred on the Secretary of State to order the stopping-up of a highway on land which was not part of the land being acquired could not form

---

[36] [1914] A.C. 569.
[37] (1965) E.G.D. 205.
[38] [1991] 13 E.G. 157.

the basis of the application of this part of the rule to the land acquired. If the argument of the acquiring authority was to prevail, it would bring within the compass of the rule a purpose to which a piece of land could be put only after obtaining some particular statutory consent such as a planning permission. To exclude any value attached to such a consent would clearly be absurd.

It should be noted, as the Uthwatt Committee pointed out, that, if the purpose is one which may also be achieved in the absence of statutory powers, its effect on value may properly be taken into account.

(ii) Land has special suitability or adaptability for a purpose for which there is no market apart from the requirements of any authority possessing compulsory purchase powers:
No account shall be taken of the special suitability or adaptability of the land for a purpose for which there is no market apart from the requirements of any authority possessing compulsory purchase powers. This part of rule (3) was added during the passage through Parliament of the Acquisition of Land (Assessment of Compensation) Bill. Its object, notes the Royal Institution of Chartered Surveyors (RICS)[39] was to ensure that when a public authority was purchasing land under compulsory powers the value should be determined by reference to the private demand for the land without regard to the fact that a public body was in the market.

However, as the Uthwatt Committee pointed out, this part of the rule fails to achieve its object:

> "it is directed to excluding special adaptability 'for a purpose for which there is no market' apart from the requirements of public authorities, rather than to excluding enhancement of value by reason of any demand by public authorities, whether or not competitive."[40]

7—11 The Committee expressed the view that any increased value due to public demand for land should be excluded in assessing the compensation payable on acquisition and went on to recommend that this part of rule (3) should be recast so as to achieve its objective. The RICS commented that the Uthwatt proposals "are too wide at a time when public authorities are increasingly competing for land which is equally suitable for private or public purposes." They concluded that there was no longer justification for excluding in all cases the consideration of public demand in assessing compensation payable for land.[41] Additional value created by a public authority was in their view sufficiently excluded by the reten-

---

[39] See *Compensation for Compulsory Acquisition*, Royal Institution of Chartered Surveyors, 1989, para. 2. 54.

[40] *Expert Committee on Compensation and Betterment: Final Report*, Cmnd. 6386 (HMSO 1942) para. 187.

[41] *Compensation for Compulsory Acquisition, supra*, para. 2. 55. See, too, M. Horton and J. Trustram Eve, in *The Planning Balance in the 1990s*, Journal of Planning & Environment Law Occasional Papers No. 18 (Sweet & Maxwell), 1991.

tion of the other limb of rule (3) (see above) and by the other statutory provisions (see Chapter 9). However, this part of the rule seems to have given rise to little difficulty in practice and there is no indication at the present time that the government are intent on its repeal.

Rule (4)

Section 5(4) of the 1961 Act provides that: 7—12

"Where the value of the land is increased by reason of the use thereof or of any premises thereon in a manner which could be restrained by any court, or is contrary to law, or is detrimental to the health of the occupants of the premises or to the public health, the amount of that increase shall not be taken into account."

Rule (4) is concerned with cases where a proportion of the market value results from what may loosely be termed an "unlawful" use. The rule provides that the value attributable to that use is to be disregarded in assessing compensation.

In *Hughes v. Doncaster Metropolitan Borough Council*[42] the House of Lords held that rule (4) applies to the assessment of compensation generally, including any element referrable to disturbance.

Just what activities are covered by rule (4) is a little uncertain, although this is not a matter which seems to have given rise to much difficulty in practice. The rule is derived from the report of the Scott Committee who recommended that "no enhancement of market value should be taken into account which arises from the use of the premises in question in a manner contrary to sanitary laws and regulations."[43] What the Committee appeared to have in mind was any value resulting from the use of premises which were overcrowded, unfit or which constituted a statutory nuisance. This sort of situation was partly covered by section 585 of the Housing Act 1985 which broadly provided that in assessing compensation for the compulsory purchase of residential property which was unfit for human habitation the assumption was that the property had no value and compensation was based on the value of the land as a cleared site. Section 585 of the 1985 Act was subsequently repealed by section 165 and Schedule 9, Part IV, paragraph 76 of the Local Government and Housing Act 1989 so that this area of overlap has now been removed. Rule (4) remains to eliminate any value due to the use of premises in a manner which is detrimental to the health of the occupants. It should be noted that, where the value of land is increased by a use which is detrimental to the health of the occupants of the premises or to the public

---

[42] [1991] 05 E.G. 133.
[43] Cd. 9229 (1918) para. 11.

health, that use does not have to be capable of restraint at law to bring rule (4) into operation.

Whether a particular use of land is one which could be restrained by a court, for example, as a nuisance, is a question to which it will not always be possible to give a precise answer. Where the matter is in doubt, it would seem, as Corfield and Carnwath suggest,[44] that the likelihood of restraint should be taken into account.

7—13   A use of land which is being carried on without planning permission but which is immune from enforcement action is not to be treated as "contrary to law" for the purposes of rule (4).[45] Such a use would attract value on a sale in the open market and to deprive the owner of such value on a compulsory purchase of the land would contravene the principle that a statute should not be held to take away private rights of property without compensation unless the intention to do so is expressed in clear and unambiguous terms.

---

[44] Sir Frederick Corfield and R.J.A. Carnwath, *Compulsory Acquisition and Compensation* (Butterworths, 1978), p. 180.

[45] *Hughes v. Doncaster Metropolitan Borough Council* [1991] 05 E.G. 133 distinguishing *LTSS Print and Supply Services Ltd v. Hackney London Borough Council* [1976] Q.B. 663. And see now s.191(2) of the 1990 Act, added by s.10 of the Planning and Compensation Act 1991 which provides that, for the purposes of that Act, if no enforcement action may be taken in respect of a use because the time for taking action has expired, the use is lawful.

Chapter 8

Development Potential

Introduction

In Chapter 7 it was pointed out that the value of land "sold in the open market   **8—01**
by a willing seller"[1] is not to be measured solely by reference to the use to which
it is being put at the time it is compulsorily acquired; account may also to be
taken of the potential which it may have for some other more profitable use.[2] As
Lord Romer observed in *Sri Raja v. Revenue Divisional Officer, Vizagapatam*:

> "No authority, indeed, is required for this proposition. It is a self-evident one. No
> one can suppose, in the case of land which is certain, or even likely, to be used in
> the immediate or reasonably near future for building purposes, but which at the valu-
> ation date is waste land, or is being used for agricultural purposes, that the owner,
> however willing a vendor, will be content to sell the land for its value as waste or
> agricultural land, as the case may be. It is plain that in ascertaining its value the
> possibility of its being used for building purposes would have to be taken into
> account."[3]

However, to realise the development potential of land in the real world, a landowner would have to abandon the existing use and incur any consequential disturbance; it is implicit in the realisation of such potential that disturbance may

---

[1] Land Compensation Act 1961, s.5(2).
[2] *McEwing v. County Council for the Council of Renfrew*, 1960 S.C. 53; 1960 S.L.T. 140, *per* Lord
President Clyde; see, also, *Commissioners of Inland Revenue v. Glasgow and South Western Rail Co.*
(1887) 14 R. (H.L.) 33, *per* Lord Chancellor Halsbury. But note the operation of rule (3) (see
Chap. 7).
[3] [1939] 2 All E.R. 317.

occur. If, therefore, land is valued on the basis of its potentiality for some other more profitable use, there should not be included in that value an element for disturbance, otherwise the claimant will receive more than his actual loss.[4] In such circumstances, as Cripps states: "the land has two values; (i) existing use value plus disturbance; (ii) potential value. The claimant is entitled to whichever is the higher."[5]

Before the introduction of planning control the assessment of the development potential of land was simply a valuation problem. Now, however, this potential depends to a very considerable extent upon the obtaining of planning permission. Planning permission is required for the development of land.[6] In some situations a purchaser may, of course, be willing to speculate on the prospect of obtaining such permission but where this occurs, any value attributable to the development potential of the land is likely to be subject to a discount because of uncertainty.

8—02 Planning permission alone, though, is not enough to create development value. As Denning M.R. observed in *Camrose (Viscount) v. Basingstoke Corporation* "it is not planning permission by itself which increases value. It is planning permission coupled with demand."[7] Thus, in *Bromilow v. Greater Manchester Council*[8] the Lands Tribunal held that a claimant, who was entitled to assume planning permission for the development of land for offices, could not obtain development value as there would be no demand for the land for that development. The site was in an area in which industrial use predominated; there was a large engineering works 50 yards away and an unattractive and obnoxious smelling bone factory 100 yards away. Because of this the tribunal concluded that there would be no demand for the land for development for offices.

On a sale in the open market, either the vendor or purchaser may test the development potential of land by submitting one or more planning applications. Where land is being acquired by a public authority, however, such an approach is likely to prove unhelpful because any application will probably be refused on the ground that the land is required for public purposes. If a claimant is to be placed in as good a position as on a sale in the open market, some alternative mechanism is required for establishing the planning position of land which is being compulsorily acquired. Such a mechanism is provided in sections 14 to 16 and Part III of the 1961 Act.

Section 14(1) provides that for the purpose of assessing compensation such one or more of the assumptions[9] as to planning permission mentioned in sections 15

---

[4] *Horn v. Sunderland Corporation* [1941] 2 K.B. 26; and see *D. M. Hoey Ltd v. Glasgow Corporation*, 1972 S.C. 200. Compensation for disturbance is discussed in Chap. 11.

[5] H. Parrish, *Cripps on Compulsory Acquisition of Land* (Stevens and Sons Ltd, London, 11th ed.), para. 4–217.

[6] Town and Country Planning Act 1990, s.57(1).

[7] [1966] 1 W.L.R. 1100.

[8] (1975) 29 P. & C.R. 517.

[9] Whether the assumptions are to be treated as cumulative or alternative for the purposes of calculating development value will depend on the physical circumstances in any particular case.

and 16 as are applicable to the land being acquired,[10] or any part of it, shall be made in ascertaining its value. However, regard is to be had in making the assumption in section 16 to any certificate issued under Part III of the Act (see paras. 8–17 to 8–25 below).[11]

There are four assumptions (see below). Their object, as Leach states, "is that, **8—03** once it has been established that any one or more of them may be made, there should be certainty in respect of permission for the relevant development or developments so that valuations can be made as if on facts and not on mere possibilities."[12] The assumptions, therefore, go some way towards relieving valuers and tribunals of the task of having to determine the planning position.

Section 14 (2) goes on to provide that any planning permission which is to be assumed in accordance with the provisions of those sections is in addition to any planning permission which may be in force at the date of the notice to treat. This includes permissions granted by development order.[13] It is immaterial whether the permission in question, which relates to the land in question taken by itself or in respect of an area including that land, is conditional or unconditional or is full or in outline.[14] Such planning permissions will, however, only assist a claimant if they are valuable.[15] A personal or time limited permission, for example, may be taken into account but is unlikely to add much value.[16]

The four assumptions in sections 14 and 16 are divided between those which are derived from the development plan (section 16) and those which are not (section 15). The assumptions are now considered in turn under these two headings.

Assumptions derived from the development plan

Section 16 of the 1961 Act provides that for the purposes of assessing compensa- **8—04** tion certain assumptions may be made about the grant of planning permission for

---

[10] The assumptions apply only to the land being acquired; the development potential of any retained land may be tested by the submission of one or more planning applications in the normal way.

[11] 1961 Act, s.14(3A) added by the Planning and Compensation Act 1991, s.70 and Sched. 15, para. 15.

[12] W. A. Leach, "Compulsory Purchase Valuation: The Six Assumptions of Planning Permission" [1973] J.P.L. 454 and 527.

[13] See Art. 3 and Sched. 2 to the Town and Country Planning (General Development) Order 1988.

[14] An outline planning permission means a planning permission for the carrying out of building or other operations which is granted subject to a condition requiring subsequent approval to be obtained from the planning authority for one or more reserved matters.

[15] See, for example, *J. Davy Ltd v. London Borough of Hammersmith* (1975) 30 P. & C.R. 469; *Bromilow v. Greater Manchester Council* (1975) 31 P. & C.R. 398; and *David Bell v. Glasgow Corporation*, decision of an Official Arbiter Ref. No. 2/1969.

[16] But see *McArdle v. Glasgow Corporation*, 1972 S.C. 41. See, too, *Wilson v. West Sussex County Council* [1963] 2 Q.B. 764; *Waverley District Council v. Secretary of State for the Environment* [1982] J.P.L. 105; and *Williamson and Stevens (Executors of Walter Williamson deceased) v. Cambridgeshire County Council*

development which accords with the provisions of the development plan in the form in which that plan is in force at the date of the notice to treat.[17] The development plan is prepared by the appropriate local planning authority(ies) and sets out policies and proposals for the development and use of land in the plan area. There are three kinds of development plan. Outside the metropolitan areas the development plan comprises two tiers. First of all, there is the structure plan. This is prepared by the county planning authority and is a written statement setting out strategic policies and proposals for the area. The second tier comprises one or more local plans. The county and the district planning authorities prepare local plans in accordance with a local plan scheme administered by the county. A local plan comprises a map and written statement setting out detailed proposals for the development and use of land in the plan area. Of the two tiers, the local plans are likely to be more specific about the identification of land for development and will, consequently, have a more pronounced effect on value.

In Greater London and the metropolitan counties there is a one tier development plan called a 'unitary' development plan. This is prepared by the appropriate London borough or metropolitan district council. It comprises a statement of their general policies for the area and of their proposals for the development and other use of land in their area.

There are four assumptions and it will be necessary to consider which, if any, are applicable in the circumstances of any particular case.

(1) If the land acquired or any part of it consists of or forms part of a site allocated in the current[18] development plan for a particular purpose, it is to be assumed that planning permission would be granted for the development of the land for that purpose (section 16(1)).[19] For example, the land may be defined in the development plan as the site for a school, a hospital or a road. In view of the nature of these purposes, this assumption is not often of much value to a claimant. If the land is shown in the development plan as subject to comprehensive development then, regardless of whether it is allocated for a particular purpose, the appropriate assumption is that in section 16(4) (see below).

8—05 (2) If the land acquired or any part of it consists of or forms part of an area allocated in the current development plan primarily for a specified use, for example, residential, industrial or commercial, it is to be assumed that planning permission would be granted for the development of all or part of the land, as the case may be, for that use (section 16(2)). Such development must, however, be development for which planning permission might reasonably have been expected to be granted assuming no part of the land was to be acquired for public purposes

---

[1977] J.P.L. 529. *Cf East Suffolk County Council v. Secretary of State for the Environment* (1972) 70 L.G.R. 595.

[17] Land Compensation Act 1961, s. 39(1).

[18] See 1961 Act, s.39(1) and the Town and County Planning Act 1990, Sched. 2, Part III, para. 5. And see *City of Aberdeen District Council v. Skean Dhu plc*, 1991 S.L.T. (Lands Tr.) 22.

[19] The wording suggests that the assumption applies to the whole of the land acquired even if only part is so allocated.

(section 16 (2)(b) and (7)).[20] If the land is shown in the development plan as subject to comprehensive development then, regardless of whether it is allocated primarily for a specified use, the appropriate assumption is that in section 16(4) (see below).

The phrase "development for which planning permission might reasonably have been expected to be granted" has given rise to some difficulty in practice, although some of the difficulty may be alleviated by the new section 54A of the Town and Country Planning Act 1990 which requires planning decisions to be made in accordance with the development plan unless material considerations indicate otherwise.[21] In *Menzies Motors Ltd v. Stirling District Council*[22] Lord Cameron observed that this phrase is "not one of hypothetical assumption but is directed to the factual probabilities of a particular situation in relation to a particular site. What is 'reasonable' in a particular case one would necessarily think was a question primarily of fact and circumstance." In assessing whether permission might reasonably have been expected to be granted, regard is to be had to any contrary opinion expressed in any certificate issued under Part III of the 1961 Act.[23]

The operation of the phrase may be illustrated by the decision in *Margate Corporation v. Devotwill Investments Ltd.*[24] The claimants owned a piece of land fronting on to a main road which was allocated in the development plan for residential use. A planning application for residential development was refused because part of the land was required for a bypass scheme and development was considered to be premature until the details were finalised. The claimants subsequently served a purchase notice which was accepted. The claimants lodged a claim for compensation based on an assumed planning permission for immediate residential development comprising 20 houses with access to the main road. The corporation argued for compensation based on an assumed planning permission for immediate residential development for nine houses with permission for a further 11 houses deferred pending some resolution of the problem of traffic congestion on the main road. The Lands Tribunal reached their decision on the basis that no land of the claimants would be taken for the bypass so that it could not have been built on the line proposed. They concluded, however, that since there would still have been an urgent need for traffic relief, it had to be assumed that a bypass would have been constructed on some other line thus enabling the immediate development of the land in question for residential purposes. The House of Lords held that the tribunal had erred as a matter of law in assuming that there would inevitably be a bypass on some other line. The possibility of the construction of a bypass elsewhere was a matter which could not rest on an assumption but on

8—06

---

[20] See, for example, *Richardson Developments Ltd v. Stoke Corporation* (1971) 22 P. & C.R. 958.
[21] Added by s.26 of the Planning and Compensation Act 1991.
[22] 1977 S.C. 33.
[23] 1961 Act, s.14(3A) added by the Planning Compensation Act 1991, s.70 of Sched. 15, para. 15.
[24] [1970] 3 All E.R. 864 H.L. See, too, *City of Aberdeen District Council v. Skean Dhu plc*, 1991 S.L.T. (Lands Tr.) 22.

an examination of all the relevant factors. The case was remitted to the Lands Tribunal to reconsider what planning permission might reasonably have been expected to be granted in all the circumstances.

8—07   A further illustration of the difficulties to which this phrase has given rise is provided by the decision of the Lands Tribunal for Scotland in *James Miller and Partners Ltd v. Lothian Regional Council*.[25] The case concerned a small plot of land allocated in the development plan, along with other surrounding land, for residential purposes. The plot was acquired by the regional council as sewerage authority for the provision of a pumping station to service the claimant's housing scheme on the surrounding land. The regional council argued, on a voluntary reference to the Lands Tribunal, that a pumping station was required for residential development and that without it planning permission could not reasonably have been expected to be granted and compensation should be assessed accordingly. The Lands Tribunal, however, concluded that further inquiry was needed to establish whether planning permission for housing would be allowed over all or any part of the land assuming no part of it was to be acquired for a pumping station. After further inquiry the conclusion was that the pumping station would have been sited elsewhere and that permission for residential development would have been likely to be granted but with a restricted access and with part of the land being set aside for the planting of a tree belt.[26]

In determining whether planning permission might reasonably have been expected to be granted, it is to be assumed in assessing compensation, where land is being acquired for or in connection with the construction[27] of a highway[28], that if the land were not to be so used no highway would be constructed to meet the need or substantially the same need for which it is being acquired.[29] Although this sounds complicated, the assumption is intended to resolve a difficult practical problem.

Where land is being acquired by a highway authority, it will be necessary to disregard, in assessing development potential, any value attributable to the road improvement scheme for which the land is being acquired. The need for the road improvement scheme will, however, still exist and in order to establish the development potential of the land the practice has been to consider in all the circumstances what, if any, alternative scheme the authority would have been most likely to pursue if they had not acquired the subject land. Such speculation is unsatisfactory and it is now provided that in assessing such potential it is to be

---

[25] 1981 S.L.T. (Lands Tr.) 3.

[26] 1984 S.L.T. (Lands Tr.) 2.

[27] References to the construction of a highway include its alteration or improvement (s.14(8) of the 1961 Act, added by s.64 of the Planning and compensation Act 1991).

[28] For the definition of "highway" see the Highways Act 1980, s.328(1).

[29] The same assumption is to be made where compensation is being assessed with regard to land which is being considered by a highway authority for use for or in connection with the construction of a highway. This might arise following the service of a purchase notice or a blight notice under Part VI of the Town and Country Planning Act 1990.

assumed that no alternative scheme would be undertaken to meet the same, or substantially the same, need.[30]

Although the planning assumption in section 16(2) of the 1961 Act is designed to place a claimant as nearly as possible in the position in which he would have found himself on a sale in the open market, it in fact places a claimant in a position of slight advantage. As the Lands Tribunal for Scotland observed in *James Miller and Partners Ltd*; "a situation in which planning permission for housing might reasonably have been expected (without having been obtained) might still cause a valuer to make some discount from value to reflect the possibility of a refusal. However, section 24(2) [the equivalent Scottish provision] also directs 'it shall be assumed that planning permission would be granted' in these circumstances—so the assumption becomes absolute affecting value."

It is, of course, conceivable that inquiry may show that the development is not **8—08** one for which planning permission might reasonably have been expected to be granted. As Leach comments "it is well known that where an area is allocated to a use in a development plan permission for development for that use would not necessarily be granted for every plot of land within that area."[31] Thus, in *Provincial Properties (London) Ltd v. Caterham and Warlingham Urban District Council*[32] claimants owned an estate consisting of a house together with grounds of over six acres along the top of a ridge. The estate was allocated for residential development in the development plan. Whilst planning permission was granted for residential development on some of the land, permission was repeatedly refused both by the local planning authority and by the Minister on appeal for the development of the land at the top of the ridge because of the harmful effect which such development would have on the visual amenity of the surrounding area. A purchase notice was subsequently served and confirmed. The claimants argued that compensation should be assessed on the basis that planning permission could be assumed, in accordance with the provisions of the development plan, for residential purposes. The Court of Appeal concluded that on the evidence planning permission could not reasonably have been expected to be granted so that the condition upon which the assumption rested had not been fulfilled. Similarly, in *O'Donnell v. Edinburgh District Council*[33] the Lands Tribunal for Scotland concluded on the evidence that, with changes in planning policy, planning permission for industrial use (the allocation in the current development plan) would be unlikely to be granted so that the assumption in section 24(2) of the Land Compensation (Scotland) Act 1963 Act could not be made.

The likelihood or otherwise of planning permission being sought and implemented would seem to be irrelevant for the purposes of making the assumption

---

[30] Section 14(5)–(7) of the 1961 Act, added by s.64 of the Planning and Compensation Act 1991.

[31] W. A. Leach, "Compulsory Purchase Valuation: The Six Assumptions of Planning Permission" [1973] J.P.L. 454 and 527.

[32] [1972] 1 Q.B. 453.

[33] 1980 S.L.T. (Lands Tr.) 13. See, too, *City of Aberdeen District Council v. Skean Dhu plc*, 1991 S.L.T. (Lands Tr.) 22.

contained in section 16(2).[34] The subsection provides that if the preconditions are satisfied the assumption is to be made. However, the assumed planning permission will not, of itself, increase the value of the land[35] and the likelihood of demand for the land with that permission will clearly be relevant to the assessment of value.

8—09   (3) If the land acquired or any part of it consists of, or forms part of, an area allocated in the current development plan primarily for a range of two or more specified uses, for example, residential and commercial, or commercial and industrial, it is to be assumed that planning permission would be granted for the development of all or part of the land, as the case may be, for any one of the range of uses (section 16(3)). As with the preceeding subsection, such development must, however, be development for which planning permission might reasonably have been expected to be granted assuming no part of the land was to be acquired for public purposes (section 16(3)(*b*) and (7)). The comments made regarding the corresponding provision in section 16(2) apply equally to this subsection. If the land is shown in the development plan as subject to comprehensive development then the appropriate assumption is that in section 16(4) (see below).

(4) If the land acquired or any part of it is allocated in the current development plan for comprehensive development,[36] it is to be assumed that planning permission would be granted for the development of all or any part of the land, as the case may be, for any one of the planned range of uses shown in the development plan for the area, whether or not the use is indicated in the plan for the land acquired (section 16(4) and (5)).[37] Such development must, however, be development for which planning permission might, in the circumstances mentioned below, reasonably have been expected to be granted assuming no part of the land was to be acquired for public purposes (section 16(4) and (7)). The comments made earlier regarding the corresponding provision in section 16(2) apply equally to this subsection.

The circumstances referred to above are those that would have existed if: (i) the area in question had not been allocated in the development plan as one for comprehensive development and no particulars or proposals relating to the area had been comprised in the plan (section 16(5)(*a*)); and (ii) in a case where, at the date of the service of the notice to treat, land in that area has already been

---

[34] *Sutton v. Secretary of State for the Environment* [1984] J.P.L. 647.

[35] *Bromilow v. Greater Manchester Council* (1975) 31 P. & C.R. 398; *J. Davy Ltd v. London Borough of Hammersmith* (1975) 30 P. & C.R. 469; and *David Bell v. Glasgow Corporation*, decision of an Official Arbiter Ref. No. 2/1969.

[36] Any reference in the 1961 Act to an area allocated for comprehensive development is to be construed as a reference to a comprehensive development area or an action area for which a local plan or a unitary development plan is in force (Town and Country Planning Act 1971, Sched. 23, Part I, as amended by the Local Government Act 1985, Sched. 1). And see now the Town and Country Planning Act 1990, s.36(4).

[37] See *McArdle v. Glasgow Corporation*, 1972 S.C. 41; *Menzies Motors Ltd v. Stirling District Council*, 1977 S.C. 33. For the definition of "the planned range of uses" see the 1961 Act, s.16 (5).

developed or redeveloped in accordance with the plan, no land in that area had been so developed on or before that date (section 16(5)(*b*)).

In *Menzies Motors v. Stirling District Council*[38] the claimants attempted to distin-   **8—10**
guish the reference to a reasonable expectation of a grant of planning permission in section 24(4) of the Land Compensation (Scotland) Act 1963 from the corresponding provisions in section 24(2) and (3). The absence of the conjunction "and" immediately preceding the provision in section 24(4), it was argued, meant that it was unnecessary to establish that planning permission might reasonably have been expected; it could be assumed. The Second Division rejected this argument. The absence of the conjunction has no significance; "expectation" is a prerequisite in the circumstances specified.

Section 16(6) goes on to provide that in respect of any of the assumptions as to planning permission which may be derived from the development plan (see section 16(2) to (4) above), it is also to be assumed that the permission would be subject to such conditions, if any, as might reasonably have been expected to be imposed in the circumstances mentioned in the relevant subsection; furthermore, if the development plan indicates that any such planning permission would be granted only at a future time then it is to be assumed that the grant of planning permission would be postponed to that time.

Assumptions not derived from the development plan

In assessing compensation for the compulsory acquisition of land there are three   **8—11**
assumptions that may be made as to the grant of planning permission which are not derived directly from the development plan (section 15). These are:

(i) that planning permission would be granted for the development of the land in accordance with the proposals of the acquiring authority;

(ii) that planning permission would be granted for development of any class specified in para. 1 or 2 of schedule 3 of the Town and Country Planning Act 1990; and

(iii) that planning permission would be granted for the development or classes of development stated in a certificate of appropriate alternative development.

These assumptions are considered in turn.

---

[38] 1977 S.C. 33. See, too, *Camrose (Viscount) v. Basingstoke Corporation* [1966] 1 W.L.R. 1100.

1. DEVELOPMENT IN ACCORDANCE WITH PROPOSALS OF THE ACQUIRING AUTHORITY

8—12   Section 15(1) of the 1961 Act provides that where land is being taken to implement development proposals of the acquiring authority on all or part of the land and planning permission for that development is not in force at the date of the service of the notice to treat,[39] it is to be assumed that planning permission would be granted such as would permit the development of the land, or part as the case may be, in accordance with the proposals of the acquiring authority. Unlike the assumptions as to planning permission in section 16(2) to (4) where it is necessary to show that the development is one for which planning permission might reasonably have been expected to be granted, section 15(1) simply provides that planning permission is to be assumed for development in accordance with the proposals of the acquiring authority.

At first sight it might appear that this assumption entitles a claimant to participate in the social worth of the scheme; compensation would seem to be based on value to the purchaser. However, such a proposition was disposed of in *Myers* v. *Milton Keynes Development Corporation*.[40]

The claimant in that case owned a 323 acre estate in an area designated as a new town. At the date of valuation, the new town master plan designated the estate for residential development 10 years hence. The Lands Tribunal concluded that the operation of the assumption conflicted with the so-called *Pointe Gourde* principle which states that "compensation for the compulsory acquisition of land cannot include an increase in value which is entirely due to the scheme underlying the acquisition."[41] The Court of Appeal disagreed. Denning M.R. explained the relationship between these two provisions in this way:

> "In valuing the estate, you are to disregard the effect of the scheme, but you are to assume the availability of planning permission. This is best explained by taking an imaginary instance. A scheme is proposed for building a motorway across Dartmoor with a service station every five miles. Suppose that land is taken on which a service station is to be built as soon as possible. In assessing compensation, you are to disregard any increase due to the proposed motorway, or service stations . . . you are to assume that he would have been granted planning permission for a service station . . . And you are to value that land with that permission in the setting in which it would have been if there had been no scheme. If it would have been a good site for a service station, there would be a great increase in value. If it would have been in an inaccessible spot on the wild moor, there would be little, if any, increase in value, because there would be no demand for it."

---

[39] No account, however, is to be taken of any planning permission which does not run with the land (1961 Act, s.15(2)).

[40] [1974] 1 W.L.R. 696. And see W.A. Leach, "The Milton Keynes Case" (1974) 230 E.G. 281.

[41] *Pointe Gourde Quarrying and Transport Co.* v. *Sub-Intendent of Crown Lands* [1947] A.C. 565.

A further illustration is provided by the decision of the official arbiter in *W.M.* **8—13**
Leggat v. East Kilbride Development Corporation.[42] The development corporation
had compulsorily acquired 130 acres of farmland for industrial development in
accordance with the new town master plan. The claimant was accordingly entitled
to assume planning permission for the industrial development of land. However,
it was necessary to consider whether in the absence of the new town there would
have been any demand for industrial development. On the facts of the case, the
arbiter concluded that there would have been no such demand and compensation
was assessed on the existing use value of the land for agriculture.

It is apparent, said Lord Denning in *Myers*,

> "that the valuation has to be done in an imaginary state of affairs in which there is
> no scheme. The valuer must cast aside his knowledge of what has in fact happened
> in the past eight years due to the scheme. He must ignore the development which
> will in all probability take place in the future ten years owing to the scheme. Instead,
> he must let his imagination take flight to the clouds. He must conjure up a land of
> make-believe, where there has not been, nor will be, a brave new town: but where
> there is to be supposed the old order of things continuing."

The effect of the assumption in section 15(1) is that the valuer may, as one commentator observed,[43] find himself assessing the value of a greenfield site with a
positive planning permission to be assumed but with an inadequate system of
roads and services and little or no infrastructure. In such circumstances, he will
need to quantify the cost of providing these and compare the result with the
dead-ripe value of the land. This may or may not produce a positive development
value.

2. Schedule 3 development

Section 15(3)[44] of the 1961 Act provides that planning permission is to be assumed **8—14**
in respect of the land acquired or any part of it:

(i) for any development of a class specified in para. 1 of Schedule 3 to the
Town and Country Planning Act 1990; and
(ii) for any development of a class specified in para. 2 of the said Schedule 3.

To understand this assumption it is necessary to go back to the Town and Country
Planning Act 1947. Under the 1947 Act a development charge was payable where

---

[42] Ref. No. 2/1961. See, too, *City of Aberdeen District Council v. Skean Dhu plc*, 1991 S.L.T. (Lands
Tr.) 22.
[43] M. Clark, Valuation Aspects of Land Taken Under a Scheme—1" in *Compensation for Compulsory
Purchase*, Journal of Planning and Environment Law Occasional Paper (Sweet & Maxwell, 1975).
[44] As substituted by s.31(4) and Sched. 6, para. 1 to the Planning and Compensation Act 1991.

a grant of planning permission for new development unlocked development value. However, it was considered unreasonable that the development charge should apply to certain categories of development closely related to the existing use of the land. To avoid the development charge, these categories of development were classified in the Third Schedule to the 1947 Act as "Development Not Constituting New Development". Their value remained with the landowner and was, accordingly, taken into account in assessing compensation for compulsory purchase.

Perhaps more importantly, a failure to realise the value of certain of these categories of development as a result of a refusal of planning permission or the imposition of onerous conditions rendered the landowner eligible for compensation from the local planning authority. This arrangement continued with occasional modification until 1991. Because of the effect which the threat of a compensation claim might have on planning decisions for such development and because of the potential for abuse, the entitlement to compensation following an adverse decision was removed by section 31(2) of the Planning and Compensation Act 1991. At the same time, the categories of "Development Not Constituting New Development" were reduced to two.[45] These are set out in paras. 1 and 2 of Schedule 3 to the Town and Country Planning Act 1990. The value of the development described in these paragraphs is still treated as belonging to the landowner and it is to be assumed in assessing compensation for compulsory acquisition that planning permission would be granted for such development.[46]

8—15   The classes of development set out in paras. 1 and 2 of Schedule 3 are as follows:

1. The carrying out:
   (a) of rebuilding as often as occasion may require, including making good war damage, of any building which was in existence on 7 July, 1948, or which was in existence before that date but was destroyed or demolished after January 7, 1937;
   (b) of rebuilding as often as occasion may require of any building which was erected after July 1, 1948 and which was in existence at the date by reference to which the Schedule falls to be applied (referred to as "the material date");[47]
   (c) for the maintenance, improvement or other alteration of any building, of works which affect only the interior of the building, or do not materially affect the external appearance of the building, and are works for making good war damage.
2. The use as two or more separate dwellinghouses of any building which at a material date was used as a single dwellinghouse.

---

[45] Planning and Compensation Act 1991, Sched. 6, para. 40.
[46] 1961 Act, s.15(3).
[47] Town and Country Planning Act 1990, Sched. 3, para. 12.

There are two provisos to para. 1. First of all, the cubic content[48] of the original building[49] must not be exceeded by more than one-tenth or 1750 cubic feet (whichever is the greater) in the case of a dwelling-house and in any other case by more than one-tenth. Secondly, the permission which may be assumed is subjected to the limitations on increase in gross floor space laid down in Schedule 10 to the 1990 Act.

Given the relatively minor nature of these categories of development, the **8—16** assumption in section 15(3) of the 1961 Act is unlikely to give much assistance to a claimant.

3. DEVELOPMENT REFERRED TO IN A CERTIFICATE OF APPROPRIATE ALTERNATIVE DEVELOPMENT[50]

Section 15(5) of the 1961 Act provides that where a certifcate of appropriate **8—17** alternative development (C.A.A.D.) is issued under Part III of the Act, planning permission is to be assumed[51] for the development or classes of development which, according to the certificate, would have been granted permission if the land was not being acquired for public purposes. If the certificate indicates that such permission would have been subject to specified conditions or would have been granted only at some specified future time, those constraints are also to be assumed.[52]

The certificate procedure may assist a claimant in certain cases where the statutory assumptions, particularly those arising from the development plan, are of little or no value. For example, the development plan may be out of date and simply show the land in question as "white land" where the existing uses are expected to remain undisturbed, notwithstanding that development has recently been permitted nearby.

Section 14(3) of the 1961 Act makes it clear that the statutory assumptions as to planning permission are not necessarily exhaustive. In attempting to establish that land has development value a claimant may base his claim upon the prospect that some other planning permission would be likely to have been granted but for the compulsory acquisition of the land.[53] However, such a claim for what is generally referred to as "hope value" will be subject to some discount for uncer-

---

[48] Measured externally (1990 Act, Sched. 3, para. 10).

[49] As defined in the 1990 Act, Sched. 3, para. 13.

[50] See generally in connection with such certificates, W.A. Leach, "Compensation on Compulsory Purchase: Section 17 Certificates" [1985] J.P.L. 291.

[51] For all or part of the land as the case may be.

[52] See, for example, the DoE appeal decision noted at [1971] J.P.L. 48.

[53] It should be noted, however, that s.14(3A) requires account to be taken of any contrary opinion expressed in a C.A.A.D. It would seem, therefore, that a claimant should not lightly embark on the certificate procedure; an adverse decision may well prejudice any subsequent claim for "hope value" under s.14(3).

tainty. This is, inevitably, a speculative area which will involve valuers and the Lands Tribunal in arguments about planning policies and proposals. Section 17 of the 1961 Act gives the claimant an opportunity, by way of an application for a C.A.A.D., to dispose of this uncertainty. The intention is that arguments about the hypothetical planning position of the land should be settled before an appropriate forum and in advance of the negotiations over compensation. If a "positive" certificate of appropriate alternative development (see below) is granted (sometimes referred to as a "valuable" certificate), planning permission is to be assumed for valuation purposes for the development or classes of development referred to in the certificate (section 15(5)). The object of the procedure, as Lord McDonald observed in *Grampian Regional Council v. Secretary of State for Scotland* [54] "is to remove the hardship which a landowner might sustain in comparison with similar landowners who are able to develop their land profitably outwith the shadow of compulsory acquisition."

8—18   Section 17 of the 1961 Act provides that where an interest in land is proposed to be acquired[55] by an authority possessing compulsory purchase powers, either the claimant or the acquiring authority may apply to the local planning authority[56] for a C.A.A.D. Where, however, a notice to treat has been served or agreement has been reached for the sale of the land to the acquiring authority and the amount of the compensation has been referred to the Lands Tribunal for Scotland to determine, no application for a certificate may be made without the consent of the other party or without leave of the tribunal.

There is no prescribed form of application for a certificate but it must be in writing and must include a plan or map sufficient to identify the land to which it relates.[57] The application is to specify what classes of development[58] would, in the applicant's opinion, be appropriate for the land in question if it were not being acquired for public purposes; it must also specify the time at which such development would be appropriate (section 17(3)(a)). The applicant must state the grounds for holding that opinion (section 17(3)(b)). The application is to be

---

[54] 1984 S.C. 1; 1984 S.L.T. 212.

[55] As substituted by s.65 (1) of the Planning and Compensation Act 1991, as amended. Leach argues that an application cannot be made where the interest has already been acquired, for example, by way of general vesting declaration (see W. A. Leach, "Compensation on Compulsory Purchase: Section 17 Certificates" [1985] J.P.L. 291). This argument was rejected by the Secretary of State for Scotland in SDD appeal decision (ref. P/AAC/TC/3); the use of the words "proposed to be acquired" in the corresponding Scottish provision is explained, it was said, by the fact that at the date of the deemed notice to treat the words reflect the status of the acquiring authority. See, too, *Young v. Lothian Regional Council*, unreported, Lands Tribunal for Scotland, May 9, 1990.

[56] For the meaning of 'local planning authority' see the Local Government Act 1972, Sched. 16, para. 55.

[57] The Land Compensation Development Order 1974, reg. 3 (1).

[58] The reference to "classes" is not linked in any way to the Town and Country Planning (Use Classes) Order 1987. It simply means that all development may be classified in one way or another (*Sutton v. Secretary of State for the Environment* [1984] J.P.L 647; *Essex Construction Co. Ltd v. Minister of Housing and Local Government* [1968] R.V.R. 818).

accompanied by a statement specifying the date on which a copy of the application has been or will be served on the other party (section 17(3)(c)).

On receipt of an application, the local planning authority must (not sooner than 21 days from the date on which a copy of the application was served on the other party (section 17(4), but not later than two months from the date of receipt of the application or such extra period as may be agreed in writing)[59] issue to the applicant a certificate stating one of two things; either (i) that, in their opinion, planning permission for development of one or more classes specified in the certificate would have been granted and for any development for which the land is to be acquired[60] (a "valuable" or "positive" certificate); these may or may not be the class or classes specified in the application and the certificate may indicate that any permission would have been subject to specified conditions or granted at a specified future time;[61] (ii) that, in their opinion, planning permission would not have been granted for any development other than that for which the land is being acquired (section 17(4) (a "nil" or "negative" certificate)).

It should be noted that the test for a valuable certificate is what planning per-   **8—19**
mission "would have been granted." This test was first introduced in the Community Land Act 1975. Prior to that it was only necessary to state the purpose or purposes for which planning permission "might reasonably have been expected." The present test would seem to be more stringent.

If the local planning authority fail to issue a certificate within the prescribed time, the applicant may lodge an appeal (see below) against a deemed "nil" certificate (section 18(4)).[62]

Establishing the relevant date for determining what, if any, alternative development would have been appropriate may be important. Is it permissible, for example, for the local planning authority to have regard to planning circumstances which were extant at the time of the decision on the certificate but had not been at the time of the proposal to acquire the land? It would appear that a distinction must be made between the relevant date for applying planning policies and the relevant date for considering physical factors.

As regards the former, the decision in *Robert Hitchins Builders Ltd v. Secretary of State for the Environment*[63] indicates that the application of planning polices should coincide as nearly as possible with the date of assessment of compensation. Thus, planning policies should be applied as at the date of entry[64] or the date of decision on the application for a C.A.A.D. (or on appeal), whichever occurs first.[65]

---

[59] The 1974 Order, reg. 3 (2); 1961 Act, s.18(4).

[60] Planning permission may in any event be assumed for the purposes for which the land is being purchased by the acquiring authority under s.15(1) of the 1961 Act.

[61] 1961 Act, s.17(5).

[62] The two month period for issuing a certificate may be extended by agreement of the parties in writing (1961 Act, s.18 (4)).

[63] (1978) 37 P. & C.R. 140. See, too, an appeal decision by the Secretary of State for the Environment under reference APP/5193/D/83/13 and PLUP 2/5193/B/1862 reported at (1984) 272 E.G. 659.

[64] See appeal decision noted in [1987] J.P.L. 659.

[65] See appeal decisions noted at [1987] J.P.L. 66 and [1988] J.P.L. 47.

However, in *Fox v. Secretary of State for the Environment*[66] Roch J. declined to follow *Hitchens* and held that both the physical condition of the land and planning policies should be looked at at the same time (see para. 6–26), that is to say by reference to whichever of the three circumstances set out in section 22(2) of the 1961 Act applies (see below).

The relevant date for considering physical factors falls to be determined by reference to section 22(2) of the 1961 Act. Thus, regard should be had to the state of the subject land at whichever of the three following dates is appropriate:

(i) where an interest in land is being compulsorily acquired, the date of publication of notice of the making of the compulsory purchase order,[67] or

(ii) where an interest in land is being acquired as a result of the service of a purchase notice[68] or a blight notice,[69] the date on which the notice to treat is deemed to have been served; or

(iii) where an interest in land is being acquired as a result of a written offer to negotiate, the date of that offer.[70]

8—20   In determining whether planning permission for any particular class of development would have been granted in respect of any land, the planning authority must disregard the prospect of the land being acquired by any authority possessing compulsory purchase powers.[71] Furthermore, the local planning authority must not rule out that class of development simply because it would have involved development of the land contrary to the provisions of the development plan (section 17(7)).[72] To treat the provisions of the development plan as conclusive of the issue would defeat many applications because the development plan may simply allocate the land for the purpose for which it is being acquired. However, it does not follow that the development plan provisions should be ignored. The provisions may be taken into account as a material but not a conclusive factor.[73] Thus in *Skelmersdale Development Corporation v. Secretary of State for Environment*[74] Griffith J. considered that it was perfectly proper for a local planning authority, in determining what alternative development should be specified in a certificate

---

[66] [1991] 40 E.G. 116.

[67] See appeal decision noted at [1987] J.P.L. 659.

[68] See the Town and Country Planning Act 1990, ss.137 *et seq*. And see appeal decision noted at [1987] J.P.L. 660.

[69] See the Town and Country Planning Act, 1990, ss.149 *et seq*.

[70] See *Jelson Ltd v. Minister of Housing and Local Government* [1970] Q.B. 243. Also *Grampian Regional Council v. Secretary of State for Scotland*, 1984 S.L.T. 212.

[71] *Grampian Regional Council v. Secretary of State for Scotland*, [1983] 1 W.L.R. 1340. And see ss.15(5) and 17(3)(*a*) of the 1961 Act (both as amended).

[72] See appeal decision noted at [1987] J.P.L. 660.

[73] *Skelmersdale Development Corporation v. Secretary of State for the Environment* [1980] J.P.L. 322; and the appeal decisions noted at [1987] J.P.L. 659, 660. See also SDD appeal decisions ref. P/AAC/GC/4; P/AAC/LD/1; P/AAC/FA/1. Section 54A of the Town and Country Planning Act 1990 appears to have no application to a decision on an application for a CAAD as this is not a determination to be made under the planning Acts.

[74] [1980] J.P.L. 322. See, too, the appeal decision noted at [1987] J.P.L. 659.

for land in a new town, to have regard to the operative master plan for the new town. A decision on an application for a certificate may be consistent with the provisions of the development plan but that does not mean that it was reached solely because of the plan.[75]

If the local planning authority issue a certificate otherwise than for the classes of development specified in the application or contrary to representations in writing made to them by either the claimant or the acquiring authority, the certificate must include their reasons for so doing.[76] On issuing a C.A.A.D. to either of the parties directly concerned, the local planning authority must serve a copy of the certificate on the other party (section 17(9)). A county planning authority must send a copy of every certificate issued by them to the district planning authority for the area in which the land is situated; and a district planning authority must send a copy of every certificate issued by them which specifies a class of classes of development relating to a county matter to the county planning authority.[77]

Section 18 of the 1961 Act makes provision for an appeal to the Secretary of State against a certificate. The certificate must give particulars of the manner in which and the time in which an appeal may be made.[78] An appeal may be made either by the claimant or by the acquiring authority and notice of the appeal must be lodged in writing with the Secretary of State within one month of the date of the receipt of the certificate or of the expiry of the period for issuing the certificate.[79] Copy of the notice of appeal must be given by the appellant to the other party, and to the local planning authority to whom the application was made; and where the issue of a certificate falls to be determined by a local planning authority other than the one to which the application was made, the copy notice of appeal shall be forwarded to the local planning authority concerned.[80] Within one month of giving notice of appeal, or within such longer period as the Secretary of State may allow, the appellant must furnish the Minister with a copy of the application to the planning authority, and the certificate (if any) together with a statement of the grounds of appeal.[81] Failure to furnish the Minister with these documents within the time prescribed will result in the appeal being treated as withdrawn.[82]

On an appeal against a certificate, the Secretary of State is to deal with the matter as if the application for the certificate had been made to him in the

8—21

---

[75] *Bell v. Lord Advocate*, 1968 S.C. 14. See, too, *Skelmersdale Development Corporation, supra.*
[76] The 1974 Order, reg. 3(3).
[77] 1974 Order, reg. 3 (4) as substituted by S.I. 1986 No. 435
[78] The 1974 Order, reg. 3(3). Failure to do so will vitiate the certificate (*London and Clydeside Estates Ltd v. Aberdeen District Council*, 1980 S.C. (H.L.) 1; 1980 S.L.T. 81).
[79] The 1974 Order, reg. 4(1). Note that the period for issuing the certificate may be extended by the parties by agreement in writing in which case the time for lodging an appeal runs from the expiry of the extended period.
[80] The 1974 Order, reg. 4(2).
[81] The 1974 Order, reg. 4(3).
[82] The 1974 Order, reg. 4(4).

first instance.[83] He may confirm the certificate, vary it, or cancel it and issue a different certificate in its place (section 18(2)). However, before determining an appeal, the Minister must afford the claimant and the acquiring authority an opportunity of appearing before and being heard by a person appointed by him for the purpose.[84]

8—22   The certificate procedure is a fictional exercise related to the assessment of compensation and not a factual exercise in planning. Its sole purpose, as Lord Bridge observed in *Grampian Regional Council v. Secretary of State for Scotland*,[85] is "to provide a basis for determining the development value, if any, to be taken into account in assessing compensation payable on compulsory acquisition."[86] This may be illustrated by the decision in *Grampian Regional Council*.[87] Developers applied for, and were granted, planning permission for the layout of a new suburb of Aberdeen. Plans accompanying the application earmarked two sites for schools and in due course Grampian Regional Council, as education authority, offered to purchase the two sites from the developers in order to construct a primary and secondary school. The offers were accepted, the price to be determined as for a compulsory acquisition. The developers considered that had it not been for the proposals of the education authority, the two sites would have had development potential and this should be reflected in the price. However, no assistance could be derived from the assumptions in the development plan as the plan was out of date. The developers accordingly applied to the planning authority pursuant to section 25 of the Land Compensation (Scotland) Act 1963 for a C.A.A.D. The planning authority issued a "nil" certificate stating that in their opinion, planning permission would not have been granted for any development other than that proposed to be carried out by the education authority. On appeal by the developers, the Secretary of State substituted "valuable" certificates to the effect that planning permission would have been granted in respect of the primary school site for residential development and in respect of the secondary school site for residential or commercial development, in each case subject to conditions.

8—23   The planning authority and the education authority applied unsuccessfully

---

[83] See appeal decision noted at [1987] J.P.L. 660.

[84] The 1961 Act, s.18(3). The hearing is generally in the form of a public local inquiry. Expenses reasonably incurred by a claimant in connection with the issue of a certificate, including expenses incurred in connection with an appeal where any of the issues on the appeal are determined in the claimant's favour, are to be taken into account in assessing compensation (s.17(9A) of the 1961 Act added by s.65(3) of the Planning and Compensation Act 1991).

[85] [1983] 1 W.L.R. 1340.

[86] However, as with the other planning assumptions, a valuable certificate will not, of itself, enhance the value of the land; demand must also be shown (*Bromilow v. Greater Manchester Council* (1975) 31 P. & C.R. 398; *J. Davy Ltd v. London Borough of Hammersmith* (1975) 30 P. & C.R. 469; and *David Bell v. Glasgow Corporation*, decision of an Official Arbiter, Ref. No. 2/1969).

[87] [1983] 1 W.L.R. 1340. See, also, the appeal decision noted at [1987] J.P.L. 660. Also the SDD appeal decisions ref. P/AAC/GA/4; and P/AAC/GA/3&5.

under section 29 of the 1963 Act to the Inner House, and from there to the House of Lords, to have the Minister's decision quashed on the ground that it was not within the powers of the Act. The authorities argued that, although in determining an application for a certificate the planning authority were obliged to ignore the actual proposal by the education authority to buy the two sites, the underlying requirement to devote those sites to the needs of public education remained and afforded a complete answer to the claims for "valuable" certificates. This argument was rejected. To accept it, said Lord Bridge, would "defeat the essential purpose of the procedure for obtaining certificates of appropriate alternative development, as part of the overall scheme of the Act to secure the payment of fair compensation to landowners who were expropriated . . . Assuming," he continued, "that every compulsory purchase of land could be justified by reference to the public purpose for which the land was required, to allow reliance on that public requirement to determine the question raised by an application under section 25 would lead to the issue of a negative certificate in every case."[88]

The argument advanced by the planning authority and the education authority in *Grampian Regional Council* was taken up by Lothian Regional Council in an appeal to the Secretary of State against the issuing of a valuable certificate by the West Lothian District Council as planning authority in respect of land being acquired by the region for a primary school.[89] If, as is required, it is to be assumed that the subject land was not being acquired for the construction of the school, it was difficult, argued the regional council, to see how it could be regarded as appropriate for residential development. There was no alternative site upon which the school could be constructed and in the absence of a school it would be inappropriate to permit residential development. This argument was rejected by the Secretary of State. The 1963 Act did not require and was not intended to require the planning authority, or the Secretary of State on appeal, to consider where the school would have been located if it were not to go on the subject land. In the hypothetical situation imposed by section 25(3) of the Act, it was enough to assume that a school site would be provided to serve the residential area and it was not necessary to point to a site either identified in the development plan or which was otherwise feasible to justify a certificate for residential use of the subject land.

Consideration of alternatives may, however, be material to the determination **8—24** of an application for a certificate where the subject land forms part of a wider scheme of public works. Leach, commenting on the operation of the corresponding English legislation, suggests that the assumption that the subject land is not being acquired for public purposes may "cause either the whole scheme to fail, to be carried out wholly on other land, or carried out with modifications with or without the addition of fresh land, or the problem to be overcome in some other

---

[88] See, too, *Scunthorpe Borough Council v. Secretary of State for the Environment* [1977] J.P.L. 653.
[89] Ref. P/AAC/LD/1.

manner . . . to the extent that the scheme would go ahead it would have to be taken into account in deciding what developments of the relevant land would be permitted in that setting.'[90] This point cropped up in respect of an application for a C.A.A.D. for land being acquired for the construction of the Perth Western Bypass. The applicant appealed to the Secretary of State against a "nil" certificate issued by the planning authority. On appeal, the planning authority argued, *inter alia*, that, in considering what development, if any, would have been appropriate on the subject land were it not being acquired for the road scheme, it was necessary to consider the likely effect on the scheme of the assumed non-availability of the subject land. The planning potential of the subject land should be judged on the basis of that effect. The Secretary of State in his decision letter[91] accepted that it was in order for him to consider the possibility of an alternative line for the bypass and the effect which such an alternative line might have had on the development potential of the ground being acquired.

Because of the difficulty of assessing how the need for road improvements would be met, if at all, in the absence of the land being acquired, it is now to be assumed in assessing development potential for compensation purposes that no highway would be constructed to meet the need or substantially the same need.[92] This restriction only applies as regards land being acquired for or in connection with the construction[93] of a highway[94].

In considering what classes of alternative development would have been appropriate, regard may properly be paid not only to the possibility of development on the subject land but also to the prospect of its development as a part of a larger area, whether or not that larger area is under the control of the applicant.[95] The likelihood of such permission being sought or implemented is irrelevant; the legislation presupposes that an application will be made.[96]

Whether or not any permission which may be assumed under section 15(5) of the 1961 Act as a result of the issuing of a valuable C.A.A.D. will in fact increase the value of the land is a matter for the claimant and the acquiring authority to determine, or falling agreement for the Lands Tribunal to decide.[97] In *David Bell*

---

[90] W.A. Leach, "Compensation on Compulsory Purchase: Section 17 Certificates" [1985] J.P.L. 291.

[91] Ref. P/AAC/TC/3. See, too, *Young v. Lothian Regional Council*, unreported, Lands Tribunal for Scotland, May 9, 1990.

[92] s.14(5)–(7) of the 1961 Act, added by s.64 of the Planning and Compensation Act 1991.

[93] Construction of a highway includes its alteration or improvement s.14(8) of the 1961 Act, added by s.64 of the 1991 Act.

[94] The same assumption is to be made where compensation is being assessed with regard to land which is being considered by a highway authority for use for or in connection with a highway. This might arise following the service of a purchase notice or blight notice under Part VI of the Town and Country Planning Act 1990.

[95] *Sutton v. Secretary of State for the Environment* [1984] J.P.L. 647.

[96] *Ibid.* The likelihood of the permission being implemented may well be relevant to the question of demand.

[97] See *Bromilow v. Greater Manchester Council* (1975) 31 P. & C.R. 398;

v. Corporation of Glasgow[98] an official arbiter rejected the view that demand as well as permission could be assumed and concluded in the circumstances of that case that there would have been no demand for certain of the activities referred to in the C.A.A.D. And in *Davy Ltd v. London Borough of Hammersmith*[99] the Lands Tribunal held that a prospective purchaser of the tail end of a lease would not have been prepared to pay anything for planning permission for a petrol filling station since it was too speculative.

Section 21 of the 1961 Act provides that any person aggrieved by a decision **8—25** of the Secretary of State on an appeal under section 18 or the planning authority may, within six weeks of the date of the decision, question its validity by way of an application to the High Court on the grounds that it is not within the powers of the Act or that any procedural requirements have not been complied with.

The cost of obtaining a C.A.A.D., including expenses incurred in connection with any appeal under section 18 where any of the issues on the appeal are determined in the claimant's favour, is an expense that may be recovered as part of the claim for compensation[1].

Compensation where permission for additional development granted after acquisition

Cases sometimes arise where land is acquired for a particular form of development and compensation is assessed accordingly but, in the light of changed circumstances, it is subsequently decided to use the land for an alternative form of development. The effect of the grant of planning permission for the alternative development may be to increase the value of the land above that on which the original award of compensation was based. Where an increase in value occurs in this way, it seems reasonable that the original owner of the land should be in a position to benefit. Part IV of the Land Compensation Act 1961 makes provision for such benefit[2].

Section 23 of the 1961 Act provides for the payment of additional compensation where an interest in land is compulsorily acquired or is sold to an authority possessing compulsory purchase powers and, before the end of the period of ten

---

[98] Ref. No. 2/1969. See, too, *Young v. Lothian Regional Council*, unreported, Lands Tribunal for Scotland, May 9, 1990.

[99] (1975) 30 P. & C.R. 469.

[1] s.17(9A) of the 1961 added by s.65(3) of the Planning and Compensation Act 1991 partly reversing the decision in *Hull and Humber Investment Co. Ltd v. Hull Corporation* [1965] 2 Q.B. 145.

[2] Added by s.66 and Sched. 14 to the Planning and Compensation Act 1991. The provisions revive in modified form Part IV of the 1961 Act repealed by the Land Commission Act 1967.

years beginning with the date of completion, a planning decision is made granting permission for the carrying out of additional development on the land.[3] The additional compensation is payable in response to a claim[4] where the original compensation or price is less than it would have been if the permission had been in force at the date of the notice to treat. The additional compensation is assessed under the provisions of Part 1 of the 1961 Act[5] and is equal to the difference. Provision is made for claims by successors in title (section 23(4)).

No additional compensation is payable in respect of a planning decision relating to land acquired:

— under sections 142 or 143 of the Local Government, Planning and Land Act 1980;
— under the New Towns Act 1981;
— where the compulsory purchase order included a direction under section 50 of the Planning (Listed Building and Conservation Areas) Act 1990.

8—26   The additional compensation will carry interest at the rate prescribed under section 32 of the 1961 Act from the date of the planning decision until payment.

To facilitate the making of a claim under section 23, the person entitled may give the acquiring authority an address for service (section 24(1)). The acquiring authority must then give notice to the person in the event of the making of a planning decision which would trigger a section 23 claim (section 24(2)).

A section 23 claim will be of no effect if it is made more than six months after the date of the notice referred to in section 24(2) or, if no address for service has been given, six months after the date of the planning decision (section 24(4)). If there is an appeal against the planning decision, including an appeal made under section 78(2) of the Town and Country Planning Act 1990, time runs in the second case from the date of the decision on the appeal.

Where the acquiring authority cease to be entitled to the whole or part of the land in question, that authority must arrange with the local planning authority to give notice to them of any planning decision so that they (the acquiring authority), will in turn be able to give notice under section 24(2) (section 24(6) and (7)).

The provisions of sections 23 and 24 are applied to any planning permission granted or deemed to be granted in the circumstances mentioned in column 1 of the Table as if a planning decision granting that permission had been made on the date shown in column 2 (section 25(1)):

---

[3] 'Additional development' is defined in s.29(1) of the 1961 Act, added by s.66 and Sched. 14 to the 1991 Act.
[4] As to who may claim, see s.23(1) and (4) and the Third Schedule to the 1961 Act, paras 4–7, added by s.66 and Sched. 14 to the 1991 Act.
[5] And see paras. 1–3 of the Third Schedule to the 1961 Act, added by s.66 and Sched. 14 to the 1991 Act.

Planning permission	Date of decision
Permission granted by a development order	When development is initiated
Permission granted by the adoption or approval of a simplified planning zone scheme	When the scheme is approved or adopted
Permission granted by an order designating an enterprise zone	When the designation takes effect
Permission deemed to be granted by a direction under s.90 of the Town and Country Planning Act 1990	When the direction is given
Permission deemed to be granted by a local planning authority	The occurrence of the event in consequence of which the permission is deemed to be granted

Where, in such a case, the development is proposed to be carried out by the acquiring authority, or by some other person who has notified the acquiring authority, the authority must give notice of the proposal to any person who has left an address for service under section 24(1) so that a claim for additional compensation under section 23 may be made (section 25(2)). However, such a claim will have no effect if made more than six months after the date of a notice given under section 25(2). If no such address for service has been left with the acquiring authority, the six month period will run from the date shown in column 2 of the Table (section 25(4)).

The provisions of sections 23 and 24 are applied by section 26 to additional development initiated by or on behalf of the Crown or initiated in right of a Crown or Duchy interest in the land. A Crown or Duchy interest refers to an interest belonging to the Queen in right of the Crown or of the Duchy of Lancaster, or belonging to the Duchy of Cornwall, or belonging to a government department or held in trust for her Majesty for the purposes of a government department (section 26(7)).

The form of any notice to be given under Part IV may be prescribed by regulations made by the Secretary of State (section 28(1)).

Chapter 9

Disregarding the Scheme

Introduction

9—01 Actions or decisions of government bodies may affect the value of land. The Uthwatt Committee referred to an increase in the value of land from such actions or decisions as "betterment"[1]; a decrease in value is generally referred to either as "worsenment," "injurious affection" or "blight." The purpose of this chapter is to consider whether, and if so to what extent, such increases or decreases may be reflected in compensation for the compulsory acquisition of land.

In Chapter 8. It was pointed out that in assessing the market value of the land account may be taken of the potential which it may have for some other more profitable use and the way in which such potential may be established for compensation purposes was examined. It is important to bear in mind, however, that what is being compensated is the claimant's loss and the claimant cannot, as Denyer-Green observes, "add to this by taking advantage of the statutory purchaser's needs and requirements which might give the land in the purchaser's hands a higher value."[2] In assessing the potential of the land the claimant must disregard any increase in value which is due to the scheme for which it is being acquired; that is the value of the land to the purchaser.

---

[1] *Expert Committee on Compensation and Betterment: Final Report*, Cmd. 6386 (1942).

[2] B. Denyer-Green, "The Pointe Gourde Principle" (1978) 8 Kingston L.R. 101. And see *Penny v. Penny* (1868) L.R. 5 Eq. 227; *Stebbing v. Metropolitan Board of Works* (1870) L.R. 6 Q.B. 37. One aspect of this has already been seen in the discussion of rule (3) in Chap. 7. Rule (3) provides that, in assessing compensation, no account is to be taken of certain potential which land may have because of its special suitability or adaptability. As to the interrelation of rule (3) and betterment arising from the scheme, see *Batchelor v. Kent County Council*, [1990] 14 E.G. 129.

Thus in *Fraser v. City of Fraserville*,[3] part of a river, including a waterfall, was acquired from the claimant for a hydroelectric scheme. The intention was to construct a dam on other land higher up the river with a view to increasing the flow of water over the waterfall at certain times so as to generate power. The claimant argued that compensation should reflect the value of the waterfall to those promoting the electricity generating scheme. The Judicial Committee of the Privy Council rejected this approach and held that any increase in the value of the land to the acquiring authority as a result of its scheme was to be ignored. Lord Buckmaster said:

> "the value to be ascertained is the value to the seller of the property in its actual condition at the time of expropriation with all its existing advantages and with all its possibilities excluding any advantage due to the carrying out of the scheme for which the property is compulsorily acquired. The question of what is the scheme being a question of fact for the arbitrator in each case."[4]

Considerable difficulty, however, arises where the subject land is just one part of a much wider area of land being acquired for the scheme of development and the development or prospect of development of the other land in implementation of the scheme enhances or depreciates the value of the land being acquired. Consider as a relatively straightforward example the facts in *MacDonald v. Midlothian County Council*.[5] MacDonald's house was compulsorily purchased as part of a redevelopment scheme in Kirknewton, a scheme involving the improvement of some houses, the demolition and rebuilding of others and the improvement and realignment of certain roads. The Lands Tribunal for Scotland found that the result of improvements already carried out in the area under the scheme was to put up the value which a willing seller would have been likely to have obtained for MacDonald's property in the open market by some £1,660. Similarly, the presence of houses on either side of MacDonald's which had been acquired under the scheme for redevelopment but which had been vandalised in the interim would have depressed the value of MacDonald's property in the open market by about £300. For reasons which will be explained shortly, these effects on value resulting from the scheme were disregarded in the assessment of compensation. The point to be made at this stage is that the adjustment in value, although caused by the redevelopment scheme, would have been reflected in a sale of the house by a willing seller in the open market.

In *MacDonald* the adjustments were to the existing use value of the land but such adjustments may also be made to the potential which the land has for some

9—02

---

[3] [1917] A.C. 187.
[4] In 1919, Parliament, as explained in Chapter 4, substituted a hypothetical willing seller for the actual seller in an effort to achieve a more objective measure of compensation (s.2 of the Acquisition of Land (Assessment of Compensation) Act 1919) but it did not otherwise alter the basis of compensation.
[5] 1975 S.L.T. (Lands Tr.) 24.

other use. A local authority scheme for the development of a greenfield site for residential purposes may increase the value of other greenfield sites in the vicinity due to expectations about their future allocation for similar purposes.

The question is, given the analogy with a sale by a willing seller in the open market which rule (2) strives to achieve, should these adjustments in value be reflected in compensation when the land is acquired for the scheme? If not, why not?

9—03   In *South-Eastern Railway Co. v. London County Council*[6] in 1915 the Court of Appeal held that in the absence of specific statutory authority no adjustment was to be made to the compensation for land taken for a road improvement scheme to reflect the appreciation in the value of other neighbouring land belonging to the claimants resulting from the scheme. Eve J. at first instance pinpointed the difficulty of adjusting compensation on account of betterment. It would unfairly discriminate between a landowner whose land was compulsorily acquired and a neighbour whose land was not acquired but was similarly increased in value as a result of the scheme. It would, he said:

> "bring about some startling results; the most obvious one being that it would upset all uniformity of value, inasmuch as the value of the identical piece of land in the hands of one vendor might be assessed at many times its value in the hands of another, and this, not from any intrinsic distinction, but by reason solely of extraneous considerations. Moreover, it would be calculated to work injustice in that a vendor compelled to sell, and who the legislature intended should be compensated for being compelled to sell, might have to accept from the undertakers a price far less than he would have obtained from any other purchaser, and out of all proportion to the true value of the land had it been ascertained without reference to the fortuitous circumstances of his also being interested in the contiguous land."[7]

Similarly, in *Walker's Trustees v. Caledonian Railway Company*[8] the trustees claimed compensation for the depreciation in the value of their premises caused by the adverse effects, on their access, of the construction of a railway. The railway company argued that, in assessing compensation, the beneficial effects on the value of the premises from the location of a railway station in the immediate neighbourhood should be taken into account. In the Court of Session, Lord Young rejected the railway company's argument. "This contention is," he said, "admittedly novel, and I content myself with saying that it is in my opinion inadmissable."[9]

The Pointe Gourde principle

9—04   However, the decision of the Judicial Committee of the Privy Council in *Pointe Gourde Quarrying and Transport Co. Ltd v. Sub-Intendent of Crown Lands*[10] in 1947 is

---

[6] [1915] 2 Ch. 252.
[7] *Ibid.* at p. 259.
[8] (1881) 8 R. 405.
[9] Although the case went to the House of Lords this particular line of argument was not pursued.
[10] [1947] A.C. 565.

widely regarded as authority for the proposition that compensation should be adjusted to account for betterment arising from the scheme. The facts of the case were that the Crown compulsorily acquired the company's stone quarry in Trinidad for use in the construction of a nearby naval base. The ordinance under which the compensation was assessed followed closely the provisions of the Acquisition of Land (Assessment of Compensation) Act 1919. The total claim for the quarry as a going concern amounted to $101,000. Of this, $15,000 represented additional value reflecting the increased profits which an operator of the quarry could have expected to make selling stone for the construction of the nearby naval base had it not been expropriated by the Crown. The point at issue was whether the item of $15,000 was allowable in law as a part of the compensation. Much of the argument centred on whether the item was excluded by the local equivalent of rule (3). The court held that it was not. However, Lord MacDermott, giving judgment for the court, went on to say: "But it does not follow that this part of the award can stand. It is well settled that compensation for the compulsory acquisition of land cannot include an increase in value which is entirely due to the scheme underlying the acquisition." The court held that the sum of $15,000 represented an increase in value due to the scheme and it was disallowed. As authority for his statement, Lord MacDermott cited dicta by Eve J. in *South-Eastern Railway* and by Lord Buckmaster in *Fraser*. However, in the former case, the increase in the value of the remaining land caused by the scheme was not set off against the compensation; and the latter was concerned with excluding value to the purchaser.

Different views have been expressed about the correctness of the decision in **9—05** *Pointe Gourde*.[11] But whatever view is taken about the correctness of the decision, it is important because, as Denyer-Green observes, "for the first time betterment to market value caused by the scheme of the acquiring authority was disregarded for the purpose of assessing compensation for the land taken."[12] The converse of the decision is that worsenment, the depreciation in the value of land resulting from the scheme underlying the acquisition, should also be brought into account so as to increase the compensation. In *Jelson Ltd v. Blaby District Council*[13] Lord Denning accepted that the *Pointe Gourde* principle applies not only to appreciation in value but also to depreciation in value. And in the Privy Council decision in *Melwood Units Property Ltd v. Commission of Main Roads*[14] Lord Russell of Killowen held that "In their Lordships' opinion it is a part of the common law deriving as a matter of principle from the nature of compensation for resumption or compulsory acquisition, that neither relevantly attributable appreciation nor depreciation in value is to be regarded in the assessment of land compensation."

---

[11] See, for example, Keith Davies, "The Pointe Gourde Rule" *The Conveyancer and Property Lawyer*, 1975, p. 414, and B. Denyer-Green, "The Pointe Gourde Principle" (1978) 8 Kingston Law Review 101 and 184.

[12] B. Denyer-Green, "Recapture of Betterment" (1980) 255 E.G. 615.

[13] [1978] 1 All E.R. 548. See, too, *Birmingham City District Council v. Morris and Jacombs* (1976) 33 P. & C.R. 27; and *Abbey Homesteads (Developments) Ltd v. Northamptonshire County Council* [1992] 26 E.G. 140.

[14] [1979] A.C. 426. See, too, W.A. Leach, "Pointe Gourde Principle" (1979) 250 E.G. 966.

Statutory expression of the Pointe Gourde principle

9—06   The proposition that the effects of betterment or worsenment due to the scheme on the value of land being acquired should be disregarded in assessing compensation was subsequently given statutory expression. Section 6 of the Land Compensation Act 1961, as amended, now provides that no account is to be taken of any increase or decrease in the value of land which is attributable to the scheme as defined in Schedule 1.

To explain section 6 it is necessary to go back to the Town and Country Planning Act 1954 which introduced a dual price system in land (see Chapter 5). While private sales were to be at market value, compensation on the compulsory acquisition of land was to be restricted to existing use value plus any "unexpended balance of established development value" together with a sum representing interest. This dual price system was a clear departure from the principle of equivalence and it provoked considerable unease. "The dual price system," notes Cullingworth, "was inherently unstable, and disquiet about its operation rapidly mounted—from the land professions, from organisations of land-owners, from local authorities, from government departments, and from government back-benchers."[15] Eventually, the government felt compelled to alter the arrangements. The obvious solution was to restore market value as the measure of compensation. However, fears were expressed about the increased cost which would fall upon public authorities in acquiring land, one of the principal reasons for the introduction of the dual price system in the first place. "It was thought," says Cullingworth, "that this would expose the Government to the criticism of impeding municipal development, which would be particularly embarrassing in relation to slum clearance in Glasgow and other congested urban areas. Moreover, a Bill which increased the level of compensation for compulsory acquisition but made no attempt to deal with the problem of betterment would be likely to revive public interest in the whole question of the taxation of land values."[16] The upshot was that market value was restored as the measure of compensation by the Town and Country Planning Act 1959 and limited provision was made in the Act to enable public authorities to recover betterment generated by their schemes by way of deduction from the compensation payable. No account was to be taken in assessing compensation of increases (and decreases) in value due to the scheme as defined. This was thought to be in line with practice recognised by the Privy Council in *Pointe Gourde*.[17] The provision in the 1959 Act is now to be found in section 6 of the 1961 Act, as amended.

---

[15] J.B. Cullingworth, *Environmental Planning* (HMSO, 1980) Vol. IV. See, too, *Report of the Committee on Administrative Tribunals and Inquiries*, Cmnd. 218 (1957), para. 278.

[16] J.B. Cullingworth, *supra*, p. 195.

[17] *Ibid.* at p. 205 citing the "Notes on clauses".

Section 6 is a complex provision. In *Camrose (Viscount) v. Basingstoke Corporation*[18] **9—07** Russell L.J. observed "The drafting of this section appears to me to be calculated to postpone as long as possible comprehension of its purport." The section needs to be read in conjunction with Schedule 1 to the 1961 Act. Part I of Schedule 1 is divided into two columns. The left hand column lists seven different circumstances in which land may be earmarked for acquisition for public purposes. The characteristic of each circumstance is that the land in question ("the relevant land")[19] forms part only of a wider area earmarked for a scheme of works. The right hand column defines the extent of the scheme in the seven different circumstances. Section 16 provides that in assessing compensation for the acquisition of "the relevant interest"[20] in one of the seven circumstances listed, no account is to be taken of an increase or decrease in the value of that interest which is attributable to development under the corresponding scheme as defined. Any reference to development of any land is to be construed as including a reference to the clearing of that land.[21] Like the *Pointe Gourde* principle, section 6 modifies the effect of rule (2) by providing that in certain cases actual or prospective development is to be disregarded.

The seven circumstances and the corresponding scheme are as follows: **9—08**
Case 1: A single compulsory purchase order or special Act quite often authorises the acquisition of a number of different parcels of land with a number of different interests. In assessing the value of any one of the interests authorised to be acquired by the order or Act ("the relevant interest") it may be found that the development or prospect of development for the purposes of the scheme of any of the other land authorised to be acquired[22] has increased or decreased the value of that interest. No account is to be taken of that increase or decrease in value. The extent of the scheme is defined by the land authorised to be acquired by the order or Act but excluding the relevant land.

Case 2: In assessing the value of the relevant interest in land forming part of an action area or comprehensive development area,[23] no account is to be taken of any increase or decrease in the value of that interest which is attributable to the development or redevelopment, or the prospect of development or redevelopment, of any of the other land in accordance with the scheme for the action area or comprehensive development area. The extent of the scheme is defined by the action area or comprehensive development area but excludes the relevant land.

---

[18] [1966] 1 W.L.R. 1100.

[19] In s.39 of the 1961 Act "the relevant land" is defined as the land in which "the relevant interest" subsists; and "the relevant interest" is defined as the interest acquired in pursuance of the appropriate notice to treat.

[20] *Ibid.*

[21] s.6(3) of the 1961 Act. And see *Davy v. Leeds Corporation* [1964] 1 W.L.R. 1218; affirmed [1965] 1 W.L.R. 445.

[22] This refers to the aggregate of the land authorised to be acquired by the compulsory purchase order or the special Act (s.6(3)(*a*)). In respect of land authorised by any Act to be acquired for defence purposes, see s.6(3)(*b*).

[23] For the definition of an "action area", see the Town and Country Planning Act 1990, ss.12 and 36.

Cases 3–4B: Provision very similar to that for action areas is made in respect of land:

— which at the date of the notice to treat formed part of an area designated as the site of a new town (Case 3)[24], or as an extension of a site of a new town (Case 3A)[25],

— forming part of an area to which a town development scheme under the Town Development Act 1952 relates, being a scheme which is in operation at the date of the notice to treat (Case 4);

— forming part of an area designated as an urban development area by an order under section 134 of the Local Government, Planning and Land Act 1980 (Case 4A)[26];

— forming part of a housing action trust area established under Part III of the Housing Act 1988 (Case 4B).

It should be noted that section 6 does not apply if the development or prospect of development giving rise to the adjustment in value would have been likely to be carried out:

— as regards Case 1, if the acquiring authority had not acquired and did not propose to acquire any of the land authorised to be acquired; and

— as regards Cases 2 to 4B, if the area or areas referred to had not been so defined or designated.

9—09 Section 51 of the Land Compensation Act 1973 could operate to enlarge the scope of Cases 3 and 3A in certain circumstances. The section provides that, where the Secretary of State has made a draft order under section 1 of the New Towns Act 1981 designating any area as the site of a new town or as an extension of the site of a new town so as to provide housing or other facilities required because of the carrying out of a particular public development,[27] he may before the order is finalised give a direction specifying that development for the purposes of the section. The effect of such a direction is that in applying section 6 of the 1961 Act to Cases 3 and 3A there is also to be disregarded in the assessment of compensation any increase or decrease in the value of the relevant interest which is attributable to the carrying out or the prospect of the public development specified. It has been suggested that this provision was introduced at a time when it was thought that the third London airport would be located at Maplin and that a new town would be required to deal with the development the airport would generate.[28]

---

[24] Designated under the New Towns Act 1946. And see s.6(2) of and Sched. 1, Part II to the 1961 Act.

[25] Inserted by the New Towns Act 1966, Sched., Part I, para. 1. See, too, s.6(2) and Sched. 1, Part II of the 1961 Act.

[26] Inserted by the Local Government, Planning and Land Act 1980, s.145(1). And see s.6(2) of and Sched. 1, Part III to the 1961 Act. Part III of Sched. 1 was added to the 1961 Act by the Local Government, Planning and Land Act 1980, s.145(2).

[27] See s.51(6) of the 1973 Act.

[28] [1985] J.P.L. 78.

An illustration of the way in which section 6 and Schedule 1 may operate is provided by the decision of an official arbiter in *Mrs Leckie's Trustees v. East Kilbride Development Corporation*,[29] a case turning on the earlier provision in section 9 of the Town and Country Planning (Scotland) Act 1959. The Railway Tavern in East Kilbride was compulsorily purchased for the purposes of a new town. The construction of the new town had begun in the late 1940s and the influx of people into the area had resulted over the years in a considerable increase in the profitability of the tavern. In valuing the premises for compensation, the arbiter took the view that the profitability had been much inflated by the scheme and that in so far as this increase in profitability was reflected in the market value of the premises it should be disregarded.

A further illustration is provided by *Davy v. Leeds Corporation*[30]. The appellants **9—10** were owners of back-to-back houses in Leeds. The area in which these houses were situated was designated a clearance area by the city council under the provisions of Part III of the Housing Act 1957. A compulsory purchase order was subsequently made and confirmed for the acquisition of land in 13 clearance areas, including the one in question, together with other land for clearance and redevelopment. As the appellants' houses were unfit for human habitation compensation was assessed at that time on the value of the appellants' land as sites cleared of buildings and available for development in an area zoned for residential development. The appellants argued that, in assessing compensation regard should be had to the fact that instead of buying a site with bad housing around it, a purchaser in the open market would be buying a site in an area which was bound to be cleared and available for development. The House of Lords held that under Case 1 it was necessary to disregard the development, including the clearance of any of the land authorised to be acquired because such clearance would not have been likely to have occurred in the absence of the council's scheme. In other words, the fact that the surrounding houses which had been authorised for acquisition and would be cleared in accordance with the clearance area designation was to be disregarded. Viscount Dilhorne, referring to the dictum of Lord MacDermott in *Pointe Gourde*, observed that it seemed to him that Parliament "has given statutory expression to the principle which Lord MacDermott stated was well settled."[31]

The relationship between the Pointe Gourde principle and section 6

For a while, however, the relationship between the *Pointe Gourde* principle and its **9—11** statutory expression was not altogether clear.[32] In *Camrose (Viscount) v. Basingstoke*

[29] Ref. No. 10/1961.
[30] [1965] 1 W.L.R. 445.
[31] *Ibid.* p. 453.
[32] See *Halliwell and Halliwell v. Skelmersdale Development Corporation* (1965) 16 P. & C.R. 305; and *Kaye v. Basingstoke Corporation* (1968) 20 P. & C.R. 417.

Corporation,[33] for example, some 550 acres of land were acquired under the Town Development Act 1952 for the expansion of Basingstoke. At issue, *inter alia*, was the interpretation of section 6 and Schedule 1, Case 4 of the Land Compensation Act 1961. In defining the extent of the development, the effect of which on the value of the relevant interest is to be disregarded, Case 4 specifically excludes development of the "relevant land."[34] The claimant argued that although no regard could be paid to the effect on the value of the "relevant land" of the prospect of development of other land in the course of the town development scheme, the prospect of the development of the "relevant land" itself under the scheme was not covered by this exclusion. The section, therefore, impliedly permitted regard to be had to any increase in value due to the development of the relevant land itself under the town development scheme. The Court of Appeal held that the *Pointe Gourde* principle was left untouched by the statutory provision and that the increase in value claimed which was due to the scheme should be disregarded.

The decision in *Camrose* was subsequently followed in *Wilson v. Liverpool City Council*.[35] The city council wished to acquire some 391 acres of land for housing development. 305 acres were acquired by agreement but the remaining 86 acres, of which the claimant owned 74 acres, were the subject of a compulsory purchase order. The claimant acknowledged that any increase in the value of his land attributable to the development of any of the other land authorised to be acquired by the compulsory purchase order had to be disregarded under section 6 of and Part I of Schedule 1 to the Land Compensation Act of 1961. However, he argued, these provisions were exhaustive. There was no requirement to disregard any increase in the value of his land attributable to the prospect of the development of the 305 acres which had not been compulsorily acquired. The Court of Appeal, applying the decision in *Camrose* rejected that argument. Lord Denning said "It is suggested that that provision[36] contains a code which defines exhaustively the increases which are *not* to be taken into account: so that any other increase is to be taken into account: and, accordingly, there is no room for the *Pointe Gourde* principle. But this court has rejected that argument."

Identifying the scheme

9—12   It is clear, therefore, that section 6 of and Schedule 1 to the 1961 Act and the *Pointe Gourde* principle operate concurrently[37] and this may lead to some difficulty

---

[33] [1966] 1 W.L.R. 1100.

[34] So indeed do the other Cases.

[35] [1971] 1 W.L.R. 302.

[36] s 6 of and Sched. I, Part 1 to the 1961 Act.

[37] *Sprinz v. Kingston upon Hull City Council* (1975) 30 P. & C.R. 273.

in identifying the scheme, the effects of which on value are to be ignored. In *Wilson* the claimant argued that the *Pointe Gourde* principle could only apply where the scheme is precise and definite and is made known to all the world. Denning M.R. disagreed. "A scheme," he observed, "is a progressive thing. It starts vague and known to few. It becomes more precise and better known as time goes on. Eventually it becomes precise and definite, and known to all. Correspondingly, its impact has a progressive effect because it is so vague and uncertain. As it becomes more precise and better known, so its impact increases until it has an important effect. It is this increase, whether big or small, which is to be disregarded at the time when value is to be assessed."[38] In the same case Widgery L.J. said "It would I think be a great mistake if we tended to focus our attention on the word 'scheme' as though it had some magic of its own"; and later "It is for the tribunal of fact to consider just what activities — past, present or future — are properly to be regarded as the scheme within the meaning of this proposition."[39]

Within these broad guidelines identification of the scheme would seem to turn, as the Lands Tribunal for Scotland observed in *Mrs Fulton's Trustees v. Glasgow Corporation*[40] very largely on the facts and circumstances of each case. In that case the tribunal held that the scheme underlying the compulsory acquisition could be traced back beyond the designation of the comprehensive development area in 1972 to the written statement accompanying the quinquennial review of the development plan submitted in 1960. The statement contained proposals which were sufficiently precise and sufficiently public to constitute an identifiable scheme. In *Bird v. Wakefield Metropolitan District Council*[41] the Court of Appeal held that it was not necessary for the scheme to provide for compulsory acquisition; it was enough that it underlay the acquisition.

In *MacDonald v. Midlothian County Council*[42] the Lands Tribunal for Scotland **9—13** rejected the claimants' contention that the proposed road realignment for which his house was being acquired was the scheme. The scheme comprised the housing redevelopment being undertaken in that part of Kirknewton involving both the improvement of existing houses and the building of new ones. The road realignment was incidental to the overall redevelopment. In *Cronin and Taylor v. Swansea City Council*[43] the Lands Tribunal held that the scheme underlying the acquisition included the whole town centre development dating from 1947 of which the relevant comprehensive development area merely formed the latest phase. In that case the tribunal went on to observe that they were obliged under *Pointe Gourde* to disregard an increase in value *entirely* due to the scheme underlying the acquisition. They could, therefore, have regard to any enhancement in value due to the

---

[38] [1971] 1 W.L.R. 302 at p. 309.
[39] *Ibid.* at p. 310. And see *Fraser v. City of Fraserville* [1917] A.C. 187, *per* Lord Buckmaster at p. 194.
[40] 1976 S.L.T. (Lands Tr.) 14.
[41] (1978) 248 E.G. 499.
[42] 1975 S.L.T. (Lands Tr.) 24.
[43] (1972) 24 P. & C.R. 382.

activity of bodies other than the local authority acting in exercise of compulsory powers, so far as such enhancement was not entirely due to the scheme.

In *Bell v. Newcastle upon Tyne City Council*[44] the Lands Tribunal considered that the scheme included at least six comprehensive development areas within the city centre submitted to the Minister between 1962 to 1966 and all originating from a planning report in 1961. In that case the member concluded "I am therefore satisfied on the evidence that the Burns First Report was a scheme of works with a clear starting point in time in 1961, sufficiently precise to enable an interested party to find out its proposals which were not to be greatly changed as each succeeding CDA came into being and was implemented. I find it in no way surprising that separate CDAs were necessary for a scheme extending to more than 200 acres of mainly built-up land in the centre of the City for administrative convenience, programming and financial considerations; but that did not make each CDA a fundamentally separate 'scheme'." On the other hand, in *Sprinz v. Kingston upon Hull City Council*[45] the tribunal held that the application for planning permission for development in that case was an entirely fresh project. Provision by the council for dealing with overspill was not, on the evidence, a continuing process coming under one scheme.

9—14   In *Jelson Ltd v. Blaby District Council*[46] the Court of Appeal accepted that there could be a scheme underlying an acquisition triggered by a purchase notice so that under *Pointe Gourde* any depreciation in value resulting from the scheme had to be ignored in assessing compensation. In that case a planning application for a substantial residential development had been granted subject to the reservation of a strip for a proposed public road, the line of which was shown in the development plan. The houses were built. In the meantime, the proposal for the road was abandoned. A subsequent planning application to build houses on the reserved strip was refused because of the adverse effect such development might have on the new houses on either side of the strip. A purchase notice was served and confirmed. In awarding compensation based on the development potential of the strip, the Lands Tribunal adopted a causal approach to the identification of the scheme. It was the road scheme which underlay or was the foundation of the purchase notice and its confirmation, a view with which the Court of Appeal concurred. On the other hand, in *Birmingham District Council v. Morris and Jacombs*,[47] another purchase notice case, the Court of Appeal declined to accept that a condition on a planning permission for residential development requiring a strip of land to be reserved for vehicular access to the development could constitute a scheme. The value of the strip as an access was not due to any scheme of the local authority but simply to a condition on the planning permission.

---

[44] [1971] R.V.R. 209. See, too, *North-Eastern Housing Association Ltd v. Newcastle upon Tyne City Council* (1972) 25 P. & C.R. 178.

[45] 34 P. & C.R. 77.

[46] [1977] 1 W.L.R. 1020.

[47] (1976) 33 P. & C.R. 27. See, too, *Lawlor v. London Borough of Hounslow* [1981] J.P.L. 203.

Valuing in the "no scheme" world

Having identified the scheme it is then necessary to determine what would have **9—15** happened but for the scheme and to consider whether the scheme has, by comparison with the position in the "no scheme" world, resulted in an increase or decrease in the value of the subject land. Visualising the circumstances that would have prevailed in the "no scheme" world is for the valuer, as one commentator observed "perhaps the most difficult of the preliminaries to valuation with which he is confronted, for although he will study whatever evidence is available to him, in the end it must be inevitably a matter of conjecture."[48] Lord Denning in *Myers v. Milton Keynes Development Corporation*[49] expressed the valuer's predicament in more graphic but possibly less helpful terms: "It is apparent, therefore," he said, "that the valuation has to be done in an imaginary state of affairs in which there is no scheme. The valuer must cast aside his knowledge of what has happened in the past eight years due to the scheme. He must ignore the developments which will in all probability take place in the future ten years owing to the scheme. Instead, he must let his imagination take flight to the clouds. He must conjure up a land of make-believe, where there has not been, nor will be, a brave new town but where there is to be supposed the old order of things continuing."[50] Because of the difficulty in establishing pre-scheme value in areas of urban regeneration, the RICS, in a submission to the Department of the Environment in July 1993, argued that it was no longer realistic in such cases to disregard increases or decreases in value attributable to the activities of Urban Development Corporations.

The sort of exercise that valuers and the Lands Tribunal may have to engage **9—16** in is well illustrated in *Mrs Fulton's Trustees v. Glasgow Corporation*.[51] In that case the Lands Tribunal for Scotland was called upon to determine what would probably have occurred to the relevant part of Govan in the "no scheme" world. The scene in Govan at the date of valuation 15 years after its designation for comprehensive development was one of dereliction and devastation. In support of their argument that the scheme had depressed values, the claimants cited certain streets in Paisley, where residential property had been gradually rehabilitated by owners and occupiers over a period of years, as an illustration of what would probably have happened in Govan in the absence of the local authority scheme. The tribu-

---

[48] Maurice Clark, "Valuation Aspects of Land Taken Under a Scheme — 1" in *Compensation for Compulsory Purchase*, Journal of Planning and Environmental Law Occasional Paper (Sweet and Maxwell, 1975). See, too, T.J. Nardecchia, "Valuation aspects of Land Taken Under a Scheme — 2", *ibid.*; M. Horton, "Compensation and Valuation Matters" in *The Planning Balance in the 1990s*, Journal of Planning & Environmental Law Occasional Paper (Sweet & Maxwell), 1991; and A. Baum, "Pointe Gourde: The Valuation Problems" [1981] J.P.L. 726.

[49] [1974] 1 W.L.R. 696.

[50] *Ibid.* at p. 704.

[51] 1976 S.L.T. (Lands Tr.) 14. See, too, *Domestic Hire Co. Ltd v. Basildon Development Corporation* (1969) 21 P. & C.R. 299; *Collins v. Basildon Development Corporation* (1969) 21 P. & C.R. 318.

nal rejected this comparison. Their view, on the evidence, was that dereliction as well as bad layout was the cause of the original designation of Govan for comprehensive development and selected clearance would probably have occurred in the area notwithstanding the change of emphasis towards rehabilitation of property in the housing legislation in the intervening years. There was evidence of closing and demolition orders being issued in respect of property all around the relevant land both before and after the designation of the area for comprehensive development. As the claimants' property was below the tolerable standard, action by the local housing authority would have been likely and discretionary improvement grants would probably not have been available in the circumstances. "Our general conclusion," said the tribunal, "is that background conditions in Govan coupled with the ordinary operation of housing legislation would probably have deterred private investors from purchasing the reference subjects, either for the purpose of improvement or in the hope of obtaining vacant possession of some of the houses for resale." This view of the "no scheme" world enabled the tribunal to determine that the local authority's scheme had done little to detract from the market value of the tenement properties in question to the private investor purchaser. There had, in other words, been no depreciation due to the scheme.

In *Hugh MacDonald's Representatives v. Sutherland District Council*,[52] on the other hand, the Lands Tribunal for Scotland concluded on the evidence of that case that in the "no scheme" world the subject property would have had potential for improvement with grant aid and arrived at a market value, based on comparisons with other cottages in the vicinity which had been sold, somewhat above that calculated by the acquiring authority.

9—17 In *Abbey Homesteads (Developments) Ltd v. Northamptonshire County Council*[53] the subject land was compulsorily acquired as a site for a school. It was subject to a restrictive covenant (a planning agreement) reserving the land for school purposes. Glidewell L.J., giving judgment for the Court of Appeal, said that the Lands Tribunal had been entitled to accept the claimants' hypothesis that in the "no scheme" world a situation would be reached in which a potential purchaser of the subject land would be entitled to say that there was a very good chance that the restrictive covenant would be discharged and that chance would be reflected in the purchase price. There would be an expectation in the no scheme world that, since the authority had either purchased an alternative site or had not purchased the subject land, they were no longer seeking to acquire the subject land for a school.

In *North-Eastern Housing Association Ltd v. Newcastle upon Tyne City Council*[54] what was in issue was an appreciation in value due to the scheme. The subject premises, a 70 year old inter-terrace dwelling extensively altered and extended for use as offices, was valued for compensation purposes by reference to the prices

---

[52] 1977 S.L.T. (Lands Tr.) 7.
[53] [1992] 26 E.G. 140.
[54] (1972) 25 P. & C.R. 178.

obtained on the sale of four comparable properties in the open market. The council argued that there had been an increase in the prices paid in those transactions due to the scarcity of office property created by the council's comprehensive development scheme. The tribunal agreed that no account should be taken of this increase since the acquisitions by the acquiring authority which had resulted in the scarcity of office property was a manifestation of the comprehensive development scheme in action.

In *MacDonald* the Lands Tribunal for Scotland found that there was both an appreciation and a depreciation in the value of the subject property to be disregarded. The tribunal found that the result of improvements already carried out in the area under the scheme was to put up the value which a willing seller would have been likely to have obtained for MacDonald's property in the open market by some £1,660. Similarly, the presence of houses on either side of MacDonald's which had been acquired under the scheme for redevelopment but which had been vandalised in the interim would have depressed the value of MacDonald's property in the open market by about £300.[55]

It may, of course, be the case at the end of the day that, as in *Mrs Fulton's Trustees*, the value of the land on a notional sale in the open market in the "no scheme" world will not be substantially different from its value having regard to the scheme.

Comment on the operation of the principle and its statutory expression

In *Wilson* Widgery L.J. commented that "the purpose of the so-called *Pointe Gourde* rule is to prevent the acquisition of the land being at a price which is inflated by the very project or scheme which gives rise to the acquisition."[56] This would seem also to underlie its statutory expression in section 6 of and Schedule 1 to the 1961 Act. In a memorandum presented by the then Minister of Housing and Local Government to the Cabinet in October 1957, when the Cabinet were considering the restoration of market value as the measure of compensation for compulsory acquisition, the Minister said: **9—18**

> "But we must pause and see what it would involve. Take the case of agricultural land which acquires building value through the provision, at public expense, of roads and sewers and water supply. If it is then agreed that the land is suitable for building, its

---

[55] This would seem to depart from the general rule that the risk of damage does not pass to the acquiring authority until the date of valuation (see Chap. 6). See J. Rowan-Robinson and E. Young, "Compulsory Acquisition, Compensation and Risk of Damage to Property" (1985) 30 J.L.S. 312; and R. Carnwath, "Vandalism and 'the Scheme'" [1974] R.V.R. 562.

[56] [1971] 1 W.L.R. 302 at p. 310.

value may be increased from (say) £50 an acre to as much as £1,000 an acre, or even more in areas where, as a result of planning restrictions, building land is in short supply. If that land is then needed for any public purpose, the public—whether as taxpayer or as ratepayer—in effect has to pay twice."[57]

As Cullingworth observes "unearned increment on the scale indicated was hard to defend, and had considerable political implications."[58]

However, as Davies argues "it is very doubtful whether the *Pointe Gourde* principle is either sound or just."[59] That it is not just may be illustrated by reference to the decision in *Wilson*. In applying the *Pointe Gourde* principle, the tribunal, with the subsequent approval of the Court of Appeal, made their valuation by taking note of some comparable land next door to the subject land which had been sold not long before for £6,700 an acre. It had been sold by a private owner to a private developer at its dead-ripe value. That value was an enhanced value because the seller and the purchaser knew that the corporation would install sewage works and so forth of which the developers could take advantage. Making all allowances, and deducting the enhancement in value due to the scheme, the tribunal valued the comparable subject land at £4,615 per acre. It seems hardly just that the betterment should accrue (subject possibly to taxation) to the neighbouring landowner selling in the open market but not to the landowner whose land is being compulsorily acquired.

9—19   Similar criticism may be levelled at the statutory expression of the *Pointe Gourde* principle in section 6 of and Schedule 1 to the 1961 Act. In *Mrs Leckie's Trustees v. East Kilbride Development Corporation*, applying the corresponding Scottish legislation, for example, the increased profitability of the public house due to the development over the years of the new town which would have been reflected in the value of the premises on a sale in the open market was disregarded on the compulsory sale of the premises to the development corporation. And in *North-Eastern Housing Association Ltd* the solicitor for the claimants pointed out that they had had to purchase their office premises in the "real" open market as affected by the acquiring authority's incursions but were now liable to be expropriated at a hypothetical but lower price presumed to represent the value of the premises in a hypothetically unaffected market.[60]

The criticism that the rule is not sound follows from the way in which it can come into conflict with the basic measure of compensation: "the amount which

---

[57] Cited in J.B. Cullingworth, *Environmental Planning* (HMSO, 1980), Vol. 4, p. 180.

[58] *Ibid.* See, too, *Second Report of the Committee Dealing with the Law and Practice relating to the Acquisition and Valuation of Land for Public Purposes*, Cd. 9229 (1918), para. 32; and *Final Report of the Expert Committee on Compensation and Betterment*, Cmd. 6386 (1942), para. 188.

[59] Keith Davies, *Law of Compulsory Purchase and Compensation* (Butterworths, 4th ed.), p. 131.

[60] See, too, *Kaye v. Basingstoke Development Corporation* [1968] R.V.R. 744. Also T.J. Nardecchia, "The Valuation Aspects of Land Taken Under a Scheme—2" in *Compensation for Compulsory Purchase*, Journal of Planning and Environmental Law Occasional Paper (Sweet & Maxwell, 1975). It should be noted that the principle and its statutory expression may, in some cases, operate to the benefit of a claimant by requiring a decrease in value due to the scheme to be disregarded.

the land if sold in the open market by a willing seller might be expected to realise" (rule (2)). It is abundantly clear that in *Wilson, Mrs Leckie's Trustees* and *North-Eastern Housing Association Ltd.* the claimants did not receive in compensation what they could have expected on a sale of their property in the open market. There is no way in which the dispossessed owners could have gone out into the market and purchased with their compensation money a property roughly similar to that which had been acquired unless they were prepared to move to similar property in an area wholly unaffected by the scheme. Furthermore, the awards would appear to transgress the principle of equivalence which requires that claimants should be paid neither more nor less than their loss.[61] There would seem to be much to be said for Davies' comment that "in so far as the *Pointe Gourde* rule coincides with the willing seller rule . . . it is redundant. In so far as it conflicts with that rule it is mischievous."[62]

Depreciation due to the prospect of compulsory acquisition

In *Jelson Ltd v. Blaby District Council*,[63] which was referred to earlier in this chapter, **9—20** Lord Denning in the Court of Appeal concluded that the depreciation in the value of the strip of land caused by its earmarking in the development plan for a proposed public road, later abandoned, had to be disregarded in assessing compensation both as a result of the *Pointe Gourde* principle and because of section 9 of the Land Compensation Act 1961. Section 9 provides that:

> "No account shall be taken of any depreciation of the value of the relevant interest which is attributable to the fact that (whether by way of allocation or other particulars contained in the current development plan,[64] or by any other means[65]) an indication has been given that the relevant land is, or is likely, to be acquired by an authority possessing compulsory purchase powers."

Although there may be circumstances where the *Pointe Gourde* principle and section 9 overlap, the latter appears to be directed at a narrower and rather more specific cause of depreciation. The fact that land is to be compulsorily acquired

---

[61] *Horn v. Sunderland Corporation* [1941] 2 K.B. 26.
[62] Keith Davies, "The Pointe Gourde Rule", *The Conveyancer and Property Lawyer*, 1975, p. 414.
[63] [1977] 1 W.L.R. 1020.
[64] For the meaning of the "current development plan" see s.39 (1).
[65] For an example of depreciation in value attributable to an indication "by any other means" that land is likely to be acquired see *Abbey Homesteads (Developments) Ltd v. Northamptonshire County Council* [1992] 26 E.G. 140; *Thornton v. Wakefield Metropolitan District Council* [1991] 48 E.G. 138; and *London Borough of Hackney v. MacFarlane* (1970) 21 P. & C.R. 342. In *Abbey Homesteads* Glidewell L.J. said that an indication given "by any other means" must provide information which is available not merely to the landowner-vendor but also to a potential purchaser.

will have an adverse effect on its market value but, if the analogy with a sale by a willing seller in the open market is to be sustained, the blighting effect of the compulsory purchase must be ignored. This illustrates what Davies describes as "a paradox which lies at the heart of the law of compulsory purchase of land . . . to say that compulsory purchase compensation is to be assessed at 'market value' is to say that a state of affairs is to be visualised in terms of its direct opposite."[66] Any assessment of compensation based on the value which the land might be expected to realise if sold in the open market must necessarily disregard any depreciation in value due to the prospect of the compulsory acquisition of land. That would seem to be implicit in rule (2). Presumably for the avoidance of doubt, section 9 of the 1961 Act specifically requires such depreciation to be disregarded. Thus, for example, if a house is earmarked in a local authority plan for demolition to make way for a road improvement, the depressing effect on value resulting from the earmarking will be ignored in assessing compensation upon its eventual acquisition.

9—21   Section 9 would appear to extend not only to depreciation in the value of the land put to its existing use[67] but also to "depreciation" resulting from a failure to realise development value.[68] For example, in *Trocette Property Co. Ltd v. Greater London Council*[69] the claimants were lessees under a long lease of a disused cinema. The lease was due to expire in 1984. Planning permission for redevelopment of the site for a supermarket, shops and a bowling centre was granted in 1963. Before embarking on such a scheme, the lessees sought early renewal of the lease. Renewal seemed likely until the county council as highway authority produced a plan for a new road which would affect the cinema site at which point negotiations were broken off. To bring matters to a head, the lessees then applied for planning permission for the erection of a shop on the site. As anticipated, this was refused on the ground that the application was premature because of the road proposal and Trocette thereupon served a purchase notice which was accepted. Trocette's claim for compensation was based on the "marriage value" of the freehold and leasehold interests, *i.e.* there would have been little prospect of development unless both interests merged and the sum of the merged interests would be greater than the value of each continuing separately. The council argued that a prospective assignee would offer nothing for marriage value because the lessor had actually broken off negotiations. Trocette responded that the negotiations had been broken off as a result of an indication that the compulsory acquisition of their leasehold interest was likely and that under section 9 no account was to be taken of any depreciation in the value of their interest resulting from that

---

[66] Keith Davies, *Law of Compulsory Purchase and Compensation, supra,* p. 128.

[67] See by way of example *Sukmanski v. Edmonton Borough Council* (1961) 12 P. & C.R. 299. Also *Spence v. Lanarkshire County Council,* 1976 S.L.T. (Lands Tr.) 2 (depreciation held not to be attributable to such an indication).

[68] *Grampian Regional Council v. Secretary of State for Scotland,* [1983] 1 W.L.R. 1340.

[69] (1974) 28 P. & C.R. 408. But see *Davy v. London Borough of Hammersmith* (1975) 30 P. & C.R. 469.

indication. The majority of the Court of Appeal agreed that section 9 applied and marriage value was allowed. Megaw L.J. observed that the phrase "attributable to" in section 9 of the Act of 1961 is deliberately used to ensure greater scope for flexibility in its application than would have been achieved by other phrases such as "caused by."[70]

A similar view was taken in *Jelson Ltd* v. *Blaby District Council*.[71] As mentioned earlier, a purchase notice was served following a refusal of planning permission for development of a strip of land which had been reserved for a proposed road but which proposal was subsequently abandoned. The district council argued that the compensation should reflect the fact that the strip had no development potential. The claimants argued that had it not been for the public road proposal, permission for residential development of the strip could have been anticipated at the outset. The refusal of permission was due to an indication that the land was to be acquired by an authority possessing compulsory purchase powers and under section 9 of the 1961 Act no account should be taken of the resulting depreciation in value. The Court of Appeal, following the flexible construction of the words "attributable to" applied in *Trocette*, found for the claimants.

Both the Lands Tribunal and the Court of Appeal accepted in *Jelson* that the link between the scheme and the loss of value was sufficiently direct nothwithstanding that the road scheme had been abandoned some years before the deemed compulsory acquisition took effect. Nonetheless, it is at least arguable that it was stretching the elastic of section 9 of the 1961 Act overmuch to suggest that there was depreciation in value attributable to an indication that the land was to be compulsorily acquired. As Davies points out, the disputed strip was no longer "indicated" for compulsory acquisition. This was the very reason why the purchase notice was used.[72] The claimants' remedy lay in invoking the purchase notice procedure in connection with the initial reservation of the strip for the road scheme.

9—22

---

[70] *Ibid.* p. 417.
[71] 34 P. & C.R. 77.
[72] Keith Davies, *Law of Compulsory Purchase and Compensation, supra,* p. 132.

Chapter 10

Special Values

10—01   In Chapter 5 we stated that the courts initially measured compensation for compulsory purchase by the extent of the loss to the claimant. Since the Acquisition of Land (Assessment of Compensation) Act 1919, Parliament has provided that the extent of that loss is to be assessed by reference to the "amount which the land if sold in the open market by a willing seller might be expected to realise" together with disturbance and severance and other injurious affection, if appropriate. However, that measure is of no assistance where, as occasionally happens, land is devoted to a purpose for which there is no general demand or market. In these circumstances some alternative way of assessing the loss is required. This was recognised in the 1919 Act which provided for compensation in such cases to be calculated on the basis of the reasonable cost of equivalent reinstatement, a provision which has been repeated in the Land Compensation Act 1961.

There are also circumstances in which Parliament, for whatever reasons of policy, has decreed that compensation is to be measured by reference to some standard other than the market value of the land. For example, section 50 of the Planning (Listed Buildings and Conservation Areas) Act 1990 provides that where a direction for minimum compensation is made in connection with the compulsory acquisition of a listed building which has been deliberately allowed by the proprietor to fall into disrepair so as to justify its demolition, the compensation is to be assessed on the assumption that planning permission would not be granted for any development or redevelopment of the site of the building and that listed building consent would not be granted for any works for the demolition, alteration or extension of the building other than development or works necessary for restoring it to, and maintaining it in, a proper state of repair.

Such a direction is uncommon. Rather more common, however, is the compulsory acquisition of houses that are "unfit for human habitation" within the meaning of section 604 of the Housing Act 1985. The compensation provisions

166

in such cases used to operate broadly on the assumption that such buildings had no value; the maximum compensation payable, subject to certain supplements, was the value of the land as a cleared site. Although the cleared site value provisions do not apply to an order declaring a house to be unfit made since April 1, 1990, they still apply to orders made before that date and will be relevant in cases where the compensation remains to be settled.

This chapter examines these cases where a claimant's loss is measured by reference, not to the market value of land, but to equivalent reinstatement value or to the cleared site value.

Equivalent Reinstatement

The assessment of compensation for the value of land prior to 1919 was not based **10—02** on rigid rules but on what would best achieve restitution for a claimant. In some cases, the cost of equivalent reinstatement was considered a more appropriate measure than market value. For example, in *A and B Taxis Ltd v. Secretary of State for Air*[1] the claimants were garage proprietors operating from premises particularly well suited to their purposes. The premises were requisitioned by the Government for defence purposes. The claimants bought alternative premises which they equipped for use as a garage. On restoration to them of the original premises, they sold the substitute premises and claimed as compensation the difference between the sale price and the cost of fitting out the substitute premises. Banks L.J. in the Court of Appeal observed that "[i]t is well recognised that there are claims for compensation in which the principle of reinstatement affords the only proper basis of compensation".[2] In the Scottish case *Lanarkshire and Dumbartonshire Railway Co. v. Thomas Main*[3] the claimant had spent considerable sums of money on preparing garden ground for the growing of fruit trees. Before he could put the ground to use, part of it was compulsorily acquired for the construction of a railway. As other land contiguous to the remainder of the garden was available to the claimant, the arbiter awarded compensation on the basis of the cost of reinstatement on this contiguous land. The Court of Session confirmed this approach to the assessment of compensation in the circumstances of that case. In *McEwing and Sons Ltd v. The County Council of the County of Renfrew*, Lord President Clyde commented that the decision in *Main* was "indeed a typical case of a common practice under the 1845 Act of using reinstatement value, instead of market value, to fix the compensation."[4]

---

[1] [1922] 2 K.B. 328.
[2] *Ibid.*, p. 336.
[3] (1895) 22 R. 912. But see *Corporation of Edinburgh v. North British Railway*, unreported, but cited in H. Parrish, *Cripps on Compulsory Acquisition of Land* (Sweet & Maxwell, 11th ed.), para. 4–016.
[4] 1960 S.C. 53 at p. 63.

This method was used generally in cases where it was considered that the income derived, or probably to be derived, from the land would not constitute a fair basis for assessing the value to the owner.[5] The Scott Committee, in their report in 1918,[6] recognised that compensation based on the value which a willing seller would realise for property in the open market would not provide a just measure of compensation for property for which there was no general demand. Examples of such property are churches or chapels, schools, cemeteries, theatres, hospitals and clubs. The owner in such a case, says Cripps, "cannot be placed in as favourable a position as he was before the exercise of compulsory purchase powers, unless such a sum is assessed as will enable him to replace the premises or lands taken by premises or lands which would be to him of the same value."[7] The Scott Committee accordingly recommended that where property was used for a purpose for which there was no general demand, compensation should be assessed not on the fictional basis of a notional sale in the open market but on the factual basis of equivalent reinstatement.[8] This recommendation was given effect in the Acquisition of Land (Assessment of Compensation) Act 1919 and was re-enacted as rule (5) in section 5 of the Land Compensation Act 1961.

Rule (5) provides that:

"Where land is, and but for the compulsory acquisition would continue to be, devoted to a purpose of such a nature that there is no general demand or market for land for that purpose, the compensation may, if the Lands Tribunal is satisfied that reinstatement in some other place is bona fide intended, be assessed on the basis of the reasonable cost of equivalent reinstatement."

In *Sparks and Others (Trustees of East Hunslet Liberal Club) v. Leeds City Council*[9] the Lands Tribunal spelt out the essentials of a rule (5) claim:

"There are four essentials in rule (5) to be satisfied by the claimants, on whom is the burden of proof:
(i) that the subject land is devoted to the purpose, and but for the compulsory acquisition would continue to be so devoted;
(ii) that the purpose is one for which there is no general demand or market for the land;
(iii) the bona fide intention to reinstate on another site; and
(iv) these conditions being satisfied, that the tribunal's reasonable discretion should be exercised in their favour."

---

[5] *Compulsory Acquisition and Planning Restrictions*, Chartered Land Societies Committee, 1968, para. 21.
[6] *The Second Report of the Committee Dealing with the Law and Practice relating to the Acquisition and Valuation of Land for Public Purposes*, Cd. 9229 (1918).
[7] *Cripps on Compulsory Acquisition of Land, supra*, para. 4–047.
[8] Para. 12.
[9] (1977) 244 E.G. 56.

These four "essentials" are now considered in turn.[10]

1. DEVOTED TO A PURPOSE

A distinction is to be made between land which is "devoted to a purpose" and **10—03** land which is simply "used for a purpose." The former introduces a conception of intention.[11] Thus in *Trustees of the Central Methodist Church, Todmorden v. Todmorden Corporation*[12] rule (5) was held to be inapplicable where surplus church premises were leased to a local authority for use for their school meals service. The purpose was not one to which the premises had deliberately and voluntarily been put by the claimants.

However, in *Aston Charities Trust Ltd v. Stepney Corporation*,[13] rule (5) was applied notwithstanding that the charitable and religious work carried on by the claimants in the premises had been curtailed by war damage and most of the premises had been let for other purposes. A distinction was drawn between the *de facto* use of the premises at the date of the notice to treat and the intended purpose which had been temporarily disrupted.

The date of the notice to treat is the date at which it must be shown that premises are devoted to a purpose for which there is no general demand or market.[14] In *Zoar Independent Church Trustees v. Rochester Corporation*[15] church premises were vested in trustees for the purposes of worship by Protestant dissenters. In the early 1960s, the trustees, faced with a dwindling congregation, sought to raise money to move the centre of worship elsewhere by submitting a planning application for a change of use of the premises for community purposes. Permission was refused and in 1964 a purchase notice was served and accepted. In the meantime, because of lack of funds the premises remained as a centre of worship although there were no more than 12 and the pastor in the congregation. The structure fell into disrepair and in 1966 the roof fell in and the building ceased to function as a church. The Lands Tribunal concluded that there was no likelihood of the premises continuing to be devoted to the purpose of worship in view of the declining congregation. The Court of Appeal, however, held that at the date of the deemed notice to treat (*i.e.* the date on which the purchase notice was accepted) the premises were devoted to the purpose of worship and that because of lack of funds it appeared that they would continue to be devoted to that

---

[10] See, generally, on rule (5) W.A. Leach, "Equivalent Reinstatement" (1980) 253 E.G. 1331; (1980) 254 E.G. 107, 277 and 391.

[11] *Aston Charities Trust v. Stepney Corporation* [1952] 2 Q.B. 642.

[12] (1959) 11 P. & C.R. 32.

[13] (1952) 3 P. & C.R. 82 L.T.; [1952] 2 Q.B. 642 C.A.

[14] But note that compensation falls to be assessed by reference to the date when reinstatement of the premises first becomes reasonably practicable (*Birmingham Corporation v. West Midland's Baptist (Trust) Association (Inc.)* [1963] 3 W.L.R. 398 H.L.).

[15] [1974] 3 W.L.R. 417.

purpose indefinitely. "Devoted," said Buckley L.J. "does not signify that land must be committed to that use for any particular length of time, definite or indefinite." He went on to add that the probable duration of the continuance of use was a matter which might affect the tribunal's decision on whether to exercise its discretion to apply rule (5).

10—04   Not only must land be shown to be devoted to such a purpose at the appropriate date, but it must be shown that devotion to that purpose would have continued but for the compulsory acquisition. In *Zoar Independent Church Trustees* Russell L.J. observed "The requirement of continuity of devotion is not directed to perpetuity; I regard it as sufficiently complied with if it appears that at the time of the notice to treat it is then intended by the owners of the site to continue to devote it to the relevant purpose with no future time-limit." In *Trustees of the Nonentities Society v. Kidderminster Borough Council*[16] the necessary continuity was held to have been established notwithstanding an earlier threat by the trustees to terminate the purpose to which the premises were devoted, in that case a theatre, because of financial difficulties. The evidence showed that the threatened closure was intended as a shock tactic to generate support for the theatre and that there had been a clear intention to continue the use but for the acquisition.

2. No General Demand or Market

10—05   The second "essential" has given rise to some difficulty in practice. In *Harrison and Hetherington Ltd v. Cumbria County Council*,[17] for example, the subject of the claim was a livestock auction mart in Carlisle. Evidence was given to the effect that since 1957 there had been no more than 18 transactions in England and Wales relating to the 16 marts and that "a kind of equilibrium had been reached" in the supply of marts to meet the needs of the community. Lord Fraser of Tullybelton, giving judgment for the House of Lords, held that the word "land" where it appeared the second time in rule (5) referred to the land in general and not the subject land. Accordingly the first requirement of rule (5) was not satisfied merely by showing demand for the subject land. As Waller L.J. observed in *Wilkinson v. Middlesbrough Borough Council*,[18] "it is not sufficient that there should be demand for the land in question but that there must be a general demand, *i.e.* a demand not only for that land but for other land elsewhere for the same purpose." In *Harrison and Hetherington* the evidence showed that there was no market for land devoted to the purpose of a livestock mart; that was the inevitable inference from the very small number of transactions in land devoted to that purpose. There could not be a market, said Lord Fraser, unless both supply and demand existed.

---

[16] (1970) 22 P. & C.R. 224.
[17] (1985) 278 E.G. 457.
[18] (1982) 45 P. & C.R. 142. And see *Vaughan (Viscount) v. Cardiganshire Water Board* (1963) 185 E.G. 949.

There could, however, be a general demand[19] although there was no supply and the issue to be decided was whether a general demand existed for land devoted to that purpose. Although there was no evidence of a present general demand, the Lands Tribunal had considered that it was enough that a latent demand could be inferred in the event of a profitable mart being offered for sale. Lord Fraser rejected that argument on two grounds. First of all, rule (5) by using the word "is" requires a presently existing general demand. Secondly, there was no evidence of a general demand but only a special demand which would arise in particular circumstances. The first requirement of rule (5) was satisfied and, the other requirements being satisfied, compensation could be assessed on the basis of equivalent reinstatement if the tribunal, in their discretion, thought fit.

It is not entirely clear whether, as Leach argues,[20] the benefit of rule (5) is **10—06** related to the precise purpose of the evicted owner or whether, in considering the application of the rule, account is to be taken of any other purpose for which the land may be suitable. In *Trustees of the Manchester Homeopathic Clinic v. Manchester Corporation*[21] the Lands Tribunal found that, although the premises in question were purpose built for consultation and treatment in homeopathy, they could with no more than slight structural alterations equally be used as a clinic for general medical consultation and diagnosis. It was in respect of that wider purpose that the question of a general demand or market had to be considered. Leach, however, argues that the possibility of disposing of the premises as a general medical clinic was not relevant to the question whether the land was devoted to a purpose for which there was no general demand or market; rather it was a factor to be taken into account in the exercise of the tribunal's discretion on the application of rule (5). Similarly, in *Bathgate Football Club v. Burgh of Bathgate*[22] the club claimed compensation amounting to £3,650 being the reasonable cost of equivalent reinstatement following the compulsory purchase of their football ground. The arbiter rejected the claim and awarded £1,351 being the open market value of the ground under rule (2) of section 12 of the Scottish Act as a "sports ground." It was, he said, the general rather than the specific purpose for which the property is devoted which is relevant for the purpose of rule (5).

The fact that premises devoted to a particular purpose do not come onto the market in the ordinary way does not preclude the existence of a general demand or market for the land for that purpose. In *Wilkinson v. Middlesbrough Borough Council*[23] the Court of Appeal upheld the decision of the Lands Tribunal that the normal method of disposal of veterinary practices in an area by taking partners into the firm pointed to the existence of a market even though the practices were not bought or sold in the open market.

---

[19] The word "general" in rule (5) was held to qualify only "demand" and not "market."
[20] W.A. Leach, "Equivalent Reinstatement" (1980) 254 E.G. 107.
[21] (1970) 22 P. & C.R. 241.
[22] Decision by an Official Arbiter Ref. No. 6/1932.
[23] (1981) 45 P. & C.R. 1422.

3. BONA FIDE INTENTION TO REINSTATE

10—07 In *Zoar*, the Court of Appeal were called upon to consider whether there was a bona fide intention to reinstate as required by rule (5). After the roof of the existing building had fallen in and it had ceased to function as a church, one of the church trustees bought property and temporarily established a new church with similar purposes to Zoar. The congregation at the new church included one member from Zoar. The trustees of Zoar, as prospective purchasers of that property, were subsequently granted planning permission for a new church at that site. The Lands Tribunal concluded that there could be no bona fide intention to reinstate because the new premises had effectively attracted a different congregation. However, the Court of Appeal, Lawton L.J. dissenting, held that it was the purpose and not the congregation that had to be reinstated and the evidence showed a sufficient intention to reinstate the purpose which the former chapel served. Furthermore, the fact that the realisation of the intention to reinstate was dependent upon the receipt of compensation assessed under rule (5) did not, in Lord Russell's view, "deprive the intention of any necessary quality."[24]

A similar situation arose in *Trustees of the Nonentities Society v. Kidderminster Borough Council*[25] where a theatre was acquired for highway purposes. Although there was an intention to reinstate the purpose elsewhere, the intention was to be implemented by a new trust. The acquiring authority argued that, in the circumstances, the present trustees could not be said to have an intention to reinstate. The Lands Tribunal held that as the new theatre was designed to fulfil the purpose of the old there was a sufficient intention to reinstate. It was the purpose, not the trust, which had to be reinstated.

10—08 In *Edgehill Light Railway Co. v. Secretary of State for War*,[26] however, the Lands Tribunal were not satisfied that reinstatement was bona fide intended, the only indication to that effect being a resolution passed by the company on the advice of counsel in pursuing their rule (5) claim. By contrast, in *Trustees of the Nonentities Society*, a threat by the trust to close the theatre was regarded in the light of the evidence as simply a shock tactic designed to generate financial support for the theatre and did not of itself show an intention not to reinstate.

---

[24] See, too, *Sparks and Others (Trustees of East Hunslet Liberal Club) v. Leeds City Council* (1977) 244 E.G. 56; and *Trustees of the Nonentities Society v. Kidderminster Borough Council* (1970) 22 P. & C.R. 224. But see *Festiniog Railway Co. v. Central Electricity Generating Board* (1962) 13 P. & C.R. 248, *per* Harman L.J. The Royal Institution of Chartered Surveyors recommended that it be made clear by legislation that reinstatement can be bona fide intended although it is conditional upon an award under rule (5) (*Compensation for Compulsory Acquisition*, 1989, para. 2.74). They also suggested that the Lands Tribunal should be given power to direct that the whole or part of the sum awarded should be retained and paid as and when reinstatement takes place (para. 2.67).

[25] (1970) 22 P. & C.R. 224.

[26] (1956) 6 P. & C.R. 211.

4. THE TRIBUNAL'S DISCRETION

Even where a claimant satisfies the first three "essentials" for a rule (5) claim, an **10—09** award is at the discretion of the tribunal. Rule (5) states that compensation *may* be assessed on the basis of the reasonable cost of equivalent reinstatement.[27] In *Festiniog Railway Co. v. Central Electricity Generating Board*.[28] Harman L.J. observed that "reinstatement is usually resorted to in cases where the displaced undertaking was some non-productive enterprise such as a church or a hospital which was not intended to make a profit but to perform some public service to the community which could not equally well be performed in another situation." He went on to say that "There are, however, cases in the books which show that reinstatement may be applied to a commercial concern." In *Festiniog*, the tribunal declined to exercise its discretion to award rule (5) compensation in respect of the compulsory purchase of part of a light railway line, notwithstanding that the claim satisfied the other requirements of rule (5). Equivalent reinstatement would have involved a diversion of the line costing £180,000. The tribunal concluded that this would have imposed a heavy burden of compensation upon the acquiring authority, particularly bearing in mind that the claimants were conducting what was essentially a business venture and the cost of reinstatement would far exceed the total value of the assets of the railway company. The decision was upheld by the Court of Appeal, Ormerod L.J. observing that "if the undertaking in question is a business undertaking, then the question of the relation between the cost of reinstatement and the value of the undertaking is relevant and may be paramount in considering the question of reasonableness."

In *Sparks and Others (Trustees of East Hunslet Liberal Club) v. Leeds City Council*,[29] on the other hand, the tribunal exercised its discretion in favour of the claimant and awarded rule (5) compensation of £97,832; compensation assessed under rules (2) and (6) would have amounted to £9,000. The social purpose of the club was contrasted with the commercial venture carried on in the *Festiniog* case.

The decision in *Festiniog* raises the question whether the measure of compensation in such cases can truly be said to reflect equivalence. How, as the Scott Committee acknowledged in 1918,[30] can rule (2) provide a satisfactory measure in a case where it is acknowledged that the land is devoted to a purpose for which there is no general demand or market? It is difficult to see that the purpose of compensation in such cases can be said to be the placing of the claimant in as favourable a position as he was in before the exercise of compulsory purchase

---

[27] But see the Land Compensation Act 1973, s.45 which entitles a person with an interest in a dwelling which has been specially adapted for a disabled person to elect to have compensation assessed on the basis of equivalent reinstatement.

[28] (1962) 13 P. & C.R. 248.

[29] (1977) 244 E.G. 56.

[30] Cd. 9229, para. 12.

powers. This would seem to have been acknowledged by Lord Pearson in *Festiniog*. The governing consideration, he said, "for deciding to apply or not to apply the reinstatement basis of assessment must be to consider whether it would produce a measure of compensation which would be just as between the claimant and the authority." That is a different measure from equivalence.

5. EQUIVALENT REINSTATEMENT

10—10   Where the four "essentials" referred to in *Sparks and Others (Trustees of East Hunslet Liberal Club)* are satisfied, compensation is to be assessed on the basis of the reasonable cost of equivalent reinstatement. Difficulties can arise in determining what is reasonable. As Davies observes "The replacement of monumental Victorian architecture by a modern functional construction often makes it difficult to decide on what is in truth 'equivalent' or comparable."[31] In similar vein, JUSTICE commented "One significant effect of the application of this rule is that owners could find themselves in possession of property more valuable than that which had been taken from them. This seems to be unavoidable, since to provide otherwise would make the rule either impossible or extremely difficult to apply."[32] However, as Leach points out,[33] what is being reinstated under rule (5) is the "purpose"; the question to be asked is what accommodation is required "to continue the purpose as effectively both in scale and manner as it would have been continued if it had not been disturbed by the acquisition . . . but allowing for any previous change in scale or manner attributable to pending acquisition." This would suggest that the replacement building need not necessarily be comparable in size and quality with the one which has been compulsorily acquired.

The point arose in *Trustees of Zetland Lodge of Freemasons v. The Tamar Bridge Joint Committee*.[34] The acquiring authority argued that the requirement of rule (5) in respect of a masonic hall would be satisfied by a new purpose built hall with an equivalent number of smaller rooms. This argument was rejected by the Lands Tribunal in the circumstances of the case but the tribunal commented that had the smaller rooms simply eliminated wasted height or passage space that would have been a factor for consideration.

In *Trustees of Old Dagenham Methodist Church v. Dagenham Borough Council*[35] the question in issue was whether the cost of enhanced facilities at the new premises, in this case car parking space, could properly form part of a rule (5) claim. The tribunal held that it could as the cost of reinstatement had been increased by a

---

[31] *Law of Compulsory Purchase and Compensation* (Butterworths, 4th ed.), p. 143.
[32] *Compensation for Compulsory Acquisition and Remedies for Planning Restrictions together with a Supplemental Report* (Stevens, 1973), para. 12.
[33] W.A. Leach, "Equivalent Reinstatement" (1980) 265 E.G. 277.
[34] (1961) 12 P. & C.R. 326.
[35] (1961) 179 E.G. 295.

requirement of the planning permission. Where, however, the cost of reinstatement is increased through choice by the claimant, that increase may not be reflected in the claim for compensation. It is well established that claimants must minimise, not maximise, their loss.[36]

Acquisition of unfit houses

1. INTRODUCTION

Special provision used to be made where the land being acquired comprised a **10—11** house which in the opinion of the acquiring authority was unfit for human habitation.[37] The compensation was not to exceed the value of the site of the house as a cleared site available for development. The provision has been repealed except in relation to an order declaring a house to be unfit made before 1 April 1990.[38] As claims for compensation linked to orders made before that date may, in some instances, still be alive, the provision is described in detail below.

The explanation for this provision lies in the slum clearance programmes of the late nineteenth century.[39] A royal commission set up in 1884 to look into worsening slum conditions concluded that the normal compensation arrangements for the acquisition of unfit houses put a premium on neglect. As a consequence, the Housing of the Working Classes Act 1890 provided that compensation for the acquisition of a house that was unfit and not reasonably capable of being made fit was to be assessed on the value of the land and any materials from the buildings.

Progress with slum clearance remained slow and Cullingworth states that by "1919 the Government had become satisfied that no solution to the slum problem could be achieved unless the cost of closing property was in some way reasonably commensurate with the value of the land."[40] The Housing, Town Planning, Etc. Act 1919 accordingly provided that compensation for an unfit house, whether reasonably capable of repair or not, was to be the value of the land as a cleared site and this continued as the basis of compensation in subsequent slum clearance legislation. Owners of slum dwellings were to receive no compensation beyond the value of the site, a provision which "no doubt owed a good deal in its origin to moral indignation at slum landlordism."[41]

Because of the hardship which this basis of compensation sometimes imposed **10—12**

---

[36] See, for example, *Service Welding Ltd v. Tyne and Wear County Council* (1979) 38 P. & C.R. 352.
[37] Defined in the Housing Act 1985, s.604.
[38] Local Government and Housing Act 1989, s.194(4) and Sched. 12.
[39] See. J.B. Cullingworth, *Environmental Planning*, (HMSO, 1980) Vol. 4, App. A.
[40] *Ibid*. p. 423.
[41] *Ibid*. p. 450.

on owners of slum property, provision was subsequently made for certain supplementary payments. The Housing Act 1935 introduced well-maintained payments "to encourage owners of substandard houses to maintain them for as long as they stood."[42] More problematic was the position of owner-occupiers of slum property who because of housing shortages had been compelled to buy substandard housing but had nonetheless paid a substantial sum reflecting the scarcity value of housing and who still had substantial mortgage commitments. For them, cleared site value could represent considerable hardship. The Slum Clearance (Compensation) Act 1956 addressed this problem by providing that an owner-occupier living in an unfit house purchased between the outbreak of the Second World War and the end of 1955 would on compulsory acquisition of the house at any time in the subsequent ten years receive in compensation the amount that would have been received had the house not been declared unfit. Subsequently, the government introduced a general provision in the Housing Act 1969 for the payment of a supplement to owner-occupiers who had owned their homes for two years equivalent to the amount by which the market value of the home exceeded the value derived under the existing statutory framework.

These concessions did not satisfy everyone. The Chartered Land Societies Committee in a memorandum to the Ministry of Housing and Local Government in 1968 recommended on the grounds of simplicity and equity that the cleared site value basis of compensation for unfit houses "should be abolished and that the normal rules governing the assessment of compensation should apply to such houses."[43] And the Royal Institution of Chartered Surveyors commented that "in spite of the steps that have been taken to mitigate the harshness of this rule, it still causes serious inequities and the Institution has for a long time considered that there is no longer justification for retaining this basis of compensation for unfit dwellings."[44] Furthermore, dissatisfaction with the level of compensation may give rise to more sustained opposition to the compulsory purchase.

The government acknowledged that site value compensation could give rise to anomalies and the provision was repealed by the Local Government and Housing Act 1989[45] except in relation to orders declaring houses to be unfit made before 1 April 1990.

What follows is a detailed explanation of this basis of compensation in so far as it is still relevant.

2. COMPENSATION NOT TO EXCEED CLEARED SITE VALUE

10—13 The provisions governing the assessment of compensation for the compulsory acquisition of unfit houses, in so far as they remain relevant, are to be found in

---

[42] *Ibid.* p. 425.
[43] *Compensation for Compulsory Acquisition and Planning Restrictions* (1968), para. 47.
[44] *Compensation for Compulsory Acquisition* (1989) para. 23. See, too, B. Denyer-Green, "Unfit Houses — The Injustice of Bare Site Value to Owner-Occupiers" N.L.J., January 8, 1981, p. 30.
[45] Section 194(4) and Sched. 12.

section 10 of and Schedule 2 to the Land Compensation Act 1961 as substituted by the Housing (Consequential Provisions) Act 1985. They apply to the compulsory acquisition of such a house under the following legislation:

(i) an acquisition under Part IX of the Town and Country Planning Act 1990 or sections 47–52 of the Planning (Listed Buildings and Conservation Areas) Act 1990;

(ii) an acquisition under section 6 of the Town Development Act 1952;

(iii) an acquisition pursuant to Part VI of the Town and Country Planning Act 1990 or sections 32–37 of the Planning (Listed Buildings and Conservation Areas) Act 1990;

(iv) an acquisition of land within the area designated by an order under section 1 of the New Towns Act 1981 as the site of a new town;

(v) an acquisition by a development corporation or a local highway authority or the Secretary of State under the New Towns Act 1981 or under any enactment as applied by any provision of that Act;

(vi) an acquisition by means of an order under section 141 of the Local Government, Planning and Land Act 1980 vesting land in an urban development corporation; and

(vii) an acquisition by such a corporation under section 142 of that Act.

(viii) an acquisition by the Land Authority for Wales under section 104 of the Local Government, Planning and Land Act 1980;

(ix) an acquisition of land by an acquiring authority under the new towns code within the meaning of the Development of Rural Wales Act 1976;

(x) an acquisition under the provisions of Part VIII of the Housing Act 1985 relating to general improvement areas.[46]

Broadly, Schedule 2 of the 1961 Act, as substituted, applies to such acquisitions the provisions relating to cleared site value, owner-occupier supplement and well-maintained payments which apply to the compulsory acquisition of unfit houses under Part XVII of the Housing Act 1985. Curiously, the provisions are not applied to the acquisition of unfit houses under the Highways Act 1980.

Where an order declaring that a house is unfit has been confirmed by the **10—14** Secretary of State either before or concurrently with the confirmation of the related compulsory purchase order,[47] the provisions of sections 585–592 and Schedules 23 and 24 apply. Section 585 provides that compensation shall not exceed the value, at the time when the valuation is made, of the site of the house

---

[46] Land Compensation Act 1961, Sched. 2 as substituted by the Housing (Consequential Provisions) Act 1985. See, too, the Planning (Consequential Provisions) Act 1990, s.4 and Sched. 2, para. 9.

[47] With blight notices, purchase notices and listed building purchase notices the order must be made before the date on which the notice to treat is deemed to have been served and is subsequently confirmed by the Secretary of State. With an order coming into force under s.141 of the Local Government, Planning and Land Act 1980, the order must be confirmed before or concurrently with that order (1961 Act, Sched. 2, para. 3(1)(b) as substituted by the Housing (Consequential Provisions) Act 1985.

as a cleared site[48] available for development in accordance with the requirements of the building regulations for the time being in force in the district.[49] In other words, the claimant receives the lesser of two bases of compensation, cleared site value or market value. Where, for example, because of scarcity, the market value of the house exceeds the value of the land as a cleared site, the latter is the basis of compensation. Where, on the other hand, the market value of the land encumbered with the building is less than the value of the land as a cleared site, the former is the measure. Two valuations of the subjects will therefore be required. However, provided the person entitled to the relevant interest was in occupation of the house on the date of the making of the compulsory purchase order and continues to be entitled to the relevant interest at the date of the service of the notice to treat, the amount of compensation is not in any event to be less than the gross value of the dwelling.[50]

Before submitting an order declaring a house to be unfit to the Secretary of State for confirmation,[51] the acquiring authority must serve notice on the owner, and any mortgagee stating the effect of the order and specifying the time within which, and the manner in which, objection may be made.[52] Before reaching a decision on the order, the Minister must consider any such objection and, if either the objector or the acquiring authority so request, must make provision for a hearing. It should be noted that there is no subsequent opportunity to object to site value compensation and this is sometimes a cause of considerable hardship in practice where an owner does not appreciate the compensation implications of such an order.

10—15 In calculating both the market value of the property in question and the cleared site value, the valuation must be made in the normal way under rule (2) having regard to any potential for improvement but ignoring any appreciation or depreciation in value due to the compulsory acquisition and to the scheme behind it.[53] For example, in the Scottish case *Spence v. Lanarkshire County Council*[54] a demolition order was placed on a dwelling, part of a tenement block, below the tolerable standard. Later, and quite separately, the whole tenement was compulsorily

---

[48] In *Hugh MacDonald's Representatives v. Sutherland District Council*, 1977 S.L.T. (Lands Tr.) 7 the Lands Tribunal for Scotland held that the words "as a cleared site" which appeared in earlier Scottish legislation required an assumption to be made that the site had already been cleared of buildings down to ground level and, accordingly, no further deduction was to be made for demolition.

[49] The site may, of course, be too small to permit rebuilding in accordance with the building regulations and may, therefore, have no more than a nominal value.

[50] Housing Act 1985, s.589(2). In calculating the amount of compensation for the purposes of s.589(2) of the Act account is to be taken of any payment made under Schedules 23 and 24 to the 1985 Act. The gross value of the dwelling is to be determined in accordance with the provisions of s.589(3)–(6) of the 1985 Act; and see the Local Government Finance Act 1988, s.119.

[51] The order is to be in such form as may be prescribed.

[52] 1961 Act, Sched. 2, para. 2 (2), as substituted by the Housing (Consequential Provisions) Act 1985.

[53] 1961 Act, s.6; *Pointe Gourde Quarrying and Transport Co. v. Sub-Intendent of Crown Lands* [1947] A.C. 556.

[54] 1976 S.L.T. (Lands Tr.) 2.

acquired by the local authority to make way for a car park. The value of the dwelling was depreciated as a result of its designation for demolition but as the demolition order was not made in pursuance of the scheme behind the acquisition, that depreciation was to be taken into account; in other words, a purchaser in the open market would have known that there was no prospect of the renovation of the property with an improvement grant. At the valuation date, the only value was in the site itself. The most likely use of the site in the circumstances would be for private housing. The site was valued on that basis taking account of the demolition costs and the liability for ground burdens and the resulting figure was divided between the proprietors of the tenement to arrive at the claimant's share.

In *Hugh MacDonald's Representatives v. Sutherland District Council*[55] the premises in question, one of a row of fishermen's houses in Golspie, were acquired compulsorily following the declaration of the row as a housing treatment area to be dealt with by way of demolition. The tribunal considered that in the absence of the scheme an improvement grant would probably have been available and, notwithstanding the cost, the premises would have had a value in the market to a person interested in the shell of the cottage for improvement of £700. The alternative valuation as a cleared site available for development, assuming under section 23(3) of the Scottish Act of 1963 that planning permission would be granted to rebuild a dwelling on the site, was £300. In view of the cleared site value ceiling, compensation was awarded at the lower figure.

In *Davy v. Leeds Corporation*[56] the claimants owned back-to-back houses in Leeds in an area zoned in the development plan for residential development. The corporation declared the area to be a clearance area and decided to acquire the houses compulsorily. There were 12 other clearance areas in the immediate neighbourhood. In valuing their land as sites cleared of buildings and available for development in an area zoned for residential development, the claimants argued that a willing purchaser would have regard to the fact that all the other buildings in the clearance areas would be cleared away and this would be reflected in the value of their land. The House of Lords concluded that in the absence of the corporation's scheme there was no prospect of clearance and that any increase in value as a result of the clearance by the corporation was to be ignored as an increase in value due to the scheme.

Special provision is made where a house is compulsorily acquired at restricted **10—16** value and on the date of the order the house is occupied in whole or in part as a private dwelling by a person who throughout the relevant period[57] holds an interest in the house which is subject to a mortgage or charge or is party to an agree-

---

[55] 1977 S.L.T. (Lands Tr.) 7.
[56] [1965] 1 W.L.R. 445 H.L.
[57] This is the period from the date of the making of the compulsory purchase order to the date of the notice to treat or deemed notice to treat (or if the purchase is effected without service of a notice to treat, the date of completion of that purchase) or, if earlier, to the date of the death of the person (1985 Act, s.592(5)).

ment to purchase the house by instalments. Any party to the mortgage, charge or agreement may apply to the county court which, after giving other parties an opportunity to be heard, may make an order discharging or modifying, any outstanding liabilities of the occupier arising from the mortgage, charge or agreement.[58] The order may be subject to terms and conditions including conditions with respect to the payment of money. In determining what order, if any, to make the court is to have regard in particular, in the case of a mortgage or charge, to whether the mortgagee or person having the benefit of the charge acted reasonably in advancing the principal sum on the terms of the mortgage or charge.[59] He will be deemed to have acted unreasonably if, at the time when the mortgage or charge was created, he knew or ought to have known that the terms of the mortgage or charge did not afford sufficient security for the principal sum advanced. Regard will also be had, where the mortgage or charge secures a sum representing all or part of the purchase price for the interest, to whether the purchase price was excessive.[60]

In the case of an agreement to purchase by instalments the court will have regard in particular to how far the amount or aggregate amount already paid by way of principal together with so much, if any, of the compensation in respect of the compulsory purchase as falls to be paid to the seller represents an adequate price for the purchase.[61]

3. OWNER-OCCUPIER SUPPLEMENT

10—17   Section 587 and Schedule 24 of the Housing Act 1985[62] provides that where a house has been compulsorily acquired at site value in the circumstances described at paragraph 10–13 above, then, subject to the following pre-condition being satisfied, the acquiring authority will make a supplementary payment to the claimant equal to the difference between the full compulsory purchase value and the site value. The full compulsory purchase value of the interest being acquired must, of course, be greater than the site value for any supplement to be paid. Any question as to such value is to be determined by the Lands Tribunal.

The "full compulsory purchase value" in relation to an interest in a house means the compensation which would be payable in respect of the compulsory purchase of that interest if the house was not being dealt with as unfit.[63] "Site

---

[58] 1985 Act, s.591(2).
[59] 1985 Act, s.592(2).
[60] 1985 Act, s.592(4).
[61] 1985 Act, s.592(5).
[62] As applied by the Land Compensation Act 1961, Sched. 2 as substituted by the Housing (Consequential Provisions) Act 1985.
[63] 1985 Act, Sched. 24, para. 4(2)(a).

value" refers to compensation not exceeding the value of the site as a cleared site available for development.[64]

The pre-condition to be satisfied is that on the relevant date and throughout the qualifying period the house must have been occupied as a private dwelling, and the person so occupying the house (or, if during that period it was so occupied by two or more persons in succession, each of those persons) must have been a person entitled to an interest[65] in that house or a member of the family[66] of a person so entitled.

The "relevant date" is the date on which the order was made declaring the house to be unfit.[67]

The "qualifying period" means the period of two years ending with the   **10—18**
relevant date.[68]

Where an interest was acquired by a person on or after August 1, 1968 but less than two years before the relevant date as defined above and a supplementary payment would have been made had the qualifying period been a period beginning with the acquisition and ending with the relevant date, the authority concerned will nonetheless make such a payment provided the following conditions are satisfied. The authority must be satisfied that the first owner, before acquiring the interest, made all reasonable inquiries to ascertain whether the event by reference to which the "relevant date" is defined (above) was likely to occur within two years of the acquisition and had no reason to believe that it was likely; and the person entitled to the interest at the date when the house is purchased must be the first owner or a member of that person's family.[69]

Determining whether the pre-condition referred to above has been satisfied has given rise to considerable difficulty. Questions of entitlement have been referred in practice to the Lands Tribunal both in England and Wales and in Scotland to determine although it is not altogether clear that such matters are within their jurisdiction. In *Hugh MacDonald's Representatives v. Sutherland District Council*[70] the Lands Tribunal for Scotland was prepared to adopt a pragmatic approach: "A reference to the tribunal in a compulsory purchase case requires us to determine the total compensation due, and it would be cumbersome if the question of entitlement had to be referred to another forum."

The interpretation of "continuity of occupation" during the qualifying   **10—19**
period has proved to be the most troublesome aspect of the pre-condition. Where there has been a break in continuity during the course of a single

---

[64] 1985 Act, Sched. 24, para. 4(2)(b).
[65] "Interest" does not include the interest of a tenant for a year or any less period or of a statutory tenant (1985 Act, Sched. 24, para. 5(i)).
[66] Defined in the 1985 Act, Sched. 24, para. 6.
[67] Land Compensation Act 1961, Sched. 2, para. 4(e) substituted by the Housing (Consequential Provisions) Act 1985.
[68] 1985 Act, Sched. 24, para. 2(1)(a). See, also, para. 3.
[69] 1985 Act, Sched. 24, para. 2(2). For the definition of "family" see Schedule 24, para. 6.
[70] 1977 S.L.T. (Lands Tr.) 7.

occupation, tribunals appear to have been slow to disqualify a claimant. Thus in *Manzur Hussain v. Tameside Metropolitan Borough Council*[71] the qualifying period ran from July 5, 1976, to July 4, 1978. The claimant was in occupation at the beginning of the qualifying period and until he went to Pakistan in August 1977 because his mother was ill. During his absence, his wife moved temporarily to another house and he therefore arranged for a couple to live in as caretakers. On his return to England in December 1977, there was some delay in securing alternative accommodation for the caretakers but he and his wife resumed occupation of the house in February 1978 and remained there until the end of the qualifying period. The tribunal concluded that occupation included occupation enjoyed vicariously through furniture and caretakers and constructively through control of the subject premises so that the claimant was entitled to the supplementary payment.

In *Begum Bibi v. Blackburn Borough Council*[72] the qualifying period ran from February 8, 1983 to February 7, 1985. In February 1984 the claimant took her children on holiday to Pakistan. During her absence the house was damaged by fire. Delay on the part of the insurers meant that repairs could not be effected for some time and on her return to England she lived first of all with friends and subsequently in a local authority house. She nonetheless kept her furniture in the damaged house, visited it regularly to keep an eye on it and intended to return there once necessary repairs had been carried out. She was still waiting for a settlement from the insurers at the end of the qualifying period. The tribunal held she was entitled to a supplementary payment. The fact that the house was damaged by fire did not alter the character of the occupation. The claimant continued in occupation through her furniture and her intention to return.[73]

The legislation expressly contemplates successive owner-occupation during the qualifying period. It is, however, unrealistic to expect that a purchaser will always take up residence on the day the vendor leaves so that there is no break in occupation. Nonetheless, in this respect tribunals appear to have interpreted "continuity of occupation" more strictly. Thus in *Reeve v. Hartlepool Borough Council*[74] claims for supplementary payments in respect of six houses were rejected. Each house had changed hands during the qualifying period and in each case there was a period of delay between the vendor leaving the house and the claimant taking up residential occupation ranging from five weeks to 10 months. In each case, void periods had been allowed by the rating authority. The fact that in three cases there was no gap between the date on which the vendor vacated the house and the claimant began to occupy

---

[71] [1982] J.P.L. 252. See, too, *Abdul Aziz* v. *Tameside Metropolitan Borough Council* [1982] J.P.L. 252.
[72] [1988] J.P.L. 418.
[73] *Cf., Westerman v. St Helens Metropolitan Borough Council* (1983) 46 P. & C.R. 236 where the owner was considered unlikely to return.
[74] (1975) 30 P. & C.R. 517.

it for the purposes of repair and improvement was not sufficient. It did not give the occupation the necessary residential quality.

A similar approach was adopted in *Laundon v. Hartlepool Borough Council*.[75] In **10—20** that case there was a break of one month between the vendor vacating the house and the purchaser taking up residence. The purchaser had nonetheless bought furniture from the vendor which remained after the latter had moved out and during the break of one month the purchaser was engaged in decorating the house. The Court of Appeal declined to accept that the mere presence of furniture in the house constituted occupation of the house as a private dwelling. The court went on to indicate, however, that where the gap between successive residential occupiers was of the order of no more than a week or 10 days, the *de minimis* rule would apply. Such a gap would be too insignificant to destroy the quality of occupation as a private dwelling.

A rather more sympathetic view was taken by the Lands Tribunal for Scotland in *Hugh MacDonald's Representatives v. Sutherland District Council*[76] The house in question was occupied originally during the qualifying period by the claimant's brother who was ill. The claimant, herself, stayed at the house every two or three months during her brother's illness. Her sister, who lived nearby, called to see him nearly every day and the sister's husband, who worked together with the brother on the fishings, kept belongings at the house and continued to do so after the brother's death. The claimant kept her furniture in the house throughout the qualifying period even though for part of the period her main residence was a furnished let elsewhere. Following her brother's death, the claimant continued to keep her furniture in the house and to reside there from time to time until eventually moving in permanently.

The acquiring authority's contention, that in order to qualify for the supplementary payment the claimant or her sister should have moved in immediately following the brother's death, was rejected by the tribunal. The tribunal concluded that it was not directed by the legislation to consider whether the relevant occupation was by a qualifying person as her sole or main residence. There was sufficient evidence to establish that during the qualifying period the house was occupied as a private dwelling in the general sense required by the legislation. The supplementary payment was designed to offset the restricted compensation. "As such it should be liberally construed in the spirit of the statute so as to enable displaced householders to receive the full market value of their houses which is the normal measure of compensation."

It is not essential that the owner-occupier should occupy the whole house provided the rest of the house is, nonetheless, occupied for residential purposes, for example, by a tenant.[77] Neither is it necessary to show that all the normal

---

[75] [1978] 2 All E.R. 307 C.A.
[76] 1977 S.L.T. (Lands Tr.) 7.
[77] *Hunter v. Manchester City Council* (1975) 30 P. & C.R. 58.

incidents of residential occupation are carried on in order to establish the residential quality of the occupation.[78]

4. WELL-MAINTAINED PAYMENTS

10—21 Section 586 of the Housing Act 1985, as applied by Schedule 2 of the Land Compensation Act 1961,[79] provides that, where an acquiring authority are satisfied that a house which is being acquired and which is unfit has been well-maintained, they shall make a payment in respect of the house calculated in accordance with Schedule 23 of the 1985 Act. However, no such payment will be made where an owner-occupier's supplement is to be paid under section 587 and Schedule 24 of the 1985 Act (above).[80] Both payments together, when added to the compensation for the acquisition of the interest, would give a claimant more than he would have received if the house had not been unfit and thus more than his actual loss.

Where the house is occupied by the owner the well-maintained payment is made to him; otherwise it is paid to the person or persons liable to repair and maintain the house and if there is more than one such person it will be shared in such portions as the acquiring authority consider to be equitable in the circumstances.[81] Where, however, any other person satisfies the authority that the good maintenance of the house is attributable to a material extent to work carried out by him or at his expense, the payment may be made in whole or in part to him.

The acquiring authority will give notice whether or not they propose to make a well-maintained payment and such notice will accompany the notice of the making of the compulsory purchase order.[82] Any person aggrieved by a notice which states that no such payment is to be made, may within the period within which an objection may be made to the order concerned, refer the matter to the Secretary of State. The Secretary of State may arrange for an inspection of the house and, if he thinks it appropriate to do so, direct the authority to make such a payment.[83]

10—22 The amount of the well-maintained payment will be equal to the rateable value of the house multiplied by a multiplier prescribed from time to time by an order made by the Secretary of State.[84] The payment is not in any case to exceed the

---

[78] *Patel v. Leicester City Council* (1981) 259 E.G. 985 (meals not taken on the premises).
[79] As substituted by the Housing (Consequential Provisions) Act 1985.
[80] 1985 Act, s.588.
[81] 1985 Act, Sched. 23, para. 3(2).
[82] 1985 Act, Sched. 23, para. 7.
[83] 1985 Act, Sched. 23, para. 8.
[84] 1985 Act, Sched. 23, para. 4. As regards the calculation of the rateable value following the Local Government Finance Act 1988, see s.119 of that Act. The multiplier is at present 14 (Housing (Payments for Well Maintained Houses) Order 1982).

amount, if any, by which the full compulsory purchase value of the house[85] exceeds its value.[86] Any dispute as to value is to be determined, in default of agreement, by the Lands Tribunal.

---

[85] Defined in the 1985 Act, Sched. 23, para. 4(5).
[86] *Ibid.*

Chapter 11

Disturbance

The entitlement to disturbance compensation

11—01   Where an interest in land is compulsorily acquired the person dispossessed may incur losses as a consequence of the acquisition in addition to the value of the land itself. He may incur fees and other costs in finding and taking alternative accommodation, removal expenses, costs in adapting the new premises so that they are suitable for use, loss of goodwill, and so on, all as a direct result of the acquisition. These items, generally referred to as "disturbance", may form a substantial part of a dispossessed person's loss, in some cases more than the value of the land itself. If the person is to receive the financial equivalent of his loss he must be compensated for disturbance.

A claimant must, as mentioned in an earlier chapter, be able to point to statutory authority to support his claim (see Chapter 5). The only specific statutory reference to compensation for disturbance is to be found in rule (6) of section 5 of the 1961 Act. This provides: "The provisions of rule (2) shall not affect the assessment of compensation for disturbance or any other matter not directly based on the value of land."

Rule (6) is not, however, an authority for the payment of compensation. In *Horn v. Sunderland Corporation*[1] Greene M.R. observed 'Now rule (6) does not confer a right to claim compensation for disturbance. It merely leaves unaffected the right which the owner would before the Act of 1919 have had in a proper case to claim that the compensation should be increased on the ground that he had been disturbed."[2] It is, therefore, necessary to refer back to the 1845 Act and

---

[1] [1941] 2 K.B. 26.
[2] pp. 33–34.

186

the interpretation placed upon it by the courts to find the authority for disturbance compensation.

In *Horn*, Scott L.J. stated that "the judicial eye which has discerned that right **11—02** in the Act must inevitably have found it in . . . the fair purchase price for the land taken."[3] In other words, as section 63[4] of the 1845 Act only recognised two components in a compensation claim, *i.e.* the value of the land to be purchased or taken and damage arising from injurious affection, disturbance must inevitably form part of the value of the land. "Such compensation," says Cripps,[5] "may flow from an application of the principle that the basis on which compensation for lands taken is the value of the lands to the owner." Authority for this is to be found in *Commissioners of Inland Revenue v. Glasgow and South-Western Railway Co.*[6] In that case the question at issue was whether a jury's separate award under section 48 of the Scottish Act of 1845 of £9,500 for loss of business following the compulsory acquisition of business premises was to be regarded as part of the "consideration for the sale" of those premises for the purposes of charging *ad valorem* duty under the Stamp Act 1870. Lord Chancellor Halsbury explained the position in this way:

"The two things — and the only two things — which are within the ambit and contemplation of the statute are the value of the lands and such damage as may arise to other lands held therewith by reason of the particular land which is being taken from them . . . It is admitted therefore impliedly that the only thing which the jury had here to assess was the value of the land . . . In treating of that value, the value under the circumstances to the person who is compelled to sell (because the statute compels him to do so) may be naturally and properly and justly taken into account, and when such phrases as 'damages for loss of business,' or 'compensation for the goodwill' taken from the person, are used in a loose and general sense, they are not inaccurate for the purpose of giving verbal expression to what everybody understands as a matter of business, but in strictness the thing which is to be ascertained is the price to be paid for the land — the land with all the potentialities of it, with all the actual use of it by the person who holds it, is to be considered by those who have to assess the compensation."[7]

In other words, the price to be paid for the land on a compulsory purchase is to include not only its market value but also any personal loss imposed on the owner by the forced sale, otherwise the claimant will not be fully compensated. This has been referred to as its "extended value."[8]

---

[3] [1941] 2 K.B. 26 at p. 43.
[4] Now reenacted by s.7 of the Compulsory Purchase Act 1965.
[5] H. Parrish, *Cripps on Compulsory Acquisition of Land* (Stevens and Sons Ltd, 11th ed.) para. 4–215.
[6] (1887) 14 R. (H.L.) 33.
[7] pp. 33 and 34. See, too, *Birmingham City Corporation v. West Midland Baptist (Trust) Association Inc.* [1970] A.C. 874 *per* Lord Reid at p. 893; and *Palatine Graphic Arts Co. Ltd v. Liverpool City Council* [1986] Q.B. 335, *per* Glidewell L.J. at p. 341. See, also, *Jubb v. Hull Dock Co.* (1845) 9 Q.B. 443.
[8] *Hughes v. Doncaster Metropolitan Borough Council*, [1990] 1 EGLR 40.

11—03   Recent endorsement of the view that a disturbance claim forms part of the value of the land to the seller is to be found in the decision of the House of Lords in *Hughes v. Doncaster Metropolitan Borough Council*[9]. Lord Bridge of Harwich, giving judgment for the Court, said "[i]t is well-settled law that whatever compensation is payable to an owner on compulsory aquisition of his land in respect of disturbance is an element in assessing the value of the land to him, not a distinct and independent head of compensation:

In that case the site in question was used by the claimants as merchants dealing in scrap metal and rags. No planning permission had ever been obtained for the use. The site was compulsorily aquired by the local authority. In assessing compensation the authority argued that rule (4) of the 1961 Act applied to eliminate any value attributable to such use as the use was "contrary to law".[10] The claimants argued that rule (4) applied only to the market value of the land acquired and not to the assessment of compensation for disturbance. That being so, they were entitled to a sum in compensation for the loss of the goodwill of the scrap metal and rag merchant's business. Lord Bridge rejected the claimants' argument on this point.

> "[A]lthough compensation in respect of the market value of land acquired and compensation for disturbance must in practice be separately assessed, the courts have consistently adhered to the principle, both before and after the present rules were introduced by the Act of 1919, that the two elements are inseparable parts of a single whole in that together they make up "the value of the land" to the owner, which unless he retains other land depreciated by severance or injurious affection, was the only compensation which the 1845 code awarded him."

A similar conclusion was arrived at in the Scottish case of *McArdle v. Glasgow Corporation*.[11] A publican obtained planning permission to use a dwelling as an extension to his public house, subject to the condition that the permission was limited to the period expiring on December 31, 1967. He converted the dwelling into a lounge bar and it was used as such by him and after his death by his widow until 1965 when the whole premises were acquired compulsorily by the local authority. In a claim for compensation by the widow the authority conceded that by reason of sections 22(1) and 24(4) of the Scottish Act of 1963 it had to be assumed in assessing the value of the premises under rule (2) that permission for the change of use of the dwelling had been granted without limit of time (see Chapter 8), but they contended that that assumption did not fall to be made in assessing compensation for disturbance. The Court of Session, affirming the decision of the Lands Tribunal for Scotland, held that the assumption applied to the assessment of compensation for disturbance, as well as to the value of the

---

[9] *Ibid.*

[10] The acquiring authority were unsuccessful on this point. See para. 7–13.

[11] 1972 S.C.41. See, too, *Woolfson v. Srathclyde Regional Council*, 1978 S.C. (H.L.) 90, *per* Lord Keith at p. 96.

premises, as disturbance was an element in the total value of the "relevant interest." Lord President Clyde said "[t]he distinction which the acquiring authority seek to make between a disturbance claim and a claim for the value of the land is thus a false distinction. They are both elements in the value of the relevant interest within the meaning of that phrase in this series of Acts of Parliament."

Rule (6) in section 5 of the 1961 Act, therefore, lends support for the view that disturbance is to be treated as part of the value of the land to the owner. Rule (6) is intended to preserve the entitlement to disturbance in the face of rule (2). Rule (2) provides that compensation for the value of the land shall be assessed by reference to the amount which a notional willing seller, not the actual owner, might be expected to realise on a sale in the open market. That hypothesis leaves no grounds for assuming that a claim for disturbance is involved as part of the value of the land. It is, therefore, necessary to spell out in rule (6) that that hypothesis is not to be taken as affecting the entitlement to disturbance.

The Chartered Lands Societies Committee in a memorandum in 1968[12] **11—04** observed "it may be thought somewhat surprising that a right of such importance should still depend on decisions by judges whose 'judicial eye' (to use Lord Justice Scott's expression) 'discerned' such a right in a statute of 1845 which made no express reference to it." They went on to recommend that "the time has come to put the right to compensation for consequential loss on a firm independent statutory foundation." There is, however, a risk that a detailed statutory provision might unduly inhibit claims for consequential loss and this recommendation was not pursued by the Royal Institution of Chartered Surveyors in their recent paper reviewing the law on *Compensation for Compulsory Acquisition*.[13]

It should be noted that rule (6) in section 5 of the 1961 Act refers not only to disturbance but also to "any other matter not directly based on the value of the land." In *Lee (Judge) v. Minister of Transport*[14] Lord Denning considered that disturbance in the corresponding provision in the English legislation referred to the right to receive compensation for the personal loss sustained by reason of having to vacate the premises; other matters not directly based on the value of the land were held in that case to include professional fees incurred in the preparation of the claim for compensation.[15]

In *McLaren's Discretionary Trustee v. Secretary of State for Scotland*[16] the Lands Tribunal for Scotland declined to accept the argument that "any other matter" was confined to expenditure incurred in preparing a claim. Although there was a tendency now to refer to any claim under rule (6) not directly based on the value of land as a "disturbance claim," "disturbance" in its narrower sense referred to

---

[12] "Compensation for Compulsory Acquisition and Planning Restrictions," paras. 43 and 44.
[13] *Compensation for Compulsory Acquisition* (1989) para. 4.9 and 4.10.
[14] [1966] 1 Q.B. 111.
[15] See, too, *London County Council v. Tobin* [1959] 1 W.L.R. 354; and *Redfield Hardware Ltd v. Bristol Corporation* (1963) 15 P. & C.R. 47.
[16] 1987 S.L.T. (Lands Tr.) 25.

the disturbance of an occupier upon dispossession.[17] To give "any other matter" such a limited interpretation did not square with the reference in *Lanarkshire and Dumbartonshire Railway Co. v. Thomas Main*[18] to "full compensation for all loss."

The rule (6) claim must be consistent

11—05   As what is commonly referred to generically, and will for convenience be referred to hereafter, as a "rule (6) claim" or a "disturbance claim" goes to build up the global sum of purchase money or compensation, all heads of claim, whether under rules (2) or (6), must be interrelated and not duplicatory otherwise the claimant will receive more than the financial equivalent of his loss. Where, for example, land which is being compulsorily acquired has potential beyond its present use which can only be realised by disturbing the present use, the claimant is entitled, if he chooses, to compensation assessed on the potential value of the land but may not in those circumstances also claim disturbance compensation otherwise he will receive more than his real loss.[19] As Cripps points out, the land in such a case has two values to the claimant: (i) the existing use value and a right to compensation for disturbance; and (ii) the potential value. The claimant is entitled to whichever is the higher.

Thus in *Horn v. Sunderland Corporation*[20] the Court of Appeal held[21] that the claimant could not in Cripps' words[22] "claim that the land for the purposes of valuation be treated as building land and for purposes of disturbance as agricultural land, those claims being inconsistent with one another.'[23]

11—06   Similarly, in *Prestwick Hotels Ltd v. Glasgow Corporation*[24] the Court of Session held that the claimants were not entitled to relocation expenses where compensation had been awarded on the basis of the total extinguishment of the business. The claimants carried on the business of a licensed hotel in premises which they owned. The hotel was compulsorily acquired as part of a comprehensive development scheme. Although the claimants intended to carry on their business else-

---

[17] See, too, *Hull and Humber Investment Co. Ltd v. Hull Corporation* [1965] 2 Q.B. 145, *per* Pearson L.J. at p. 161.

[18] (1895) 22 R. 912 at p. 919.

[19] *Cripps on Compulsory Acquisition of Land*, paras. 4–217 and 4–228.

[20] [1941] 2 K.B. 26. See, too, *Mizen Bros. v. Mitcham U.D.C.*, Divisional Court, July 19, 1929, unreported, cited with approval in *Horn.*

[21] Goddard L.J. dissenting.

[22] Para 4–217.

[23] For criticism of the decision in *Horn* see B. Denyer-Green, *Compulsory Purchase and Compensation* (Estates Gazette Ltd, 2nd ed.) p. 176; and M. Horton & J. Trustram Eve, "Compensation and Valuation Malters" in *The Planning Balance in the 1990s* (Sweet & Maxwell, 1991), Journal of Planning and Environment Law Occasional Paper No. 18.

[24] 1975 S.C. 105.

where, the arbiter considered the circumstances were such that compensation should be awarded on the basis that the business, including the entire goodwill, was being extinguished. He proposed also to award compensation in respect of the costs to be incurred by the claimants in professional fees and personal outlays in searching for, locating and acquiring another hotel as a going concern. On appeal the court held that compensation awarded on the basis of the total extinguishment of the business would represent the full price for the premises and the business as a going concern, thus putting the claimants in a financial position equivalent to the position they would have been in if their land had not been taken. To give them an additional sum representing relocation costs would result in the total compensation being greater than the measure of the whole loss suffered. Relocation costs could only arise if there was something to relocate. In this case there had been a notional transfer of the entire business to the acquiring authority so there was nothing to relocate.

On the other hand, in *D. M. Hoey Ltd v. Glasgow Corporation*[25] where the question of consistency was raised, the Court of Session held that the claimants were entitled to disturbance compensation in addition to the agreed value of retail premises. The level of profits made by the claimants in the four years preceding compulsory acquisition had been unduly low. The value of the premises for business purposes was based on the anticipated level of profits which could be made. The authority argued that the compensation was based therefore on the potential value of the premises and that, on the strength of the decision in *Horn*, the owner was being inconsistent in claiming disturbance as well. This argument was rejected on the ground that the local authority were confusing the distinction between economic and uneconomic use with the distinction between existing use and potential use. In this case there was no question of a change in the existing use and the disturbance claim was allowed.

The limits of a disturbance claim

Subject to what is said below in connection with remoteness, a person who **11—07** receives and is entitled to receive a notice to treat may lodge a rule (6) claim in respect of all consequential loss. In the leading Scottish case on disturbance, *Venables v. Department of Agriculture for Scotland*.[26] Lord Justice-Clerk Alness referred to the claimant's right to "all consequential loss occasioned by his dispos-

---

[25] 1972 S.C. 200. And in *Palatine Graphic Arts Co. Ltd v. Liverpool City Council* (1986) 42 P. & C.R. 308 the Court of Appeal held that although compensation for compulsory acquisition was not to exceed the actual loss sustained, this did not mean that regional development grant payable on relocation had to be deducted from the disturbance claim.

[26] 1932 S.C. 573 at p. 591. See, too, *Lanarkshire and Dumbartonshire Railway Co. v. Thomas Main* (1895) 22 R. 912, *per* Lord Kinnear at p. 919.

session." Persons having no greater interest in land than as a tenant for a year or from year to year are not entitled to receive a notice to treat and have no entitlement to rule (6) compensation.[27] If, however, such a person is required to give up possession before the expiration of their term or interest, they are entitled to compensation for any loss or injury they may sustain.[28]

A disturbance claim is made once and for all in respect of all consequential loss both present and prospective as at the date of assessment.[29] Although the content of a disturbance claim will depend very much on the particular circumstances of each case, it may sometimes be possible to trace the consequences of dispossession through a seemingly endless series of events. In such cases the courts and tribunals have had to define the limits of a disturbance claim. The object of compensation, like damages, is to put the claimant, so far as money can do it, in the same position as he would have been in had the dispossession not occurred.[30] It is not surprising, therefore, that in defining these limits recourse has been had to concepts derived from the law relating to damages. Concepts such as causation, remoteness and mitigation have all been applied to disturbance claims to determine the limits of loss occasioned by dispossession.[31] The defining and refining of these limits are described in McGregor on *Damages*[32] as producing the most difficult problems in the whole field of damages. The same comment appears to apply equally to the application of these limits to the assessment of disturbance compensation.

11—08   Disentangling questions of causation from remoteness of loss and questions of remoteness from mitigation may not be easy. Causation is concerned with the question whether the acquisition of the land by the acquiring authority caused the claimant's loss. If this question is answered in the claimant's favour, it is then necessary to consider whether the law protects the claimant from the particular loss which has been suffered or whether it is too remote. As Lord Wright commented in *Liesbosch Dredger v. S.S. Edison*[33] "[t]he law cannot take account of everything that follows a wrongful act; it regards some subsequent matters as outside the scope of its selection, because 'it were infinite for the law to judge the cause of causes' or consequences of consequences." Finally, the question must be asked whether the claimant has taken all reasonable steps to mitigate the loss to him consequent upon the acquisition. There will, of course, be cases where

---

[27] *Newham London Borough Council v. Benjamin* [1968] 1 W.L.R. 694.

[28] Compulsory Purchase Act 1965, s.20. Where, however, the acquiring authority purchase the landlord's interest and simply allow the tenant's interest to expire following the service of a notice to quit, the tenant may be entitled to a disturbance payment under ss.37 and 38 of the Land Compensation Act 1973 (see Chap. 13).

[29] Agreement may sometimes be reached in practice to defer certain aspects of a claim for disturbance until the extent of loss is clearer.

[30] *Ricket v. Metropolitan Railway Co.* (1865) 34 L.J.Q.B. 257, *per* Erle C.J. at p. 261; *Palatine Graphic Arts Co. Ltd v. Liverpool City Council* [1986] Q.B. 335, *per* Glidewell L.J. at pp. 342 and 343.

[31] For a useful discussion of the application of these concepts to disturbance see P.H. Clarke, "Remoteness of Loss in Disturbance Compensation" [1977] J.P.L. 138; and E. Young, "Remoteness, Impecuniosity and Disturbance" [1981] J.P.L. 707.

[32] Harvey McGregor, *McGregor on Damages* (Sweet & Maxwell Ltd, 15th ed.), para. 103.

[33] [1933] A.C. 449 at p. 460.

these distinctions, particularly that between causation and remoteness, are more theoretical than real. Nonetheless, they provide a framework within which some of the decisions in this complex area may be considered.

1. CAUSATION

In *McGhee v. National Coal Board*[34] Lord Reid commented that the legal concept **11—09** of causation "is not based on logic or philosophy. It is based on the practical way in which the ordinary man's mind works in the everyday affairs of life."[35] Whether a loss may be said to be caused by an acquiring authority will depend on the particular circumstances of a case. The onus is upon the claimant to establish by evidence all the items of his disturbance claim.[36]

Consequential loss may take many different forms;[37] indeed, it is probable, as Davies remarks,[38] that the categories of disturbance are never closed. Nevertheless, grouping decisions in this field under a number of separate headings may help to give some indication of, to borrow Lord Reid's words, the practical way in which the test of causation has been applied in the everyday operation of the compensation code. The exercise may also give some idea of the possible scope of a disturbance claim.

(1) Increased operating costs: In *J. Bibby and Sons Ltd v. Merseyside County* **11—10** *Council*[38a] the Court of Appeal accepted that increased operating costs consequent on the removal to new premises could form the subject of a disturbance claim provided there was no alternative to incurring them and provided also that no benefit was derived by the claimant as a result of the extra operational costs which made it worthwhile to incur them. In that case the court refused to interfere with the finding of the Lands Tribunal that the claimants had failed to satisfy the second proviso. And in *Eastern v. Islington Corporation*[39] a claim for increased outgoings at the new premises in the form of increased rent and rates was disallowed on the same basis. As Cripps says, "loss therefore can only be the reasonable consequence of the taking of the land if the increased rent or other expenses of the new premises are unproductive to the claimant."[40] Duplicate operating costs incurred

---

[34] 1973 S.C. (H.L.) 37.

[35] *Ibid.* at p. 53.

[36] *Bede Distributors Ltd v. Newcastle upon Tyne Corporation* (1973) 26 P. & C.R. 298; *Campbell Douglas and Co. Ltd v. Hamilton District Council*, 1984 S.L.T. (Lands Tr.) 44.

[37] For a comprehensive discussion of the different forms of consequential loss see W.A. Leach, *Disturbance on Compulsory Purchase* (Estates Gazette Ltd, 3rd ed.) with supplement.

[38] K. Davies, *Law of Compulsory Purchase and Compensation* (Butterworths, 4th ed.) p. 202.

[38a] (1979) 251 E.G. 757.

[39] (1952) 3 P. & C.R. 145.

[40] *Cripps on Compulsory Acquisition of Land*, para. 4–232. And see *Rought (W.) Ltd v. West Suffolk County Council* [1955] 2 Q.B. 338; *Rutter v. Manchester Corporation* (1974) 28 P. & C.R. 443.

while a business is transferred from one set of premises to another would be recoverable in an appropriate case.[41]

(2) Fees and expenses: The expense of obtaining professional advice in preparing and negotiating the compensation claim is generally accepted as a direct consequence of dispossession;[42] so also are professional fees incurred in searching for and acquiring alternative accommodation.[43] However, in *Hull and Humber Investment Co. Ltd v. Hull Corporation*[44] the costs incurred in pursuing a successful appeal to the Secretary of State in connection with a certificate of appropriate alternative development were disallowed. Such costs were incurred not to ascertain the value of the land but to increase the value. This decision has now been overtaken by section 17(9A) of the 1961 Act (added by section 65(3) of the Planning and Compensation Act 1991) which provides that there shall be taken into account in assessing compensation any expenses reasonably incurred by the claimant in connection with the issue of a certificate. This includes expenses incurred in connection with an appeal under section 18 of the 1961 Act where any of the issues on the appeal are determined in the claimant's favour.

Claimants, themselves, are likely to devote considerable time to protecting their interests during the period of dispossession and it would seem that the cost of this time may be a proper item of claim.[45]

(3) Interest and charges: In *Service Welding Ltd v. Tyne and Wear County Council*[46] the Court of Appeal disallowed bank interest and charges on an overdraft for financing the capital progressively laid out in the preparation of the site to which the claimant was intending to remove and the building of a factory. The interest and charges were regarded as part of the price for the factory. The court considered that a person selling a factory on the open market would include interest charges incurred during construction as part of the cost. Bridge L.J. said:

> "What the authorities . . . very clearly establish, however, is that when an occupier, whether residential or business, does, in consequence of disturbance, rehouse himself in alternative accommodation, *prima facie* he is not entitled to recover by way of compensation for disturbance or otherwise, any part of the purchase price which he

---

[41] For example, see *Mogridge (W.J.) (Bristol 1937) Ltd v. Bristol Corporation* (1956) 8 P. & C.R. 78; *Sloan v. Edinburgh District Council* 1988 S.L.T. (Lands Tr.) 25.

[42] *London County Council v. Tobin* [1959] 1 W.L.R. 354.

[43] *Harvey v. Crawley Development Corporation* [1957] 1 Q.B. 485. In that case professional fees incurred in abortive negotiations over alternative accommodation were also allowed. And in *Smith v. Strathclyde Regional Council*, 1982 S.L.T. (Lands Tr.) 2 professional fees incurred in connection with an abortive scheme to preserve part of the subject premises were allowed.

[44] [1965] 2 Q.B. 145.

[45] See, for example, *D.B. Thomas and Son Ltd v. Greater London Council* (1982) 262 E.G. 991 and 1086; *Smith v. Birmingham Corporation* (1974) 29 P. & C.R. 265. See, also, the RICS paper, *Compensation for Compulsory Purchase* (1989), paras. 4.37–4.47.

[46] (1979) 251 E.G. 1291.

pays for the alternative accommodation to which he removes, whether that accommodation is better or worse than, or equivalent to, the property from which he is being evicted. The reason for that is that there is a presumption in law, albeit a rebuttable presumption, that the purchase price paid for the new premises is something for which the claimant has received value for money."

A similar view was taken by the Lands Tribunal with regard to a claim for bank **11—11** charges and interest on bridging finance in *D.B. Thomas and Son Ltd v. Greater London Council*.[47] In *Sloan v. Edinburgh District Council*,[48] on the other hand, compensation for additional interest and rates was awarded by the Lands Tribunal for Scotland. The claimants wished to buy another house and decided to sell their existing house. They were, however, unable to sell the existing house as it was discovered that the local authority were going to include it in a housing action area and that demolition was a possibility. They nonetheless proceeded to buy the alternative house on the assumption that the authority would buy the existing house. Negotiations with the authority over the existing house were protracted and the claimants were left in the position of incurring two sets of loan interest and rates over a prolonged period. Eventually, the claimants served a blight notice which was accepted and lodged a claim for the additional interest and rates paid over a period of two and a half years. The claim was referred to the Lands Tribunal for Scotland for determination. The tribunal concluded that the payments were entirely due to the authority's scheme of acquisition and should be compensated.[49]

(4) Adaptations: The cost of carrying out adaptations to new premises to make them suitable for use by the claimants has been allowed by the Lands Tribunal.[50] However, in the light of the comments by Bridge L.J. in *Service Welding Ltd, supra*, it would seem that where the adaptations are reflected in the value of the premises, the claimant will be presumed to have obtained value for money and the cost would not form part of the disturbance claim.[51]

(5) Removal costs: Losses incurred through the necessity of removing to alternative premises are a common item in a disturbance claim. These may include the

---

[47] (1982) 262 E.G. 991 and 1086. See, too, *Simpson v. Stoke-on-Trent City Council* (1982) 263 E.G. 673; and *Emslie and Simpson v. Aberdeen District Council*, [1994] 18 E.G. 136. Contrast *Roberts v. Greater London Council* (1949) 229 E.G. 975. And see, generally, *Service Welding Ltd, supra*.

[48] 1988 S.L.T. (Lands Tr.) 25.

[49] See, too, *Cole v. Southwark London Borough Council* (1979) 251 E.G. 477.

[50] *Powner and Powner v. Leeds Corporation* (1953) 4 P. & C.R. 167. See, too, *Tamplin's Brewery Ltd v. County Borough of Brighton* (1971) 22 P. & C.R. 746.

[51] See *Bresgall and Sons Ltd v. London Borough of Hackney* (1976) 32 P. & C.R. 442; and *Smith v. Birmingham Corporation* (1974) 29 P. & C.R. 265.

loss of trade fixtures to a tenant,[52] loss on the forced sale of equipment,[53] actual removal costs, adaptations to carpets, curtains and blinds,[54] re-installation of cooker and telephone,[55] notification of change of address, and depreciation of machinery caused by its unseating, removal and reseating.[56]

11—12   **(6) Loss of profits:** In *McEwing and Sons Ltd v. Renfrew County Council*[57] the claimants, a firm of builders, in addition to claiming for the market value of the subject land with the benefit of planning permission for residential development, claimed for the loss of future profits they would have enjoyed if they had been left to erect and sell houses on the subject land. The Court of Session rejected the claim on the ground that the profitability of the land was reflected in the compensation for the value of the land. As Lord Moulton aptly observed in *Pastoral Finance Association Ltd v. Minister (New South Wales)*[58] "no man would pay for land in addition to its market value the capitalised value of the savings and additional profits which he would hope to make by the use of it.[59] It would seem, therefore, as Cripps says,[60] that there is no right to claim for disturbance of land in relation to its potentiality. An owner can only be disturbed from an actuality.

However, it appears that, if a business is so disrupted by dispossession that it has to discontinue all or part of its operations for a period, a claim for temporary loss of anticipated profits may be competent.[61] To borrow Cripps' phraseology, the claimant in these circumstances may be said to be disturbed from an "actuality."

In *Emslie and Simpson v. Aberdeen District Council*[62] shop premises were acquired for a city centre redevelopment scheme. The tenants included in their claim an item of £54,446 for loss of profits in the year prior to vesting, resulting from the blighting effect of the impending acquisition. The acquiring authority resisted the claim on the ground that this was not a loss caused by the dispossession of the claimant. They were losses due to the blight caused by the underlying scheme over a period of years and would have been no different even if they had not

---

[52] *Evans v. Glasgow District Council*, 1978 S.L.T. (Lands Tr.) 5. The case concerned a disturbance payment under ss.34 and 35 of the Land Compensation (Scotland) Act 1973. However, the measure of the payment is essentially the same as for disturbance compensation (see Chap. 13).

[53] *Venables v. Department of Agriculture for Scotland*, 1932 S.C. 573; 1932 S.L.T. 411.

[54] See, for example, *Harvey v. Crawley Development Corporation* [1957] 1 Q.B. 485.

[55] *Bryce v. Motherwell District Council* [1980] R.V.R. 282.

[56] *Mogridge, W.J. (Bristol 1937) v. Bristol Corporation* (1956) 8 P. & C.R. 78.

[57] 1960 S.C. 53.

[58] [1914] A.C. 1083 at p. 1088.

[59] See, too, *Collins v. Feltham U.D.C.* [1937] 4 All E.R. 189; *George Wimpey and Co. Ltd v. Middlesex County Council* [1938] 3 All E.R. 781; *Watson v. Secretary of State for Air* [1954] 3 All E.R. 582.

[60] *Cripps on Compulsory Acquisition of Land*, para. 4–228.

[61] See, for example, *West Suffolk County Council v. W. Rought Ltd* [1957] A.C. 403; *Evans v. Glasgow District Council*, 1978 S.L.T. (Lands Tr.) 5; *Bede Distributors Ltd. v. Newcastle upon Tyne Corporation* (1973) 26 P. & C.R. 298; *Smith v. Birmingham Corporation* (1974) 29 P. & C.R. 265; *Bailey v. Derby Corporation* [1965] 1 W.L.R. 213. And see the comments of Lord Sorn in *McEwing and Sons Ltd, supra* at p. 67.

[62] [1994] 18 E.G. 136.

been displaced. Although it was accepted that compensation for disturbance may include reinbursement of expenditure incurred in anticipation of dispossession, that was not the same as compensating for losses caused by the overall blighting effect of a scheme of acquisition. The Court of Session accepted the acquiring authority's argument and rejected this item of claim.

(7) Loss of goodwill: Goodwill has been defined as "the possibility of the continu‑ **11—13** ance of a business connection."[63] This probability may depend on the personality and ability of the owner, upon the reputation of the business or upon the location of the premises in which the business is carried on. The value of the probability rests upon an objective assessment of the performance of the business and of its prospects.

Goodwill arising by virtue of the location of the premises, as for example with a public house where the goodwill may simply represent the habit of customers resorting to the premises, passes as part of the value of the land.[64] Apart from this, goodwill is a personal asset and does not pass to the acquiring authority with the land and remains with the trader. The loss or diminution in the value of the goodwill upon compulsory acquisition may be the subject of a rule (6) claim. The extent of loss or diminution will depend on the character of the business. In *Prestwick Hotels Ltd v. Glasgow Corporation*,[65] for example, the Court of Session accepted that the claimants, who carried on the business of licensed hoteliers, were unlikely to find other premises near enough to their present site to enable them to move any of their goodwill to the new premises. In the circumstances, the claimants were entitled to compensation for the total extinguishment of the goodwill. On the other hand in *London County Council v. Tobin*,[66] where an opti‑ cians business was relocated, it was accepted that there had been no more than a partial loss of goodwill.[67] It may be that a wholesale business taking orders from a wide area would suffer very little or no loss of goodwill on relocation.

(8) Pre-notice to treat expenses: An area which has given rise to some uncertainty **11—14** in the past has been the competence of a claim for consequential loss arising prior to the date of the notice to treat or the deemed notice to treat. In a line of cases[68] culminating in *M. Bloom (Kosher) v. Tower Hamlets London Borough Council*[69] the Lands Tribunal declined to allow costs incurred in anticipation of dispossession as

---

[63] *Cripps on Compulsory Acquisition of Land*, para. 4–234.
[64] But see *Park Automobile Co. Ltd v. City of Glasgow Corporation* (1975) 30 P. & C.R. 491, a case concerning a filling station.
[65] 1975 S.C. 105.
[66] [1959] 1 W.L.R. 354.
[67] And see *R. v. Scard* (1894) 10 T.L.R. 545; *Remnant v. London County Council* (1952) 3 P. & C.R. 185; and *John Line and Sons Ltd v. Newcastle upon Tyne Corporation* (1956) 6 P. & C.R. 466.
[68] *Webb v. Stockport Corporation* (1962) 13 P. & C.R. 339; *Widden v. Kensington and Chelsea Royal London Borough* [1970] R.V.R. 160; *Bostock, Chater and Son v. Chelmsford Borough Council* (1973) 26 P. & C.R. 321; and *Walter, Brett Park v. South Glamorgan County Council* (1976) 238 E.G. 733.
[69] (1978) 35 P. & C.R. 423.

part of the disturbance claim. In *Bloom* the claimant's factory was compulsorily acquired as part of a clearance scheme under the Housing Act 1967. Knowing of the forthcoming clearance area declaration and of the compulsory purchase order, the claimants sought and obtained alternative premises and moved into them before the date of the notice to treat. In doing so, they incurred professional fees, capital expenditure on alterations to machinery, losses on non-transferable plant and machinery and the cost of alterations to the new premises. The claim for these expenses was rejected by the tribunal. "As a matter of causation or remoteness or indeed as a matter of meaningful English language," said the tribunal member, "I cannot accept that a loss is consequent upon an acquisition if it is incurred before there is an acquisition."[70]

The question whether the cost of taking action in anticipation of dispossession might be recovered as part of the disturbance claim was answered in quite a different way by the Lands Tribunal for Scotland in *Smith v. Strathclyde Regional Council*.[71] The claimant in *Smith* was the owner of a public house in Hamilton. In 1971 the local authority wrote to say that part of the premises would need to be demolished for a road realignment scheme. Negotiations were opened to buy necessary land. The claimant initially took the view that the whole building would have to be demolished but the local authority suggested that part could be retained and adapted. Detailed discussions took place between the authority and the claimant's advisers about alternative schemes of adaptation. In the meantime, compulsory purchase orders were promoted and confirmed for the land and notice to treat was deemed to have been served in 1973. The discussions about the adaptation of the remainder of the building came to nothing and it was eventually demolished in 1976. The claimant included an item in his disturbance claim for the professional fees incurred prior to the date of the deemed notice to treat in the abortive negotiations over adapting the rump of the premises. This item was rejected by the acquiring authority on the basis of the decision in *Bloom*.

11—15 The tribunal declined to follow *Bloom*. Founding strongly on the principle of equivalence referred to by Lord Justice-Clerk Alness in *Venables Department of Agriculture for Scotland* and by Scott L.J. in *Horn v. Sunderland Corporation* the tribunal concluded that the consequences of dispossession had to be viewed in a causal rather than a strictly temporal sense and they upheld the claim.

The decision in *Smith* was subsequently approved by the Court of Session in *Aberdeen District Council v. Sim*[72] where solicitor's fees incurred by the claimants in acquiring alternative accommodation some five years prior to the date of the deemed notice to treat were allowed as part of the disturbance claim, and followed in England by the Court of Appeal in *Prasad v. Wolverhampton Borough Council*[73]

---

[70] The decision would seem to accord with the general position at common law where damages cannot be given on account of any loss before the cause of action arises (MacGregor on *Damages*, Chap. 9).

[71] 1982 S.L.T. (Lands Tr.) 2.

[72] [1982] R.V.R. 251; 1983 S.L.T. 250.

[73] [1983] Ch. 333.

where a disturbance payment was allowed in respect of loss incurred in moving out of a house prior to the date of the notice to treat.[74] Stephenson L.J., with whom Fox L.J. and Kerr L.J. agreed, cited the decision in *Smith* at some length because "it exactly expresses better than I can my opinion of the authorities and the principle to be drawn from them and applied to costs and loss incurred in obtaining alternative accommodation to that which is threatened with compulsory acquisition."

The decisions in *Smith*, *Sim*, and *Prasad*, nonetheless, place a claimant in an anomalous position in that expenses incurred at an early stage in a scheme of acquisition will not be recoverable unless a notice to treat or deemed notice to treat is subsequently served. They also raise difficult questions about how far back the consequences of dispossession may be traced, a matter which now falls to be determined in the light of the test of remoteness (below)[75] and about the extent to which a claimant may be expected to take steps prior to the notice to treat to mitigate loss (below). The decisions sacrifice certainty for principle but in the circumstances that would seem more equitable.[76]

2. REMOTENESS OF LOSS

Having established that an acquiring authority's action has caused a particular loss, **11—16** it is then necessary to consider whether the loss may be recovered as part of the disturbance claim. Some losses may be too remote and, therefore, beyond recovery.

The test for remoteness in disturbance cases which has been widely adopted[77] is that laid down by Romer L.J. in *Harvey v. Crawley Development Corporation*.[78] Influenced in particular by the decision in *Venables*, he stated:

> "any loss sustained by a dispossessed owner (at all events one who occupies his house) which flows from a compulsory acquisition may properly be regarded as the subject of compensation for disturbance, provided, first, that it is not too remote and,

---

[74] See, too, *Campbell Douglas and Co. Ltd v. Hamilton District Council*, 1984 S.L.T. (Lands Tr.) 44; *Park Automobile Co. Ltd v. Strathclyde Regional Council*, 1984 S.L.T. (Lands Tr.) 14; and *Sloan v. Edinburgh District Council*, 1988 S.L.T. (Lands Tr.) 25.

[75] See *Sim* and *Smith*, *supra*.

[76] For comment on the question of pre-notice to treat expenses see E. Young and J. Rowan-Robinson, "Disturbance Compensation: Flexibility and the Principle of Equivalence," 1984 J.R. 133; W.A. Leach, "Disturbance — the 'Prasad' case" (1983) 267 E.G. 669; B. Denyer-Green, "Disturbance before notice to treat," *Chartered Surveyor Weekly*, March 24, 1983, p. 661; the Royal Institution of Chartered Surveyors, *Compensation for Compulsory Acquisition* (1989) paras. 4.11–4.22; N. Macleod, "Compensation for Disturbance on Compulsory Acquisition" [1989] J.P.L. 891; and letters at (1981) 257 E.G. 663; (1983) 265 E.G. 744; and (1983) 266 E.G. 7.

[77] See, for example, *Sim* and *Smith*, *supra*.

[78] [1957] 1 Q.B. 485.

secondly, that it is the natural[79] and reasonable consequence of the dispossession of the owner."[80]

It is not altogether clear from this statement whether there are two separate tests or whether the two tests referred to by Romer L.J. are simply the opposite sides of the same coin. In *J. Bibby and Sons Ltd v. Merseyside County Council*,[81] Megaw L.J., after referring to the passage in Romer L.J.'s judgment, said "I do not find it necessary to pause here to consider whether there are, as the law has now developed, separate considerations relating to being 'too remote', on the one hand, and being not 'the natural and reasonable consequence,' on the other hand. It may be that those two have now merged."[82] The decisions in this field do not appear to show any clear separation between them.

The operation of the test of remoteness may be illustrated by reference to two different questions which have arisen in connection with disturbance. The first concerns the categories of claimant who may be disturbed; the second concerns the circumstances of the claimant and their effect on the disturbance claim.

11—17 **(1) Who may be disturbed:** A person who receives and is entitled to receive a notice to treat (see Chapter 4) may claim compensation for any consequential loss. However, it would seem that, until recently, such person had to be in occupation. This is no longer so.[83] This former requirement of occupation appears to have been derived from what the Lands Tribunal for Scotland in *McLaren's Discretionary Trustee v. Secretary of State for Scotland*[84] described as a narrow view of disturbance as the loss caused to an occupier on dispossession. There are dicta to support this view. In *Venables* Lord Justice-Clerk Alness referred to "compensation for all loss occasioned to him by reason of his dispossession;" in *McArdle* Lord President Clyde referred to "a right to compensation for his enforced removal and the disturbance which this entails to him;" and in *Woolfson v. Strathclyde Regional Council*[85] Lord Wheatley in the Second Division stated "compensation for disturbance is payable to the occupier of the premises."[86]

---

[79] In *Evans v. Glasgow District Council*, 1978 S.L.T. (Lands Tr.) 5 the Lands Tribunal for Scotland commented that "natural" in damages cases was interpreted as "according to the ordinary course of things" which may, said the tribunal, include reasonable human conduct (*S.S. Baron Vernon v. S.S. Meta Gamma*, 1928 S.C. (H.L.) 21; 1928 S.L.T. 117, *per* Lord Haldane L.C. at p. 118; *Steel v. Glasgow Iron and Steel Co.*, 1944 S.C. 273; 1945 S.L.T. 70, *per* Lord Justice-Clerk Cooper at p. 74).

[80] Page 494. Denning L.J. at p. 492 applied a somewhat different test of remoteness: "all damage directly consequent on the taking of the house under statutory powers."

[81] (1979) 39 P. & C.R. 53.

[82] *Ibid.* at p. 65.

[83] See the Planning and Compensation Act 1991, s.70 and Sched. 15, para. 2 which adds a new s.10A to the Land Compensation Act 1961 providing for compensation for the expenses of owners not in occupation.

[84] 1987 S.L.T. (Lands Tr.) 25.

[85] 1977 S.C. 84; 1977 S.L.T. 60.

[86] See, too, Romer L.J. in *Harvey* at p. 494; and Davies L.J. in *Lee (Judge) v. Minister of Transport* [1966] 1 Q.B. 111 at p. 122.

Thus in *Roberts v. Coventry Corporation*[87] an owner of land who was also the principal shareholder of the company which occupied the land was unable to claim for the depreciation in the value of her shares which she claimed was the consequence of the compulsory acquisition of the land.[88] "I am content," said Lord Goddard C.J., "to put my judgment on the short ground that the damage is far too remote for the appellant to be able to claim compensation in respect of it."[89]

The requirement that a claimant had to be in occupation resulted in an inability to recover losses which in the ordinary sense of the words could be said to be the natural and reasonable consequence of the compulsory acquisition. In particular, a landlord who was not in occupation could recover professional expenses incurred in preparing and negotiating his claim for the value of his interest in the land acquired (these being treated as other matters not directly based on the value of the land) but he was unable to recover the costs of reinvestment. In *Harvey* Denning L.J. said:

> "Supposing a man did not occupy a house himself but simply owned it as an investment. His compensation would be the value of the house. If he chose to put the money into stocks and shares, he could not claim the brokerage as compensation. That would be much too remote. It would not be the consequence of the compulsory acquisition but the result of his own choice in putting the money into stocks and shares instead of putting it on deposit at the bank. If he chose to buy another house as an investment, he would not get the solicitors' costs on the purchase. These costs would be the result of his own choice of investment and not the result of the compulsory acquisition."

It was, however, difficult to see what difference there was in principle between a person who invested his savings in a house from which he derived a regular income and who would as a result of the compulsory acquisition of the house, have to consider incurring the costs of investing in another house and a person who occupied a house who would have to consider incurring the costs of finding another house to occupy. As Mann stated,[90] it was hard to see why such costs were not recoverable "so long as the act of reinvestment is a natural and reasonable step for the investor to take and one which he would not have taken but for the acquisition." As long ago as 1918 the Scott Committee recommended that "where the claimant can prove that, acting reasonably, he is put to special expense for reinvestment, the cost of a single reinvestment should be allowed as an item

11—18

---

[87] [1947] 1 All E.R. 308.
[88] A somewhat similar argument was advanced, *inter alia*, before the House of Lords by the claimant in *Woolfson* (1978 S.C. (H.L.) 90; 1978 S.L.T. 59) with equal lack of success.
[89] [1947] 1 All E.R. 308 at p. 309.
[90] M. Mann, "Adequacy of the Law of Disturbance to meet Actual Losses" in *Compensation for Compulsory Purchase* (Sweet & Maxwell), Journal of Planning and Environment Law Occasional Paper, 1975; also N. Macleod, "Compensation for Disturbance on Compulsory Acquisition," [1989] J.P.L. 891.

of claim,"[91] a view which received endorsement from the Royal Institution of Chartered Surveyors.[92] The government accepted the inequity of the position and the Planning and Compensation Act 1991, s.70 and Sched. 15, para. 2 added a new section 10(A) to the 1961 Act. Section 10(A) provides that where the acquiring authority acquire an interest of a person who is not then in occupation of the land and that person incurs incidental charges or expenses in acquiring an interest in other land in the United Kingdom, the charges or expenses are to be taken into account in assessing that person's compensation as they would be taken into account if the person were in occupation of the land. The incidental charges or expenses incurred in acquiring the interest in other land must, however, be incurred within the period of one year beginning within the date of entry.

There was until 1973 a further difficulty over the question who may be disturbed. This was highlighted in the decision of the Lands Tribunal for Scotland in *Lander Equipment Co. v. Glasgow Corporation.*[93] The corporation compulsorily acquired premises which included a ground floor shop. The shop premises were owned by a husband and wife partnership under the name Lander Equipment Co. The occupier of the shop was a limited company, Bothwell Electric Supplies (Glasgow) Ltd., the entire share capital of which was held by the husband and wife. The husband and wife were compensated for the value of their interest in the shop as landlords but received nothing for disturbance as they were not legally in occupation, notwithstanding their plea that the company was merely their *alter ego*. Unfortunately, the company as occupier was also unable to claim disturbance as there was no lease between the company and the partnership so the company had no interest in the premises entitling it to receive a notice to treat. As the tribunal commented, "[i]n considering this part of the claim the Tribunal is dealing with a region of valuation in which the application of the law as it exists is not infrequently regarded as giving rise to unfortunate results."

11—19   The decision in *Lander* highlights a not uncommon situation in which a claimant does not occupy the property which is being acquired but nonetheless has such a commanding interest in the occupation of the property as to be the person who is really adversely affected by the disturbance. There have been instances where, in connection with a compensation claim, courts and tribunals have been prepared to "lift the corporate veil" of a limited company in order to expose the *alter ego* underneath.[94] However, the decision of the House of Lords in *Woolfson v. Strathclyde Regional Council*[95] suggests that the courts will be slow to deny the

---

[91] *Second Report of the Committee dealing with the Law and Practice relating to the Acquisition and Valuation of Land for Public Purposes,* (Cd. 9229, HMSO) para. 17.

[92] *Compensation for Compulsory Acquisition* (1989) para. 4.52.

[93] 1973 S.L.T. (Lands Tr.) 8. See, too, *Taylor v. Greater London Council* (1973) 25 P. & C.R. 451.

[94] *Smith, Stone and Knight Ltd v. Birmingham Corporation* [1939] 4 All E.R. 116; *D.H.N. Food Distributors Ltd v. London Borough of Tower Hamlets* [1976] 3 All E.R. 462; *Wharvesto Ltd v. Cheshire County Council* (1984) 270 E.G. 149.

[95] 1978 S.C. (H.L.) 90; 1978 S.L.T. 59.

legal effects of incorporation[96] and that it will only be appropriate to lift the corporate veil where special circumstances exist indicating that a company is a mere facade concealing the true facts.

In *Woolfson* a company, M. & L. Campbell Ltd, traded as a shop from five premises, three of which were owned by Mr Woolfson and two by Solfred Holdings Ltd. (a company all the shares in which were owned by Mr and Mrs Woolfson). Mr Woolfson owned 999 shares of the 1,000 issued shares in Campbell Ltd., the remaining share being owned by his wife. The premises were compulsorily acquired by Glasgow Corporation. As Campbell Ltd never occupied the premises under a formal lease it was, when displaced, a tenant at will with no entitlement to rule (6) compensation. Before the Lands Tribunal for Scotland it was argued that the business carried on in the premises was truly that of the claimants (Mr Woolfson and Solfred Holdings Ltd) which Campbell Ltd conducted impliedly as their agents.[97] The claimants were the true occupiers of the premises and entitled as such to disturbance compensation amounting to £95,469. The tribunal held, after considering the circumstances, that there were no special factors concerning the relationship between the claimants and the company which justified denying the legal effects of incorporation and the claim was rejected.[98] On appeal to the Court of Session, Mr Woolfson pursued a different line of argument to the effect that he, Campbell Ltd. and Solfred Holdings Ltd. should all be treated as a single entity embodied in himself,[99] thus entitling him to disturbance compensation. This argument, too, was rejected both by the Second Division[1] and on appeal to the House of Lords,[2] Lord Justice-Clerk Wheatley commenting that if someone decided "so to organise things to produce what he considered the best way of securing his own interests, then he must accept the consequences of that policy, however unfortunate for him that may be."

An occupier in the sort of situation described in *Lander* and *Woolfson* may, nonetheless, be entitled under section 20 of the Compulsory Purchase Act 1965 to compensation for "any loss or injury they may sustain" if they are required to give up possession before the expiration of their term (see Chapter 13). If, however, the acquiring authority purchase the landlord's interest and bring the tenant's interest to an end through the service of a notice to quit, the occupier faces similar consequential loss but until 1973 had no *right* to any redress under the compulsory purchase code, although he might receive a "disturbance payment" at the *discretion* of the acquiring authority.[3] JUSTICE in a report in 1973 commented of such a

11—20

---

[96] *Salomon v. A. Salomon and Co. Ltd* [1877] A.C. 22. And see B.C. Cunningham, "Lifting the Veil: An English — Scottish Contrast" (1977) 22 J.L.S. 52.

[97] Reliance being placed on the decision in *Smith, Stone and Knight Ltd v. Birmingham Corporation, supra.*

[98] 1976 S.L.T. (Lands Tr.) 5.

[99] Reliance being placed on the decision in *D.H.N. Food Distributors Ltd v. London Borough of Tower Hamlets, supra.*

[1] 1977 S.C. 84; 1977 S.L.T. 60.

[2] 1978 S.C. (H.L.) 90; 1978 S.L.T. 59.

[3] Land Compensation Act 1961, s.30.

payment: "if justice requires that it be paid, it should be paid as of right."[4] Sections 37 and 38 of the Land Compensation Act 1973 now provide for the making of "disturbance payments" as of right to displaced occupiers without compensatable interests (see Chapter 13) and these should overcome in many cases the sort of hardship encountered in *Lander* and *Woolfson*.

11—21 **(2) The circumstances of the claimant:** As Mann points out,[5] a person's age, health and financial position can each in reality affect his ability to mount a response to a compulsory acquisition and the question arises whether in considering what are the natural and reasonable consequences of dispossession the acquiring authority must, as in personal injury cases, take the claimant as they find him.

In *Evans v. Glasgow District Council*[6] the claimant carried on a printer's business in premises occupied under a yearly tenancy in Ballater Street, Glasgow. The premises were compulsorily acquired and, in due course, the claimant transferred his business elsewhere. The business did not prosper in its new location and was disposed of some two years later. The claimant sought a disturbance payment under sections 34 and 35 of the Land Compensation (Scotland) Act 1973 which included an item of £14,512 for temporary loss of profits. Although a disturbance payment under the 1973 Act is quite distinct from disturbance compensation under rule (6) (see Chapter 13), the Court of Session held in *Glasgow Corporation v. Anderson*[7] that such a claim could properly include "all reasonable expenses, reasonably incurred as the direct and natural consequence of, and in, the compulsory removing, in addition to the expenses strictly referrable to 'the removal' itself."[8] In *Evans* the Lands Tribunal for Scotland concluded that in assessing such payments the test of remoteness laid down in *Harvey* and in *Anderson* should be applied.

The claim for loss of profits in *Evans* was attributed in part to lack of capital which made it difficult for the claimant to adapt his business to the new premises. The tribunal after hearing evidence was not altogether satisfied that the lack of capital had contributed to the loss of profits but, in so far as it had, the tribunal considered that this was not a consequence of the displacement, any more than it would be regarded as consequential in a claim for damages. In reaching this conclusion, the tribunal was influenced by the decision of the House of Lords in *Liesbosch Dredger v. S. S. Edison*.[9]

---

[4] *Compensation for Compulsory Acquisition and Remedies for Planning Restrictions together with a Supplemental Report* (Stevens, 1973), para. 113.
[5] M. Mann, "Adequacy of the Law of Disturbance to meet Actual Losses," *supra*; and N. Macleod, "Compensation for Disturbance on Compulsory Acquisition" [1989] J.P.L. 891.
[6] 1978 S.L.T. (Lands Tr.) 5.
[7] 1976 S.L.T. 225.
[8] Although *Glasgow Corporation* was concerned with a claim under s.35(1)(a) of the Scottish Act of 1973, the Lands Tribunal for Scotland considered in *Evans* that the same broad approach applied to a claim under section 35(1)(b).
[9] [1933] A.C. 449.

In that case, the *Liesbosch Dredger* was sunk as a result of the negligence of the   **11—22**
master of the steamship *Edison*. The dredger had been engaged on a contract
which provided for heavy penalties in the event of delay. For want of funds, the
owners of the dredger were unable to buy a replacement and, therefore, had to
hire one to complete the contract. In an action for damages, the owners of the
dredger were awarded its market value but were unable to recover the cost of
hiring a second dredger to complete the contract. The House of Lords held that
that cost arose from the claimants' own impecuniosity, a matter which was not
traceable to the respondents' acts and which was, as a result, outside the legal
purview of the consequences of those acts.[10]

The decision in the *Liesbosch Dredger* was subsequently applied by the Lands
Tribunal for Scotland in *Bryce v. Motherwell District Council*.[11] Mr Bryce was displaced from his council house and had to move to another in circumstances which
qualified him for a disturbance payment. Being a man of limited means, he found
he could not, after spending money on carpets, blinds, and so on, afford the cost
of immediately reinstalling the telephone at his new house. The telephone was
finally reinstalled some two years after the move, by which time the installation
cost had risen from £32.40 to £48. The local authority refused to pay the difference and the tribunal, when the matter came before it, held that it was the claimant's own admitted impecuniosity which had caused the delay and led to the
increased cost. The increase "was not reasonably incurred as a direct and natural
consequence of, and in, his compulsory removing."[12] In *Emslie and Simpson v.
Aberdeen District Council*[13] a figure of £4,505 was claimed representing interest on
additional borrowings which the claimants had been forced to make in the year
prior to vesting because of poor trading conditions resulting from the running
down of the area because of the scheme. The item was rejected by the Lands
Tribunal for Scotland on the ground, *inter alia*, that the need to borrow was the
result of the claimants' impecuniosity and was, therefore, too remote.

A similar approach was taken by the Court of Appeal in *Bailey v. Derby Corpora-*   **11—23**
tion[14] with regard to loss resulting from the poor state of health of the claimant.
A builder's yard and workshop were compulsorily acquired. Ill health, not the
result of the expropriation but an "unhappy coincidence," prevented him from
re-establishing his business on another site. He sought compensation based on the
total extinguishment of his business, a basis of assessment which would have pro-

---

[10] In recent years the courts seem to have circumvented a rigorous application of the decision in the
field of damages. See, for example, *Martindale v. Duncan* [1973] 1 W.L.R. 574; *Dodd Properties v.
Canterbury City Council* [1980] 1 W.L.R. 433; *Bunclark v. Hertfordshire County Council* (1977) 243
E.G. 381 and 455; *Perry v. Sidney Phillips and Son* (1982) 263 E.G. 888.

[11] [1980] R.V.R. 282.

[12] Contrast the decision in *Bede Distributors Ltd v. Newcastle upon Tyne Corporation* (1973) 26 P. &
C.R. 298 in which the Lands Tribunal held it was not unreasonable for a company without liquidity
to go into liquidation instead of removing to an alternative site (see *"Mitigation"* below). See, too,
the decision in *Knott Mill Carpets v. Stretford Borough Council* (1973) 26 P. & C.R. 129.

[13] [1994] 18 E.G. 136.

[14] [1965] 1 All E.R. 443.

duced an award considerably in excess of disturbance compensation based on relocation of the business in alternative premises. This approach was rejected on the ground that the corporation were not acquiring the business; this was not a loss flowing from the acquisition. Denning L.J. said of the claim:

> "I am quite clear in this case that the loss which is the 'natural and reasonable consequence' of the acquisition is the cost of removal and the loss of profits immediately and directly consequent on his having to move. In so far as any loss is due, not to the acquisition, but to the state of health of the claimant, that seems to me to be an extraneous and independent matter which must be put on one side. It should not be taken into account in assessing the compensation. It is comparable to the impecuniosity mentioned in the *Edison*."

It would seem from the decisions in *Bailey, Bryce* and *Evans* that the application of the test of remoteness laid down by Romer L.J. in *Harvey* does not involve the acquiring authority taking the claimant as they find him. Loss resulting on expropriation as a result of the particular financial or physical circumstances of the claimant are not treated as the "natural and reasonable consequence" of the acquisition.

It has been argued that this does not accord well with the principle of equivalence. Young in an interesting discussion of the *Bryce* decision points out that "a person who is forced, as a result of action taken in the interests of the community at large, to leave the property he occupies has a right to expect that he will be left no worse off than he was prior to the dispossession. *Bryce* appears to show that if the *Liesbosch* principle is applied, such expectations may not be fulfilled where the claimant is short of money."[15] And JUSTICE, in a comment on the decision in *Bailey*, recommended that "the personal circumstances of the claimant, such as age and state of health, be taken fully into account" in assessing compensation for disturbance.[16]

11—24   The position of some claimants has now been eased following the introduction of section 46 of the Land Compensation Act 1973. This provides that disturbance compensation for a person carrying on a trade or business on land which is or forms part of a hereditament the annual value of which does not exceed a prescribed amount,[17] who is required in consequence of the compulsory acquisition of the land to give up possession and who on the date of giving up possession has attained the age of 60, shall be assessed on the basis of the total extinguishment

---

[15] E. Young, "Remoteness, Impecuniosity and Disturbance" [1981] J.P.L. 707.

[16] *Compensation for Compulsory Acquisition and Remedies for Planning Restrictions together with a Supplemental Report* (Stevens, 1973) paras. 41 and 42. See, also, M. Mann, "Adequacy of the Law of Disturbance to meet Actual Losses," *supra*; and N. Macleod, "Compensation for Disturbance on Compulsory Acquisition" [1989] J.P.L. 891.

[17] This is the amount prescribed for the purposes of s.149(3)(a) of the Town and Country Planning Act 1990 (interests affected by planning proposals: blight) and currently stands at £18,000 (Town and Country Planning (Blight Provisions) Order 1990). For the definitions of "annual value" and "hereditament" see the 1990 Act, s.171(1).

of the business. The person must not have disposed of the goodwill of the trade or business and must undertake that he will not dispose of the goodwill and that he will not, within such area and for such period of time as the acquiring authority may require, directly or indirectly engage in or have an interest in any other similar trade or business. Compensation so assessed will usually be more generous than compensation based on the cost of transferring the business elsewhere.[18]

3. MITIGATION

It may not be enough to show that the loss is the natural and reasonable consequence of dispossession. Claimants are also under a duty to mitigate their loss. This derives from the well-established principle in the law of damages that:

> "the plaintiff must take all reasonable steps to mitigate the loss consequent upon the defendant's wrong and cannot recover damages for any such loss which he could thus have avoided but has failed, through unreasonable action or inaction, to avoid. Put shortly, the plaintiff cannot recover for avoidable loss."[19]

This principle also applies to disturbance. In *Service Welding Ltd, v. Tyne and Wear County Council*[20] Bridge L.J. said:

> "It is clear, however, that where as here a business occupier is in a position to find alternative accommodation in which to carry on his business and prevent its extinction, he is under a duty to mitigate his disturbance compensation by removing his business to the alternative accommodation."[21]

Indeed, as the Lands Tribunal for Scotland pointed out in *Smith*, compulsory purchase cases differ from delict (the Scottish equivalent of tort) in that pending loss, prior to the acquisition, can often be seen from afar; so anticipatory action to mitigate loss becomes more feasible.

A further illustration of the duty to mitigate loss is provided by the decision in *Park Automobile Co. Ltd v. Strathclyde Regional Council*.[22] A garage and petrol station was compulsorily acquired and the premises vested in the acquiring authority in May 1975. The claimant company, anticipating dispossession, had purchased an

11—25

---

[18] Where a person has disposed of the goodwill of part of a trade or business, the provisions may nonetheless operate on the remainder.

[19] McGregor on *Damages*, para. 275. And see *British Westinghouse Co. v. Underground Railway* [1912] A.C. 673, *per* Viscount Haldane L.C. at p. 689.

[20] (1979) 38 P. & C.R. 352.

[21] *Ibid.* at p. 357.

[22] 1984 S.L.T. (Lands Tr.) 14. See, too, *J. Shulman (Tailors) Ltd v. Greater London Council* (1966) 17 P. & C.R. 244; *Simpson v. Stoke-on-Trent City Council* (1982) 263 E.G. 673; *Thomas and Son Ltd v. Greater London Council* (1982) 262 E.G. 991 and 1086; *Sloan v. Edinburgh District Council*, 1988 S.L.T. (Lands Tr.) 25.

alternative property assisted by an advance payment of compensation from the authority. However, the claimants were allowed by the acquiring authority to remain in occupation as tenants of the original premises and for business reasons they chose to do this and they continued to trade profitably. Subsequently, as the local authority showed no signs of requiring possession of the garage, the claimants sold their alternative premises. The six year time bar from the date of divestiture for referring disputed claims for compensation to the Lands Tribunal for Scotland[23] eventually compelled the claimants to lodge a claim for anticipated disturbance although at that time the loss had not actually arisen. The claim was based on the notional total extinguishment of the business as at the date of vesting. The tribunal considered that the claimants were not entitled to absolve themselves from all duty to find alternative accommodation by choosing to stay on. That was not minimising but maximising the authority's liability for compensation. The claimants could have relocated the business at the date of vesting. It was a business decision to stay where they were. That was not mitigating their loss; it was a decision not to do so. They could not, therefore, claim for more than they would have obtained had they taken reasonable steps to relocate.

11—26   The duty to mitigate loss would seem to be no more than a duty to act reasonably in the circumstances.[24] What is reasonable is a question of fact depending on the circumstances in each case.[25] The onus appears to be upon the acquiring authority to demonstrate that the claimant has not acted reasonably.[26] *In Simpson v. Stoke-on-Trent City Council*[27], for example, the claimant included an item in his claim of £1,068.07 representing back interest on a bridging loan obtained to enable him to purchase another house following service of notice to treat and notice of entry. The Lands Tribunal held that the sum could not be recovered from the acquiring authority because it was not reasonable in the circumstances for the claimant to have taken a bridging loan, nor was he bound to do so. Having decided to negotiate for another house, he could have made a reference to the tribunal to have the compensation determined and could have taken an advance payment from the local authority. In *Millar v. Strathclyde Regional Council*[28] the Lands Tribunal for Scotland had to consider whether the claimant's decision not to relocate his business was a reasonable one in all the circumstances. The claimant had made no attempt to find suitable alternative property. After examining possible alternatives put forward by the acquiring authority, the tribunal concluded that there were no suitable alternative premises available at the date of displacement and the claimant had not acted unreasonably and was entitled to compensation on the basis of the extinguishment of the business.

---

[23] Town and Country Planning (Scotland) Act 1972, Sched. 24, para. 36(1).
[24] *Millar v. Strathclyde Regional Council*, 1988 S.L.T. (Lands Tr.) 9; *MacLeod v. Strathclyde Regional Council*, Lands Tribunal for Scotland, May 18, 1987, unreported.
[25] *Payzu Ltd v. Saunders* [1919] 2 K.B. 581.
[26] *MacLeod v. Strathclyde Regional Council, supra; Millar v. Strathclyde Regional Council, supra.*
[27] (1982) 44 P. & C.R. 226. And see MacGregor on *Damages*, para. 289.
[28] 1988 S.L.T. (Lands Tr.) 9.

The duty to mitigate loss does not, however, require a claimant to subject **11—27** himself to unreasonable commercial risks especially if lacking the financial means to do so. In *Knott Mill Carpets Ltd v. Stretford Borough Council*[29], for example, the claimants sought compensation of £9,000 for the total extinguishment of their business. They had owned a carpet shop in a shopping area. The shopping area had been replaced by a heated shopping precinct as a result of the activity of the acquiring authority. Although negotiations had taken place over possible relocation within the new precinct, they had come to nothing because the claimants did not think they could increase their turnover sufficiently to pay the higher rents and still maintain their net profits. The Lands Tribunal held that in the circumstances a claim based on the total extinguishment of the business rather than on its notional removal was reasonable. In *MacLeod v. Strathclyde Regional Council*[30] the Lands Tribunal for Scotland concluded that the claimant, who had carried on a business retailing, servicing, repairing and reconditioning Hoover equipment, was entitled to compensation based on the total extinguishment of the business. Alternative premises were available in a good retail position but the evidence showed that it would be economically hazardous to move to such a position paying either a retail rent or a retail purchase price, with appropriate rates, when the requirement was for a workshop with no more than a limited retail facility. And in *Bede Distributors Ltd v. Newcastle upon Tyne Corporation*[31] the Lands Tribunal held that it was not unreasonable for a company without liquidity to go into liquidation instead of removing.

Unlike the test for remoteness (above), it seems from the decisions in *Knott Mill Carpets, MacLeod* and *Bede* that in considering whether a claimant has discharged his duty to mitigate his loss, account may be taken of his financial circumstances. This is in line with the law of damages. In *Clippens Oil Co. Ltd v. Edinburgh and District Water Trustees*[32] Lord Collins said "in my opinion the wrongdoer must take his victim *talem qualem*, and if the position of the latter is aggravated because he is without the means of mitigating it, so much the worse for the wrongdoer, who has got to be answerable for the consequences flowing from his tortious act."[33] It is important to note that Lord Collins, here, was dealing not with the measure of damage but with the victim's duty to minimise damage.[34] It is, therefore, necessary as Young observes "to draw a distinction between, on the one hand, a loss which is too remote because it was *caused* by the victim's lack of means and, on the other hand, a loss which the victim was unable to *mitigate* because of his lack of means."[35]

---

[29] (1973) 26 P. & C.R. 129.
[30] Lands Tribunal for Scotland, May 18, 1987, unreported.
[31] (1973) 26 P. & C.R. 298.
[32] 1907 S.C. (H.L.) 9.
[33] *Ibid.* at p. 14.
[34] See the comment by Lord Wright in *Liesbosch Dredger v. S.S. Edison* [1933] A.C. 449 at p. 461.
[35] E. Young, "Remoteness, Impecuniosity and Disturbance" [1981] J.P.L. 707. R.G. Lawson in "The Status of the Edison" (1974) 124 N.L.J. 240 comments that "the distinction between a separate loss caused by straightened means, and one which is simply a loss not abated . . . is superficial at

11—28   The corollary of the duty to take all reasonable steps to mitigate loss is that where a claimant takes such steps, he can recover for loss incurred in so doing. This would seem to be so, even if the steps prove to be abortive or the resulting loss is greater than it would have been if the mitigating steps had not been taken.[36] In the words of Lord Collins in *Clippens Oil Co.* "I think the wrongdoer is not entitled to criticise the course honestly taken by the injured person on the advice of his experts, even though it should appear by the light of after events that another course might have saved loss." In *Evans v. Glasgow District Council,*[37] for example, the Lands Tribunal for Scotland, in dealing with a claim for temporary loss of profits, considered the claimant's conduct in seeking to carry on the family business in new premises to have been reasonable, even though the business failed at the end of the day. And in *Smith v. Strathclyde Regional Council*[38] the tribunal allowed as part of the disturbance claim professional fees incurred in abortive plans to retain and shore up part of a public house, the whole of which was eventually acquired. On the other hand, in *Simpson v. Stoke-on-Trent City Council*[39] the Lands Tribunal disallowed interest on a bridging loan as part of a disturbance claim. The claimant had not acted reasonably in taking out the loan to buy another house. The need for a loan could have been avoided by referring the compensation claim for the value of the land to the tribunal for determination and taking a 90 per cent. advance payment on the compensation (see Chapter 13).

---

best, for each is, at bottom, a case of damage arising where ample funds would have dictated otherwise."

[36] McGregor on *Damages*, para. 276.
[37] 1978 S.L.T. (Lands Tr.) 5.
[38] 1982 S.L.T. (Lands Tr.) 2.
[39] (1982) 263 E.G. 673. See, too, *Thomas v. Greater London Council* (1982) 262 E.G. 991 and 1086.

Chapter 12

Remaining Land

It will sometimes be the case that an acquiring authority take part only of a parcel of land in which an interest subsists. The scheme of public works for which the part has been acquired may affect the value of the remaining land. It may enhance its value by opening up the prospect of development for some more profitable use; or it may reduce its value because of nuisance arising from the scheme. The actual physical severance of the part taken may also give rise to some reduction in the profitability in continuing the existing use of the remaining land which is reflected in its value. The question is whether such increase or decrease in the value of the remaining land should be taken into account in assessing compensation. This chapter is given over to consideration of this question. It is divided into two parts. The first part examines the extent to which an enhancement in the value of the remaining land may be set-off against the compensation for the land taken. The second part considers whether depreciation in the value of the remaining land may form part of the overall claim for compensation arising from the compulsory acquisition.

Set-off

In the absence of any express statutory provision, the courts have not been prepared to countenance the suggestion that an increase in the value of remaining land resulting from the scheme of the acquiring authority should be set-off against compensation for the land taken. In *South-Eastern Railway Co. v. London County*

Council,[1] referred to in Chapter 9, Eve J. spelt out the objection to set-off. It would, he said:

> "Upset all uniformity of value, inasmuch as the value of the identical piece of land in the hands of one vendor might be assessed at many times its value in the hands of another, and this, not from any intrinsic distinction, but by reason solely of extraneous considerations. Moreover, it would be calculated to work injustice in that a vendor compelled to sell, and who the legislature intended should be compensated for being compelled to sell, might have to accept from the undertakers a price far less than he would have obtained from any other purchaser, and out of all proportion to the true value of the land had it been ascertained without reference to the fortuitous circumstances of his also being interested in the contiguous land."[2]

12—02 Neither have the courts been prepared to imply such a provision in dealing with claims for compensation for injurious affection to land no part of which has been the subject of compulsory acquisition (see Chapter 16). In *Senior v. Metropolitan Railway Co.*[3] Wilde B. said "if the company were entitled to set-off the benefit derived from proximity to the station, one individual would be made to pay something for that, whereas his neighbour would pay nothing. It is the first time such an idea has been brought forward, and I see no reason for giving countenance to it." A similar argument was subsequently rejected in Scotland by the Court of Session in *Walker's Trustees v. Caledonian Railway Co.*[4] There Lord Young said

> "[t]he third question regards the contention of the complainers that they are entitled to set the benefits which they have conferred on the respondents' property against the damage which they have done to that property of a character entitling them to compensation under the statute. This contention is admittedly novel, and I content myself with saying that it is in my opinion inadmissable."[5]

Over the years, however, express provision for set-off has appeared in specific legislation. Such provision first appeared in the Turnpike Roads Act (Scotland) 1831,[6] section 64 of which provided that in assessing compensation for land taken for making or improving roads, the assessing authority was to take into consideration "all the circumstances of the case and particularly the advantages arising to the proprietors and occupiers by new or altered roads." Other provisions for set-off subsequently appeared in Acts such as the Artizans and Labourers Dwellings Act (1868) Amendment Act 1879, the Light Railways Act 1896, the Development and Road Improvement Funds Act 1909, the Restriction of Ribbon

---

[1] [1915] 2 Ch. 252.
[2] *Ibid.* p. 259.
[3] (1863) 32 L.J. Ex.Ch. 225. See, too, *Eagle v. Charing Cross Railway Co.* (1867) L.R. 2 C.P. 638.
[4] (1881) 8 R. 405.
[5] This particular point was not pursued in the subsequent appeal to the House of Lords.
[6] Referred to in the *Final Report of the Expert Committee on Compensation and Betterment* (Cmd. 6386, 1942) para. 265.

Development Act 1935, and the Highways Act 1959. The Metropolitan Management Act 1858 adopted a rather different approach by making no provision for compensation for depreciation resulting from the public works apparently on the ground that the depreciation would effectively be compensated for by the benefit arising from the works.[7]

The possibility of introducing a general set-off provision into compensation legislation was considered by both the Scott[8] and Uthwatt[9] Committees. The former, although advocating the recovery of betterment by promoters, rejected set-off in favour of an alternative approach based upon scheduled betterment areas. The Uthwatt Committee, while acknowledging the principle of set-off to be equitable, drew attention to two perceived defects.[10] First of all, it could only be collected from landowners from whom land had been acquired for the scheme. It was thus "very much a hit and miss method of recovery and is unfair as between one owner and another." Secondly, the maximum amount which can be collected is the actual cost to the promoter of the particular parcels of land which are being acquired. In view of these imperfections, the committee concluded that the balance of advantage was against this method of collecting betterment. They advocated instead recovery by way of a periodic levy on increases in annual site values. However, if that was not accepted, they recommended the introduction of a general provision for setting off betterment against compensation on the basis that "something is better than nothing."

12—03

A general provision for set-off was subsequently introduced in the Town and Country Planning Act 1959[11] when the government abandoned the dual price system and restored market value in land as the measure of compensation for compulsory purchase (see Chapter 5). In introducing the provision the government were clearly influenced by the extent to which express provision for set-off was made in specific Acts. As Cullingworth observes "[t]he honourable ancestry of set-off was clearly an important factor in this decision."[12] Section 9 of and Schedule 1 to the 1959 Act were subsequently replaced by sections 7 and 8 of and Schedule 1 to the Land Compensation Act 1961 (below).

Express provision for set-off may, however, still be encountered in specific public and general Acts which incorporate their own compensation arrangements. For example, section 261 of the Highways Act 1980 makes special provision for compensation including set-off in respect of the acquisition of land for the construction and improvement of roads.

12—04

And express set-off provisions may also be found in private and local Acts, the Zetland County Council Act 1974, providing for the acquisition of land in con-

---

[7] *Second Report of the Committee Dealing with the Law and Practice relating to the Acquisition and Valuation of Land for Public Purposes*, (Cd. 9229, 1918), App. 3.
[8] *Ibid.*
[9] *The Final Report of the Expert Committee on Compensation and Betterment*, *supra*.
[10] *Ibid.* para. 285.
[11] s.9 and Sched. 1.
[12] J.B. Cullingworth, *Environmental Planning* (HMSO, 1980) Vol. IV, p. 207.

nection with the construction of the Sullom Voe oil terminal, being a notable example.

Section 7 of the 1961 Act[13] provides that where, on the date of service of the notice to treat, the person from whom land is being acquired is also entitled in the same capacity to contiguous or adjacent land,[14] there is to be deducted from the compensation for the land acquired any increase in the value of the contiguous or adjacent land which, in the circumstances described, is attributable to and which would not have occurred but for the scheme as defined. The circumstances in which land may be earmarked for acquisition for public purposes are described in column 1, Part I of Schedule 1 to the 1961 Act; and the scheme for the purposes of each such circumstance is defined in column 2. These are set out in detail at para. 9–07 to 9–09 above.[15] It would seem that it is only when those circumstances apply that a set-off is to be made;[16] there is no judicial authority corresponding to the *Pointe Gourde* principle[17] which allows for the recovery of betterment in this way in other circumstances.[18] In other words, the definition of "the scheme" for the purposes of the remaining land will in some cases be narrower than it is for the land taken (see Chapter 9).

12—05   Section 7 is not to apply to an acquisition under a "corresponding enactment"[19] or a private or local Act which makes separate provision for set-off.[20]

It should be stressed that for the set-off provisions to apply it must be shown that the increase in the value of the remaining land would not have occurred but for the scheme. In the Scottish case *James Miller and Partners Ltd v. Lothian Regional Council (No. 2)*[21] the claimants owned some 40 acres of land allocated in the development plan for residential development. Planning permission was granted in accordance with the allocation. The plans attached to the grants of planning permission earmarked a small part of the site (0.42 of an acre) for a sewage pumping station. In due course, the regional council as sewerage authority, in discharge of their duty under section 1 of the Sewerage (Scotland) Act 1968, acquired the site in order to construct the pumping station. The parties disagreed over the price and the matter came before the Lands Tribunal for Scotland by voluntary

---

[13] Which is expressed to be subject to the provisions of s.8 (see below).

[14] A person is entitled to two interests in land in the same capacity in the circumstances set out in s. 39(6) of the 1961 Act.

[15] The definition of the scheme in column 2 in each case is modified by the omission of the words "other than the relevant land" (s.7(2)).

[16] *South-Eastern Railway Co. v. London County Council* [1915] 2 Ch. 252.

[17] See, also, *Camrose (Viscount) v. Basingstoke Corporation* [1966] 1 W.L.R. 1100; and *Wilson v. Liverpool City Council* [1971] 1 W.L.R. 302.

[18] But see *Melwood Units Property Ltd v. Commissioner of Main Roads* [1979] A.C. 426 as regards *depreciation* in the value of the remaining land.

[19] See s.8(7) of the 1961 Act.

[20] s.8(5) of the 1961 Act. S.8(6) provides that where any such local Act includes a provision restricting the assessment of the increase in value by reference to existing use, the Act is to have effect as if it did not include that provision.

[21] 1984 S.L.T. (Lands Tr.) 2. See, too, *Laing Homes Ltd v. Eastleigh Borough Council* (1979) 250 E.G. 350 and 459; and *Young v. Lothian Regional Council*, 1992 S.L.T. (Lands Tr.) 17.

reference. The council argued that they were entitled under the corresponding provision in section 14 of the Scottish Act of 1963 to set-off the value of the pumping station against any increase in the value of the claimant's adjoining land due to the construction of the pumping station. The presence of the pumping station, they argued, enabled the residential development to proceed and consequently raised the value of the adjoining land by over £150,000, thus effectively extinguishing any compensation for the land taken. The question the tribunal had to answer was whether the claimant's housing scheme would still have been likely to have been carried out if the authority had not acquired the subject land for a pumping station. Their conclusion was that the authority would have been able to provide and would have been likely in terms of their statutory duty to provide a sewage disposal unit on other land so that the residential development could have proceeded. Accordingly, there was no set-off to be made.

In their interpretation of the somewhat differently worded set-off provision in **12—06** what was section 222(6) of the Highways Act 1959 (now section 261 of the Highways Act 1980) the Lands Tribunal have taken a fairly strict view of what is meant by benefit to remaining land attributable to the purpose for which the land is acquired. In *Cooke v. Secretary of State for the Environment*[22] farmland was compulsorily acquired for a road improvement. The acquiring authority sought to deduct from the compensation for the land taken the sum of £4,200 (net) paid by the contractors for the right to tip surplus soil from the roadworks onto the claimant's land. The tribunal held that the set-off provision did not apply since the true purpose of the acquisition was the establishment of a road and the retained land had benefitted, not from the construction of the road, but from the dumping of soil which was purely incidental to the construction of the road. The tribunal member went on to say that he thought the purpose of section 222(6) of the 1959 Act was to set-off any value which the land would have, particularly for development purposes, by reason of having a new or improved access to it. And in *Portsmouth Roman Catholic Diocesan Trustees v. Hampshire County Council*[23] land at Winchester was acquired for a distributor road. The question before the Lands Tribunal was whether the value of the planning permission for development of the claimant's remaining land which was a virtual certainty upon completion of the road should be set-off against the compensation for the land taken. The tribunal concluded that the grant of a planning permission was not the kind of benefit to which it was required to have regard under section 222(6) of the 1959 Act. "The kind of benefit to which the tribunal is required to have regard," said the tribunal member, "is, in my opinion, one which is directly referable to the purpose for which the land is authorised to be acquired, such as where the coming of the road will provide access to the retained land of a new or improved kind (including the creation of a frontage to a widened highway), which benefit increases the value of that land. It appears to me that the grant of planning permis-

---

[22] (1973) 27 P. & C.R. 234.
[23] (1980) 253 E.G. 1236 and 1347.

sion by the local planning authority in respect of the green land was an indirect effect of the purpose for which the land taken was acquired; it was too remote."[24]

12–07   Where the enhancement in the value of the remaining land exceeds the compensation for the land taken there is no provision for recovery of the excess. This is one of the imperfections of this method of recovering betterment to which the Uthwatt Committee referred (see above). For example, in *Cotswold Trailer Parks Ltd v. Secretary of State for the Environment*[25] a small piece of land forming part of a site with permission for the erection of a motel was acquired for a road scheme. The severance of the small piece of land in no way prejudiced the motel proposal but in the absence of the road scheme some improvement would have been required to the existing road network to enable it to proceed. Because of the road scheme this was no longer necessary. The benefit accruing to the remaining land as a result of the scheme was far in excess of the value of the land taken so the compensation awarded was nil.

When it operates, the set-off provision is, as the Uthwatt Committee observed "unfair as between one owner and another."[26] Why should two landowners, both of whom own land which has benefitted from a scheme of public works, be treated differently solely because of the coincidence that one of them has had part of his land acquired for the scheme? Furthermore, the provision can cause hardship in practice. Bell cites the example of bypass schemes with small areas of remaining farmland between the village and the bypass being assessed for increased hope value because of the apparent improvement in their prospect of development. Such increased hope value may be set-off against compensation at the date for valuing the land being taken notwithstanding that the owner may have no intention of realising the potential or may subsequently be unable to obtain planning permission. Betterment, suggests Bell, should not be levied until it arises.[27]

Section 8 of the 1961 Act complements section 7. Its object is to avoid the possibility of betterment to remaining land arising from a scheme being set-off twice against compensation. The section applies to a subsequent acquisition where the interest acquired is the same as the interest previously taken into account[28] or is an interest deriving from that interest (section 8(3)).

12—08   The section is directed at two different circumstances. First of all, where remaining land which has been the subject of set-off is, itself, subsequently acquired in whole or in part for the scheme, section 8 provides that, in assessing compensation, the increase in value due to the scheme is *not* to be left out of account by virtue of section 6 or taken into account by virtue of section 7. Secondly, where remaining land which has been the subject of compensation for

---

[24] See, also, *Lorbright Ltd v. Staffordshire County Council* (1979) 254 E.G. 53. But see the letter from W.A. Leach at (1980) 254 E.G. 1730.

[25] (1974) 27 P. & C.R. 219.

[26] *Final Report of the Expert Committee on Compensation and Betterment, supra,* para. 285.

[27] M. Bell, "Agricultural compensation: The Way Forward" [1979] J.P.L. 577.

[28] Although the subsequent acquisition need not extend to the whole of the land in which that interest previously subsisted (s.8(3)(a)).

injurious affection is, itself, subsequently acquired in whole or in part for the scheme, then, in assessing compensation, the decrease in value due to the scheme is not to be left out of account by virtue of section 6. Section 8 applies even if the subsequent acquisition is by agreement (section 8(4)).

Injurious affection

As mentioned earlier, the compulsory acquisition of part only of land in which an interest subsists may result in harm to what remains. The construction and use on the land taken, perhaps in conjunction with other land, of major public works such as roads, airports, urban redevelopment schemes, sewage works and so on will in many cases cause intentional harm to the remaining land. These activities are ostensibly promoted in the public interest. To what extent are private rights expected to yield to the public interest? Activities which seriously interfere with a person's use or enjoyment of land or of some right connected with the land may be the subject of damages or restraint as a private nuisance; such activities are considered to be a violation of a person's private rights.[29] Are major schemes of public works open to restraint at common law at the suit of the disturbed neighbour?

12—09

The plea of "public interest" is not, of itself, a sufficient answer to an action at common law.[30] It has, however, long been established that where an activity is authorised expressly or by implication by an Act of Parliament, or by an instrument of delegated legislation, then, subject to what is said below, the body carrying on the activity will be immune from an action at common law.[31] The Act authorising the activity does not usually confer an express immunity: rather it is the inevitable consequence of the authorisation.[32]

However, for anything done in excess of or contrary to such authorisation, the common law remedy remains.[33] Furthermore, certain consequences may not flow inevitably from the authorisation. The Act may merely authorise something to be done in respect of which nuisance is not a necessary incident.[34]

---

[29] *Hals. Laws*, 4th Edn., Vol. 34, para. 307.
[30] *R. v. Morris* (1830) 1 B & Ad 441; *R. v. Ward* (1836) 4 Ad & El 384.
[31] *R. v. Pease* (1832), 4 B. & Ad. 30; *Caledonian Railway Co. v. Ogilvy* (1856) 2 Macq. 229, *per* Lord Chancellor Cranworth at p. 236; *Vaughan v. Taff Vale Railway Co.* (1868) 5 H. & N. 679; *Hammersmith and City Railway Co. v. Brand* (1869) L.R. 4 H.L. 171; *City of Glasgow Union Railway Co. v. Hunter* (1870) 8 M. (H.L.) 156; *Lord Blantyre and Others v. Clyde Navigation Trustees* (1871) 9 M. (H.L.) 6; *Allen v. Gulf Oil Refining Ltd*. [1981] 1 All E.R. 353.
[32] *Hammersmith and City Railway Co. v. Brand* (1869) L.R. 4 H.L. 171; *Allen v. Gulf Oil Refining Ltd* [1981] 1 All E.R. 353.
[33] *Jones v. Festiniog Ry. Co.* (1868) L.R. 3 Q.B. 733.
[34] *Metropolitan Asylum District v. Hill* (1881) 6 App. Cas. 193; *Manchester Corporation v. Farnworth* [1930] AC 171; *Rapier v. London Tramways Co.* [1893] 2 Ch. 588.

12—10   Certain activities may be excluded by the authorising statute. For example, section 114 of the Railways Clauses Consolidation Act 1845 provides that "[e]very locomotive steam engine to be used on the railway shall, if it uses coal or other similar fuel emitting smoke, be constructed on the principle of consuming and so as to consume its own smoke." Statutory authority would be unlikely in such circumstances to provide a defence to an action for excessive disturbance caused by smoke from passing trains.

Where a body carrying out a scheme of public works is rendered immune by statutory authority from an action at common law in respect of the consequences of the scheme, it is reasonable to expect that Parliament will make provision for compensation in lieu. Such provision is to be found in respect of injury to remaining land in section 7 of the Compulsory Purchase Act 1965, re-enacting section 63 of the Lands Clauses Consolidation Act 1845. This section provides that in assessing the compensation to be paid:

> "regard shall be had not only to the value of the land to be purchased by the acquiring authority, but also to the damage, if any, to be sustained by the owner of the land by reason of the severing of the land purchased from the other land of the owner, or otherwise injuriously affecting that other land by the exercise of the powers conferred by this or the special Act."

Although the section does not constitute a specific direction to compensate for injury to remaining land, the Act recognises such loss as a separate head of claim and, given the judicial presumption that an intention to take away the property of a subject without giving him a legal right to compensation for the loss of it is not to be imputed to the legislature unless that intention is expressed in unequivocal terms (see para. 5–02), that would seem to be sufficient.

The term "severance" used in section 7 of the 1965 Act refers to the harm caused to the remaining land by the physical loss of the land taken. The most notable cases of severance arise from the construction of major roads through farm land. The result may be to separate the farm buildings from the farm land and to require the reorganisation of the farm enterprise, if it is to continue, along with the rearrangement of access, land drainage, fencing and so on. Severance may, of course, also affect industrial, commercial or residential property

12—11   If the harm resulting from severance is particularly severe, a proprietor may prefer, instead of claiming compensation, to serve a notice objecting to the severance. The statutory provisions governing the service of such a notice are to be found partly in the Compulsory Purchase Act 1965, section 8, partly in the Compulsory Purchase (Vesting Declarations) Act 1981, section 12 and Schedule 1 and partly in the Land Compensation Act 1973.[35] These provisions, which vary

---

[35.] ss.53–57.

according to the nature of the land affected and the procedure adopted for acquiring title, are explained in Chapter 4.

"Otherwise injuriously affecting" in section 7 refers to the adverse effect on the remaining land arising from the construction and use of the works for which the land was acquired. For example, the construction and bringing into use of a major road may render an access to property very much less convenient, may spoil a good view and result in loss of privacy and may give rise to noise, fumes and disturbance from lights at night-time from traffic using the road.

These adverse effects may be just as serious for proprietors who have had no land taken as they are for those who have had part of their land acquired for the scheme. Other injurious affection does not discriminate between those who have had their land taken and those who have not. The entitlement to compensation, however, differs. The position of a proprietor who has had no land taken for the scheme is discussed in Chapter 16.

The reference in the 1965 Act to severance and *other* injurious affection indicates that severance is to be treated simply as one form, albeit a somewhat specialised form, of injurious affection. The requirements to be satisfied are the same for both.

In addition to the general provisions for injurious affection compensation in section 7, the 1965 Act makes certain special provisions. Section 19 specifically provides that where part only of lands comprised in a lease for a term of years unexpired is acquired, the lessee is entitled to compensation for damage to his interest arising from severance or "otherwise by reason of the execution of the works."[36] And section 20 makes special provision for a person having no greater interest in land than as a tenant for a year or from year to year. Such a person has no compensatable interest for the purposes of section 7 (see Chapter 13). Where such a person is required to give up possession of part of the land in which he has an interest before the expiration of his term, he is entitled to compensation for, *inter alia*, the damage done by severance or other injurious affection.

Section 16 of the 1965 Act deals with the position where part only of land **12—12** subject to a mortgage is acquired. If the value of the land acquired is less than the sums outstanding under the security and the holder of the security considers that the remaining land does not provide a sufficient safeguard for such sums, the value of the part acquired and the compensation to be paid in respect of severance or otherwise are to be settled by agreement between the lender and the borrower on the one hand and the acquiring authority on the other, or, failing agreement, by the Lands Tribunal; and the amount of such value or compensation is to be paid to the lender in satisfaction, so far as adequate, of the sums outstanding.

---

[36] It is not clear whether the words "by reason of the execution of the works" are intended to limit the extent of a claim for injurious affection in such cases by excluding damage arising from the *use* of the works. Cripps suggests that the provision in the Lands Clauses Act did not exclude the application of the general provisions in that Act relating to injurious affection (para. 4–250).

Section 18 makes provision for apportioning a rent charge (by agreement or in default by the Lands Tribunal) where part only of land subject to such a charge is acquired.[37]

1. LANDS HELD THEREWITH

12—13 Section 49 of the Lands Clauses Consolidation Act 1845, which set out the way in which juries were to deliver their verdict following an inquiry into the amount of compensation to be paid, began "[w]here such inquiry shall relate to the value of lands to be purchased, and also to compensation claimed for injury done or to be done, to the *lands held therewith*. . ." The phrase in italics has been taken to mean that to succeed in a claim for compensation for injurious affection, the claimant must show that the land affected was held together with the land which has been acquired. In the Scottish case *Caledonian Railway Co. v. Lockhart*[38] Lord Chancellor Campbell observed in this connection: "[t]he right to compensation depends on 'cause and effect', not on 'distance or proximity'."

This is well illustrated by the decision in *Holt v. Gas Light and Coke Co.*[39] There the plaintiffs, a volunteer corps, had leased land on which they had constructed a rifle range. They had also of necessity to have control of the land beyond the butts in order to operate the range safely. They had secured a verbal agreement regarding the use of the marsh land immediately behind the butts and a lease of the marsh meadows beyond. The defendants compulsorily acquired part of the marsh meadows for the construction of a road to their plant. The formation and bringing into use of the road rendered it impossible to use the range. In addition to compensation for the land taken the plaintiffs sought compensation for severance and other injurious affection reflecting the closure of the rifle range. The defendants argued that there was no actual severance of land from the rifle range; the plaintiffs' interest in the intervening marsh land governed by the verbal agreement was little more than precarious. The court held that although the land taken and the remaining land were separated by the intervening marsh land, they were held together for the purposes of the legislation. The land so taken was, said Cockburn C.J., "held at the same time and for a common purpose, and was connected with the land which has been left."[40]

12—14 It would seem, therefore, that contiguity is not the test. In *Cowper Essex v. Acton Local Board*[41] Lord Watson in the House of Lords said "I cannot assent to

---

[37] s.12 and Sched. 1 of the Compulsory Purchase (Vesting Declarations) Act 1981 Act deals with the position where land, the subject of such a charge, is acquired by a general vesting declaration.

[38] (1860) 3 Macq. 808.

[39] (1872) L.R. 7 Q.B. 728.

[40] *Ibid.* p. 735. Lush J. in the same case said "I think it means lands connected together in use as regards the purpose for which the owner has applied them" (p. 740).

[41] (1889) 14 App. Cas. 153.

the argument that there can be no severance within the meaning of the Act unless the part taken and the parts left were in actual contiguity." In that case land taken for the construction of a sewage works was separated from other building land belonging to the claimant which would be adversely affected by the works. Lord Watson went on to say "where several pieces of land owned by the same person are, though not adjoining, so near to each other and so situated that the possession and control of each gives an enhanced value to all of them, they are lands held together within the meaning of the Lands Clauses Consolidation Act 1845 ss. 49 and 63."[42]

Where a claimant is unable to satisfy this test, it may still be possible to claim compensation in respect of injurious affection on the same basis as a claim where no land has been taken (see Chapter 16).

Where, however, the claim for the land taken is based on its value for a purpose which could only be realised by reducing the value of the remaining land, the claimant is effectively acknowledging that the remaining land is not "held together" with the land taken and such reduction in value could not form the subject of a claim for injurious affection. A claim for injurious affection must, in other words, be consistent with the claim for the land taken,[43] otherwise the claimant will be compensated for more than his real loss.

2. MEASURE OF LOSS

Although injurious affection compensation is referred to separately in the 1965 **12—15** Act from compensation for the value of the land taken, it is nonetheless just one element of the overall price[44] and is measured by the depreciation in the value of the remaining land.[45] Mere personal inconvenience is not, therefore, a matter for compensation unless the inconvenience to owners and occupiers is such as would be reflected in the value of the land. In the Scottish case *Caledonian Railway Co. v. Ogilvy*[46] the claimants, in addition to a claim for the acquisition of land for the construction of a railway through part of an estate, sought compensation for "very material injury done to the place as a residence and deterioration to the amenity and value of the house and policy by the railway crossing the approach to the lodge and gate on the level immediately in front of and within a few yards of the

---

[42] In the Scottish case *City of Glasgow Union Railway Co. v. Hunter* (1870) 8 M. (H.L.) 156 it was held that the mere fact that the two parcels of land were held under the same title was not sufficient to support a claim for injurious affection. And see *Oppenheimer v. Minister of Transport* [1942] 1 K.B. 242.

[43] H. Parrish, *Cripps on Compulsory Acquisition of Land* (Stevens and Sons Ltd, 11th ed.) para. 4–257.

[44] *Oswald v. Ayr Harbour Trustees* (1883) 10 R. 472, *per* Lord Young at p. 489.

[45] H. Parrish, *Cripps on Compulsory Acquisition of Land, supra*, 4–276. See, too, *Re Stockport, Timperley, and Altrincham Railway Co.* (1864) 33 L.J.Q.B. 251; *Cowper Essex v. Acton Local Board* (1889) 14 App. Cas. 153; *Buccleuch (Duke) v. Metropolitan Board of Works* (1872) L.R. 5 H.L. 418.

[46] (1852) 2 Macq. 229 overruling *Scottish Central Railway Co. v. Cowan's Hospital* (1850) 12 D. 999.

gate." This part of the claim was rejected by the House of Lords partly because it did not constitute an injury to remaining land. "[A]ll attempts at arguing that this is damage to the estate is a mere play upon words," said Cranworth L.C. "It is no damage at all to the estate, except that the owner of that estate would oftener have a right of action from time to time than any other person, inasmuch as he would traverse the spot oftener than other people would traverse it."[47]

12—16 As mentioned at the beginning of this chapter, compensation for "other injurious affection" may be viewed to an extent as a substitute for a nuisance action. It would seem, however, that a claim for "other injurious affection" under the 1965 Act may be made in respect of *any* depreciation in the value of the remaining land resulting from the construction or use of the works for which the land was acquired — regardless of whether the cause of the depreciation could have founded an action at common law in the absence of the statutory authority for the works.[48] This is a matter upon which initially there was some uncertainty. In *Caledonian Railway Co. v. Ogilvy*,[49] referred to above, a claim for injurious affection was lodged in respect of the inconvenience to the estate caused by the construction and use of a level crossing on a public highway giving access to the estate. In the House of Lords, Lord Chancellor Cranworth asserted "the construction that is put upon this expression, 'injuriously affected', in the clauses in the Act of Parliament which gives compensation for injuriously affecting lands, certainly does not entitle the owner of lands which he alleges to be injuriously affected, to any compensation in respect of any act which, if done by the Railway Company without the authority of Parliament, would not have entitled him to bring an action against them."[50]

In other words, the view initially taken appears to have been that a claim for "other injurious affection" was coextensive with an action for nuisance. There had to be *damnum cum injuria*. While that seems still to be the position for a claim for compensation for injurious affection where no land has been taken (see Chapter 16), it is no longer the position as regards a claim for "other injurious affection" under section 7 of the 1965 Act.

12—17 Subsequently, in *Re Stockport, Timperley and Altrincham Railway Co.*[51] a distinction was drawn between claims for injurious affection where land had been taken and claims in cases where no land had been taken. In that case compensation was awarded for depreciation arising from the risk of fire to a cotton mill from the use of a railway where it passed over ground acquired from the mill. It was

---

[47] *Ibid*, at p. 603.

[48] *Re Stockport, Timperley and Altrincham Railway Co.* (1864) 33 L.J.Q.B. 251; *Cowper Essex v. Acton Local Board* (1889) 14 App. Cas. 153 H.L.; *Buccleuch (Duke) v. Metropolitan Board of Works* (1872) L.R. 5 H.L. 418. Contrast the position of a claimant for injurious affection where no land has been taken (*Penny v. South-Eastern Railway Co.* (1857) 7 E. & B. 660; *Hammersmith and City Railway Co. v. Brand* (1869) L.R. 4 H.L. 171; and *City of Glasgow Union Railway Co. v. Hunter* (1870) 8 M. (H.L.) 156; and see Chap. 16).

[49] (1852) 2 Macq. 600.

[50] *Ibid*. p. 602.

[51] (1864) 33 L.J.Q.B. 251.

argued by the railway company that exposing property to damage by fire was not actionable *per se*; neither would a fire which occurred without negligence give rise to any liability. No claim to compensation could arise in respect of an activity sanctioned by Parliament for which no action could have been maintained in the absence of Parliament's sanction. In his judgment for the claimants, Crompton J. held that that rule did not apply where the mischief complained of is caused by what is done on the land taken.

> "Where, however, the mischief is caused by what is done on the land taken, the party seeking compensation has a right to say, "it is by the Act of Parliament, and the Act of Parliament only, that you have done the acts which have caused the damage; without the Act of Parliament, everything you have done, and are about to do, in making and using the railway, would have been illegal and actionable, and is, therefore, matter for compensation according to the rule in question".[52]

The judgment of Crompton J. was subsequently approved unanimously by the House of Lords in *Cowper Essex v. Acton Local Board*.[53] Part of the claimant's land was acquired for a sewage works. There was evidence that the existence of the sewage works, even if conducted so as not to create a nuisance, depreciated the value of the claimant's remaining land for building purposes. Their Lordships confirmed the distinction made by Crompton J. and held that the damage in this case was not too remote even though no nuisance might be caused.[54]

The scope of a claim for injurious affection compensation under section 7 of the 1965 Act is not, therefore, coextensive with a nuisance action and may include the full consequential loss in so far as it is reflected in depreciation in the value of the remaining land. Although the list of activities which may be recognised by the law as a nuisance is open-ended, there are some activities which in the ordinary sense of the words could be said to disturb a person in the enjoyment of his property and which may depress the value of the property but which will not be regarded as a nuisance. Loss of a good view and loss of privacy are examples.[55] These may nonetheless form part of a claim for "other injurious affection" under section 7. In other words *damnum* alone would appear to be sufficient to support such a claim.

In the *Stockport* case Crompton J. referred to the mischief "caused by what is **12—18** done on the land taken." For many years the position was that a claim for compensation for "other injurious affection" was limited to the mischief caused by what was done on the land taken from the claimant; it could not encompass any

---

[52] *Ibid.* at p. 253.
[53] (1889) 14 App. Cas. 153 H.L.
[54] Lord Chancellor Halsbury and Lords Watson and Bramwell considered that the distinction had already been settled by the decision of the House of Lords in *Buccleuch (Duke) v. Metropolitan Board of Works* (1872) L.R. 5 H.L. 418. The difficulty with that decision is that although their Lordships agreed on the result, they did not appear to arrive at that result upon the same general construction of the provisions of the Act.
[55] *Penny v. South-Eastern Railway Co.* (1857) 7 E. & B. 660.

injury caused by what was being done on other land acquired by the promoter. Thus in the Scottish case *City of Glasgow Union Railway Co. v. Hunter,*[56] where a parcel of land was acquired from the claimant for the construction of a railway, compensation was claimed under section 48 of the Scottish Act of 1845 for depreciation in the value of the remaining land arising from the use of the railway. The claim under section 48 was rejected as the land taken was not held together with the land retained (see above). Lord Chelmsford pointed out that "[a]s no part of the property of the respondent has been injured by anything done on his land over which the railway runs, his right to compensation for damage appears to me to be precisely the same as if none of his land had been taken by the company."[57]

More recently, in *Edwards v. Minister of Transport*[58] some 302 square yards of land were compulsorily acquired from a householder for the construction of a trunk road. The householder claimed compensation on the basis of the injurious affection to his house from the annoyance caused by traffic on the new road. The Court of Appeal held he was entitled to compensation for injurious affection only in respect of that attributable to traffic on the small plots of land acquired from him.[59]

12—19　　The decision of the House of Lords in *Buccleuch (Duke) v. Metropolitan Board of Works*[60] might, at first sight, appear to depart from this position. The claimant was the lessee of a large house with grounds running down to the Thames. There was a causeway and landing place belonging to the house which provided access to and from the river. The causeway and landing place were acquired to make way for the Victoria Embankment which was constructed between the garden and the river. The claimant sought compensation not only for the loss of the causeway and landing place but also for depreciation resulting from the conversion of the land between the house and the river into a highway and the consequent public use of it. In the light of the discussion above, one might have expected the claim for injurious affection to have been limited to mischief arising on the small bit of land taken for the scheme. However, their Lordships unanimously agreed that compensation was due for the proximity of the embankment and all the consequences of its use as a public highway. The grounds upon which this conclusion was arrived at are not clear but the explanation for the decision may lie in the judgment of Lord Cairns who held that the claimant was entitled to the whole loss because of the acquisition of his rights as riparian owner to the undisturbed

---

[56] (1870) 8 M. (H.L.) 156.

[57] *Ibid.* at p. 163.

[58] [1964] 1 All E.R. 483.

[59] See, too, *R. v. Mountford, ex p. London United Tramways (1901) Ltd* [1906] 2 K.B. 814; *Horton v. Colwyn Bay and Colwyn Bay U.D.C.* [1908] 1 K.B. 327; *Sisters of Charity of Rockingham v. R.* [1922] 2 A.C. 315. It would seem that the claim for "other injurious affection" in *Ogilvy* might equally have been rejected on this ground.

[60] (1872) L.R. 5 H.L. 418. The decision in this case much influenced three of the judgments in the House of Lords in *Cowper Essex v. Acton Local Board, supra.*

flow of the river along the whole frontage of the property.[61] If that is the explanation, the decision is consistent with those discussed above.

The result of these decisions, as Cripps observes, was that "no compensation is payable in respect of what is done on lands other than those taken from the claimant."[62] The decision in *Edwards* provoked considerable dissatisfaction[63] and the government agreed to introduce amending legislation.[64] Section 44 of the Land Compensation Act 1973 now provides that where land is acquired from any person for the purpose of works which are to be situated partly on that land and partly elsewhere, compensation for a claim for injurious affection under section 7 of the 1965 Act[65] is to be assessed by reference to the whole of the works and not only the part situated on the land acquired or taken from him.

It would seem that the measure of compensation based upon land as an invest- **12—20** ment rather than as a factor of production may cause hardship to farmers faced with severance, particularly where the market value of the retained land remains high. As Hamilton states, "the severance may cause greater damage to the profitability of working the land than it does to the value of the land itself."[66] This may be illustrated by the decision in *Cooke v. Secretary of State for the Environment.*[67]

A farm already severed by the A40 trunk road, found the effects of severance considerably aggravated by the carrying out of improvements to that road in the form of the construction of a large roundabout and a new dual carriageway. As a result of the improvement it was no longer possible to drive cattle across the road, the farmhouse was severed from the land, all the farm buildings with the exception of a modern corn store had to be demolished as they were located on the land acquired, and the area of the farm was reduced by nine acres. The claimants based their claim for severance on the amount required to reinstate the farm as a working holding and included a substantial proportion of the cost of the new buildings, the whole cost of constructing a concrete farmyard and a new farm road and an outfall sewer, the cost of transporting stock across the A40 and the capitalised cost of travelling by car to the site of the new farm buildings. The whole claim, including the value of the land taken was assessed at £19,373. The

---

[61] This was the explanation of the decision advanced in *Edwards, supra.*

[62] H. Parrish, *Cripps on Compulsory Acquisition of Land, supra,* para. 4–263.

[63] JUSTICE, *Compensation for Compulsory Acquisition and Remedies for Planning Restrictions together with a Supplemental Report* (Stevens, 1973) para. 54; Chartered Lands Societies Committee, *Compensation for Compulsory Acquisition and Planning Restrictions* (1968) s.5.

[64] Cmnd. 5124, para. 29.

[65] s.44 of the 1973 Act applies also to claims for severance and other injurious affection under s.20 of the 1965 Act by a person who has no greater interest in land than as a tenant for a year or from year to year.

[66] R.N.D. Hamilton, *Compensation for Compulsory Acquisition of Agricultural Land* (RICS, 1980) para. 39. See, too, M. Bell, "Compensation: Can money do it?" Chartered Surveyor Rural Quarterly, 1978, No. 6, p. 3; M. Bell, "Agricultural Compensation: The Way Forward" [1979] J.P.L. 577; B. Denyer-Green, "Agricultural Compensation: The Injustice of Market Value in Severance Cases" [1980] J.P.L. 505; and *Compensation for Compulsory Acquisition*, RICS, 1984, para. 3.10.

[67] (1973) 27 P. & C.R. 234.

tribunal considered that the basis of the claim was misconceived. Compensation for severance was to be measured by the depreciation in the market value of the land not taken. They awarded £3,376 for the land taken and £3,048 for severance.[68]

12—21   It may, however, be possible to recover some of the consequences of severance under the heading of disturbance (see Chapter 11),[69] but if the expense has been taken into account in the valuation of the remaining land for a severance claim, it cannot also form part of a disturbance claim. In *McLaren's Discretionary Trustee v. Secretary of State for Scotland*[70] the Lands Tribunal for Scotland were asked to decide whether the cost of meeting the future maintenance and renewal of accommodation works (see below) was an item of injurious affection to the retained land or of disturbance. The tribunal decided that as the accommodation works were intended to mitigate what would otherwise be a much larger claim for injurious affection, and as they became fixtures and thus a part of the owner's property, what was being valued was a proprietary interest in land. "So in calculating the claimant's overall loss in the present case, it was not unfair to do so under Rule 2 by reference to the overall diminution in the value of the retained land — provided this is estimated by taking into account the likely future expenditure involved to provide a guide to the amount by which notional purchasers in the market would be likely to lower their offers."

Compensation for injurious affection is assessed on a "before and after" basis. This involves calculating the difference between the market value of the land not taken before severance and other injurious affection and the value after that date. There would seem to be some flexibility in approach to the calculation of this sum.[71]

12—22   In *Cuthbert v. Secretary of State for the Environment*[72] the Lands Tribunal suggested that a valuer should assume that immediately before the date of valuation a notional purchaser had agreed to buy the whole estate at a particular price; that at the date of valuation he was told of the intended acquisition of part of the estate and the agreement to purchase became void; and that immediately after the date of valuation he made a fresh bid for the estate less the land being acquired. The Lands Tribunal for Scotland, however, declined to follow this approach in *McLaren's Discretionary Trustee*,[73] a case which turned on the compensation payable to cover the future costs of maintaining and renewing accommodation works (see above) on retained land. The tribunal considered that it would be unfair in the

---

[68] For a possible approach to assessing depreciation in the value of remaining land which will reflect decreased profitability see R.N.D. Hamilton, *Compensation for Compulsory Acquisition of Agricultural Land, supra,* para. 39; also *Compensation for Compulsory Acquisition,* Royal Institution of Chartered Surveyors (1989) paras. 3.10–3.14.

[69] See H. Parrish, *Cripps on Compulsory Acquisition of Land, supra,* para. 4–283; and R.N.D. Hamilton, *Compensation for Compulsory Acquisition of Agricultural Land, supra,* para. 44.

[70] 1987 S.L.T. (Lands Tr.) 25.

[71] *Executors of J.R. Bullock, deceased v. Minister of Transport* [1969] R.V.R. 442.

[72] (1979) 252 E.G. 1178.

[73] 1987 S.L.T. (Lands Tr.) 25.

circumstances to assess compensation for injurious affection by reference to the test adopted in *Cuthbert*. The hypothetical purchaser might well shrug off such a relatively minor expenditure when bidding for a large sporting estate. "While there may be other possible valuation approaches, the Tribunal prefer, therefore, a more down to earth approach involving a build-up of various items of injurious affection (on a 'before and after valuation') to those specified parts of the retained land which the accommodation works were actually designed to serve."

The Royal Institution of Chartered Surveyors in a discussion paper raised two questions about valuation for injurious affection.[74] 1. Should the land taken be valued as severed or as part of the whole? 2. Is severance compensation payable only in respect of the land retained by the claimant or in respect of the land taken and the land retained?

The decision of the Lands Tribunal in *Abbey Homesteads Group Ltd v. Secretary of State for Transport*[75] suggests that the land taken should be valued as severed[76] and that severance compensation is payable only in respect of the land retained.[77] This, as the RICS point out, may result in a claimant receiving compensation for less than the full loss suffered.[78] In the *Abbey Homesteads* case some farmland was acquired for the construction of the Witney Bypass. The claimants argued that, because the land taken had no development potential on its own but only in conjunction with the retained land, it was right to value the entirety of the land and apportion its value to the several parts. In other words, they advocated assessing the totality of the loss and apportioning it to the relevant statutory provisions. The Lands Tribunal held that as a matter of law a separate assessment of compensation was required for the land taken, although in making that separate assessment regard could be taken of any value attributable to the prospect of "marrying" the land taken with the land retained. The overall compensation for the land taken and for the damage to the land retained was not to be ascertained by deducting the value of what was left to the owner after the acquisition from the aggregate value of the entirety immediately prior to the acquisition.

12—23

Prospective value may sometimes be an important element in a claim for injurious affection. In assessing compensation for injurious affection a claimant may, in the words of Cockburn C.J. in *R. v. Brown*,[79] "take into account not only the present purpose to which the land is applied, but also any other more beneficial purpose to which in the course of events at no remote period it may be applied, just as an owner might do if he were bargaining with a purchaser in the market."[80]

---

[74] "Compensation for Compulsory Purchase: Revisions to the Law on Severance and Injurious Affection Where Land is Taken" (1983) paras. 7–11.

[75] (1982) 263 E.G. 983. See, too, *A.D.P.& E. Farmers v. Department of Transport* (1988) 8818 E.G. 80; 8819 E.G. 147; and 8820 E.G. 104.

[76] But see H. Parrish, *Cripps on Compulsory Acquisition of Land, supra,* para. 4–279 for a contrary view.

[77] *Hoveringham Gravels Ltd v. Chiltern District Council* (1979) 252 E.G. 815.

[78] See W.A. Leach, "Market Value Under Rule (2): A Fresh Appraisal" (1974) 231 E.G. 907; G.S. Sarns, "Severance and the Land Taken" (1982) I Journal of Valuation 9.

[79] (1867) L.R. 2 Q.B. 630.

[80] *Ibid.* at p. 631. And see *Bolton Metropolitan Council v. Waterworth* (1981) 259 E.G. 625.

Thus in *Ripley v. Great Northern Railway Co.*,[81] where the railway company acquired land from the claimant on which cotton mills would probably have been built, it was held that compensation for severance was properly awarded on the basis of the profits which might have been derived from supplying water to the mills from a reservoir built by the claimant on land remaining in his ownership.

12—24 In assessing the development potential of the remaining land, no assistance may be obtained from the statutory planning assumptions set out in sections 14–16 of the Land Compensation Act 1961 (see Chapter 8). These apply only to the "relevant land" (sections 14(1) and 39(2)). Furthermore, the procedure for applying for a certificate of appropriate alternative development (see Chapter 8) would seem to be available only in respect of the land acquired.[82] A claimant may, however, test the development potential of the remaining land by applying for planning permission in the normal way.

In assessing the value of the remaining land "before" severance, the effect of the scheme underlying the acquisition must be ignored.[83] In *Clark v. Wareham and Purbeck Rural District Council*[84] 2.69 acres of land were acquired for the construction of a new sewage works. The claimant sought compensation for depreciation in the value of his remaining land resulting from the scheme. The claim was based on the difference in the value of the remaining land having regard to the actual state of affairs (the "with scheme world") and the state of affairs that would have existed in the absence of the scheme underlying the acquisition (the "no scheme world"). The Lands Tribunal agreed with the claimant that the correct yardstick for measuring injury from injurious affection was the difference between the value of the remaining land in the "with scheme world" and its value in the "no scheme world" but disagreed that there would have been any difference in value in the circumstances of the case.

12—25 Although, as indicated at the beginning of this chapter, it is not possible in the absence of an express statutory provision to set-off any increase in the value of the remaining land due to the scheme against the compensation for the land taken, it would seem that any such increase should be set-off against the compensation for injurious affection. In *George Wimpey and Co. Ltd v. Middlesex County Council*[85] land was acquired from the claimants for open space purposes. Adjoining land belonging to the claimants was damaged by the loss of access to a main road. However, in assessing compensation for this damage, the court held that account should be taken of the increase in the value of the adjoining land resulting from

---

[81] (1875) 10 Ch. App. 435.

[82] A certificate granted in respect of land acquired may, however, be persuasive as to the development potential of the land retained (*Abbey Homesteads Group Ltd v. Secretary of State for Transport* (1982) 263 E.G. 983; and *A.D.P.& E. Farmers v. Department of Transport* [1988] 18 E.G. 80; 19 E.G. 147; and 20 E.G. 104).

[83] *Pointe Gourde Quarrying and Transport Co. Ltd v. Sub-Intendent of Crown Lands* [1947] A.C. 565.

[84] (1972) 25 P. & C.R. 423. See, too, *Melwood Units Property Ltd v. Commissioner of Main Roads* [1979] A.C. 426.

[85] [1938] 3 All E.R. 781.

the provision of open space. It is common practice for an acquiring authority to undertake with the agreement of the claimant what are generally termed "accommodation works" designed to mitigate the damage to remaining land by injurious affection. Such works often take the form of fencing, walling, drainage, screening, planting and the provision of alternative forms of access. These works must be taken into account when assessing compensation for injurious affection. The cost of future maintenance and renewal of accommodation works may be a factor in formulating a claim for injurious affection.[86] Account should also be taken of any steps to mitigate the injurious effect of public works carried out in accordance with the provisions of Part II of the Land Compensation Act 1973.

The claim for injurious affection should embrace all damage both present and prospective.[87] In *Croft v. London and North-Western Railway*[88] Cockburn C.J. said in the context of a claim under the Lands Clauses Act:

> "The statute provides that compensation, in respect of land taken, and in respect of land injuriously affected, shall at once and, as it appears to me, for all be settled; and there is no provision whatever for any further damage presenting itself, not contemplated by the parties at the time of compensation by the jury, or not entered upon before the jury. I think if the Act of Parliament had intended that the inquiry should be renewed from time to time, if that, which at the time of the first inquiry might more or less be speculative, should be afterwards realised, there certainly would have been some provision in some of the statutes.[89]"

In determining a claim for damage for severance the Lands Tribunal have applied the general principle that applies to the assessment of damages at common law established in *Bwlfa and Merthyr Dare Steam Collieries (1891) Ltd v. Pontypridd Waterworks Company*[90] to the effect that in assessing damages it is unnecessary to speculate on what might be the measure of loss if at the time of the trial the true loss has become a fact.[91]

Because of the difficulty in formulating a claim in respect of future or contingent damage, the Uthwatt Committee recommended that a claim for injurious affection should be deferred until the authorised works have been completed and in operation for an appreciable time.[92] "Facts are better than predictions" was

12—26

---

[86] *McClaren's Discretionary Trustee v. Secretary of State for Scotland*, 1987 S.L.T. (Land Tr.) 25.
[87] *Sisters of Charity of Rockingham v. R.* [1922] 2 A.C. 315; *Caledonian Railway Co. v. Lockhart* (1860) 3 Macq. 808, *per* Lord Chancellor Campbell, para. 813; *Croft v. London and North-Western Railway Co.* (1863) 32 L.J.Q.B. 113.
[88] (1863) 32 L.J.Q.B. 113.
[89] *Ibid.* at pp. 119 and 120.
[90] [1903] A.C. 426.
[91] See *Bolton Metropolitan Borough Council v. Waterworth* (1978) 251 E.G. 963 and 1071; and (1981) 259 E.G. 625; also *A.D.P.& E. Farmers v. Department of Transport* [1988] 18 E.G. 80; 19 E.G. 147; and 20 E.G. 104.
[92] *Final Report of the Expert Committee on Compensation and Betterment* (Cmd. 6386, HMSO 1942) para. 211.

their view.[93] Although there is no requirement to defer a claim, agreement is sometimes reached in practice to reserve certain aspects of a claim for injurious affection until the impact of the scheme of works is clearer.[94] Subject to that, it would seem that no further claim may be made in respect of damage arising later which could be foreseen at the date of valuation.

Conclusion

12—27 "In our opinion," said the Scott Committee, "the principle of Betterment, *i.e.* the principle that persons whose property has clearly been increased in market value by an improvement should specially contribute to the cost of such an improvement, and the principle of Injurious Affection, *i.e.* the principle that persons whose properties are damaged by the construction or user of the promoters' works shall be entitled to receive compensation, are correlative."[95] It would seem logical, therefore, to treat them as such. However, with the exception of section 6 of the 1961 Act (see Chapter 9), Parliament has not treated betterment and injurious affection as correlative. It will be apparent from this chapter that set-off and "other injurious affection" are concerned broadly with converse positions; yet general provision for compensating injurious affection has been available since 1845, while the general provision for recovering betterment accruing to remaining land was not introduced until 1959.

There is, furthermore, an important difference in the operation of the provisions for recovering betterment and compensating injurious affection. The latter is measured by the full loss to the remaining land arising from the scheme;[96] the former, as the Uthwatt Committee observed,[97] is measured by the cost to the public authority of the part of the land acquired.[98]

The Uthwatt Committee also regarded set-off as unfair in principle "between one owner and another." It discriminates against a person whose land is being compulsorily acquired. The increase in the value of the land left is set-off against

---

[93] See, too, "Compensation for Compulsory Purchase: Revisions to the Law on Severance and Injurious Affection Where Land is Taken," Royal Institution of Chartered Surveyors Discussion Paper (1983) paras. 12–17.

[94] See R.N.D. Hamilton, *Compensation for Compulsory Acquisition of Agricultural Land, supra,* para. 42.

[95] *Second Report of the Committee Dealing with the Law and Practice relating to the Acquisition and Valuation of Land for Public Purposes* (Cd. 9229, 1918) para. 32.

[96] *Re Stockport, Timperley and Altrincham Railway Co.* (1864) 33 L.J.Q.B. 251; *Cowper Essex v. Acton Local Board* (1889) 14 App. Cas. 153.

[97] *Final Report of the Expert Committee on Compensation and Betterment* (Cmd. 6386, 1942) para. 285.

[98] There also appears to be a further difference in that set-off and injurious affection may not necessarily arise in respect of the same land. Section 7 of the 1961 Act refers to set-off in the context of "contiguous or adjacent" land. Injurious affection is concerned with land "held together" with the land taken.

the compensation for the land taken. A neighbour who has had no land taken for the scheme enjoys the full benefit of any betterment that accrues.[99]

Compensation for "other injurious affection" may also be regarded as unfair between one owner and another although the advantage is reversed. The injurious effects of a scheme do not discriminate between those who have had land taken and those who have not. Yet the entitlement to compensation differs (see Chapter 16); and a person who has land acquired may be compensated more generously for these effects than one who has not. In *Buccleuch* Mr Justice Hannen sought to explain the distinction on the ground that the landowner who has had land acquired for the scheme "was possessed of something without which the proposed public purpose could not be accomplished."[1] Whilst this may be a ground for awarding some special element in the compensation for the land taken, it has very little to do with injury to the land retained.

For these reasons the present arrangements for recovering betterment and com-   **12—28**
pensating "other injurious affection" may be regarded as both illogical and confusing.[2] The law relating to compensation for compulsory purchase would be much simpler if these elements of gain and loss were removed from the legislation; they are not a direct consequence of compulsory acquisition. There would seem to be something to be said for a separate code of legislation which treated like cases alike rather than making artificial distinctions because of the coincidence that a person has had land acquired for the scheme.

---

[99] Subject to prevailing fiscal policy.
[1] (1872) L.R. 5 H.L. 418 at p. 445.
[2] These criticisms are not directed at compensation for severance which is part of the consequential loss arising from compulsory acquisition.

Chapter 13

Compensation: Other Matters

Short tenancies

13—01 Section 20 of the Compulsory Purchase Act 1965 is a self-contained provision dealing with the interests of short tenants. A "short tenant" is one who has no greater interest in land than as a tenant for a year or from year to year. Because such tenancies are short, the acquiring authority may content themselves with persuading the landlord to serve a notice to quit or with purchasing the landlord's interest and giving such a notice themselves. If a tenant's interest simply expires in this way there is no entitlement to compensation under the compulsory purchase legislation as there has been no compulsory acquisition or compulsory extinguishment of the interest.[1] It merely terminates under the contractual terms of the tenancy.

Where, however, the acquiring authority require early possession they may be unable to wait for the contractual arrangements to run their course. In that event, having served a notice of entry,[2] they may enter on the land and extinguish the tenant's interest and pay compensation under section 20 for the extinguishment of that interest.

Subject to what is said below about the general vesting declaration procedure, short tenants are not entitled to a notice to treat under section 5 of the 1965 Act as that interest is not being acquired but simply extinguished. As was said in

---

[1] *Syers v. Metropolitan Board of Works* (1877) 36 L.T. 277. But note the right of a person served with notice to quit an agricultural holding to opt in prescribed circumstances for notice of entry compensation (Land Compensation Act 1973, s.59); see para. 13–38.
[2] Compulsory Purchase Act 1965, s.11.

Greenwood's Tyre Services Ltd v. Manchester Corporation[3], "this procedure did not involve the acquisition of an interest in land; a short tenancy did not become *acquired*, it became simply *snuffed out* by entry." However, as a matter of practice, acquiring authorities may serve such a notice to announce their intention to take the land or to clarify particulars of interests which may not be known to them. Service of a notice to treat on a short tenant in these circumstances does not alter the basis of compensation.[4]

Where a general vesting declaration has been executed in respect of any land, **13—02** short tenancies are excluded from the deemed notice to treat and divestiture provisions. The right of entry which arises upon vesting is not exercisable in respect of any land in which a short tenancy subsists.[5] The authority must first serve a notice to treat on such tenants followed by a notice of entry before possession can be taken. This is an exception to the general rule that a short tenant is not entitled to a notice to treat but here, too, service of such a notice does not alter the basis of compensation.[6]

Section 20 provides that a short tenant will be entitled upon extinguishment of his tenancy to compensation:

(i) for the value of his unexpired term;
(ii) for any just allowance which ought to be made to him by an incoming tenant;
(iii) for any loss or injury he may sustain;
(iv) where part only of the land is required, compensation for damage arising from severance and other injurious affection.

In *Greenwood's Tyre Services Ltd* it was held that in the case of a periodic tenancy the "unexpired term" was the period which would have elapsed from the date on which the acquiring authority actually took possession until a notice to quit deemed to have been given on that date would have expired. Further, in *Smith and Waverley Tailoring Co. v. Edinburgh District Council*[7] the Lands Tribunal for Scotland concluded that, where a general vesting declaration had been executed, a short tenancy subsisting at the date of divestiture automatically terminated at its next term date without a formal notice to quit. In that case, although the claimants continued in occupation after that date they did so at the will of the acquiring authority who could displace them at any time. They accordingly had no extant claim in respect of an unexpired term on their eventual displacement.

---

[3] (1971) 23 P. & C.R. 246.
[4] *Newsham London Borough Council v. Benjamin* [1968] 1 W.L.R. 694.
[5] Compulsory Purchase (Vesting Declarations) Act 1981 s.9(2).
[6] *Smith and Waverley Tailoring Co. v. Edinburgh District Council* (1976) 31 P. & C.R. 484.
[7] *Ibid.*, a decision on the application of Sched. 24, para. 8(b) of the Town and Country Planning (Scotland) Act 1972.

Compensation falls to be assessed under section 20 when the tenant is required to give up possession.[8] A number of points may be made regarding the assessment of compensation.

13—03   First of all, a person with a short tenancy of business premises with a rateable value not exceeding the prescribed amount[9] who is over the age of 60 and who does not wish to relocate the business is entitled, subject to giving certain undertakings[10], to have compensation assessed on the basis of the total extinguishment of the business (1973 Act, section 46).

Secondly the position of a short tenant whose interest is ended under either of the above procedures was not, prior to the Land Compensation Act 1973, entitled to compensation which reflected the right of the tenant to any security of tenure under any legislation relevant to the tenancy. In the case of a business tenant, section 39 of the Landlord and Tenant Act 1954 expressly provided that the right of the tenant to obtain a new tenancy under that Act was to be disregarded in assessing compensation on compulsory taking of possession. This rule was reversed, however, by section 47 of the Land Compensation Act 1973 which requires the right of a business tenant to apply for a new tenancy to be taken into account. In assessing compensation, the scheme giving rise to the taking of possession is to be disregarded (section 47(1)). In addition, a short tenant of business premises enjoys a guarantee that compensation under section 20 of the 1965 Act shall not be less than that which he would have been entitled to receive if the tenancy had been terminated in accordance with the procedure contained in the Landlord and Tenant Act 1954.[11]

13—04   Similar arrangement have been made for a tenant of an agricultural holding. Such a tenant was formerly denied recognition of his right to continue in possession of the holding.[12] The Land Compensation Act 1973 repealed this provision and provides that the compensation payable to the tenant shall be assessed irrespective of any right to serve a notice to quit (section 48(3)). Since the tenant's prospects of remaining in possession are therefore to be included, these prospects require evaluation. An example of this is provided by *Anderson v. Moray District Council*[13] in which the yearly tenant of an agricultural holding was displaced to make way for council house development. In assessing the value of the unexpired term the Lands Tribunal had to estimate how long, having regard to the tenant's circumstances and the security of tenure afforded by the Agricultural Holdings Act, the tenant might remain in possession had the local authority not needed the land for council housing. The Tribunal concluded on the evidence that in the absence of the local authority requirement, the land was near ripe for residential development. Provided the landlord had first obtained planning permission to

---

[8] *Newham London Borough Council v. Benjamin* [1968] 1 W.L.R. 694 *per* Denning L.J. at p. 700.
[9] See the Land Compensation Act 1973, s.46(2).
[10] See para. 11–24.
[11] Landlord and Tenant Act 1954, s.39(2).
[12] Agriculture (Miscellaneous Provisions) Act 1968, s.42.
[13] [1980] R.V.R. 19.

develop the land for that purpose, he would have been able to terminate the tenancy not less than one year and not more than two years from the term date and section 25(2)(c) of the Agricultural Holdings (Scotland) Act 1949 would then operate to dispense with the consent of the Scottish Land Court. The unexpired term was accordingly taken to be two years.

The reference to any just allowance and to any loss or injury in section 20 **13—05** would seem to encompass the sort of matters that may be the subject of a disturbance claim under rule (6) (see Chapter 11).[14] The whole claim must, however, be consistent within itself so that any claim for loss or injury must be based on the unexpired term.[15] It may be that loss incurred in anticipation of displacement is now recoverable.[16]

As regards severance and other injurious affection, section 20(2) provides that the tenant is entitled to compensation for the damage done to him by severing land held by him or otherwise injuriously affecting it. This provision was amended by the Planning and Compensation Act 1991 to enable the tenant to recover compensation for damage suffered in respect of land held under a separate tenancy, since, as originally enacted, section 20 was limited to compensation for damage "in his tenancy". This was interpreted by the Lands Tribunal in *Warlock v. Sodbury Rural District Council*[17] to have a restrictive effect preventing payment of compensation in respect of land held under another tenancy. An earlier reform, effected by section 44 of the 1973 Act, reversed the effect of the decision in *Edwards v. Minister of Transport*,[18] so that compensation for injurious affection will have regard to the whole of the work and not only the part situated on the land from which the tenant has been displaced.

Home loss payments

Sections 29, 29A, 30, 32 and 33 of the Land Compensation 1973 Act[19] make **13—06** provision for home loss payments. The object of such payments is to make some recompense for the personal upset and distress which people suffer when they are compulsorily displaced from their homes. As Lord Widgery C.J. observed, the purpose of the payment is "to make some compensation to a man for the loss of

---

[14] For an illustration of the sorts of items that might be comprised in such a claim see *Anderson v. Moray District Council (supra)*.

[15] See *Greenwood's Tyre Services Ltd v. Manchester Corporation* (1971) 23 P. & C.R. 246.

[16] *Smith v. Strathclyde Regional Council*, 1982 S.L.T. (Lands Tr.) 2; *Aberdeen District Council v. Sim*, 1983 S.L.T. 250.

[17] (1961) 12 P. & C.R. 315.

[18] [1964] 2 Q.B. 134.

[19] Section 29A was inserted and the other provisions cited were amended by ss.68 and 69 of the Planning and Compensation Act 1991.

his home as opposed to the loss of any interest he might have in the particular dwelling which he formerly occupied."[20] The provisions stem from a recommendation in the report of the Urban Motorways Committee that an additional head of compensation should be payable to the occupiers of dwellings in recognition of the real personal disturbance that is inflicted on them when they are required to move.[21] In the White Paper *Development and Compensation — Putting People First,*[22] the Government acknowledged that "the principle of a lump sum payment of this sort, quite independent of the payment for the interest acquired" was right.

13—07   Section 29(1) provides that a person will be entitled to a home loss payment from the acquiring authority[23] where he is displaced from a dwelling on any land in consequence of:

    (i) the compulsory acquisition of an interest in the dwelling;
    (ii) the making, or acceptance of a housing order or undertaking, *i.e.*:
       — a demolition or closing order, or an obstructive building order, under Part IX of the Housing Act 1985 (slum clearance);
       — a closing order under section 368(4) of that Act (closing of multi-occupied house with inadequate means of escape from fire);
       — an undertaking accepted under section 368 of the 1985 Act; or
    (iii) the carrying out of any improvement to the dwelling[24] or of redevelopment on the land[25] where the land has previously been acquired by an authority possessing compulsory purchase powers or appropriated by a local

---

[20] *R. v. Corby District Council ex p. McLean* [1975] 1 W.L.R. 735 at p. 736.

[21] *New Roads in Towns,* (D of E., HMSO 1972) paras. 12.18–19. See, too, the discussion of consumer surplus in the *Final Report of the Commission on the Third London Airport* (1968–71) (HMSO, 1971). P. McAusland in *The Ideologies of Planning Law* (Pergamon Press, 1980) views the carrot of more compensation in this and other provisions of the 1973 Act as very much a utilitarian measure designed to lessen opposition and objection to public works and so speed up development (see Chap. 4).

[22] Cmnd. 5124, (1972) para. 36.

[23] Where the dwelling is not the subject of compulsory acquisition, a home loss payment can be claimed from the authority responsible for the displacement where displacement results from the use of other statutory powers, *e.g.* following the service of a blight notice under s.150 of the Town and Country Planning Act 1990.

[24] "Dwelling" is defined by s.87(1) of the 1973 Act to mean "a building or part of a building occupied, or (if not occupied) last occupied or intended to be occupied as a private dwelling.

[25] "Improvement" includes alteration and enlargement and "redevelopment" includes a change of use (s.29(7A) added by the Housing Act 1974, s.130 and Sched. 13, para. 42). In *R. v. Corby District Council, ex p. McLean* [1975] 1 W.L.R. 735 it was held that the carrying out of redevelopment would include the act of demolition which preceded the substitution of new buildings which were to come under a redevelopment scheme. The applicant was accordingly treated as displaced in consequence of the carrying out of redevelopment and thus entitled to a home loss payment. In *Greater London Council v. Holmes* [1986] 1 All E.R. 739 the Court of Appeal held that in the circumstances of that case displacement to make way for demolition and clearance of property as an essential step in the sale and redevelopment of the land was displacement as a result of "redevelopment." See, too, *Follows v. Peabody Trust* (1983) 10 H.L.R. 62.

authority and is for the time being held by the authority for the purposes for which it was acquired or appropriated;[26]

(iv) the carrying out of any improvement to the dwelling or of redevelopment on the land by a housing association which has previously acquired the land and at the date of displacement is registered;[27]

(v) the making of an order for possession of the dwelling under ground 10 or 10A in Part II of Schedule 2 to the Housing Act 1985 to enable the landlord to demolish or reconstruct or carry out substantial work on the building, or the dwelling is in an area which is the subject of a redevelopment scheme approved by the Secretary of State or the Housing Corporation in accordance with Part V of Schedule 2, and the landlord intends to dispose of the dwelling within a reasonable time of obtaining possession.[28]

A person is not to be treated as displaced from a dwelling in consequence of the acceptance of an undertaking or the carrying out of any improvement to it unless he is permanently displaced from it (section 29(3)(A)).[29] Nor is a person to be treated as displaced from a dwelling in consequence of the compulsory acquisition of an interest if he gives up occupation of it before the date on which the acquiring authority were authorised to acquire the interest (section 29(3)). Apart from that, a person is entitled to a payment, whether or not he has been required by the authority to give up his occupation of the dwelling. Section 29(6) makes it clear that a tenant is entitled to a payment where the authority acquire the landlord's interest by agreement, provided he does not give up occupation before the date of the agreement. **13—08**

To qualify for a home loss payment a person must have been in occupation of the dwelling or a substantial part of it as his only or main residence by virtue of an interest or right to which section 29 applies (below) throughout a period of not less than one year ending with the date of displacement (section 29(2)).[30] The relevant authority nevertheless have a discretionary power to make a home loss payment where the claimant satisfies the qualifying conditions at the date of the displacement, other than the one year occupation requirement.

The interests or rights to which section 29 applies are:

---

[26] "Purposes for which it was acquired" refers to the broad and general purposes for which the authority acquired the land rather than the precise scheme envisaged at the time of acquisition (*Greater London Council v. Holmes* [1986] 1 All E.R. 739).

[27] Under the Housing Associations Act 1985.

[28] The references to ground 10A and to a redevelopment scheme were inserted by section 9 of the Housing and Planning Act 1986.

[29] Added by the Housing Act 1974, s.130, Sched. 13, para. 42(2).

[30] The previous residence qualification of five years was criticised as an arbitrary cutting off point which made no attempt to develop a graduated scale based on length of residence (see D. Farrier and P. McAusland, "Compensation, Participation and the Compulsory Acquisition of 'Homes'", in *Compensation and Compulsory Acquisition*, J.F. Garner (ed.). In the consultation paper *Land Compensation and Compulsory Purchase Legislation* (1989), the Government proposed that the qualifying period be reduced to one year (para. 5), a reform which was implemented by s.68(1) of the Planning and Compensation Act 1991.

(i) any interest in the dwelling;

(ii) a right to occupy the dwelling as a statutory tenant within the meaning of the Rent (Agriculture) Act 1976 or the Rent Act 1977, or under a restricted contract;[31]

(iii) a right of occupation under a contract of employment;

(iv) a right to occupy the dwelling under a license if the right is to occupy as a protected occupier under the Rent (Agriculture) Act 1976, or if Part IV of the Housing Act 1985[32] applies to the licence, or the license is an assured agricultural occupancy within the meaning of Part I of the Housing Act 1988 (section 29(4)).[33]

13—09 A person who has been in occupation within the meaning of section 29(2) for only part of the qualifying period (referred to as 'the claimant's own qualifying period') but who nonetheless, in some other capacity resided in the dwelling, or a substantial part of it, as his only or main residence for a period immediately before that may still be entitled to a home loss payment. He must show, however, that another person, or other persons successively, were in occupation within the meaning of section 29(2) throughout the preceding period. In that event, the claimant's own qualifying period will be treated as including that preceding period for the purposes of section 29(2)).

Aggregation of periods of residence is also permitted to include residence in other dwellings if the conditions of section 29(2) are satisfied (other than the one year residence requirement) in respect of the dwelling from which the displacement occurs. The qualifying conditions, must, however have been satisfied in respect of the former dwelling or dwellings.[34]

Where the claimant has successively occupied different rooms in the same building,[35] section 27(2) has effect as if those rooms constituted the same dwelling (section 32(5)).

If two or more persons are entitled to make a claim to a home loss payment in respect of the same dwelling, the payment to be made on each claim will equal the whole amount of the home loss payment divided by the number of such persons (section 32(6)).

13—10 If a person entitled to a home loss payment dies without having claimed it, a claim may be made by any person, aged 18 or over, who throughout a period of not less than one year ending with the date of displacement of the deceased, resided in the dwelling or a substantial part of it as his only or main residence. That person must, however, be entitled to benefit by virtue of a testamentary

---

[31] Within the meaning of section 19 of the Rent Act 1977.

[32] Part IV of the Housing Act 1985 applies to secure tenancies granted by local authorities, housing associations and other public bodies.

[33] As regards occupation of a dwelling by a person beneficially entitled under a trust, see s.29(8) of the 1973 Act.

[34] See s.32(3)(3A) of the 1973 Act.

[35] s.32(5) refers to different "dwellings" being dwellings consisting of a room or rooms not constructed or adapted for use as a separate dwelling.

disposition or the right of survivorship under a joint tenancy, or the operation of the law of intestacy as applied to the death of the deceased (section 32(4)).

Entitlement to claim a home loss payment by a deserted spouse who has a right of occupation under the Matrimonial Homes Act 1983 is conferred by section 29A of the 1973 Act.[36] If the claiming spouse's right of occupation continues and the claimant is in occupation to the exclusion of the other spouse, the claimant is treated as occupying the dwelling by virtue of an interest in it. This interest is not, however, an owner's interest (see below) and hence the maximum home loss payment is restricted to £1,500.

The Urban Motorways Committee considered whether such payments **13—11** should be tailored to individual circumstances or whether they should be calculated on the basis of a generalised formula. Their conclusion was that the former would give rise to very considerable complexity.[37] Section 30(1), therefore, initially adopted a generalised formula. The amount of a home loss payment was to be equal to the rateable value of the dwelling multiplied by a multiplier prescribed from time to time by the Secretary of State. The maximum amount of a payment was fixed initially at £1,500 and the minimum at £150. The adoption of the formula meant that, as Farrier and McAuslan point out,[38] the payment "bears no relationship at all to the value placed by this person on his house." Denyer-Green drew attention to a further shortcoming in the formula, commenting "if the purpose of the home loss payment is to provide some solution for the forced displacement from a home, it seems necessarily unfair that those displaced from dwellings with higher rateable values get more than those from dwellings with lower rateable values."[39] Following the abolition of rates on domestic property by the Local Government Finance Act 1988, the government adopted the former maximum of £1,500 as a flat rate home loss payment with effect from April 1, 1989.[40]

The 1989 arrangements were short-lived, however, and were replaced on the enactment of section 68(3) of the Planning and Compensation Act 1991 which substituted a revised section 30 into the 1973 Act, the effect on which was to raise the maximum home loss payment to £15,000 and the minimum to £1,500 using a formula based on market value, and making a distinction between claims made by owners and claims made by non-owners.[41] Where the claimant has an "owner's interest" (one who has the power to dispose of the fee simple or who has a lease of which at least three years are unexpired at the date of displacement) the amount of the home loss payment is 10 per cent of the market value of his

---

[36] Inserted by section 69 of the Planning and Compensation Act 1991.
[37] *New Roads in Towns, supra,* para. 12.19. But see the *Final Report of the Commission on the Third London Airport, supra,* which attempted to quantify what it referred to as "consumer surplus."
[38] See "Compensation, Participation and the Compulsory Acquisition of 'Homes'," in *Compensation for Compulsory Acquisition,* J.F. Garner (ed.), *supra.*
[39] *Compulsory Purchase and Compensation* (The Estates Gazette Ltd, 2nd ed.) p. 192.
[40] See the Home Loss Payments Order 1989 (S.I. 1989 No. 24).
[41] These figures are variable by statutory instrument made under s.30(5).

interest in the dwelling, subject to a maximum of £15,000 and a minimum of £1,500. Other claimants (those without an owner's interest) are entitled to the flat figure of £1,500; in such cases the market value of the interest is not relevant. In the case of a claim based on an owner's interest, the market value of the interest in the dwelling[42] is the amount assessed for the purposes of compulsory acquisition of the interest, but if the displacement is caused otherwise than by compulsory purchase the valuation is based on the assumption that a notice to treat was served on the date of displacement (section 30(3)).

13—12   A claim for a home loss payment must be made in writing accompanied by such particulars as may be required to enable the responsible authority to determine both the entitlement to and the amount of the payment (section 32(1)). The payment must be made within three months of the date of the claim, or the date of the displacement, or the day on which the market value of the property is agreed or determined if the claim is based on an owner's interest, whichever is the latest (section 32(2)). No reduction in the amount of compensation payable in respect of the compulsory acquisition of an interest is to be made on account of such payment (section 50(1)) and (3)). Section 9 of the Limitation Act 1980 applies to an obligation to make a home loss payment so as to extinguish the obligation in the absence of a claim at the expiration of six years from the date of displacement (section 32(7A)).[43]

No entitlement to a home loss payment arises when an authority possessing compulsory purchase powers acquire an interest in a dwelling by agreement. However, in such circumstances, the authority have a discretion to make to the person from whom the interest is acquired a payment corresponding to a home loss payment (section 32(7)).[44] Department of the Environment Circular 73/1973 indicates[45] that this provision is intended for use only where there is an element of compulsion in the transaction so that no payment should be made in exercise of the discretion if there is no corresponding power of compulsory purchase. The effect of the provisions, as McAuslan points out, may be to penalise the co-operative person. By co-operating with the public authority, the person loses the statutory right to a home loss payment and has to rely on their discretion.[46]

13—13   Section 33 adapts the provisions of home loss payments (including discretionary payments) to the circumstances of a person residing in a caravan who is displaced from a caravan site[47] and for whom no suitable alternative site for stationing a caravan is available on reasonable terms.

---

[42] "Dwelling" includes any garden, yard, outhouses and appurtenances belonging to or usually enjoyed with the dwelling: s.30(4).

[43] Inserted by the Local Government, Planning and Land Act 1980, s.114(4)(5)(6).

[44] See s.29(6) (above) as regards the position of a tenant where the landlord's interest is acquired by agreement.

[45] See para. 22.

[46] P. McAuslan, *Ideologies of Planning Law* p. 115.

[47] "Caravan site" means land on which a caravan is stationed for the purpose of human habitation and land which is used in conjunction with land on which a caravan is so stationed (s.33(7)).

Advance payment of a home loss payment can be made at any time if the claim is by virtue of an owner's interest. In such a case the full amount of the payment is determined in accordance with the market value of the interest in the dwelling. Such valuation will in most cases be agreed or determined after the date of displacement and hence the responsible authority is required to make an advance payment before the displacement occurs or expiration of three months from the making of the claim, whichever is the later. Such an advance payment will be based on an estimate of the market value of the interest; 10 per cent of the estimate is payable unless this exceeds £15,000 in which case the payment will be £15,000.[48]

The home loss payment is a move back towards the pre-1919 position where a supplement was paid to claimants on account of the compulsory nature of the acquisition.[49] The Royal Institution of Chartered Surveyors have recommended that the time has come to amend rule (1) of the Land Compensation Act 1961 Rules which provides that no allowance shall be made on account of the acquisition being compulsory and that an additional allowance should be payable to *all* claimants to compensate for the factor of compulsion and in recognition that the claimant is an unwilling seller. The amount of the allowance should be calculated on a sliding scale and be payable on the total compensation. The Institution suggest that the home loss payment should be retained and that the allowance should be whichever is the higher of the additional amount so assessed or the home loss payment.[50]

Disturbance payments

When premises are subject to a tenancy, an acquiring authority may, as mentioned earlier,[51] purchase the landlord's interest and leave the tenancy to expire when possession is required by effluxion of time. In that event, the tenant has no entitlement to compensation for there has been neither a compulsory acquisition nor a compulsory extinguishment of the interest; merely a termination under the contractual terms of the tenancy. Yet in practice the disturbance suffered by the tenant in these circumstances may be very similar to that experienced upon compulsory acquisition. He may incur removal expenses and other business losses.

The potential hardship arising from this "notorious defect in compensation law"[52] was recognised in section 37 of the Land Compensation Act 1973 which

13—14

---

[48] See s.32(2A) (2B) (2C) of the Land Compensation Act 1973, inserted by s.68(4) of the Planning Compensation Act 1991.

[49] See Chap. 5.

[50] *Compensation for Compulsory Purchase: Revisions to the Statutory Rules*, para. 6–13.

[51] See para. 13–01.

[52] *Woolfson v. Strathclyde Regional Council*, 1976 S.L.T. (Lands Tr.) 5.

conferred a discretionary power upon acquiring authorities to pay to a person displaced from premises in such circumstances a reasonable allowance towards expenses incurred in removing and towards disturbance of any trade or business being carried on by him in the premises. It is in the nature of discretionary powers that their application tends to be uneven and JUSTICE, in their review of the compensation provisions for compulsory purchase, suggested that "[i]f justice requires that it be paid, it should be paid as a matter of right."[53] This suggestion was taken up in the subsequent White Paper *Development and Compensation — Putting People First*[54] and the entitlement to what is described as a "disturbance payment" was conferred by sections 37 and 38 of the 1973 Act.

13—15 The sections provide that where a person suffers loss and expense because of displacement[55] from any land, other than land used for the purposes of agriculture (section 37(7)), in consequence of specified public sector actions (below), he will be entitled to receive a disturbance payment from the appropriate authority.[56] The specified actions are similar to those which may trigger a home loss payment (above) although in this case they may be directed not just at dwellings but at other buildings. They are:

(i) the acquisition of the land by an authority possessing compulsory purchase powers (section 37(1)(a));[57]
(ii) the making, or acceptance of a housing order or undertaking in respect of a house or building on the land:
— a demolition, or closing order, or an obstructive building order, under Part XI of the Housing Act 1985 (slum clearance);
— a closing order under section 368(4) of that Act (closing of multi-occupied house with inadequate means of escape from fire);
— an undertaking accepted under section 368 of that Act; (section 37(1)(b);
(iii) the carrying out of any improvement to a house or building on the land or of redevelopment[58] of the land where the land has previously been acquired by an authority and is for the time being held by the authority for the purposes for which it was acquired or appropriated (section 37(1)(c));[59]

---

[53] *Compensation for Compulsory Acquisition and Remedies for Planning Restrictions together with a Supplemental Report* (Stevens, 1973) para. 113.
[54] Cmnd. 5124 (1972) paras. 47 and 50.
[55] Defined in s.37(1).
[56] In *Smith & Waverley Tailoring Co. v. Edinburgh District Council (No.2)*, 1977 S.L.T. (Lands Tr.) 29, the Lands Tribunal for Scotland were prepared to treat a claimant as displaced in consequences of acquisition of land even though the claimant was allowed to remain in occupation for several years following acquisition. The acquisition was the real cause of ultimate displacement.
[57] The displacement must be permanent (s.37(3A)).
[58] "Improvement" includes alteration and enlargement and "redevelopment" includes a change of use (ss.29(7A) and 37(9) of the 1973 Act added by the Housing Act 1974, s.130 and Sched. 13, para. 42). See *R. v. Corby District Council, ex p. McLean* [1975] 1 W.L.R. 735; *Greater London Council v. Holmes* [1986] 1 All E.R. 739; and *Follows v. Peabody Trust* (1983) 10 H.L.R. 62.
[59] See *Greater London Council v. Holmes* [1986] 1 All E.R. 739.

(iv) the carrying out of any improvement to a house or building on the land or of redevelopment on the land by a housing association which has previously acquired the land and at the date of displacement is registered[60] (section 37(1)(d)).

In *Prasad v. Wolverhampton Borough Council*[61] the Court of Appeal held that the **13—16** words "displaced from any land in consequence of" were to be construed causatively rather than temporally so that where a person threatened with inevitable dispossession because of compulsory purchase acted reasonably in moving to other accommodation before he was given notice to treat, or before his land was actually acquired by compulsory purchase, he was displaced in consequence of the acquisition.[62] Where displacement occurs due to an order for possession following arrears of mortgage repayments, a claim for a disturbance payment arising from acceptance of a blight notice by a local authority will fail if the notice is served after the order for possession has been made: *McTaggart v. Bristol and West Building Society and Avon County Council*[63]

To qualify for a disturbance payment a claimant must show that he was in lawful possession of the land from which he was displaced (section 37(2)(a)). In *Prasad* Stephenson L.J. referring to the use of the word "displaced" observed that "[i]f its use instead of "dispossessed" has any significance, it is to get rid of the notion which "dispossessed" might convey, that what is being considered is the termination of legal possession as opposed to actual possession, the ending of rights and interests in the land as opposed to occupation of it."[64] In *Smith and Waverley Tailoring Co. v. Edinburgh District Council (No. 2)*[65] the Lands Tribunal for Scotland similarly took the view that a person who occupies premises with the consent of the proprietor of the premises is in "lawful possession" of them even though he has no legal title beyond the proprietor's consent.

Where a person is displaced in consequence of the acquisition of land he must **13—17** show, in order to qualify for a payment, that he has no interest in the land for the acquisition or extinguishment of which he would be entitled to compensation under any other enactment (section 37(2)(b)).[66] Similarly, where the displacement

---

[60] Under the Housing Associations Act 1985.
[61] (1983) 265 E.G. 1073. Stephenson L.J., with whom Fox L.J. and Kerr L.J. agreed, was strongly influenced in his conclusion by the decisions of the Lands Tribunal for Scotland in *Smith v. Strathclyde Regional Council*, 1982 S.L.T. (Lands Tr.) 2 and of the Court of Session in *Sim v. Aberdeen District Council* 1983 S.L.T. 250 on the scope of disturbance compensation which he regarded "as of high persuasive authority on a point of law which affects many inhabitants on each side of the Border." (See Chap. 11). See, also, *Millar v. Strathcylde Regional Council*, 1988 S.L.T. (Lands Tr.) 9.
[62] For a discussion of the decision in *Prasad* see W.A. Leach, "Disturbance — the 'Prasad' case" (1983) 267 E.G. 669.
[63] (1985) 50 P. & C.R. 184.
[64] (1983) 265 E.G. 1073 at p. 1078. See also *Wrexham Maelor Borough Council v. MacDougal* [1993] R.V.R. 141 ("lawful possession" includes a mere licensee).
[65] 1977 S.L.T. (Lands Tr.) 29. See, too, *Millar v. Strathcylde Regional Council*, 1988 S.L.T. (Lands Tr.) 9.
[66] See *Smith and Waverley Tailoring Co. v. Edinburgh District Council (No. 2)*, 1977 S.L.T. (Lands Tr.) 29. A tenant of business premises, who is entitled to claim compensation for disturbance under s.37 of the Landlord and Tenant Act 1954 on termination of his tenancy, may claim compensation

is in consequence of the making, or acceptance of a housing order, or undertaking, there must be no entitlement to a payment under section 584A(1) of the Housing Act 1985 (compensation payable in respect of closing and demolition orders).

In the case of displacement in the circumstances set out in section 37(1)(a), (c), or (d), a claimant must also show, in the case of land acquired under a compulsory purchase order, that he was in lawful possession not only at the date of displacement but also at the time when notice of the *making* of the order was first published or, if it is an order which does not require confirmation, at the time of the preparation of the order in draft.[67] In the case of land acquired by agreement the relevant time is when the agreement was made (section 37(3)). But in *R. v. Islington London Borough Council; ex p. Knight*[68] it was held that a claimant who surrendered her secure tenancy on the allocation of a new house by the local authority was not entitled to a disturbance payment. The surrender of the tenancy extinguished her interest; there was no acquisition by agreement.

In the case of displacement under section 37(1)(b), the claimant must have been in lawful possession at the time when the order was made, or the undertaking was accepted (section 37(3)).

13—18 Where a person is displaced from any land in the circumstances mentioned in section 37(1) but has no entitlement to a disturbance payment or to compensation for disturbance under any other Act the authority responsible for displacement may made a discretionary disturbance payment (section 37(5)). If the authority decide to make such a payment, the amount is determined in accordance with the provisions of section 38(1) and (3) (below).[69]

The amount of a disturbance payment is to be equal to the reasonable expenses of the person entitled to the payment incurred in removing from the land (section 38(1)(a));[70] and, if the person was carrying on a trade or business on the land, the loss that will be sustained as a result of the disturbance of the trade or business consequent on having to quit the land (section 38(1)(b)). In estimating trade or business loss, regard must be had to the period for which the land might reasonably have been expected to be available for that purpose and to the availability of other land suitable for that purpose (section 38(2)).[71]

---

under the 1954 Act or the 1973 Act, at his option, but is not entitled to both payments: s.37(4) of the 1973 Act.

[67] In the case of land acquired under an Act specifying the land as subject to compulsory acquisition, the relevant time is when the provisions of the Bill for that Act were first published s.(37(3)(b)).

[68] [1984] 1 All E.R. 154.

[69] 1973 Act, s.37(5). It would seem that any dispute as to the amount of a discretionary payment is to be determined by the Lands Tribunal: *Gozra v. Hackney London Borough Council* (1988) 57 P. & C.R. 211 (Court of Appeal). See, however, *Glasgow District Council v. Mackie* [1992] 20 E.G. 114 (Court of Session).

[70] It must be doubtful whether the provision is wide enough to cover the cost of any structural modifications to the new accommodation (*Glasgow Corporation v. Anderson*, 1976 S.L.T. 225; *Nolan v. Sheffield Metropolitan District Council* (1979) 38 P. & C.R. 741).

[71] As regards a disturbance payment where a business is carried on by person aged at least 60, see the 1973 Act, s.46(7).

Although the scope of these provisions has been considered by the Lands **13—19** Tribunal, the leading case is *Glasgow Corporation v. Anderson*[72] in which the First Division of the Court of Session held that the term "reasonable expenses . . . in removing" was to be construed more generously than "any expenses in the removal." In that case a tenant was displaced from a house in good decorative condition. The local authority flat to which she moved required a certain amount of necessary decoration. In addition, as the flat was all electric, she had to buy and instal a small electric cooker. Her claim for removal expenses, the cost of reconnecting the telephone and of lifting, removing and refitting carpets was accepted by the corporation. Her claim in respect of redecoration, curtain rails, new plugs and the electric cooker was rejected. These items were allowed, although the amount for the cooker was reduced, by the Lands Tribunal for Scotland whose decision was subsequently affirmed by the First Division. Lord President Emslie said:

> "In all these circumstances, it is not unreasonable, when one comes to construe section 35(1)(a) (of the Land Compensation (Scotland) Act 1973) in a commonsense way, in the context in which it is set, to conclude that a disturbance payment may include reasonable expenses, reasonably incurred as a direct and natural consequence of and in, the compulsory removing, in addition to the expenses strictly referable to 'the removal' itself. In applying the subsection, the question of whether a particular expense claimed is or is not within the ambit of the disturbance payment will be one of circumstance and degree.[73]

Agreeing with this view, Lord Cameron observed that the payment "should in a **13—20** true sense be a 'disturbance payment' and not the mere cost of the removal operation." This decision was cited by the Lands Tribunal in *Nolan v. Sheffield Metropolitan District Council*[74] in reaching a similar conclusion about the scope of "reasonable expenses . . . in removing." In this case the claimant recovered (*inter alia*) the cost of removal expenses, telephone connection, refitting of domestic appliances, purchase of paint and filler for repairs, loss of earnings due to time off work, and loss of roses from his garden. Items which were disallowed by the Lands Tribunal included the cost of new carpets and kitchen cupboards and rent payable during the period in which the work was carried out. The cost of new carpets was also in issue in *Goss v. Paddington Churches Housing Association*[75] in which the Lands Tribunal held, disallowing the claim, that the correct measure of compensation should be the cost of lifting and relaying existing carpets or the loss incurred on forced sale.

---

[72] 1976 S.L.T. 225.
[73] *Ibid.* at p. 229.
[74] (1979) 38 P. & C.R. 741. See, also, *Barker v. Hull City Council* (1985) 275 E.G. 157 L.T.
[75] (1982) 261 E.G. 373.

Where the claim arises from disturbance to a trade or business under section 38(1)(b) a similar broad approach is taken. In *Evans v. Glasgow District Council*[76] it was held that the general approach in assessing this form of disturbance payment was the same as for a rule (6) claim[77] and the remoteness test considered in *Harvey v. Crawley Development Corporation*[78] and in *Anderson* should be applied. The Tribunal cautioned, however, that the precise wording of section 38 might operate more restrictively in some cases than the general nature of the test in *Harvey*. "[I]t would be unwise," said the Tribunal, "to commit ourselves in this particular case to any general proposition that disturbance claims under rule (6) and disturbance payments under section 38, following upon compulsory dispossession, are in all respects identical when it comes to assessing quantum."

13—21 When displacement is from a dwelling to which structural modifications have been made to meet the needs of a disabled person[79] and a local authority having duties under section 29 of the National Assistance Act 1948 have provided assistance in such modifications, or would have done so if an application had been made, the amount of the disturbance payment is to include an amount equal to the reasonable expenses incurred by the claimant in making comparable modifications to the dwelling to which the disabled person removes (section 38(3)).

A disturbance payment will carry interest at the rate for the time being prescribed under section 32 of the Land Compensation Act 1961 from the date of displacement until payment (section 37(6)).

Any dispute as to the amount of a disturbance payment is to be referred to and determined by the Lands Tribunal (section 38(4)).

Rehousing

13—22 Section 39 of the 1973 Act provides that where, in the circumstances described below, a person[80] is displaced from residential accommodation on any land and suitable alternative residential accommodation on reasonable terms is not otherwise available to that person then the local housing authority[81] have a duty to

---

[76] 1978 S.L.T. (Lands Tr.) 5.
[77] See Chap. 11.
[78] [1957] 1 Q.B. 485.
[79] Whether or not this is the person entitled to the disturbance payment.
[80] The provision does not apply to a person trespassing on the land or who has been permitted to reside in a house or building pending its improvement or demolition (s.39(3) of the 1973 Act, as amended by the Housing Act 1974, s.130 and Sched. 13, para. 40).
[81] Defined in section 39(7), as amended by the Housing (Consequential Provisions) Act 1985, s.4 and Sched. 2, para. 24(4).

secure the provision of such accommodation.[82] The duty arises where a person is displaced[83] in consequence of:

(a) the acquisition of the land by an authority possessing compulsory purchase powers (section 39(1)(a));

(b) the making, or acceptance of a housing order or undertaking[84] in respect of a house or building on the land (section 39(1)(b));

(c) the carrying out of any improvement to a house or building on the land or of redevelopment on the land[85] if it has been previously acquired by an authority possessing compulsory purchase powers or appropriated by a local authority and held for the time being for the purpose for which it was acquired or appropriated (section 39(1)(c)).

In an area designated as the site for a new town the rehousing obligation falls upon the development corporation or the Commission for the New Towns. If the displacement arises from the acquisition of land by the corporation or the redevelopment of land held by it, the duty will fall on the development corporation. Where, however, the land is redeveloped by the Commission for the New Towns the duty will fall on that authority (section 39(8)).

The duty to rehouse does not arise where the acquisition is in pursuance of a **13—23** blight notice served under section 150 of the Town and Country Planning Act 1990 (section 39(2)).[86] Nor does it extend to a person who has been displaced in the circumstances described and to whom money has been advanced either under section 41 of the 1973 Act (see below) to acquire or construct a substitute dwelling, or under the Small Dwellings Acquisition Acts 1899 to 1923, or section 43 of the Housing (Financial Provisions) Act 1958 or section 435 of the Housing Act 1985[87] or by a development corporation or the Commission for the New Towns otherwise than under section 41 of the 1973 Act.[88]

---

[82] In *R. v. Bristol Corporation, ex p. Hendy* [1974] 1 All E.R. 1047 the Court of Appeal took the view that the corporation were under a duty to act reasonably and to do their best as soon as practicable to provide suitable alternative accommodation. In the meantime, the authority discharged their obligation under the legislation by providing temporary accommodation. In *R. v. East Hertfordshire District Council ex p. Smith* (1991) 23 H.L.R. 26 the Court of Appeal held that this section did not impose a duty on the local housing authority to rehouse the displaced occupants as a family unit and that provision of temporary bed and breakfast accommodation for part of the family was sufficient. Although permanent accommodation was subsequently provided, the Court of Appeal expressed the view that there is no absolute duty to promise permanent accommodation when making temporary arrangements.

[83] *i.e.* when possession of the house is taken: *Glasgow District Council v. Douglas* (1978), unreported.

[84] Defined in s.29(7) of the 1973 Act, as amended by the Housing (Consequential Provisions) Act 1985, s.4 and Sched. 2, para. 24(1).

[85] "Improvement" includes alteration and enlargement and "redevelopment" includes a change of use (s.29(7A) of the 1973 Act, added by the Housing Act 1974, s.130 and Sched. 13, para. 42).

[86] See Chap. 16.

[87] Added by the Housing (Consequential Provisions) Act 1985, s.4 and Sched. 2, para. 24(4).

[88] s.39(4) of the 1973 Act.

A person is not to be treated as displaced in consequence of any such acquisition, improvement or redevelopment as is mentioned in section 39(1)(a) or (c) (above) unless he was residing in the accommodation in question:

(a) in the case of land acquired under a compulsory purchase order, at the time when notice of the making or preparation in draft, as the case may be, of the order was first published (section 39(6)(a));
(b) in the case of land acquired under an Act specifying the land as subject to compulsory acquisition, at the time when the provisions of the Bill for the Act specifying the land were first published (section 39(6)(b));
(c) in the case of land acquired by agreement, at the time the agreement was made (section 39(6)(c)).

13—24 Neither is a person to be treated as displaced in consequence of an order, or undertaking mentioned in section 39(1)(b) (above) unless he was residing in the accommodation at the time the order was made, the resolution was passed, or the undertaking was accepted.[89]

Section 40 of the 1973 Act imposes on local housing authorities a similar rehousing obligation in relation to a person displaced from a residential caravan on a caravan site[90] for whom neither suitable residential accommodation nor a suitable alternative site for stationing a caravan is available on reasonable terms.

Department of the Environment Circular 73/73 recognises that many local authorities already voluntarily accept responsibility for rehousing in circumstances which go beyond the statutory requirements in the Act or in earlier legislation. The circular states that: "The Secretaries of State would not wish the introduction of the new obligations to lead these authorities to adopt less generous practices. They are sure that all authorities will adopt as sympathetic an attitude as possible, bearing in mind the housing situation in their particular area, to the difficulties of displaced occupiers falling outside the scope of section 39."[91]

13—25 Section 41 of the 1973 Act enables the local housing authority, subject to such conditions as may be approved by the Secretary of State, to satisfy the rehousing obligation by making "interest only" mortgage advances repayable on maturity to displaced residential owner-occupiers. Such an advance may be made where an owner-occupier[92] of a dwelling is displaced from it in any of the circumstances mentioned in section 39(1)(a), (b) or (c) (above) and wishes to acquire or construct another dwelling in substitution for the one from which he has been displaced. The advance will be made on terms providing for the repayment of the principal

---

[89] s.39(6) of the 1973 Act.
[90] As defined in s.33(7) of the 1973 Act.
[91] Circular 73/73, para. 36
[92] Defined in s.41(9) of the 1973 Act.

at the end of a fixed period which may be extended by the authority or upon notice given by the authority, subject in either case to provision for earlier repayment on the happening of a specified event, for example, the sale of the property or the death of the borrower. An advance may be made on such other terms as the authority think fit having regard to all the circumstances. Department of the Environment Circular 73/73 suggests that this would, for example, permit an authority to transfer the advance, as secured, to a spouse or other adult member of the household on the death of the borrower.[93] An advance for the construction of a dwelling may be made by instalments linked to progress with the work (section 41(4)).

The principal of the advance, together with the interest on it, is to be secured by way of a mortgage on the borrower's interest in the dwelling. The amount of the principal is not to exceed the value of the borrower's interest or, as the case may be, the value when the dwelling has been constructed. The authority must satisfy themselves that the dwelling to be acquired or constructed is, or will on completion be, fit for human habitation.[94]

Where the displacing authority and the rehousing authority are not one and **13—26** the same, section 42 of the 1973 Act provides for the former to indemnify the latter against any net loss incurred[95] in providing or securing the provision of accommodation for any person in pursuance of section 39(1)(a) or (c) of the Act. Similar provision is made for indemnifying a net loss incurred[96] in respect of an advance made under section 41 of the Act.

Section 43 provides that where a person displaced from a dwelling[97] in consequence of any of the events specified in section 39(1)(a) or (b) has no interest in the dwelling or no greater interest than as tenant for a year or from year to year and that person wishes to acquire another dwelling as a substitute, the displacing authority may pay any reasonable expenses incurred in connection with the acquisition, other than the purchase price. The substitute dwelling must be acquired[98] not later than one year after displacement and must be reasonably comparable with that from which the person has been displaced.

Section 50(1) of the 1973 Act prohibits the reduction of compensation payable in respect of the compulsory acquisition of an interest in land on account of the provision or the securing of provision by the acquiring authority of alternative residential accommodation for the person entitled to the compensation.

---

[93] Circular 73/73, para 39.
[94] See s.604 of the Housing Act 1985.
[95] Defined in s.42(2) of the 1973 Act.
[96] Defined in s.42(4) of the 1973 Act.
[97] As regards displacement, see s.39(3), (6) and (6A) as applied by s.43(4) of the 1973 Act.
[98] A dwelling acquired pursuant to a contract is to be treated as acquired when the contract is made (s.43(3)).

Agricultural land

13—27 Although compensation claims by owners and occupiers of agricultural land are determined in accordance with the rules described earlier in this book, there are a number of special provisions relating to such claims which, for convenience, are drawn together in this section.[99]

1. AN OWNER-OCCUPIER

13—28 An owner-occupier of agricultural land will be entitled to claim under section 5 of the Land Compensation Act 1961 for the value of the land taken measured according to rule (2), and also for disturbance. Where appropriate, he may also claim compensation for severance and other injurious affection. He may also be entitled to a home loss payment (above). In addition, he may be entitled to what is called a "farm loss payment."

The White Paper *Development and Compensation — Putting People First*[1] acknowledged that "because of the long time-scale of agricultural production, its peculiar dependence on land and the complex effects of climatic and other factors on yield, owner-occupiers who lose the whole of their farms and have to move to unfamiliar land may be faced with temporary unavoidable losses." To meet this difficulty a payment, in addition to compensation, was proposed for persons displaced from agricultural land. The provisions for farm loss payments were introduced in sections 34 to 36 of the Land Compensation Act 1973 and were subsequently amended by the Planning and Compensation Act 1991.[2]

Section 34 provides that an owner-occupier[3] of land constituted or included in an agricultural unit[4] will be entitled to a farm loss payment from the acquiring authority if, in consequence of the compulsory acquisition of his interest in not less than 0.5 hectares of that land, he is displaced from the land and not more than three years after the date of displacement he begins to farm another agricultural unit elsewhere in Great Britain (section 34(1)).[5] An "owner's interest" means

---

[99] See, generally, R.N.D. Hamilton, *Compensation for Compulsory Acquisition of Agricultural Land* (RICS, 3rd ed. 1980).

[1] Cmnd. 5124 (1972) para. 55.

[2] See s.70 and Sched. 15, para. 6 to the 1991 Act, implementing recommendations of the Royal Institution of Chartered Surveyors in their paper *Compensation for Compulsory Acquisition* (1989), para. 4.93.

[3] Where the agricultural land unit containing the land is occupied for the purposes of a partnership, see s.36(2).

[4] As defined in s.171 of the Town and Country Planning Act 1990.

[5] On the date on which he begins to farm the new unit he must be in occupation of the *whole* of that unit as owner or as lessee but the interest in the new unit does not have to correspond with that which he enjoyed in that unit from which he has been displaced; it would be sufficient, therefore, to have no more than a yearly tenancy of the new unit (s.34(4)).

the interest of an owner or a lessee under a lease the unexpired period of which on the date of displacement is not less than a year (section 34(2)). An agricultural tenant holding for a year or from year to year also has a qualifying interest.

A person is to be treated as displaced from land if, and only if, he gives up **13—29** possession on a date after the making or confirmation of the compulsory purchase order but before being required to do so by the acquiring authority. He will also qualify if he is required to give up possession by the acquiring authority, or on completion of the acquisition or, where the acquiring authority permit him to continue temporarily in possession, either under a tenancy or a licence of a kind not making him a tenant as defined in the Agricultural Holdings Act 1986, on the expiration of that tenancy or licence (section 34(3)). There is no entitlement to a farm loss payment if a farmer leaves in advance of displacement as so defined.[6] Nor is there any entitlement if he acquired the interest in or the lease of the new unit before the date on which the acquisition of his original unit was authorised (section 34(4)).

No farm loss payment is to be made as a result of displacement from land of a person who is entitled to a payment under section 12 of the Agriculture (Miscellaneous Provisions) Act 1968 (section 34(5)).[7] A payment can be made, however, where a person is displaced in consequence of the service by him of a blight notice under section 150 of the Town and Country Planning Act 1990.[8]

The formula for calculating the farm loss payment is set out in section 35. The **13—30** payment is to equal the average annual profit derived from the use for agricultural purposes of the agricultural land comprised in the land acquired. The average is to be computed by reference to the profits for the three years ending with the date of displacement or for the period during which the person displaced was in occupation, whichever is the shorter (section 35(1)).[9] Where a person has been permitted by the acquiring authority to continue temporarily in possession of the original unit and on the date of eventual displacement he has been in occupation of that unit for more than three years, he may elect to compute the annual average

---

[6] As originally enacted, s.34(3) restricted "displacement by excluding a farmer who vacated the land before being required to do so because suitable alternative property was available in the market. The Royal Institution of Chartered Surveyors noted this defect in their paper, *supra*, (paras. 4.76 to 4.78). An amendment to the provision was affected by the Planning and Compensation Act 1991, s.70 and Sched. 15, para. 6 to overcome this difficulty.

[7] s.12 of the 1968 Act makes provision for a "reorganisation payment" to be made where an acquiring authority acquire the interest in the whole or part of an agricultural holding of the tenant or take possession of the whole or part of the holding (see paras. 13–37 and 13–38).

[8] The Royal Institution of Chartered Surveyors' paper, *supra*, suggested that a farmer whose interest is acquired following the service of an effective blight notice should be entitled to receive a farm loss payment, assuming he qualifies in other respects, unless it can be shown that his desire to sell his interest was unconnected with the scheme underlying the proposed acquisition by the authority (para. 49.1). This suggestion was implemented by the repeal of s.34(6) of the 1973 Act by the Planning and Compensation Act 1991, s.70 and Sched. 15, para. 6, and s.84 and Sched. 19, Part III.

[9] If the claimant's 12 month's accounting period ends not more than one year before the date of displacement, the date on which that period ends is to be treated as the date of displacement for the purposes of s.35(1).

profit by reference to the profits, not for the last three years, but for any three consecutive periods of twelve months during which he was in occupation and for which accounts have been made up, the last of which ends on or after the date of completion of the acquisition. Alternatively, if there are no such periods, the computation can be made by reference to the profits for any three consecutive years for which he has been in occupation, the last of which ends as before (section 35(3)).

In calculating the profits, there is to be deducted a sum equal to the notional rent that might reasonably be expected to be payable in respect of the agricultural land comprised in the land acquired if it was let for agricultural purposes to a tenant responsible for rates, repairs and other outgoings. The deduction is to be made whether or not the land is in fact let; and if it is let, no deduction is to be made for the rent actually payable (section 35(4)). There must also be left out of account loss of profits from any activity in respect of which an item would fall to be included in the compensation for disturbance; such loss of profits cannot be counted for both the disturbance claim and for the farm loss payment (section 35(5)).

13—31   If the value of the agricultural land comprised in the original unit exceeds the value of such land in the new unit, the farm loss payment is to be proportionately reduced (section 35(6)). When comparing values, the assessment is to be made on the basis of a freehold interest with vacant possession in the land valued solely for agricultural purposes. Account must also be taken of the condition of the land and its surroundings and to prices current, as regards the land comprised in the land acquired, on the date of displacement and, as regards land comprised in the new unit, on the date on which the person concerned begins to farm the new unit. Rules (2) to (4) of section 5 of the 1961 Act[10] apply. And the valuation is to be made without regard to the principal dwelling, if any, comprised in the same agricultural unit (section 35(7)).

An upper limit is placed on the amount of a farm loss payment. Section 35(8) provides that it is not to be greater than the amount by which the payment together with compensation for the acquisition of the interest acquired assessed on the basis of the assumptions referred to in section 5(2) to (4) of the 1973 Act[11] (including any sum for disturbance) exceeds the compensation actually payable for the acquisition of the interest. In other words, where the farm loss payment together with compensation assessed on the value of the land put to its existing use (plus disturbance) exceeds the compensation assessed on the basis of the open

---

[10] See Chap 7.

[11] The effect of s.5(2)–(4) of the 1973 Act is that planning permission may only be assumed for the classes of development specified in paras. 1 and 2 of Sched. 3 to the Town and Country Planning Act 1990. It must not be assumed that planning permission for Sched. 3 development would be granted where such development is the subject of a discontinuance order made under s.102 of the 1990 Act in respect of which compensation has become payable. If planning permission has in fact been granted for development other than such Sched. 3 development, it is to be assumed that no such permission has been granted for development that has not been carried out.

market value of the land, the payment is limited to the difference. Any dispute as to the amount of a farm loss payment is to be determined by the Lands Tribunal (section 35(9)).

A claim for such a payment, which may include any reasonable valuation or legal expenses incurred in preparing and prosecuting the claim (section 36(5)), must be lodged in writing by the person entitled[12] to it within a year of the date on which he began to farm the new unit (section 36(1)). The claim is to be accompanied by sufficient information to enable the acquiring authority to determine both entitlement and amount. A farm loss payment will carry interest at the prescribed rate[13] from the date on which the claimant begins to farm the new unit until payment (section 36(6)).

13—32

Where an interest in land is acquired by agreement by an authority possessing compulsory purchase powers there is no entitlement to a farm loss payment but the authority have a discretion to make a corresponding payment (section 36(4)). The vendor should seek to ensure at the time of acquisition that such a payment will be made if he begins farming a new unit within the stipulated three year period.

2. A LANDLORD

Where agricultural land is let, the landlord will be entitled upon the compulsory acquisition of his interest to compensation under section 5 of the 1961 Act for the value of his interest in the land taken assessed in accordance with rule (2). As he is not in occupation, he is not entitled to disturbance;[14] nor is he entitled to a home loss payment or a farm loss payment (above). In an appropriate case, he will, however, be entitled to claim in respect of severance and other injurious affection.

13—33

In assessing the value of the landlord' interest regard must be had to section 48 of the Land Compensation Act 1973. It provides that the security of tenure which the tenant would enjoy were the land not required for use by the acquiring authority is to be taken into account. The provision reverses the effect of the House of Lords decision in *Rugby Joint Water Board v. Shaw-Fox*.[15]

In that case the water board obtained a confirmed compulsory purchase order in respect of a large part of a farm for use as a reservoir. As a result of the water board's proposal, the agricultural tenant lost his security because the owner was

---

[12] Where a person, who would have been entitled to a farm loss payment, dies before the expiration of the period for making the claim, a claim may be lodged before the expiration of that period by his personal representative (s.36(3)).

[13] See para. 13–43.

[14] See Chap. 11.

[15] [1973] A.C. 202 affirming the decision of the Court of Appeal in *Minister of Transport v. Pettit* (1969) 20 P. & C.R. 344.

placed in a position whereby he could serve a notice to quit which could not be contested. Notice to treat was subsequently served on the owner who claimed compensation on the basis that his interest was subject to an unprotected tenancy. The water board contested this on the ground that the scheme had altered the nature of the owner's interest and increased its value. In other words, they said, this was an increase in value due to the scheme underlying the acquisition and fell to be ignored under the rule in *Pointe Gourde*.[16] The House of Lords, Lord Simon dissenting, held that the *Pointe Gourde* rule applied not to the ascertainment of the interests to be valued but to the value of the interests when ascertained. The change in this case had been to the interest to be ascertained and the owner was awarded compensation on the basis that at the date of the notice to treat his interest was subject to an unprotected tenancy.

13—34   To avoid a repetition of the hardship to agricultural tenants arising from the decision in *Shaw-Fox*, section 48 of the 1973 Act was introduced. This provides that, in assessing the compensation payable by an acquiring authority in respect of the acquisition of the interest of the landlord in an agricultural holding, there shall be disregarded any right of the landlord to serve a notice to quit, and any notice to quit already served by the landlord, which would not be or would not have been effective if:

    (i) in Case B in Part I of Schedule 3 to the Agricultural Holdings Act 1986 (land required for non-agricultural use for which planning permission has been granted), the reference to the land being required did not include a reference to its being required by an acquiring authority; and

    (ii) in section 27(3)(f) of the 1986 Act (proposed termination of tenancy for purpose of land being used for non-agricultural use not falling within Case B) the reference to the land being used did not include a reference to it being used by an acquiring authority (section 48(2)(a)).[17]

If the tenant has quit the holding or any part of it by reason of a notice to quit which is to be so disregarded, it is to be assumed that he has not done so (section 44(1)).

3. A TENANT

13—35   A tenant for a term of years is entitled to a notice to treat and may claim under section 5 of the 1961 Act in respect of the value of his interest, for disturbance and, where appropriate, for severance and other injurious affection. He may also be entitled to home loss and farm loss payments. However, tenancies of agricultural land are frequently on a yearly basis and, as indicated in the discussion of

---

[16] See Chap. 9.
[17] See, for example, *Anderson v. Moray District Council*, 1978 S.L.T. (Lands Tr.) 37.

"short tenancies" (above), dispossession may occur in one of two ways. First of all, the acquiring authority may persuade the landlord to serve a notice to quit or, having purchased the landlord's interest, may themselves serve a notice to quit. In such a case the tenant is entitled to compensation not for compulsory acquisition but as between landlord and tenant under the Agricultural Holdings Act 1986. There are three heads of compensation:

(i) Compensation for disturbance equal to one year's rent of the holding. With proof of loss the tenant may be able to claim an amount up to a maximum of two years' rent of the holding.

(ii) Compensation for improvements, generally referred to as "tenant right." This would include such matters as the unexhausted value of fertilisers and loss of growing crops.

(iii) A reorganisation payment under the Agriculture (Miscellaneous Provisions) Act 1968, section 12. This is a payment equal to four times the annual rent of the holding and is intended to help the tenant in the reorganisation of his affairs.

Where dispossession is from part only of the holding, provision is made for an abatement of the rent.

Alternatively, where an acquiring authority is unable to wait for a notice to quit to run its course they may serve a notice of entry and, after the expiration of 14 days, enter on the land and extinguish the tenant's interest.[18] When a general vesting declaration has been employed, the authority must first serve a notice to treat on a short tenant before serving a notice of entry and taking possession.[19] The tenant is entitled to compensation under section 20 of the 1965 Act for the extinguishment of that interest.

13—36

There are four heads of claim under section 20:

(i) The value of the unexpired term or interest in the land: in *Wakerley v. St Edmundsbury Borough Council*[20] Sir David Cairns indicated (in his dissenting judgment) that the value of the unexpired term was to be assessed in accordance with rule (2). As with the landlord's interest, section 48(3) of the Land Compensation Act 1973, reversing the effect of the decision in *Rugby Joint Water Board v. Shaw-Fox*[21] (above), provides that in making such assessment no account is to be taken of the consequences of the acquiring authority's scheme on the nature of the interest being extinguished. There is to be disregarded any right of the landlord to serve a notice to quit, and any notice to quit already served by the landlord, which would not be or would not have been effective if the appropriate grounds for possession in the Agricultural Holdings Act 1986 (Case B and section

---

[18] Compulsory Purchase Act 1965, s.11.
[19] Compulsory Purchase (Vesting Declarations) Act 1981, s.9(2).
[20] (1979) 38 P. & C.R. 551.
[21] [1973] A.C. 202.

27(3)(f)) were construed as not including a reference to the land being required or used by an acquiring authority.[22]

13—37   (ii) Any just allowance which ought to be made to him by an incoming tenant: In *Anderson v. Moray District Council*,[23] for example, an allowance was made under this head for tenant's improvements for grass seed sown with the waygoing white crop, and for unexhausted fertility.

(iii) Any loss or injury: In *Minister of Transport v. Pettit*[24] the Court of Appeal were of the opinion that section 20(1) of the Compulsory Purchase Act 1965 does not confine this head of claim to financial loss or injury. In *Anderson*, for example, the Lands Tribunal for Scotland awarded sums under this head in respect of loss on forced sale of stock, removal expenses, fees and own time and expenses.

(iv) Where appropriate, compensation for damage arising from severance and other injurious affection: The tenant's claim under this head is limited to "damage done to him in his tenancy." In *Worlock v. Sodbury R.D.C.*[25] this was construed as not extending to damage to land in any other tenancy, but the Planning and Compensation Act 1991[26] has reversed the effect of that decision to enable compensation to be claimed in respect of damage relevant to land held under another tenancy as well.

In addition to these four heads of claim, provision is made for a reorganisation payment. Section 12 of the Agricultural (Miscellaneous Provisions) Act 1968 provides that the tenant will be entitled to the tax-free reorganisation payment, for which provision is also made in section 60 of the Agricultural Holdings Act 1986, which is equal to four times the annual rent of the holding to help in the reorganisation of his affairs. Section 48(5) of the Land Compensation Act 1973, however, provides that the tenant's compensation is to be reduced by an amount equal to the reorganisation payment. Hamilton points out that "the 1968 Act payment was introduced on the assumption that the tenant had not got a protected tenancy, so that it is reasonable that he should not get both the payment and the enhanced compensation on the protected tenancy basis."[27] The reason for dealing with the payment "in this rather circuitous way of addition and subtraction" is apparently to enable the tenant to continue to enjoy the tax-free advantages of the 1968 Act payment.

13—38   Section 48(6) of the 1973 Act goes on to provide that if the tenant's compensation determined on the basis of a protected tenancy but with deduction of the reorganisation payment is less than it would have been before these provisions were introduced, it is to be increased by the amount of the deficiency. In other

---

[22] See *Wakerley v. St Edmundsbury Borough Council* (1979) 38 P. & C.R. 551; *Dawson v. Norwich City Council* (1979) 250 E.G. 1297; *Anderson v. Moray District Council*, 1978 S.L.T. (Lands Tr.) 37.

[23] 1978 S.L.T. (Lands Tr.) 37.

[24] (1969) 20 P. & C.R. 344.

[25] (1961) 12 P. & C.R. 315.

[26] Planning and Compensation Act 1991, s.70 and Sched. 15, para. 4.

[27] R.N.D. Hamilton, *Compensation for Compulsory Acquisition of Agricultural Land* (RICS 3rd ed., 1980), para. 95.

words, the tenant can be no worse off as a result of these provisions and, in some cases, he will be better off.

A yearly tenant is entitled to a farm loss payment on the extinguishment of his interest[28] and he may also qualify for a home loss payment.

There will be occasions where the compensation available upon extinguishment of the interest is more generous than that available under a notice to quit. Section 59 of the 1973 Act accordingly allows a tenant served with a notice to quit either by the landlord or by the acquiring authority after they have acquired the landlord's interest[29] to elect for notice of entry compensation. If the tenant served with a notice to quit opts for notice of entry compensation and gives up possession of the holding to the acquiring authority on or before the date on which the tenancy terminates under the notice to quit, he is entitled to have compensation assessed under section 20 of the 1965 Act as if the notice to quit had not been served and the acquiring authority had taken possession of the holding pursuant to a notice of entry on the day before that on which the tenancy terminates under the notice to quit. An election must be made by notice in writing served on the acquiring authority not later than the date on which possession of the holding is given up (1973 Act, section 59(4)).

It should be noted that a person served with notice to quit part of an agricultural **13—39** holding is not entitled both to make an election under section 59 of the 1973 Act and to give a counter-notice under section 32 of the Agricultural Holdings Act 1986 treating the notice to quit part of the holding as notice to quit the entire holding (1973 Act, section 59(6)). He may, however, elect for notice of entry compensation within two months of the date of the notice to quit, or, if later, the decision of the Agricultural Land Tribunal, and then by notice served on the acquiring authority within the same period claim that the remainder of the holding is not reasonably capable of being farmed, either by itself or in conjunction with other relevant land, as a separate agricultural unit (1973 Act, section 61(1)). Any dispute over the validity of such a notice may be referred to the Lands Tribunal. If the notice takes effect and the claimant within 12 months gives up possession of the part of the holding to which it relates, compensation under section 20 of the 1965 Act will be payable in respect of the whole (1973 Act, section 61(3)).[30]

Advance payment

Section 52 of the Land Compensation Act 1973 confers a right upon a person **13—40** who has been dispossessed of land subject to compulsory purchase to claim an

---

[28] Land Compensation Act 1973, s.34(1)(2) as amended by s.70 of and Sched. 15, para. 6 to the Planning and Compensation Act 1991.

[29] *Dawson v. Norwich City Council* (1979) 250 E.G. 1297.

[30] S.55(2)–(4) and s.56(3) are applied in relation to s.61(1)–(3) by s.61(4). For the meaning of "other relevant land" see s.55(3).

advance payment on account of any compensation payable for the compulsory acquisition of the claimant's interest.[31] The entitlement arises where an acquiring authority have taken possession of any land,[32] although it would seem that a request for such payment may anticipate possession.

A request for an advance payment is to be made in writing to the acquiring authority giving particulars of the claimant's interest in the land if this has not already been given in response to a notice to treat. In practice, satisfactory evidence of title will also be required. Such other particulars as will enable the authority to estimate the compensation in respect of which the advance payment is to be made must also be provided.

The amount of any advance payment will be equal to 90 per cent. of the compensation agreed between the claimant and the acquiring authority; or, if agreement has not yet been reached, 90 per cent. of the authority's estimate of the compensation (section 52(3)). However, no such payment will be made in respect of any land which is subject to a mortgage, the principal of which exceeds 90 per cent. of such an amount. Where the principal does not exceed 90 per cent., the advance payment will be reduced by the sum which the acquiring authority consider is required by them to secure the release of the interest of the mortgagee (section 52(6)).

13—41   The payment is to be made not later than three months after the date of the request or on possession, whichever is the later.[33] Before payment is made the acquiring authority must give details of the payment of compensation, and the interest to which it relates, to the district council (or London borough council) to enable that authority to make an appropriate entry in the register of local land charges. The acceptance of an advance payment does not prejudice the claimant's ability to dispute the amount of compensation ultimately payable.

If the amount of the advance payment exceeds the amount of the compensation as finally agreed or determined, any excess is to be repaid. Until section 52 was amended by the Planning and Compensation Act 1991, it was not altogether clear whether the converse applied and a supplementary payment could be claimed if the acquiring authority's estimate subsequently proves to be on the low side.[34] The 1991 Act clarified the position by providing[35] that if the claimant requests a further advance payment, the acquiring authority are authorised to supplement the initial advance if it appears to them that the initial estimate of compensation

---

[31] It is questionable whether this entitlement extends to a person who has no greater interest in the land than as a tenant for a year or from year to year who is required to give up possession before the expiration of the term.

[32] Or have first entered for the purposes of exercising a right which has been compulsorily acquired (1973 Act, s.52(10)).

[33] See H. St John, "Why advance payments should be claimed promptly" 1980 Chartered Surveyor, p. 208.

[34] *Compensation for Compulsory Purchase: Revisions to the Law on Disturbance and Other Matters and on Injurious Affection Where no Land is Taken from the Claimant,* Royal Institution of Chartered Surveyor's Discussion Paper, January 1985.

[35] See s.63(1) of the 1991 Act.

was too low. It seems that the acquiring authority are also empowered to make an additional further advance should it transpire that the revised estimate of compensation is also too low.

Although there is no entitlement to an advance payment prior to the taking of possession, authorities have a discretion to make a payment of up to 90 per cent. before entry. The Department of the Environment have expressed the hope that authorities will do this where claimants need money to reinstate themselves prior to giving up possession.[36] Advance payment can also be made in respect of certain home loss payments.[37]

Interest

The statutory provisions regulating the payment of interest on compensation are **13—42** inconsistent and depend on the particular statutory power, the exercise of which gives rise to the claim. In compulsory purchase proceedings which are determined by the Lands Tribunal, although there is no provision in the Lands Tribunal Act 1949 permitting the Tribunal to award interest, such an award can be made under section 20 of the Arbitration Act 1950.[38] The effect is that a sum awarded as compensation by the Lands Tribunal may, if the Tribunal so determine, carry interest as from the date of the award at the same rate as is applicable in the case of a judgment debt. But the right to interest in respect of a period prior to the award (or in the event of the parties reaching agreement on compensation) will depend on the existence of other statutory authority. The following provisions exist:

1. Where, following service of a notice of entry,[39] possession is taken of land before the payment of compensation, provision is made for the payment of interest on the compensation from the date of possession to the date of payment.[40]

   In *Chilton v. Telford Corporation*[41] where, following service of a notice of entry, physical possession of the land described in the notice (67.87 acres) was taken in eight separate parcels spread over more than two years, the Court of Appeal held that first entry on any part of the land described in

---

[36] Department of the Environment Circular 73/73, para. 52. See, too, *Development and Compensation — Putting People First*, Cmnd. 5124 (1972), para. 35.

[37] See para. 13–13.

[38] s.20 of the 1950 Act is applied to Lands Tribunal proceedings by rule 38 of the Lands Tribunal Rules 1975 (S.I. 1973 No.299).

[39] See para. 4–23.

[40] Compulsory Purchase Act 1965, s.11(1). See, also, s.11(3) of that Act.

[41] [1987] 1 W.L.R. 872.

the notice constituted entry on the whole. Accordingly, interest on the compensation for the whole land was to be calculated from the date of first entry.

2. Where, as a result of a general vesting declaration, land is vested in an acquiring authority in advance of the payment of compensation,[42] interest is payable on the compensation from the date of vesting to the date of payment,[43] notwithstanding that the taking of possession may be effected considerably later.[44]

13—43   3. Section 63 of the 1973 Act provides that compensation awarded under section 68 of the Lands Clauses Consolidation Act 1845, or section 10 of the Compulsory Purchase Act 1965, in respect of injurious affection suffered by neighbouring land not held together with land acquired for the scheme of works[45] and arising from the *construction* of the works, shall carry interest from the date of claim until payment.

4. Similarly, section 18 of the 1973 Act[46] states that an award of compensation under Part I of that Act for damage caused to neighbouring land by the *use* of works shall carry interest at the same rate from the date of service of the notice of claim (or if that date precedes the first claim day — from the first claim day) until payment.

5. Section 37(6) of the 1973 Act provides that a disturbance[47] payment shall carry interest from the date of displacement until payment.

6. Section 36(6) of the 1973 Act provides that a farm loss payment[48] shall carry interest from the date on which the claimant begins to farm another agricultural unit (being not more than three years from the date of displacement) until payment.

13—44   The rate of interest in the six circumstances referred to above is prescribed by regulations made from time to time under section 32 of the 1961 Act. In the absence of any other statutory provisions, it would seem that the Lands Tribunal has no general power to award interest in respect of a period antecedent to the date of the award.[49]

It has for some time been a bone of contention that simple, not compound, interest is paid and then only when the compensation itself is fixed. It is, of course,

---

[42] See para. 4–28.
[43] Compulsory Purchase (Vesting Declarations) Act 1981 s.10(1).
[44] This problem is illustrated by *Birrell Ltd v. Edinburgh District Council*, 1982 S.C. (H.L.) 75, 1982 S.L.T. 363.
[45] Compensation awarded for injurious affection suffered by land held together with land acquired for the scheme is part of the global sum awarded under the 1845 Act and carries interest in the circumstances described above.
[46] As amended by the Local Government, Planning and Land Act 1980, s.112(4).
[47] See para. 13–21.
[48] See para. 13–32.
[49] See, for example, *Hobbs (Quarries) Ltd v. Somerset County Council* (1975) 30 P. & C.R. 286; *Burlin v. Manchester City Council* (1976) 32 P. & C.R. 115.

not possible to make any precise calculation of the interest until the principal is known. In a consultation paper issued in March 1984, the Department of the Environment suggested that provision might be made for paying simple interest in advance of fixing the compensation in much the same way as an advance on compensation may be made under section 52 of the 1973 Act.[50] The Planning and Compensation Act 1991 did not affect the restriction of interest to simple interest only. Significant additions were made, however, to the provisions regulating payment of interest by the enactment of provisions requiring (a) payment of interest with any advance payment of compensation under section 52 of the 1973 Act, and also (b) conferring a discretionary power on an acquiring authority to make payments on account of compensation and interest. More particularly, these changes are:

1. Advance payments of compensation carry interest following the enactment **13—45** of section 52A of the 1973 Act.[51] The provision applies where compensation carries interest under section 11(1) of the Compulsory Purchase Act 1965 from the date possession is taken to the date of payment (above). If an advance payment of compensation is made under section 52 of the 1973 Act, the payment must include accrued interest, from the date of entry, on the amount of the estimated compensation. If any further advance payment is made under section 52(4A) of that Act[52] interest must be paid, from the date of entry, on the difference between the initial estimate of compensation and the revised estimate of compensation. In either case, the balance of the compensation due to the claimant is known as an unpaid balance which will continue to carry simple interest until the outstanding compensation is paid. If the interest accrued on an unpaid balance exceeds £1,000 on an anniversary of the date of payment of an advance payment, the acquiring authority must pay the claimant the amount of the accrued interest. Any interest on an advance payment of compensation paid under section 52(1) is set off against interest accruing under section 11 of the 1965 Act in order to avoid a double payment (section 52A(9)).

2. Department of the Environment Circular 15/91 *Planning and Compensation Act 1991 — Land Compensation and Compulsory Purchase* emphasises the importance of early settlement of compensation claims.[53] Since an advance payment of compensation cannot be claimed as of right until possession has been taken by the acquiring authority, a claimant on whose land no entry has been made is at a disadvantage.[54] Title may even have been acquired by means of a general vesting declaration without entry being required until

---

[50] See para. 13–40.
[51] Inserted by s.63(2) of the Planning and Compensation Act 1991.
[52] Subs. (4A) was inserted by *ibid.* s.63(1).
[53] Circular 15/91, Annex, para. 8.
[54] Circular 73/73, para. 52 indicates that acquiring authorities have a discretionary power to make an advance payment.

considerably later. Although a claimant in such a position cannot claim an advance payment as of right, he may nevertheless request the acquiring authority to exercise their power to make advance payments of compensation and interest under section the power conferred on them by 80(2) of the Planning and Compensation Act 1991. While the use of this power is discretionary it is intended that it should be used to help ensure that claimants receive as much of their entitlement as is not in dispute at the earliest opportunity.

The taxation of compensation

13—46 To what extent, if at all, should the incidence of taxation be taken into account in an award of compensation? Compensation for the compulsory acquisition of land is a capital sum realised on the disposal of an asset. Should the compensation be paid net of tax? A disturbance claim may include an item for loss of earnings or loss of profits which would have been taxable in the hands of the recipient. If the incidence of taxation is not taken into account, a claimant will arguably be compensated for more than his real loss.

Capital taxation is a relatively recent phenomenon and hence the question of what to do about the incidence of taxation first arose, not surprisingly, in the context of disturbance. In *West Suffolk County Council v. W. Rought Ltd*[55] the local authority compulsorily acquired the leasehold interest of a company in factory premises. The company claimed disturbance compensation for temporary loss of profits for the period which elapsed between the date when the local authority took possession and the date when the company was able to recommence operations in alternative accommodation. The House of Lords, applying the decision in *British Transport Commission v. Gourlay*[56] relating to the taxation of an award of damages for loss of earnings, held that the Lands Tribunal should have reduced the award by the amount of the additional taxation which the company would have had to bear if it had actually earned the amount which the acquiring authority's action prevented it from earning. In reaching this decision their Lordships were influenced by a statement from the Inland Revenue that the compensation award would not itself be subject to tax. Had it been, the claimant would have been subjected to double taxation. As it was, the company was simply denied an undeserved tax bonus.

13—47 The decision in *W. Rought Ltd* is difficult to reconcile with the legal fiction that disturbance is part of the value of the land (see Chapter 11). In other words, although disturbance items such as temporary loss of profits are income, they are

---

[55] [1957] A.C. 403.
[56] [1956] A.C. 185.

treated for compensation purposes as capital. At a time when income was taxable but capital was not, or not to the same extent, the distinction was important. But it was not a distinction that troubled the House of Lords, for as Lord Keith observed:

> "In assessing the loss under this head, liability to tax cannot, in my opinion, be ignored merely because the amount of the loss goes to make up the total compensation or purchase price for the acquisition of a capital asset."[57]

Subsequently, in *Rosenberg and Son (Tinware) Ltd v. Manchester Corporation*[58] the approach adopted in *W. Rought Ltd* was taken a step further when the Lands Tribunal permitted a deduction for tax from disturbance compensation in respect of a claim for removal expenses. It was thought by the Tribunal that such expenses were allowable in the circumstance of compulsory acquisition as an income tax deduction.

The decision in *W. Rought Ltd* was, in due course, reviewed by the Court of **13—48** Appeal in *Stoke-on-Trent City Council v. Wood Mitchell and Co. Ltd*[59] At issue was the amount payable for disturbance under the heading of temporary loss of profits while the respondents' offices and warehouse were being re-established and the question turned on whether the amount should be adjusted to take account of corporation tax. The respondent's contention was that since the decision in *W. Rought Ltd* circumstances had changed and they were now liable for either or both corporation income tax and corporation capital gains tax on the compensation; accordingly the principle laid down in *W. Rought Ltd* no longer applied. Roskill L.J., giving judgment for the court, concluded that "the principles laid down in *Roughts'* case can only be applied if after examination of the relevant statutory provisions it is clear beyond peradventure that the sum in question would not be taxable in the hands of the respondents." An examination of the relevant statutory provisions[60] showed that since the decision in *W. Rought Ltd*, a liability for capital gains tax on compensation is a capital sum received on the disposal of an asset. The provisions furthermore permitted a breakdown of that compensation into its component parts so as to apportion capital and income elements and to exclude from the computation of the capital gain any money charged to income tax as the income of the person making the disposal. The effect of this was to free the compensation for temporary loss of profits of its capital nature and enable it to be treated as a trading receipt. The situation was clearly distinguishable from that in *W. Rought Ltd* and it was held that the compensation should not be adjusted by

---

[57] [1957] A.C. 403 at p. 416.
[58] (1971) 23 P. & C.R. 416.
[59] (1978) 248 E.G. 871. And see *Pennine Raceway Ltd v. Kirklees Metropolitan Borough Council*, (No. 2) (1989) 58 P. & C.R. 482.
[60] At that time the Finance Act 1965, s.22 and the Finance Act 1969, Sched. 19, para. 11. See now the Income and Corporation Taxes Act 1988, s.70(1); also the Capital Gains Tax Act 1979, ss.20(1), 43(4), and 110.

the acquiring authority to take account of corporation tax. It should therefore be paid gross.

13—49   The Inland Revenue have since indicated that they will follow the decision of the Court of Appeal in *Wood Mitchell & Co. Ltd.* In a statement of practice SP 8/1979, issued in June 1979, the Inland Revenue indicated that any element of compensation received for temporary loss of profits for the acquisition by an authority possessing compulsory purchase powers of property used for the purposes of a trade or profession "falls to be included as a receipt taxable under Case I and II of Schedule D. Compensation for losses on trading stock and to reimburse revenue expenditure, such as removal expenses and interest, will be treated in the same way for tax purposes." The statement goes on to indicate that this practice will also apply to compensation cases where no interest is acquired (*e.g.* compensation due for damage, injury or exploitation of land, or to the exercise of planning control).

The statement of practice clarifies the position as regards disturbance items which represent income. Compensation for loss of goodwill, like compensation for the land taken and for severance and other injurious affection, represents capital and will be subject to capital gains tax in the normal way.[61]

Compensation is thus taxable both as capital and as income in respect of its different components. As *The Estates Gazette* aptly observed "the one-time windfall is taken back out of the hands of the acquiring authority into those of the claimant, and thence into the hands of the Inland Revenue, where it disappears."[62]

---

[61] See the Capital Gains Tax Act 1979, s.110, and see s.111A and B as regards roll over relief.

[62] (1978) 248 E.G. 53, Legal Notes. Note, however the decision of the Lands Tribunal in *Alfred Golightly & Sons Ltd v. Durham County Council* (1981) 260 E.G. 1045, 1135 and 1199 which allowed, as part of a disturbance claim, an item representing the claimant's increased liability to tax (in that case development land tax) which would not have arisen but for the acquisition by the local authority.

Chapter 14

The Lands Tribunal

Powers and constitution

Disputes relating to the quantum of compensation payable on compulsory acquisi- **14—01**
tion of land are determined by the Lands Tribunal. This is an expert tribunal both
in relation to valuation and also in relation to matters of law. Although not form-
ally a court of record, its decisions are widely reported and cited, and an appeal
from a decision of the Lands Tribunal lies to the Court of Appeal rather than to
the High Court. Earlier generations of lawyers and valuers were less fortunate,
however, particularly in respect of disputes arising under nineteenth century statutory powers. Thus the Lands Clauses Consolidation Act 1845 made provision
for determination of disputes by a variety of methods depending on the amount
of the claim.

Under section 23 the parties could refer disputes to arbitration. However, if
the disputed claim did not exceed £50,[1] it was to be settled by two justices
pursuant to section 22. For claims in excess of £50 the parties, unless they had
elected for arbitration, could petition the sheriff of the county to summon a jury
to determine the compensation. At a time when compulsory purchase was linked
with the entrepreneurial activity of the industrial revolution carried on for profit
as much as for the public good, it seems there was a tendency for juries to sympathise with claimants.[2] In the period of reconstruction that followed the First
World War, this generosity to claimants was considered to be misplaced. To

---

[1] This apparently humble figure, having been fixed almost 150 years ago would then have been
regarded as a substantial sum.
[2] *Second Report of the Committee Dealing with the Law and Practice Relating to the Acquisition and Valuation
of Land for Public Purposes* (The Scott Committee), Cmd. 9229 (1919), para. 8.

curb excesses and to introduce "realism" into awards, the Acquisition of Land (Assessment of Compensation) Act 1919 provided for disputed claims to be determined by official arbitrators appointed because of their expertise in valuation.[3]

14—02   The system operated reasonably well until the aftermath of the Second World War. The advent of comprehensive planning control introduced very considerable legal complexity into land valuation and the government of the day concluded that the system would have to be changed to accommodate this. "The main defect under the existing machinery," observed the Attorney-General, "is that the official arbitrators, qualified only as surveyors and valuers, have no means of providing themselves with legal advice or assistance in regard to matters of law, or indeed of securing close coordination and consistency of decisions with each other."[4] The Lands Tribunal Act 1949 accordingly made provision for the setting up of a Lands Tribunal for England and Wales.[5] The Tribunal was to bring both legal and surveying expertise to bear on disputes over land valuation.

The Lands Tribunal for England and Wales came into existence on January 1, 1950, with jurisdiction to determine matters formerly directed to be determined by official arbitrators. The jurisdiction of the official arbitrators was not, however, comprehensive, their functions being limited to compulsory acquisitions by "public authorities", a term which was restrictively defined. The jurisdiction of the Lands Tribunal became fully comprehensive, however, in 1961; section 1 of the Land Compensation Act 1961 provides that "any question of disputed compensation . . . shall be referred to the Lands Tribunal . . ." where the question arises under any statute authorising the compulsory acquisition of land. Numerous other functions are, however, discharged by the Lands Tribunal, the common factor being settlement of disputes in connection with the valuation of land. For the purposes of this chapter it is sufficient to say that the jurisdiction of the Tribunal extends to:

14—03   1. The determination of disputes over compensation where land is authorised to be acquired compulsorily; and, where any part of the land to be acquired is subject to a lease which also comprises land not to be acquired, the resolution of questions as to the apportionment of the rent payable under the lease.[6]

2. Any other question of disputed compensation under the Lands Clauses Acts, where the claim is for the injurious affection of any land.[7]

3. The determination of disputed compensation under Part I of the Land Compensation Act 1973.[8]

---

[3] s.2.
[4] H.C. Deb., 1948–49, Vol. 462, col. 43.
[5] Provision was also made for the setting up of the Lands Tribunal for Scotland, though this Tribunal was not established until 1971.
[6] Land Compensation Act 1961, s.1.
[7] Lands Tribunal Act 1949, s.1(3).
[8] Land Compensation Act 1973, s.16.

4. The determination of disputes over other payments under the Land Compensation Act 1973 such as home loss payments, disturbance and farm loss payments.[9]

5. Determining the price under a voluntary reference where the acquisition of land by a public authority is proceeding not by compulsory purchase but by negotiation.[10]

As indicated in other chapters, the Tribunal also has a role to play in resolving disputes over notices of objection to severance[11] and blight notices.[12] The Tribunal has no jurisdiction, however, in relation to matters of title.[13]

The Tribunal comprises a president and such other members as the Lord Chancellor may determine. The president of the Tribunal is to be a person suitably qualified by the holding of judicial office or by being a barrister of at least seven years' standing. The other members are to be barristers or solicitors of similar standing or persons having experience in the valuation of land appointed after consultation with the president of the Royal Institution of Chartered Surveyors. Appointments are for such periods as the Lord Chancellor may determine.[14]   **14—04**

The jurisdiction of the Tribunal may be exercised by any one or more of its members.[15] Compensation claims where no legal issues arise are generally determined by one member sitting alone. In most other cases, the Tribunal will sit with two members, one a lawyer and the other a surveyor with the former presiding, to obtain the benefits of combined expertise referred to above. Exceptionally, where cases raise matters of particular importance the Tribunal may sit with additional members. Where a case is dealt with by two or more members, the decision will be that of the majority. In the event of equality, the member presiding will have a second or casting vote.[16] Where any case before the Tribunal calls for special knowledge, the president may direct that the Tribunal will be assisted by one or more assessors.[17]

The Lands Tribunal has its own permanent staff. Its offices and court room are   **14—05** situated at 48–49 Chancery Lane, London, WC2A 1JR. The Tribunal is peripatetic but, in practice, the major cases tend to be heard in London. Proceedings can be determined without an oral hearing in some cases.

---

[9] Land Compensation Act 1973, ss.30(3), 35(9) and 38(4).
[10] Lands Tribunal Act 1949, s.1(5).
[11] See para. 4–15.
[12] See para. 16–21.
[13] *Mountgarret v. Claro Water Board* (1963) 15 P. & C.R. 53.
[14] Lands Tribunal Act 1949, s.2. By virtue of the Judicial Pensions and Retirement Act 1993, s.26 and Sched. 6, para. 31, s.2 of the 1949 Act was amended to restrict appointment to persons under the age of 70. The Lord Chancellor may, however, authorise continuance in office up to the age of 75, if he considers this to be in the public interest.
[15] *Ibid.* s.3(1).
[16] *Ibid.* s.3(3).
[17] Lands Tribunal Rules 1975, r.35.

Procedure

Rules may be made for regulating the proceedings of the Tribunal and as regards fees. The principal rules at the present time are the Lands Tribunal Rules 1975,[18] a key feature of which is the provision that no application for the determination of any question of disputed compensation may be made before the expiration of 28 days from the date of service or constructive service of a notice to treat or (where no notice to treat is served or deemed to be served) the date of service of notice of claim.[19] A person, whether the claimant or the acquiring authority, requiring to have a question or dispute determined must submit an application to the Tribunal by means of a notice of reference in accordance with Form 4 (or Form 4A in the case of a dispute relating to a purchase notice or counter-notice).[20]

A copy of the notice to treat (if such notice has been served) and of any notice of claim should accompany an application relating to the compensation payable on the compulsory acquisition of land. In any other case, a copy of the order, direction, notice, decision, authorisation or other document which is evidence of the proceedings giving rise to compensation should be submitted. The Tribunal will send copies of the application to the other parties to the question or dispute.

14—06   The Tribunal is to a considerable extent the master of its own procedure.[21] On the motion of any party to the proceedings or *ex proprio motu* it may: require a party to furnish in writing further particulars of his case; order a record to be made up; grant to a party an order for discovery of documents; and require the attendance of any person as a witness or require the production of any document relating to the question to be determined; and may appoint a time at or within which and place at which such action is to be taken.[22] Small claims, however, are likely to be dealt with informally with next to no pleadings.

With the consent of all parties the Tribunal may dispose of any application before it without a hearing.[23] Where a hearing is to be held, not less than 14 days' notice in writing must be given by the Tribunal of the date, time and place unless

---

[18] S.I. 1975 No.299, as amended by the Lands Tribunal (Amendment) Rules 1977 (S.I. 1977 No. 1820), the Lands Tribunal (Amendment) Rules 1981 (S.I. 1981 No. 105), the Lands Tribunal (Amendment No. 2) Rules 1981 (S.I. 1981 No. 600), the Lands Tribunal (Amendment) Rules 1984 (S.I. 1984 No. 793), the Lands Tribunal (Amendment) Rules 1986 (S.I. 1986 No. 1322) and the Lands Tribunal (Amendment) Rules 1990 (S.I. 1990 No. 1382).

[19] Lands Tribunal Rules 1975, r.16(3).

[20] *Ibid.* r.16(1). See the Lands Tribunal (Amendment) Rules 1990 for the appropriate fees.

[21] Lands Tribunal Rules 1975, r.52. The party making the appeal, claiming compensation, or making an application to the Tribunal, will begin the proceedings at the hearing.

[22] *Ibid.* r.38, applying s.12 of the Arbitration Act 1950. The Tribunal may not, however, require any person to produce any document or to answer any question which he would be entitled, on the ground of privilege or confidentiality, to refuse to produce or to answer if the proceedings were proceedings in a court of law. See, too, *R. v. Lands Tribunal, ex p. City of London Corporation* [1982] 1 W.L.R. 258 on the interpretation of the word "decision" in the Lands Tribunal Act 1949, s.3(4).

[23] *Ibid.* r.33A.

the parties agree to a shorter period.[24] To avoid surprises, parties to a hearing will be ordered to produce a list of any comparable properties to which reference is to be made at least one month in advance. The Tribunal will sit in public except when it is acting as arbitrator under a reference by consent, in which circumstances the procedures shall be heard in private if the parties to the reference so request.[25] A preliminary hearing can be held to determine a point of law.[26]

Any party to the proceedings before the Tribunal may appear and be heard in person or be represented by counsel or solicitor, or with the leave of the Tribunal, by any other person. There are serious objections to a surveyor also acting as his client's advocate, for as Emlyn Jones observes, "combining the role of advocate and expert witness puts an undue strain on an individual. In giving evidence he is under oath to tell the truth; as an advocate he can with complete propriety put forward arguments and submissions based on inference or interpretation."[27] Nevertheless, in small cases a combination of roles is sometimes permitted to keep down expense.   **14—07**

The proceedings before the Tribunal are conducted generally in accordance with the rules of evidence. Evidence may be given on oath and will be subject to cross examination. If the parties to the proceedings consent, or the Tribunal so orders, evidence may be given by affidavit but the Tribunal may at any stage of the proceedings require the personal attendance of any deponent for examination and cross examination.[28]

As the usual rules of evidence apply, this includes in particular the rule against hearsay evidence. This means that factual evidence by a valuer about transactions of which he has no direct knowledge and which cannot, therefore, be tested by cross examination is likely to be rejected.[29]

Not more than one expert witness on either side may be heard unless the Tribunal otherwise directs.[30] An additional expert witness may, however, be permitted, for example, to support a business disturbance claim or to give evidence on a claim for compensation relating to minerals. The Tribunal is required to determine disputed compensation claims referred to it.[31] To do this the Tribunal may need to perform an investigatory function since it cannot merely dismiss a claim for want of proof. In the absence of one party, the other party are not   **14—08**

---

[24] *Ibid.* r.32(2).
[25] Land Compensation Act 1961, s.2(2), as amended by the Local Government, Planning and Land Act 1980, s.193 and Sched. 33, para. 5; and see also the Lands Tribunal Rules 1975, r.33.
[26] Lands Tribunal Rules 1975, r.49.
[27] J.H. Emlyn Jones, *The Lands Tribunal — A Practitioners Guide* (Herbert Bewley Fund, 1982) p. 17.
[28] Lands Tribunal Rules 1975, r.39. See also *Mahboob Hussain v. Oldham Metropolitan Borough Council* (1981) 42 B.&C.R. 388.
[29] *English Exporters v. Eldonwall Ltd* [1973] 1 Ch. 415, per Megarry J. at p. 420; *Nuttall v. Leeds City Council* (1982) 251 EG 1179.
[30] Lands Compensation Act 1961, s.2(3); Lands Tribunal Rules 1975 r.42(2).
[31] Lands Tribunal Act 1949, s.1(3). The Tribunal may not, however, make an award on a basis not relied on by either of the parties: *Aquilina v. Havering London Borough Council* [1992] 32 R.V.R. 251.

automatically entitled to a determination in accordance with their calculations but must lead evidence to support them.

Previous decisions on matters of valuation do not constitute binding precedents. "Valuation is an exercise in determining facts and each case must be decided on the evidence adduced at the hearing of that case."[32] Nor is the Tribunal bound by its previous decisions on matters of law although such decisions may be very persuasive.[33] The decision of the Tribunal in any proceedings will normally be given in writing and must include a statement of the reasons for the decision. A decision and reasons can, however, be given orally in cases where the Tribunal is satisfied that no injustice or inconvenience would be caused to the parties.[34] Where an amount awarded or value determined by the Tribunal is dependent upon the decision of the Tribunal on a question of law which is in dispute in the proceedings, the Tribunal must ascertain and state in its decision the alternative amount or value (if any) which it would have awarded or determined if it had decided otherwise on the question of law.[35] This may avoid the necessity of a further hearing before the Tribunal in the event of its original decision on the question of law being subsequently overturned by the Court of Appeal.

14—09   A person dissatisfied with the Tribunal's decision on a point of law may, within four weeks of the Tribunal's decision, require the Tribunal to state a case for the court's decision.[36] The decision of the Tribunal is, however, final as to matters of valuation.

Costs

Where the acquiring authority have made an unconditional offer in writing to a claimant of any sum as compensation and the sum awarded by the Tribunal to the claimant does not exceed the sum offered, the Tribunal must, unless for some special reason it is considered inappropriate to do so, order the claimant to bear his own costs and to pay the costs of the acquiring authority so far as they were

---

[32] Douglas Frank Q.C. "Lands Tribunal Problems" in Compensation for Compulsory Purchase, Journal of Planning and Environment Law Occasional Paper (Sweet & Maxwell, 1975).

[33] See *West Midlands Baptist (Trust) Association v. Birmingham City Council* [1968] 1 All E.R. 205 C.A. *per* Salmon L.J. at p. 213 and Sachs L.J. at p. 222.

[34] Tribunals and Inquiries Act 1992 s.10(1), Sched. 1, para. 27; Lands Tribunal Rules 1975 r.54(1). In *R.A. Vine (Engineering) Ltd v. Havant Borough Council* [1989] 39 E.G. 164, Glidewell L.J., in the Court of Appeal, applying the judgment of Megaw J. in *Re Poyser and Mills Arbitration* [1964] 2 Q.B. 467 and of Sir John Donaldson (as he then was) in *Norton Tool Co. Ltd v. Tewson* [1973] 1 All E.R. 183, observed that reasons must be proper, adequate and intelligible.

[35] Lands Tribunal Rules 1975, r.54(3).

[36] Lands Tribunal Act 1949, s.3(4); Rules of the Supreme Court Ord. 61, r. 1. The question(s) of law must be defined "concisely and with reasonable precision:" Lands Tribunal Practice Note No. 1, (1993).

incurred after the offer was made.[37] Similarly, if the Tribunal is satisfied that a claimant has failed to deliver to the acquiring authority, in time to enable them to make a proper offer, a notice in writing of the amount claimed by him containing the required particulars[38] it must, unless special reasons exist, order the claimant to bear his own costs and to pay the costs of the acquiring authority so far as they were incurred after the time when, in the Tribunal's opinion, the notice should have been delivered.

Conversely, where a claimant has delivered to the acquiring authority a notice **14—10** of claim containing the appropriate particulars and has made an unconditional offer in writing to accept any sum as compensation, then, if the sum awarded to him by the Tribunal is equal to or exceeds that sum, the Tribunal must, unless for some special reason it is considered inappropriate to do so, order the acquiring authority to bear their own costs and to pay the costs of the claimant so far as they were incurred after his offer was made.[39]

In practice, unconditional offers by the acquiring authority or by the claimant, after being communicated to and rejected by the other party, are sealed and lodged with the Tribunal and are not disclosed to the Tribunal during the hearing. Having reached a determination on the disputed claim, the Tribunal will open the sealed offer and make an order as to costs according to the content.

Apart from the circumstances described above costs are at the discretion of the **14—11** Tribunal.[40] They usually follow success; in *Pepys v. London Transport Executive*[41] it was held that where there was a departure from the usual rule, the reasons for that departure must be given as the discretion with regard to the award of costs had to be exercised judicially. In *Church Cottage Investments Ltd v. Hillingdon London Borough Council (No.2)*[42] an award of costs was made against a claimant who had sought compensation of £76,000 but had been held by the Tribunal to be entitled to receive only £100 as nominal compensation. The Court of Appeal upheld an award by the Tribunal in favour of the acquiring authority as the claimant had wholly failed in his claim.

Where an award of costs is made, the Tribunal may award a lump sum or may direct that the costs of the successful party be taxed by the registrar of the Lands Tribunal on a scale specified as either the High Court of the county court scale.[43] The Tribunal may, in any case, disallow the cost of counsel.[44]

Where the Tribunal orders the claimant to pay the costs, or any part of the costs, of the acquiring authority, the acquiring authority may deduct the amount

---

[37] Land Compensation Act 1961, s.4(1)(a).
[38] *Ibid.* s.4(1)(b).
[39] *Ibid* s.4(3).
[40] Lands Tribunal Act 1949, s.3(5); Lands Tribunal Rules 1975, r.56. And see *McLaren's Discretionary Trustee v. Secretary of State for Scotland*, 1989 S.L.T. 83.
[41] [1975] 1 W.L.R. 234.
[42] [1991] 27 E.G. 127. See, also, *Wootton v. Central Land Board* [1957] 1 W.L.R. 424.
[43] Lands Tribunal Rules 1975, r.56(2).
[44] Land Compensation Act 1961, s.4(4).

so payable by the claimant from the amount of the compensation, if any, payable to him.[45]

Legal aid is available in appropriate cases under the terms of the Legal Aid Act 1988 in relation to proceedings in the Lands Tribunal.[46]

---

[45] *Ibid.* s.4(5).
[46] Legal Aid Act 1988, Part III and Sched. 2, Part I.

Chapter 15

Compensation for Regulation

Introduction

In Chapter 5 we referred to the well-established judicial presumption that an **15—01** intention to take away the property of a subject without giving him a legal right to compensation for the loss of it is not to be imputed to the legislature unless that intention is expressed in unequivocal terms. The cases which support this presumption[1] all turn on instances where ownership or, at least, possession or use of property has been taken over by the state.

The question which is examined in this chapter is the extent to which interference by the state in rights in land falling short of "taking" as defined above may be the subject of compensation. For example, should the proprietor of a factory be expected to bear the cost of installing insulation to prevent noise from disturbing neighbouring residential property? Would it make any difference if the factory had been in operation long before the houses were built? Should the operator of a quarry be expected to bear the cost of making the land suitable for some alternative use upon completion of mineral operations? Who should bear the loss of development value when land which is ripe for development is zoned in the development plan as green belt so that planning permission for development is refused? Who should bear the burden when plans for the conversion of a building are blocked following its listing as a building of special architectural or historic

---

[1] *Burmah Oil Co. (Burma Trading) Ltd v. Lord Advocate*, 1964 S.C.(H.L.) 117; 1964 S.L.T. 218; *Tiverton and North Devon Railway Co. v. Loosemore* (1884) 9 App. Cas. 480 H.L.; *Attorney General v. Horner* (1884) 14 Q.B.D. 245; *Cannon Brewery Co. Ltd v. Gas Light and Coke Co.* [1904] A.C. 331, H.L.; *Colonial Sugar Refining Co. Ltd v. Melbourne Harbour Trust Commissioners* [1927] A.C. 343 P.C.; *Bond v. Nottingham Corporation* [1940] 1 Ch. 429.

interest? Where should the loss fall when plans for afforestation of land are thwarted because of its nature conservation interest? These questions are of some importance because over the last 150 years owners and occupiers of land have had increasingly to face up to regulation of their activities in the name of public health, safety, amenity and conservation. Compliance with such regulation is regarded as essential in the interests of the wider community. The essence of the compensation problem is whether the cost of compliance should fall upon the owner of the land or whether it should be shared amongst the wider community who are benefitting from the regulation.

15—02   Although there is in such cases what might be described as an expropriation of [2] or at least an abridgement of [3] rights in property, the judicial eye has been reluctant to discern an entitlement to compensation in the absence of an express provision in the statute. "A mere negative prohibition," said Wright J. in *France Fenwick & Co. v. The King*[4] "though it involves interference with an owner's enjoyment of property, does not, I think, merely because it is obeyed, carry with it at common law any right to compensation. A subject cannot at common law claim compensation merely because he obeys a lawful order of the state."

In *Belfast Corporation v. O.D. Cars Ltd*[5] for example, planning permission was refused for the construction of industrial and commercial buildings on land in Belfast. The proposed industrial buildings were regarded as incompatible with the residential zoning of that part of the site; and the height and character of the proposed commercial buildings were considered not to be in accordance with the requirements of their part of the site. A claim for compensation for "injurious affection" under the Planning (Interim Development) (Norther Ireland) Act 1944 was rejected as it fell, because of the grounds of refusal, within the exceptions to the specific compensation entitlement in the Act. It was argued for the claimants that the exceptions in the legislation were contrary to section 5 of the Government of Ireland Act 1920 which provides that Parliament shall not make a law "to take away property without compensation." This argument was rejected by the House of Lords. Lord Radcliffe pointed out that interference with rights of development and use of land were not treated in the 1944 Act as a "taking" of property. The compensation entitlement in the Act was provided not on the basis that property or property rights had been "taken" but on the basis that property, itself retained, had been "injuriously affected."

15—03   And in *Westminster Bank Ltd v. Minister of Housing and Local Government*[6] an application for planning permission to extend bank premises by the construction of a strong room was refused on the ground that it would prejudice the future widening of the road onto which the premises fronted. An appeal was dismissed.

---

[2] *Belfast Corporation v. O.D. Cars Ltd* [1960] A.C. 490, *per* Lord Radcliffe at p. 524.
[3] *Belfast Corporation v. O.D. Cars Ltd per* Viscount Simonds at p. 519 citing Brandeis J. in *Pennsylvania Coal Co. v. Mahon* (1922), 260 U.S. 393 at p. 417.
[4] [1927] 1 K.B. 458.
[5] [1960] A.C. 490.
[6] [1971] A.C. 508.

The local authority, who were both the highway and the planning authority, had not, however, prescribed an improvement line under the Highways Act 1959 which would have entitled a person whose property was adversely affected by the line to claim compensation. The question to be determined was whether the planning authority could defeat a claim for compensation by refusing planning permission without an improvement line having been prescribed. The House of Lords held that local authorities could choose which course to pursue to safeguard land for road widening, even where the course chosen avoided the payment of compensation. In this case, the course chosen had been the refusal of planning permission and it was clear from the legislation that there was no general right to compensation for an adverse decision.

However, simple and attractive as the distinction between the "taking" of **15—04** property and the regulation of property may seem at first sight, there is no doubt that sustaining the distinction in practice presents considerable difficulty. The Uthwatt Committee, having drawn the conventional distinction, went on to acknowledge that "it will always be a matter of difficulty to draw the line with any satisfactory logic, *i.e.* to determine the point at which the accepted obligations of neighbourliness or citizenship are exceeded and an expropriation is suffered."[7] In *Westminster Bank Ltd* Lord Reid described the distinction as "too meticulous."[8] Michelman, in a wide ranging review of the criteria developed by the American courts for determining when a particular injurious result of government activity should be classed as a "taking" and thus compensatable shows, "that none of the standard criteria yields a solid and self-sufficient rule of decision — that each of them, when attempts are made to erect it into a general principle, is either seriously misguided, ruinously incomplete, or uselessly overbroad."[9] In his judgment in *Belfast Corporation* Lord Radcliffe recognised that it was not "out of the question that, on a particular occasion, there might not be a restriction of user so extreme in substance, though not in form, it amounted to a 'taking' of the land for the benefit of the public."[10]

An illustration of the difficulty of drawing the line between regulation and **15—05** expropriation is provided by a series of decisions on the validity of conditions imposed on grants of planning permission. Section 70(1) of the Town and Country Planning Act 1990 empowers a local planning authority to impose "such conditions as they think fit" on a grant of planning permission.[11] In *Hall & Co.*

---

[7] *Final Report of the Expert Committee on Compensation and Betterment*, Cmd. 6386 (1942) para. 32.
[8] [1971] A.C. 508 at p. 529.
[9] F.I. Michelman, "Property, Utility, and Fairness: Comments on the Ethical Foundations of 'Just Compensation' Law" (1967) 80 Harv. L.R. 1165. See, too, J. Sax, "Takings and the Police Power" (1964) 74 Yale L.J. 36; and J. Sax "Takings, Private Property and Public Rights," (1971) 81 Yale L.J. 149; and R.A. Epstein, "Takings, Private Property and the Power of Eminent Domain" (Harvard Univeristy Press, 1985).
[10] [1960] A.C. 490 at p. 525.
[11] For a discussion of the restrictions woven by the courts around this seemingly wide power see Michael Purdue, Eric Young and Jeremy Rowan-Robinson, *Planning Law and Procedure* (Butterworths, 1989) Chap. 9.

v. Shoreham-by-Sea UDC[12] conditions were imposed on a permission for industrial development requiring the developers to construct at their own expense a service road along the frontage of the site and to give a right of passage over the road to and from adjoining sites. The Court of Appeal held the conditions to be unreasonable. Wilmer L.J. said, "I can certainly find no clear and unambiguous words in the Town and Country Planning Act 1947, authorising the defendants in effect to take away the plaintiffs' rights of property without compensation by the imposition of conditions such as those sought to be imposed."[13] In somewhat similar vein, Lord Widgery C.J. in *R. v. London Borough of Hillingdon, ex p. Royco Homes Ltd*[14] categorised as a "fundamental departure from the rights of ownership and unreasonable" conditions which required the first occupiers of a scheme of residential development to be drawn from the local authority's housing waiting list and which provided for such persons to have security of tenure for 10 years. In *M.J. Shanley Ltd (in liquidation) v. Secretary of State for the Environment*[15] Woolf J., relying on *Hall and Co.*, held that a condition requiring the provision of 40 acres of open space for public use was unreasonable. In *Westminster Renslade Ltd v. Secretary of State for the Environment*[16] Forbes J., relying on *London Borough of Hillingdon*, held that it was wrong to refuse planning permission because the application did not contain provision for an increase in the proportion of parking spaces subject to public control. It was, he said, "perfectly simple to provide off street car parking which was under public control; the local authority could acquire the land to do so. But it was wholly illegitimate to try to seek to do that by imposing conditions on the planning consent." And in *City of Bradford Metropolitan Council v. Secretary of State for the Environment*,[17] Lloyd L.J., giving judgment for the Court of Appeal, held that a condition on a grant of planning permission for residential development which required improvements to a public road to be undertaken on land which was not owned or controlled by the developers was unreasonable. He could see no relevant distinction between that case and the decision in *Hall & Co.* It would seem to be implicit in all these decisions (and it is made explicit in *Hall & Co.*) that the conditions in question effectively overstepped the mark between mere regulation and the expropriation of land for public purposes without compensation.

15—06   On the other hand, in *Brittania (Cheltenham) Ltd v. Secretary of State for the Environment*[18] Sir Douglas Frank was prepared to accept as valid a condition which required the provision of public open space in association with a scheme of resid-

---

12 [1964] 1 W.L.R. 240.

13 *Ibid.* at p. 251. See, too, Pearson L.J. at p. 260.

14 [1974] Q.B. 720. See, too, *David Lowe and Sons Ltd v. Musselburgh Town Council*, 1973 S.C. 130; 1974 S.L.T. 5.

15 [1982] J.P.L. 380.

16 (1984) 48 P. & C.R. 255; [1983] J.P.L. 454.

17 [1986] J.P.L. 598.

18 [1978] J.P.L. 554 (subsequently quashed by the Court of Appeal on other grounds [1979] J.P.L. 534). And see also *R. v. Gillingham Borough Council, ex p. F. Parham Ltd* [1988] J.P.L. 336.

ential development. The factors which appeared to distinguish the circumstances in this case from those in *M.J. Shanley Ltd (in liquidation)* was that the condition did not require land to be dedicated to the public. Yet curiously, the economic loss imposed on the developer would be likely to be heavier in the circumstances of the *Britannia* case in view of the continuing maintenance burden. Once dedicated, the burden of maintaining open space generally passes to the local authority.[19]

However, profitable though it may sometimes be to challenge a restriction *ad hoc* in the courts on the ground that it is not within the scope of the enabling legislation and is in substance a "taking," it would seem that the courts are reluctant to discern any general entitlement to compensation for regulation in the absence of explicit provision in the statute. This is in marked contrast to the position with compulsory purchase legislation. To establish where the cost of complying with regulation falls it is therefore necessary to refer to the relevant legislation.

It would, of course, be impossible in a book such as this to canvas every code **15—07** of regulation. The size of such a task is underlined by the comment in a Government white paper that "there is no readily available measure of the number of regulations, but these run into thousands of pages of statutes."[20] The Uthwatt Committee in their report in 1942, however, summarised the general position. After describing the history of the growth of regulation, the report continued:

> "the essence of the compensation problem as regards the imposition of restrictions appears to be this — at what point does the public interest become such that a private individual ought to be called on to comply, at his own cost, with a restriction or requirement designed to secure that public interest? The history of the imposition of obligations without compensation has been to push that point progressively further on and to add to the list of requirements to be essential to the well-being of the community."[21]

Although the last 15 years have witnessed a movement towards deregulation of **15—08** some sectors of the economy and an increasing interest in self-regulation as opposed to formal regulation, this has not altered the general position as regards compensation. Where formal regulation exists the point has been reached where legislation providing for the regulation of land does not, as a general rule, confer an entitlement to compensation. In other words, the cost of complying with regulations relating to the control of pollution, fire precautions, health and safety at work, building control and so on tends to lie where it falls — upon the landowner. There are, of course, a number of exceptions to the general statement and

---

[19] It should, however, be noted that local authorities are increasingly looking for capitalised maintenance payments to accompany the dedication of open space — see J. Rowan-Robinson and M.G. Lloyd, *Land Development and the Infrastructure Lottery* (T. & T. Clark, 1988) Chap. 4.

[20] *Building Businesses . . . Not Barriers*, Cmnd. 9794 (1986) para. 3.7.

[21] *Final Report of the Expert Committee on Compensation and Betterment*, *supra*, para. 33.

some of these are discussed below. It may also be open to the landowner to alter the initial distribution of cost of passing the burden to other sectors of the community, for example through higher product prices or through deduction from taxation.

The remainder of this chapter is given over to an assessment of three areas where the distribution of the cost of complying with restrictions on the use, development and management of land have been the subject of recent scrutiny. These are development control, mineral operations and nature conservation. These areas are now considered in turn.

"Mainstream" planning control

15—09   "Mainstream" planning control refers to the general development control functions of local planning authorities under Part III of the Town and Country Planning Act 1990, and in particular to their ability to regulate the development of land. Although mineral operations are subject to control under Part III of the 1990 Act like other forms of development, there are a number of special features about the regulation of such development which deserve separate consideration. Mineral operations are, accordingly, the subject of a separate section in this chapter. The 1990 Act in Part VIII also provides for additional controls in special cases. These relate to trees, land adversely affecting the amenity of the neighbourhood ("waste land"), and advertisements.[22] The operation of these additional controls will in certain circumstances confer an entitlement to compensation but these controls are not a part of mainstream planning control and are beyond the scope of this section of the chapter.[23]

In a report in 1973, JUSTICE aptly observed that "[t]he ability or otherwise of an owner of an interest in land to claim compensation in respect of any loss he has suffered as a result of the exercise by a local planning authority of its power to control the development of land, can be explained historically but not logically."[24] It would therefore seem appropriate to devote some space to tracing the history of the compensation provisions for regulating the development of land, and to observe that many of the compensation provisions were repealed by the Planning and Compensation Act 1991. Compensation for refusal of planning permission to construct new buildings or change to a new use was always severely

---

[22] Additional controls relevant to buildings of special architectural or historic interest are contained in Part I of the Planning (Listed Buildings and Conservation Areas) Act 1990.

[23] For an explanation of the entitlement to compensation in respect of the operation of these additional controls see Michael Purdue, Eric Young and Jeremy Rowan-Robinson *Planning Law and Procedure, supra*, Chap. 18.

[24] JUSTICE, *Compensation for Compulsory Acquisition and Remedies for Planning Restrictions together with a Supplemental Report* (Stevens and Sons Ltd, 1973) para. 64.

restricted but has now been removed altogether, subject only to the possibility that a disappointed owner may require the local planning authority to purchase the land if it has become incapable of reasonably beneficial use.

1. REGULATING NEW DEVELOPMENT — DEMISE OF COMPENSATION RIGHTS

Planning control developed from the public health and housing legislation of the nineteenth century. The first planning Act, the Housing, Town Planning etc. Act 1909 enabled local authorities to prepare "schemes" for controlling the development of new housing areas so as to secure "proper sanitary conditions, amenity and convenience." The Act gave owners a right, subject to certain exceptions, to claim compensation where their property was injuriously affected by the making of a scheme. Conversely, authorities could recover betterment from a person whose property was increased in value by the operation of a scheme. It is not clear why a compensation entitlement was included in the legislation; Lord Radcliffe in *Belfast Corporation v. O.D. Cars Ltd* suggested that it may have had something to do with the shift in emphasis from "consideration of public health to the wider and more debatable ground of public amenity."[25]

    15—10

    The next significant step was the Town and Country Planning Act 1932 which enabled local authorities to make planning schemes, effectively a form of zoning plan, for almost any type of land whether built-up or undeveloped. The 1932 Act made no fundamental change in the basis of the compensation provisions but added to the list of restrictions in respect of which compensation might be excluded. The result was that compensation could be excluded, for example, in respect of a provision limiting the density of development but not in respect of a provision forbidding building altogether. The Uthwatt Committee in attempting to explain the distinction appeared to regard the outright prohibition of development as amounting almost to an expropriation of a proprietary right or interest. "The difference in treatment as regards compensation may be rested on the difference between expropriation of property on the one hand and restriction on user while leaving ownership and possession undisturbed on the other."[26]

    The report of the Royal Commission on the Distribution of Industrial Population in 1940 expressed serious misgivings about the effect of the compensation provision. "Evidence has been placed before the Commission that the difficulties that are encountered by planning authorities under these provisions are so great as seriously to hamper the progress of planning throughout the country."[27] The burden of compensation where planning considerations dictated a prohibition on

    15—11

---

[25] [1960] A.C. 490 at p. 524.
[26] *Final Report of the Expert Committee on Compensation and Betterment, supra*, para. 35.
[27] Cmnd. 6153, para. 248.

development was often far too great for local authorities to bear. The result was that planning authorities were unwilling to risk the preparation of a really strong scheme. The Commission considered a proposal for the acquisition by the State of the development rights in undeveloped land, but because of the important issues of finance and policy involved, they recommended the appointment of a body of experts to examine the whole question of compensation, betterment and development.

Such a committee (the Uthwatt Committee) was duly appointed and reported in 1942.[28] The Committee concluded that if planning control was to operate effectively, local authorities should be able to make decisions free from the shadow of compensation claims.[29] "It is clear that under a system of well-conceived planning the resolution of competing claims and the allocation of land for the various requirements must proceed on the basis of selecting the most suitable land for the particular purpose, irrespective of the existing value which may attach to the individual parcels of land."[30] As regards undeveloped land the Committee recommended the immediate vesting in the State of the rights of development on payment of fair compensation, such vesting to be secured by the imposition of a prohibition against development otherwise than with the consent of the State.[31] The recommendations as regards developed land were more complex but it is unnecessary to go into these as it was the proposals for undeveloped land upon which the subsequent legislation was built.[32]

15—12 The Town and Country Planning Act 1947, introduced by the post-war Labour Government with effect from July 1, 1948, vested in the State the right to develop land. From that time forward, development could only take place upon obtaining the consent of the planning authority. The 1947 Act provided for the payment of a charge on obtaining consent, subject to certain exceptions (see para. 15–25), to be levied by the Central Land Board. The charge, which was levied at an amount equal to the value by which the land was estimated to have increased as a result of the consent, was intended to secure the recovery of increases in value created by the efforts of the community as a whole. Differing from Uthwatt, the Government took the view that owners who were unable to realise development value as a result of the operation of the legislation were not on that account entitled to compensation. Indeed, it would have been logically inconsistent to have provided compensation for a refusal of planning permission given that any increase in value arising from a grant of planning permission was recovered by the State through the development charge. However, it was recognised that the legislation would cause hardship in many cases where land had been acquired prior to the Act in the expectation that it might be developed.

---

[28] *Final Report on the Expert Committee on Compensation and Betterment, supra.*
[29] *Ibid.* para. 25.
[30] *Ibid.* para. 22.
[31] *Ibid.* para. 56.
[32] For a detailed discussion of the events leading up to the 1947 planning legislation see J.B. Cullingworth, *Environmental Planning* (HMSO, 1975), Vol. I.

Accordingly, claims were invited against a global fund set up for Britain as a whole of £300 million from landowners who could show that their land had development value on the date the legislation came into force which prevented them from realising it. It was intended that payment of established claims would be made on a once and for all basis in 1953.

However, the incoming Conservative administration in 1951 decided to abolish **15—13** the development charge thus restoring development value in land to the land-owner in the event of planning permission for development being obtained.[33] It followed from this that there would no longer be any necessity to compensate people out of the global fund for hardship caused by loss of development value. The Town and Country Planning Act 1953 accordingly abolished the levy of a development charge on future development and repealed the provisions in the 1947 Act dealing with the distribution of the £300 million fund before any payments were made.

At this point, the Government encountered a problem.[34] There were a considerable number of existing owners of land which was ripe for development who had purchased the land at a price which reflected that expectation but who could not for whatever good planning reason obtain permission for its development. Under the financial provisions of the 1947 act they would have been in a position to claim against the global fund. Now they could not. As development value had been restored to landowners in the event of planning permission being obtained, their failure to realise development value following upon a refusal of permission would be particularly galling. Having restored development value to landowners on a grant of permission, the logical step would have been to pay compensation upon a refusal of permission. However, the Government would not contemplate the cost of such an exercise; in any event, the experience of the 1932 Act suggested that such an approach would be anathema to effective planning control. The problem was seen essentially as of a transitional nature. New acquisitions of land for development would depend on the availability of planning permission and the price paid would reflect the outcome of the application.

To meet the problem, the Town and Country Planning Act 1954 made provi- **15—14** sion for compensation to be paid, subject to certain exceptions, following an adverse planning decision on an application for new development of land in respect of which a claim had been lodged and accepted against the now defunct global fund. In other words, compensation in such cases, as Cullingworth observes, was to be only "for loss of development value which accrued in the past up to the point where the 1947 axe fell — but not for loss of development value accruing in the future."[35] Any such established claim, together with an

---

[33] The arrangements for dealing with development value have varied over the intervening years but as they have not been linked directly to the question of compensation for the regulation of land they are not described here.

[34] For a detailed discussion of the events surrounding the unscrambling of the financial provisions of the 1947 Act see J.B. Cullingworth, *Environmental Planning* (HMSO, 1980), Vol. IV.

[35] J.B. Cullingworth, *Town and Country Planning in Britain* (Unwin Hyman, 10th ed), Chap. 5.

additional sum in lieu of interest amounting to one seventh of the amount of the claim, was converted on January 1, 1955 into the "original unexpended balance of established development value" attaching to the land. Until September 25, 1991[36] compensation could be claimed from the Secretary of State in the event of an adverse planning decision relating to land in respect of which there remained an unexpended balance of established development value. The relevant provisions, now repealed, were set out in Part V of the Town and Country Planning Act 1990. The balance could be reduced or wholly expended in several ways but principally by the payment of compensation following such a decision or by deduction of development value realised following a grant of planning permission in respect of the land.

15—15   An entitlement to compensation in respect of an unexpended balance of established development was rarely encountered in the years immediately preceding the 1991 Act. This was because over the intervening years, planning permission for the development of such land (which was considered ripe for development as long ago as 1948), had been either persistently refused for whatever good planning reasons or granted. In the former case, the balance would have been extinguished following the payment of compensation; in the latter, it would have been extinguished by deduction of the development value realised. For those very few cases where an unexpended balance remained, the compensation payable for a refusal of planning permission was unlikely, based as it was on 1948 development values, to bear any relation to the development value foregone.[37] Until the 1991 Act and the repeal of Part V of the Town and Country Planning Act 1990 it was the only circumstance in which compensation was payable for the regulation of new development. "It may well be," observed the JUSTICE report in 1973, "that the real anomaly in this area of law is not that many people receive no compensation, but that a few people receive some in the shape of the 'unexpended balance of established development value' attached to their land . . . We believe that the community has now accepted that there should in general be no payment of compensation for such restrictions."[38]

2. PURCHASE NOTICE PROCEDURE — LAND INCAPABLE OF REASONABLY BENEFICIAL USE

15—16   Reference was made in the introduction to this chapter to the comment of Lord Radcliffe in *Belfast Corporation v. O.D. Cars Ltd*[39] that it was not "out of the

---

[36] The date on which s.31(1) of the Planning and Compensation Act 1991 came into force (see S.I. 1991 No. 2067).

[37] For a detailed explanation see Michael Purdue, Eric Young and Jeremy Rowan-Robinson, *Planning Law and Planning Procedure, supra,* Chap. 13.

[38] *Compensation for Compulsory Acquisition and Remedies for Planning Restrictions together with a Supplemental Report, supra,* para. 66.

[39] [1960] A.C. 490.

question that, on a particular occasion, there might not be a restriction of user so extreme in substance, though not in form, it amounted to a 'taking of the land for the benefit of the public'." The 1990 Act effectively acknowledges that the outcome of an adverse decision on an application for development may in certain circumstances be so severe as to amount to an expropriation of land by enabling an owner of land to serve what is known as a "purchase notice" on the district council (or the London borough council, as appropriate) requiring them to purchase the land at its market value. It is a form of inverse compulsory purchase.[40]

Section 137 of the 1990 Act provides that where planning permission is refused or is granted subject to conditions, and the owner claims that:

(i) the land has become incapable of reasonably beneficial use in its existing state; and

(ii) in a case where planning permission was granted subject to conditions, the land cannot be rendered capable of reasonably beneficial use by the carrying out of the permitted development in accordance with those conditions; and

(iii) in any case, that the land cannot be rendered capable of reasonably beneficial use by the carrying out of any other development for which planning permission has been granted or for which the local planning authority or the Secretary of State has undertaken to grant planning permission;

he may serve a purchase notice on the district council requiring them to purchase his interest in the land.

There is no prescribed form of notice[41] but it should be served within 12 months **15—17** of the adverse decision.[42] Within three months of service of the notice, the district council should respond (by means of a "response notice") indicating either that they or some other public body are willing to comply with the notice or that they are not willing to comply with it, stating the reasons, and that they have referred a copy to the Secretary of State for a decision (section 139). If the authority or some other public body are willing to comply with the notice, they are deemed to be authorised to acquire the interest compulsorily and to have served a notice to treat on the date of service of their response notice (section 139(2)). Compensation is to be assessed as for compulsory purchase.

In the event of the purchase notice being referred to the Secretary of State, he may confirm the notice and in doing so may substitute some other body (*e.g.* a statutory undertaker) for the district council on whom it was served. Alternatively, he may, in lieu of confirming the notice, grant planning permission for the devel-

---

[40] See generally on purchase notices, Michael Purdue, Eric Young and Jeremy Rowan-Robinson, *Planning Law and Procedure, supra,* Chap. 14.

[41] A model form of notice is contained in Appendix 1 to Department of the Environment Circular 13/83.

[42] s.137(2); and see the Town and Country Planning General Regulations 1992 reg. 12(2).

opment which was refused or, if permission was granted subject to conditions, revoke or amend the conditions. Or he may direct that planning permission be granted for some alternative development in the event of an application being made in that behalf (section 141).

15—18   The Secretary of State may refuse to confirm a purchase notice, even though he is satisfied that the land has become incapable of reasonably beneficial use, if the land has a restricted use by virtue of a previous planning permission and it appears to the Secretary of State that the land should continue to be allocated for that restricted use. Land is to be treated as having a restricted use if it is part of a larger area in respect of which planning permission was previously granted and either the application contemplated, or a condition on the permission required, that the land should remain undeveloped or be preserved or laid out as amenity land in relation to the remainder of the land (section 142). It is necessary that the relevant grant of planning permission should actually have been implemented before this power can be exercised.[43] The section is limited to land which is to be left undeveloped or laid out as amenity land.[44]

The key to the purchase notice provisions is the phrase "incapable of reasonably beneficial use." It is not enough to show that land will be of less use or value as a result of the refusal or conditions than it would have been if the full development potential could be realised.[45] That is generally the effect of an adverse planning decision. What has to be shown is that the land has become incapable of reasonably beneficial use in its existing state.[46] Where part of the land is capable of reasonably beneficial use the procedure cannot be successfully invoked in relation to the remainder.[47]

3. REGULATING THE EXISTING USE OF LAND

15—19   The system of planning control, says Davies, "rests on the assumption that the existing use of land — and the value of that use — is the owner's."[48] This is in contrast to the prospect of the development of land which as a result of the 1947 legislation belongs to the community. The scheme of the legislation is that any proposal to regulate the existing use *will* give rise to an entitlement to compensation.

---

[43] *Sheppard v. Secretary of State for the Environment* [1975] J.P.L. 352.
[44] *Strathclyde Regional Council v. Secretary of State for Scotland*, 1987 S.L.T. 724.
[45] *R. v. Minister of Housing and Local Government ex p. Chichester R.D.C.* [1960] 1 W.L.R. 587.
[46] See DoE Circular 18/83; also *Purbeck District Council v. Secretary of State for the Environment* (1982) 263 E.G. 261; and the appeal decisions noted at [1976] J.P.L. 189; [1976] J.P.L. 649; [1977] J.P.L. 256; [1980] J.P.L. 194; [1982] J.P.L. 257; [1986] J.P.L. 374; and [1988] J.P.L. 51.
[47] *Wain v. Secretary of State for the Environment* [1982] J.P.L. 244.
[48] K. Davies, *Law of Compulsory Purchase and Compensation* (Butterworths, 4th ed), at p. 271.

A claim for compensation for regulation of the existing use of land may arise on one of two (although there were formerly three) ways.[49] First of all, a planning authority may take action to secure the discontinuance of a use currently being carried on.

Secondly, an authority may revoke or modify an existing but unimplemented planning permission for development. Until the Planning and Compensation Act 1991 a third source of compensation existed in cases where planning permission was refused for one of the categories of development set out in Part II of Schedule 3 to the 1990 Act. The first two circumstances are summarised in turn and a brief commentary is made on the (now repealed) third circumstance.

1. Discontinuance: A local planning authority may, because, for example, of a   **15—20** change in policy or because of a change in the character of an area, conclude that a particular use of land should be discontinued, that conditions should be imposed on the continuance of a use or that a building should be altered or removed. They may secure this by way of an order under section 102 of the 1990 Act.[50] Such an order is of no effect unless it is confirmed by the Secretary of State. When an order is submitted to the Secretary of State for confirmation, notice must be served on the owner and on any lessee, occupier or other person who may be affected. There is a minimum period of 28 days for objection and the Secretary of State must, before confirming the order, grant a hearing to any such person, if so requested.

If such an order is confirmed, any person who can show that they have suffered damage by depreciation of the value of an interest in land or by being disturbed in the enjoyment of land is entitled to compensation from the authority (section 115(2)). Such a claim may include any cost reasonably incurred in carrying out any works required by the order. A claim should be lodged within 12 months of the making of the order or such longer period as the Secretary of State may allow.[51] Failure to comply with such an order is an offence (section 189(1)).

2. Revocation or modification: Under section 97 of the 1990 Act, a local planning   **15—21** authority may, if they consider it expedient to do so, by order revoke or modify any planning permission granted under Part III of the Act.[52] The power may be exercised in respect of building or other operations, at any time before they have been completed and in respect of a change of use, at any time before the change

---

[49] It would seem that the existing use of land may also, in certain circumstances, be regulated without payment of compensation by way of a condition on a grant of planning permission for new development (*Kingston-upon-Thames Royal London Borough Council v. Secretary of State for the Environment* [1973] 1 W.L.R. 1549; *British Airports Authority v. Secretary of State for Scotland*, 1979 S.C. 200; 1979 S.L.T. 197).

[50] See, generally, on discontinuance orders, Michael Purdue, Eric Young and Jeremy Rowan-Robinson, *Planning Law and Procedure, supra*, Chap. 15.

[51] Town and Country Planning General Regulations 1992, reg. 12(2).

[52] See, generally, on revocation orders. Michael Purdue, Eric Young and Jeremy Rowan-Robinson, *Planning Law and Procedure, supra*, Chap. 15.

of use has taken place. Once operations have been completed or a change of use has occurred the planning authority would have to have recourse to a discontinuance order under section 102 of the Act to regulate the existing use (above).

A revocation or modification order will not generally take effect unless it is confirmed by the Secretary of State although provision is made under section 99 for an expedited procedure which does not require confirmation by the Secretary of State where the owner, occupier and other affected persons have stated that they have no objection. Such procedure might be employed when a substitute planning permission is to be granted. When submitting an order to the Secretary of State for confirmation, the local planning authority must notify the owner, occupier and other affected persons, and any such person has a right to be heard by a person appointed by the Secretary of State before a decision is made regarding confirmation of the order.

15—22   Where such an order is confirmed, any person having an interest in the land who can show that he has incurred expenditure in carrying out work which is rendered abortive by the order or has otherwise sustained loss or damage, including depreciation in the value of the interest, directly attributable to the order is entitled to be compensated by the authority (section 107(1)). A claim for compensation should be submitted to the local planning authority within twelve months of the date of the order although this period may be extended by the Secretary of State.[53]

Planning permission may be granted, not only in response to an application under Part III of the 1990 Act, but by way of a development order (section 59). In particular, Article 3 of the Town and Country Planning General Development Order 1988, as amended, grants planning permission for the classes of development specified in Schedule 2. However, the Secretary of State or a local planning authority may, if they consider it expedient that any such development should not be carried out, except in response to an application for permission made in the normal way, withdraw the permission granted by the General Development Order at any time before it is implemented. This can be effected by the Secretary of State or the local planning authority making a direction under Article 4 of the order.

15—23   The direction may apply to: (i) all or any development of all or any of the classes in the Schedule in any particular specified area; or (ii) any particular specified development falling within any of the classes in the Schedule. In *Thanet District Council v. Ninedrive Limited*[54] it was held that an Article 4 direction could be made even if it applied to a single site.

A direction by the local planning authority requires the approval of the Secretary of State. There is no right of appeal. The consequence of a direction is that the specified development no longer has permission and an application for permission must be submitted to the local planning authority and approved in the normal

---

[53] Town and Country Planning General Regulations 1992, reg. 12(2).
[54] [1978] 1 All E.R. 703.

way before it can commence. If such an application is refused or subjected to conditions more onerous than those originally imposed by the development order, a claim for compensation may be lodged with the local planning authority under section 108 of the Act; compensation is assessed as for a revocation order.

A claim under section 108 may also be made where planning permission for development granted by a development order is withdrawn following the revocation or amendment of the order by the Secretary of State and where a subsequent application under Part III for planning permission for the development in question is refused or onerously conditioned. However, a claim may only be made in these circumstances if the subsequent application for planning permission is made within a year of the revocation or amendment of the order.[55]

3. Schedule 3 development: As originally enacted, Schedule 3 to the 1990 Act **15—24** listed eight categories of development. These were specified in two Parts; Part I contained categories 1 and 2 and Part II contained categories 3 to 8. A refusal or conditional grant of planning permission for the development of land for any of the purposes in Part II entitled a person with an interest in the land to compensation from the local planning authority under section 114 if it could be shown that the interest was of less value than it would have been if the permission had been granted or granted unconditionally, as the case may be. The adverse decision had to be one made by the Secretary of State either on appeal against a refusal by the local planning authority or on the reference of the application to him for a decision in the first place. An adverse decision in respect of the categories of development listed in Part I of Schedule 3 did not qualify for compensation although if the land could be shown to be incapable of reasonably beneficial use, it would then have been possible to serve a purchase notice under section 137 (above). Section 114 and Part II of Schedule 3 were repealed by the Planning and Compensation Act 1991,[56] except in relation to claims for compensation submitted before July 25, 1991.

The categories of development listed in Schedule 3 were a hangover from the **15—25** financial provisions of the 1947 legislation. When planning permission was granted under that Act, a development charge was, until 1953, imposed equal to the amount of any development value arising from the permission. However, certain categories of development listed in the third Schedule of that Act were considered to be so closely related to the existing use of the land that *as a concession* to landowners they were treated for the purposes of the legislation as part of the existing use value and thus not subject to the development charge which was only levied in respect of planning permission for "new development."[57] The converse position was that refusal of planning permission or the imposition of onerous

---

[55] 1990 Act, s.108(2).
[56] s.31(2), (4) and Sched. 6, para. 40.
[57] This term was expunged from the legislation by section 31 of and Sched. 6, para. 9 to the Planning and Compensation Act 1991.

conditions for such categories of development were treated as a derogation of existing use rights and thus eligible for compensation, at least as regards the categories of development in what was Part II of Schedule 3. These categories of development were treated as forming part of the existing use value of the land to the landowner so to that extent under the general scheme of the 1990 Act an adverse decision qualified for compensation. And it was for this reason that section 15(3) of the Land Compensation Act 1961 provides that it be assumed for the purpose of assessing compensation for the compulsory acquisition of land that planning permission would be granted for development of any class specified in Schedule 3 to the 1990 Act (Parts I and II).[58] On the repeal of Part II it is now to be assumed that planning permission would be granted for development in Part I. Thus two surviving categories of development in Part I are still relevant for valuation purposes on compulsory acquisition. These are as follows:

15—26
1. The carrying out of –
   (a) the rebuilding, as often as occasion may require, of any building which was in existence on July 1, 1948, or of any building which was in existence before that date but was destroyed or demolished after January 7, 1937, including the making good of war damage sustained by any such building;
   (b) the rebuilding, as often as occasion may require, of any building erected after July 1, 1948 which was in existence at a material date,[59]
   (c) the carrying out for the maintenance, improvement or other alteration of any building, of works which –
      (i) affect only the interior of the building, or do not materially affect the external appearance of the building, and
      (ii) are works for making good war damage, so long as the cubic content of the original building is not substantially exceeded.
2. The use as two or more separate dwellinghouses of any building which at a material date was used as a single dwellinghouse.

The first of these two categories is subject to two conditions. First of all, the cubic content of the original building[60] must not be substantially exceeded, *i.e.* by more than one-tenth or 1750 cubic feet (whichever is the greater) in the case of a dwelling-house and in any other case by more than one-tenth. Secondly, the permission which may be assumed is subject to the limitations on increase in gross floor space laid down in Schedule 10 to the 1990 Act. This has the effect of limiting the increase in gross floor space to not more than 10 per cent. of the original building.

---

[58] See Chap. 8.
[59] The date by reference to which the Schedule falls to be applied in the particular case: Sched. 3, para. 12.
[60] Building is defined by *ibid*, para. 13; cubic content is measured externally (para. 10).

4. CONCLUSION

One of the interesting features of the history of the compensation provisions for **15—27** mainstream planning control is the reverse of the compensation entitlement. A general right to compensation, such as existed prior to and under the 1932 Act is not, it seems, consistent with an effective system of regulation.

It is probable that most people today would regard as reasonable the provisions whereby compensation is payable for action initiated by a local planning authority to discontinue an existing use of land or to revoke a planning permission. The value of that use or permission belongs to the landowner. Such provisions, however, are not often invoked in practice because, as Grant observes, "[l]ocal authorities have rarely been in a position to buy environmental improvements by using the powers of direct intervention."[61]

The compensation entitlements arising from the unexpended balance and from Schedule 3 were anachronisms. As JUSTICE commented, they "can by explained historically but not logically".[62] The repeal of the relevant provisions means that mainstream planning control has been brought more firmly into line with many other codes of regulation in that the cost of compliance will, for the most part, lie where it falls — upon the landowner.

Mining operations

Mining operations are "development" within the meaning of section 55(1) of **15—28** the Town and Country Planning Act 1990 and consequently require planning permission in the normal way. As with other forms of development, the normal rule applies so that a refusal of permission or the imposition of conditions on a grant of permission will not give rise to a claim for compensation. It is in the context of the regulation of *existing operations* that the regime governing the winning and working of minerals and depositing of mineral waste departs in certain important respects from the general scheme of the planning legislation.

As mentioned above, the position under the 1990 Act is that proposals to restrict or take away an established right to use or develop land will generally entitle the landowner to compensation. That entitlement was modified by the Town and Country Planning (Minerals) Act 1981 in respect of certain changes

---

[61] M. Grant, *Urban Planning Law* (Sweet & Maxwell, 1982), First Supplement (1986) at p. 646.
[62] *Compensation for Compulsory Acquisition and Remedies for Planning Restrictions together with a Supplemental Report, supra*, para. 64.

to existing mineral operations, the relevant provisions now being contained in section 116 of the 1990 Act.[63]

15—29 The 1981 Act was the progeny of the report of the Stevens Committee on *Planning Control over Mineral Working*.[64] Stevens recognised that the winning and working of minerals could be distinguished from other operations in a number of important respects.[65] Most operations are transitory; they are simply a means to an end in that they fit land for some alternative use. Mineral operations, on the other hand, are an end in themselves; and, although not permanent, they may be carried on for a great many years. They do not fit land for some other use; indeed, they are essentially destructive of land. Furthermore, there is little scope for locational choice; such operations must, of course, locate where the minerals exist. As mineral deposits tend to coincide with some of our most interesting and beautiful landscapes, proposals for the extraction are often attended by considerable controversy. Mainstream planning control, geared as it is to once and for all decisions, proved to be incapable of adequately safeguarding the environment over the life of the mineral operations. Conditions imposed at the outset become less relevant and effective as time goes by. Because of these characteristics, Stevens recommended that certain additional controls should be applied to the winning and working of minerals. The 1981 Act implemented those recommendations in modified form.[66]

15—30 Broadly, the effect of the 1981 Act was to increase the burden of regulation on operators without compensation. This may be illustrated by reference to two provisions. Section 72 and Schedule 5 to the 1990 Act enable a mineral planning authority[67] to impose an "aftercare" condition where planning permission for mineral working or involving the deposit of mineral waste is granted subject to a condition requiring restoration of the site. Stevens considered that restoration conditions tended to lack any clear objective. Now they may be coupled with an "aftercare condition" requiring the land to be planted, cultivated, fertilised, watered, drained or otherwise treated on completion of restoration for a specified period so as to fit the land for use for agriculture, forestry or amenity.[68] Further,

---

[63] As substituted by s.21 of and Sched. 1 para. 9 to the Planning and Compensation Act 1991. The substituted section enables regulations to be made to provide (a) for circumstances in which compensation is not to be payable; (b) for modification of the basis on which compensation is assessed; and (c) for assessment of the amount to be paid on a basis different from that on which it would otherwise have been assessed.

[64] Report of the Committee under the chairmanship of Sir Roger Stevens (HMSO, 1976).

[65] *Ibid.* Chap. 3.

[66] See, generally, Michael Purdue, Eric Young and Jeremy Rowan-Robinson, *Planning Law and Procedure, supra*, Chap. 18.

[67] Defined by s.1(4) of the 1990 Act to mean the county planning authority in non-metropolitan areas. In metropolitan areas or in London, the mineral planning authority is the metropolitan district council or London borough council, respectively.

[68] See Minerals Policy Guidance Note 7, *The Relocation of Mineral Workings*, paras. 37–48. Such a condition may be added to an existing permission by way of orders under section 97 of and Sched. 5, or s.102 of and Sched. 9 to the 1990 Act, as appropriate (see below), subject to the payment of compensation. The compensation entitlement may, however, be reduced in certain circumstances (below).

section 72(5), together with Schedule 5, paragraph 1 to the Act, subjects every planning permission for mineral working to a defined life which, unless otherwise specified, is to be 60 years from the commencement of the 1981 Act[69] or the date of the permission, whichever is the later. Stevens thought it important that there should be no doubt about the time for commencement of restoration. The Committee also felt that future generations should be allowed an opportunity to review the position.[70]

A key provision is section 105 of the 1990 Act[71] which imposes a duty on **15—31** mineral planning authorities to undertake, at such intervals as they consider fit, reviews of every mineral working and sites for depositing of mineral waste in their area and to make such changes to the conditions governing the operations on each site as they consider appropriate. The intention is that such changes will be made by way of revocation and discontinuance orders under sections 97(6) and Schedule 5 (revocation or modification of planning permission) and Section 102 and Schedule 9 (discontinuance orders). Mineral workings, which are classed as "operations" under the planning legislation, are to be treated as a "use" of land for the purposes of section 102, and such an order may now secure the alteration or removal of any plant or machinery used for winning and working minerals or depositing of mineral waste.[72] Furthermore, mineral planning authorities are given power to make two other types of order — a "prohibition order" and a "suspension order" (below) to cope with the environmental problems arising from the intermittent nature of mineral working which become apparent on review.[73]

Reference was made during the discussion of "mainstream planning control" **15—32** (above) to the limited use made by local planning authorities of the power to make revocation and discontinuance orders because of the compensation entitlement. Planning authorities in their representations to the Stevens Committee made it clear that a system of review would only be effective if the compensation entitlement was modified. This could be justified, they argued, on the ground that the permissions requiring change would be likely to be those where operations had been carried on over a number of years under what, by comparison with present controls, was a relatively relaxed regime of conditions. The change would simply bring further operations on such sites into line with the position on other sites governed by modern permissions. The minerals industry accepted that these arguments had some force in relation to changes in conditions which gave rise to no more than reasonable additional costs. Stevens accordingly concluded that:

> "a mineral operator should be required to bear reasonable costs arising from a review of conditions. We are also satisfied that to require him to bear all costs in every case

---

[69] February 22, 1982.
[70] *Planning Control over Mineral Working* (HMSO, 1976) para. 7.16.
[71] Substituted by section 21 of and Sched. 1, para. 7 to the Planning and Compensation Act 1991.
[72] Sched. 9, para. 1(c) to the 1990 Act.
[73] Sched. 9, paras. 3 and 5, respectively.

might often expose him to the risk of an unjustifiable derogation from his existing rights to use or develop his land. We are consequently faced with the task of drawing a line which separates reasonable costs, which the operator will bear, from unreasonable costs, for which he should be compensated. The difficulties for drawing such a line are formidable."[74]

15—33 The Committee went on to suggest that the question whether the loss suffered by an operator on a review was substantial and should therefore attract compensation might be determined by comparing the net additional costs of complying with the modifications with the annual value of the right to work the mineral-bearing land.[75] The legislation broadly follows this suggestion (below).

The 1990 Act, as originally enacted, provided that the normal compensation entitlement will be modified where "mineral compensation requirements" are satisfied in respect of orders made following a review.[76] These requirements are complex and vary according to the type of order employed to effect the change.[77] The principal requirements, however, are that the order must not:

(i) restrict the winning and working of minerals;
(ii) modify or replace any such restriction; and
(iii) the development consisting of the winning and working of minerals must have begun not less than five years before the date of the order.

Such restriction might threaten the economic viability of the operations and the loss suffered by an operator would be likely to be substantial. Such restriction would not satisfy "mineral compensation requirements" and would therefore attract full compensation.

15—34 Section 116 of the 1990 Act empowers the Secretary of State to make regulations modifying the entitlement to compensation where "mineral compensation requirements" are satisfied. Implementation of the provisions in the 1981 Act was delayed pending the outcome of consultations over the details and the formula for determining the amount of the reduction, although for revocation and discontinuance orders a basis for the formula is provided in sections 107 and 115 of the Act.[78] The details eventually emerged in the Town and Country Planning (Compensation for Restrictions on Mineral Working) Regulations 1985.[79] Regu-

---

[74] *Planning Control over Mineral Working, supra*, para. 8.18.
[75] *Ibid.* para. 8.32.
[76] s.116, Sched. 11 and the Town and Country Planning (Compensation for Restrictions on Mineral Working) Regulations 1985. S.116 was substituted and Sched. 11 repealed by s.21 of and Scheds. 1 and 19 to the Planning and Compensation Act 1991, from September 25, 1991. Pending issue of further regulations, however, Sched. 11 continues to apply.
[77] See Sched. 11, paras. 4–8.
[78] See the DoE consultation paper "Proposals to Amend the Law Relating to Planning Control over Mineral Workings: Compensation Aspects" (September 1980). The review provisions were finally brought into effect on January 1, 1988 by the Town and Country Planning (Minerals) Act 1981 (Commencement No.4) Order.
[79] These regulations were amended by the Town and Country Planning (Compensation for Restrictions on Mineral Working) (Amendment) Regulations 1990 (S.I. 1990 No. 803).

lation 6 provides that where "mineral compensation requirements" are satisfied in relation to a revocation or discontinuance order, compensation is to be assessed in the normal way under section 107 of the 1990 Act as modified by the regulations. From the amount so assessed there is to be deducted either the sum of £3,200 or 10 per cent. of a figure calculated in accordance with a prescribed formula,[80] whichever is the greater. The deduction in any case is not to exceed £128,000. The remainder represents the compensation to be paid by the mineral planning authority in respect of the order. The formula is the product of the annual value of the right to win and work the mineral multiplied by a multiplier based on the life expectancy of the workings. The regulations detail the way in which the annual value is to be calculated, the appropriate multiplier is to be selected and the estimated life of the workings is to be assessed.[81] Provision is also made to cover the situation where two or more minerals are being worked or where two or more persons have an interest in the site.

Regulation 5 deals with the position where "mineral compensation requirements" are satisfied in respect of a prohibition or suspension order. The former may be employed where no development has been carried out to any substantial extent at a site for a period of at least two years and it appears that the resumption of development is unlikely.[82] The mineral planning authority may by order prohibit the resumption of such development and impose requirements with a view to tidying up the site. The latter may be used where no development has been carried out to any substantial extent at a site for a period of at least 12 months but it appears that a resumption of such development is likely.[83] The order will specify certain steps to be taken for the protection of the environment. Compensation in respect of such orders is to be assessed as for a discontinuance order but there is to be deducted from the amount so assessed the sum of £6,400 (or the appropriate proportion where persons in addition to the claimant have an interest in the site in question). In assessing compensation for a prohibition order, no account is to be taken of the value of any mineral which cannot be won or worked in consequence of the order (regulation 4(4)). Compensation in such a case will only arise where a planning authority impose additional requirements such as restoration and aftercare and only then if the threshold of £6,400 is exceeded. **15—35**

The redistribution of costs effected by the 1981 Act would seem to be a manifestation of the trend noted by Uthwatt to push the point at which obligations may be imposed without compensation progressively further on. It is doubtful, however, whether the redistribution will be, or is intended to be, significant. The Stevens Committee noted that substantial environmental gains can often be

---

[80] Town and Country Planning (Compensation for Restrictions on Mineral Working) Regulations 1985, regs. 6(2) and 6(3).
[81] *Ibid.* Scheds. 1 and 2.
[82] 1990 Act, Sched. 9, para. 3.
[83] *Ibid.* Sched. 9, para. 5.

obtained without imposing substantial costs on operators.[84] And in winding up the second reading debate for the Government on the Town and Country Planning (Minerals) Bill in the House of Lords, Lord Mansfield said "I accept that this is not the time to be adding significantly to industry's burdens. This Bill does not do that."[85]

Nature conservation

15—36   Nature conservation is concerned with safeguarding flora, fauna and geological or physiographical features. Its principal concern is with safeguarding of habitats rather than with species. The question at the root of this chapter is the extent to which interference by the State in rights in land falling short of "taking" may be the subject of compensation. The picture which emerges from the study of mainstream planning control and mineral operations is one of the state progressively pushing forward the point at which obligations may be imposed and rights withdrawn without compensation. Nature conservation has been selected for consideration here, however, because it presents a markedly different picture. The general position in this instance is that obligations may only be imposed upon payment of compensation. To understand how this has come about, it is necessary to trace the way in which the regime for safeguarding habitats has evolved.

Responsibility for safeguarding habitats rests primarily with the Nature Conservancy Council for England and the Countryside Council for Wales. These bodies were established by section 128 of the Environmental Protection Act 1990, which transferred to these Councils the functions formerly exercised by the Nature Conservancy Council. The new Nature Conservancy Council for England has adopted the style "English Nature" and hence this name is used in the text which follows.

15—37   One of the key mechanisms employed by English Nature for promoting nature conservation is the designation of sites to which a special safeguarding regime is to be applied. Habitats with the greatest nature conservation interest are designated as nature reserves. "Nature reserves" are defined in section 15 of the National Parks and Access to the Countryside Act 1949 as land managed for the purpose of preserving flora, fauna, or geological or physiographical features and for providing special opportunities for the study of and for research into such matters. Nature reserves are "declared" by English Nature under section 19 of the 1949 Act and safeguarded through acquisition[86] or leasing of them or through negotiation of management agreements with the landowners under section 16 of the 1949 Act.

---

[84] *Planning Control over Mineral Working, supra*, para. 8.17.
[85] H.L. Deb, Vol. 416, col. 528.
[86] Powers of compulsory acquisition are conferred by sections 17 and 18 of the 1949 Act.

The essential feature of a reserve is that it is managed primarily in the interests of nature conservation. Local authorities may also establish nature reserves under section 21 of the 1949 Act.

Section 23 of the 1949 Act originally provided that if the Nature Conservancy Council were of the opinion that any area of land, not being managed as a nature reserve, was nonetheless of "special scientific interest" by reason of its flora, fauna or geological or physiographical features, it was their duty to notify that fact to the local planning authority in whose area the land was situated.

In the case of sites notified as of special scientific interest (S.S.S.I.s), the nature conservation interest has, unlike nature reserves, to fit in with other land management objectives. Hence, it is with these sites that this chapter is principally concerned. The consequence of notification was that the local planning authority had to consult with the Nature Conservancy Council before determining any application for planning permission for the development of land, thus ensuring that the nature conservation interest is taken into account.[87] This continues to be a feature of the contemporary law, though the consultation will now be carried out with English Nature. The requirement of consultation can also extend to proposed development on land close to the boundaries of the S.S.S.I. up to a maximum of 2 kilometres where English Nature have advised that the additional land is a "consultation area". Local planning authorities should also consult if they themselves form the view than an S.S.S.I. is likely to be affected.[88] More than 4,000 S.S.S.I.s in England (and Wales) have been notified by English Nature (or its predecessors) to local planning authorities. Although the statutory provisions for notification of an S.S.S.I. have changed (below), the interaction with the development control process remains the same. **15—38**

While the notification procedure helped to safeguard S.S.S.I.s against development proposals, it was unable to protect them from actions beyond planning control. In particular, planning authorities had no control over the use of land for agriculture or forestry, the principal land uses in the great majority of designated sites.

The Town and Country Planning Act 1947, which first introduced a comprehensive system of control of the development of land, specifically excluded the use of land for agriculture or forestry from the definition or "development" and that exclusion has been carried through into section 55(2)(e) of the 1990 Act. The reason for the exclusion lies primarily in the policy which has been pursued since the Second World War until recently by successive governments of promoting agriculture, but also partly in the perception of agriculture and forestry as benign influences on the countryside. As Lowe (et al.) observe: **15—39**

> "[A]griculture's exemption occasioned no dispute at the time — reflecting the romantic view of farming encapsulated in the Scott Report and the overriding political

---

[87] Town and Country Planning General Development Order 1988, art. 18.
[88] Town and Country Planning General Development (Amendment) (No. 3) Order 1991. See also DoE Circular 1/92 "Planning Controls over Sites of Special Scientific Interest."

commitment given to the expansion of home food production at a time when rationing was still in force."[89] The threat to S.S.S.I.s was seen as coming primarily from "developers."

However, "few people," continue Lowe (et al.), "anticipated the rapid transformation in agricultural practices which was to occur in the post war period . . . agricultural intensification, fostered by government and mechanisation and the consolidation of holdings, has transformed the rural environment."[90] This transformation has been effected at very considerable cost to nature conservation interests.[91] Increasing public and parliamentary concern led to new provisions for S.S.S.I. protection being incorporated into Part II of the Wildlife and Countryside Act 1981.

15—40   The new provisions are built around a reciprocal notification procedure. Section 28 of the 1981 Act, which replaces section 23 of the 1949 Act, imposes a duty on English Nature where they are of the opinion that an area of land is of special scientific interest to notify the fact to the local planning authority, to every owner and occupier of the land and to the Secretary of State. Previous notifications to local planning authorities under section 23 remain good but as no notice was given under that provision to owners and occupiers and to the Secretary of State, such notice now has to be given. The notification to owners and occupiers will specify the features of scientific interest and list operations[92] which appear to English Nature to be likely to damage those features. Provision is made for representations or objections to be made to English Nature within a minimum period of three months; English Nature then has a further period within which to decide whether to confirm or withdraw the notification.

The S.S.S.I. is, however, safeguarded from the date of notification.[93] The consequence is that an owner or occupier[94] who wishes to carry out one of the listed operations (referred to as "potentially damaging operations" (P.D.O.'s)) must notify English Nature (the reciprocal notification). The operation may not be carried out unless:

(i) English Nature give their written consent; or
(ii) the operation is carried out in accordance with the terms of an agreement

---

[89] P. Lowe, G. Cox, M. MacEwen, T. O'Riordan and M. Winter, *Countryside Conflicts* (Gower/Maurice Temple Smith, 1986) pp. 17 and 18.

[90] *Ibid.* p. 25.

[91] *Ibid.* Chap. 3. See, too, D. Goode, "The Threat to Wildlife Habitats", 1981 New Scientist 89, 219; *Nature Conservation in Britain* (Nature Conservancy Council, 1984).

[92] "Operations" is not defined by the 1981 Act. Whether this includes an agricultural use is not clear but it is submitted that an interpretation which excludes uses of land would defeat the purpose of the amendments introduced by the Wildlife and Countryside Act 1981.

[93] Wildlife and Countryside (Amendment) Act 1985, s.2.

[94] "Occupier" does not include a person who carried out operations on the land for a few weeks since that person "has no stable relationship with the land to which the provisions could sensibly be made to apply" per Lord Mustill in *Southern Water Authority v. Nature Conservancy Council* [1992] 1 W.L.R. 775.

entered into under section 16 of the 1949 Act (a nature reserve agreement) or section 15 of the Countryside Act 1968 (an S.S.S.I. agreement); or

(iii) four months have elapsed since English Nature was notified without consent being given or an agreement being entered into.

Such an agreement can include provision for payments to be made to the person who gave the reciprocal notification.

A person who, without reasonable excuse, carries out a P.D.O. without satisfy- **15—41** ing these requirements is liable on summary conviction to a fine not exceeding £2,500. It is a reasonable excuse to carry out an operation if it was authorised by a planning permission granted under Part III of the Town and Country Planning Act 1990 (but not a development order).

Provision is made under section 29 of the 1981 Act for an extended period of protection to be given by order (known as a "nature conservation order") of the Secretary of State to certain S.S.S.I.'s which are considered by him to be of "national importance". Experience shows that such orders are made ad hoc by the Secretary of State, if he considers it appropriate in response to a request from English Nature where they anticipate or are facing difficulty in attaining nature conservation objectives in respect of a particular S.S.S.I. The maximum penalties prescribed for contravention under section 29 are rather more severe.

Part II of the 1981 Act regulates land use only in so far as it imposes a temporary **15—42** restraint on the activities of owners and occupiers. The temporary restraint gives English Nature an opportunity to assess the impact of what is proposed on the nature conservation interest and, where the impact is adverse, to attempt to persuade the owner or occupier to desist or to negotiate an agreement to safeguard that interest. The process is, however, voluntary and accordingly the provisions were described by Lord Mustill in *Southern Water Authority v. Nature Conservancy Council*[95] as "toothless" and demanding "no more from the owner or occupier of an S.S.S.I. than a little patience". Owners and occupiers are under no obligation to fall in with the wishes of English Nature and may persist in proceeding with their activity at the end of the period of restraint.[96] The government, nonetheless, believe that "the best guarantee of the future of Britain's landscape lies in the natural feel for it possessed by those who live and work in it. This is why the heart of the Wildlife and countryside Act is fashioned from a policy of consent.[97] Those who live and work on the land are thus seen as stewards of the nature conservation interest on behalf of the nation. The regime under Part II is effectively one of self-regulation; this is manifested in the Code of Guidance issued by the Government in 1982 (subsequently withdrawn) which emphasised that the

---

[95] [1992] 1 W.L.R. 775.

[96] A power of compulsory acquisition is conferred on English Nature by section 29(7) of the 1981 Act. This can only be exercised, however, where the Secretary of State has exercised his power to make a nature conservation order under s.29(1).

[97] *Operation and Effectiveness of Part II of the Wildlife and Countryside Act 1981; The Government's Reply to the First Report from the Environment Committee*, Cmnd. 9522 (May 1985).

conservation and proper management of S.S.S.I.s is vital to the maintenance of Britain's wildlife and urged owners and occupiers to co-operate.[98]

15—43   The regime provides a considerable incentive for owners and occupiers to co-operate with English Nature. An agreement under section 16 of the 1949 Act or section 15 of the 1968 Act may provide for payments to be made in accordance with guidelines provided by the Secretary of State.[99] Indeed, section 32(2) of the 1981 Act goes so far as to provide that where an application for a farm capital grant has been made under section 29 of the Agriculture Act 1970 in respect of expenditure incurred or to be incurred for the purposes of activities notified to English Nature under sections 28 or 29 of the Act, and the Secretary of State refuses to make a grant in consequence of an objection from English Nature, that authority *must* offer to enter into an agreement imposing restrictions on such activities and providing for the making of payments to the applicant in accordance with the guidelines. And English Nature have indicated that they will voluntarily apply the provisions of section 32(2) to applications made for all types of farm capital grant and for grants for felling permission under forestry legislation.[1]

15—44   Financial guidelines for management agreements were issued by the Government in 1983.[2] Their objective was to establish a means by which a fair balance could be struck which did not place the land user at a financial disadvantage while at the same time ensuring that the interests of the community at large who foot the bill were properly protected.[3] Owners and occupiers may choose between a lump sum or annual payments; tenants are eligible for annual payments only. For agreements, other than those relating to forestry operations, the lump sum payment represents the difference between the restricted and unrestricted value of the claimant's interest calculated having regard to the rules set out in section 5 of the Land Compensation Act 1961. Annual payments reflect the net profits foregone because of the agreement. As regards agricultural operations, it is to be assumed in calculating the payment that farm capital grant would have been payable. For agreements relating to forestry operations, lump sum payments are to be determined by individual assessments of net revenue foregone based generally on a comparison of discounted streams of expenditure and income over the period of the agreement and calculated (a) with, and (b) without, the constraints imposed by the particular management agreement. The claimant may, alternatively, elect to receive payment based on the depreciation in value of the land or woodlands concerned assessed according to the rules in section 5 of the 1961 Act. Where

---

[98] *Code of Guidance for Sites of Special Scientific Interest*, DoE, M.A.F.F., Scottish Office and Welsh Office, 1988.

[99] The financial regime of Part II of the 1981 Act was based on compensation guidelines developed to promote moorland preservation on Exmoor. See Lowe *et al, Contryside Conflicts, supra*, Chap. 8

[1] D o E Circular 4/83 "Wildlife and Countryside Act 1981 — Financial Guidelines for Management Agreements" (1983) Appendix, para. 4.

[2] *Ibid.*

[3] "Wildlife and Countryside Act 1981 — Review of Financial Guidelines", DoE consultation paper, April 1987, para. 2.

annual payments are to be made, these are to be derived from the lump sum calculated as above and amortised to produce a flow of annual payments based on an estimate of current market rates of interest over the period of the agreement. If forestry grant would have been payable, this should be taken into account in assessing the appropriate payment.

Experience of the guidelines in operation led to criticism that they were com- **15—45** plex, imprecise and overgenerous.[4] Consultants were commissioned to examine the operation and effectiveness of the guidelines and they reported in September 1985.[5] At the time of writing, the guidelines are currently under review.[6]

The compensation provisions relating to the operation of Part II of the 1981 Act could be viewed as in accord with the general scheme for compensating landowners under the planning legislation for restrictions on the existing use of land. The use of land for agriculture and forestry is excluded by section 55(2)(e) from the definition of "development" under the Town and Country Planning Act 1990; the right to undertake such activity was not vested in the State under the 1947 planning legislation. The value of such activity belongs to the landowner; any restriction on the realisation of that value is properly the subject of compensation.

Such a view, to borrow Lord Reid's words, is arguably "too meticulous."[7] The mere fact that the value of an activity belongs to a landowner has not prevented successive governments from imposing restrictions on the activity without compensation. As the Uthwatt Committee observed, the trend has been to push the point at which obligations may be imposed without compensation progressively further forward. Examples of this may be seen, as mentioned earlier, in the fields of building control, health and safety at work, fire precautions and the control of pollution. The decision to couple compensation to an exercise of self-regulation reflects a political decision to employ subsidy rather than formal regulation to promote behaviourial change.

This is not, of itself, a cause for criticism. There is a case to be made of the use **15—46** of economic incentives rather than formal regulation as a mechanism for securing behaviourial change.[8] And the government have extended the role of such incentives in the countryside in the form of payments to farmers operating in environmentally sensitive areas.[9] for continuing with or adopting farming methods which are environmentally benign.

---

[4] See the arguments rehearsed in the First Report from the Environmental Committee of the House of Commons, *Operation and Effectiveness of Part II of the Wildlife and Countryside Act*, Session 1984–85 (HMSO, 1985), Vol. 1.

[5] *Wildlife and Countryside Act 1981: Financial Guidelines for Management Agreements*, Final Report by Lawrence Gould Consultants Ltd, DoE September 1985.

[6] "Wildlife and Countryside Act 1981 — Review of Financial Guidelines", DoE consultation paper, April 1987.

[7] *Westminster Bank Ltd v. Minister of Housing and Local Government* [1971] A.C. 508.

[8] J.K. Bowers and P. Cheshire, *Agriculture, The Countryside and Land Use: an Economic Critique* (Methuen, 1983), p. 143.

[9] Designated under the Agriculture Act 1986, s.18.

However, experience with the compensation provisions of the Town and Country Planning Act 1932 (above) suggest that public bodies are not generally well-placed to buy control and that, if conservation is not to be compromised, the employment of economic incentives must be coupled with a commitment to increase resources. It was estimated, for example, that the annual cost to the public purse of agreements for the whole of the U.K. would be somewhere between £14–18 million by 1989–90.[10]

15—47   The principal criticism of the financial arrangements for safeguarding nature conservation is their illogicality. As the Environment Committee of the House of Commons commented: "[t]he illogicality of one part of government (MAFF) offering financial inducement to someone to do something which another part of government (D. of E. and related bodies) then has to pay him not to, is clear.[11] The 1981 Act may also be seen as giving legal expression "to the surprising notion that a farmer has a right to grant aid from the tax payer: if he is denied it in the wider public interest, he must be compensated for the resulting, entirely hypothetical, losses."[12] The Government's explanation of this "surprising notion" is that it would be unfair to put the particular farmer who happens to be in a conservation area at a disadvantage just because of that reason, as opposed to the farmer next door who might be getting the grant.[13] The explanation is unconvincing. The government have not shown themselves so sensitive to the plight of the developer who is refused planning permission for development because land is designated as a green belt or as a conservation area.

Conclusion

15—48   In the introduction to this chapter, we highlighted the question raised by the Uthwatt Committee — at what point does the public interest become such that a private individual ought to be called on to comply, at his own cost, with a restriction or requirement? This chapter shows that there is no clear cut answer. Although the trend has been towards placing the whole cost of compliance on the individual, the trend is by no means consistent. There are differences, as will

---

[10] Grant aid to the Nature Conservancy Council increased from £12.7 million in 1983–84 to £36.5 million in 1987–88: 13th Report of the N.C.C., April 1, 1986 — March 31, 1987.

[11] *Operation and Effectiveness of Part II of the Wildlife and Countryside Act, supra,* para. 46.

[12] Letter from the Director of the Council for the Preservation of Rural England to *The Times* cited in P. Lowe *et al, Countryside Conflicts, supra,* p. 147. But see in this connection *Palatine Graphic Arts Co. Ltd v. Liverpool City Council* (1986) 56 P. & C.R. 308, a case which turned on the question whether the payment of a discretionary regional development grant should be deducted from disturbance compensation.

[13] The Hon. W. Waldegrave M.P., cited in the First Report of the Environment Committee of the House of Commons, *Operations and Effectiveness of Part II of the Wildlife and Countryside Act, supra,* para. 14.

be apparent from the sections on mainstream planning control and on mineral operations, in the distribution of the burden between the individual and the wider community, while the section on nature conservation provides an example of a code where the cost of compliance is borne entirely by the community. The decision whether or not to compensate for the imposition of restrictions is, at the end of the day, a political one.[14] The factors which have influenced political choice, although touched on in places, are beyond the scope of this book.[15]

---

[14] But see possible models for determining this question discussed in F.I. Michelman, "Property, Utility and Fairness: Comments on the Ethical Foundations of 'Just Compensation' Law" (1967) 80 Harv. L.R. 1165; J. Sax, "Takings and the Police Power", (1964) 74 Yale L.J. 36; and "Takings, Private Property and Public Rights", (1971) 81 Yale L.J. 149; and R.A. Epstein, *Takings, Private Property and the Power of Eminent Domain* (Harvard University Press, 1985).

[15] For an insight into these factors as regards mainstream planning control, see J.B. Cullingworth, *Environmental Planning* (HMSO, 1975), Vol. I and Vol. IV, 1980; and as regards nature conservation, P. Lowe *et al, Countryside Conflicts, supra.*

Chapter 16

Blight

Introduction

16—01 "Blight" is a term which means different things to different people. In general it refers to the depressing effect on property values of public sector actions and decisions. A nuclear power station or a major road, for example, may have a depressing effect on the value of land required for or located near to the works. This depressing effect is sometimes referred to alternatively as "injurious affection" or "worsenment."

Of course not all public sector actions and decisions serve to depress the value of land. Some may have the reverse effect. Land allocated for industrial use or for a hotel, for example, may increase in value if the public road network serving the site is significantly improved. This increase in value is generally referred to as "betterment". The way in which betterment is dealt with in the context of compulsory acquisition was considered in Chapters 9 and 12.

There would seem to be something to be said for looking at the topics of betterment and worsenment in the round. In Chapter 12 we have referred to the opinion of the Scott Committee that "the principle of Betterment, *i.e.* the principle that persons whose property has clearly been increased in market value by an improvement should specially contribute to the cost of such an improvement, and the principle of Injurious Affection, *i.e.* the principle that persons whose properties are damaged by construction or user of the promoters' works shall be entitled to receive compensation are correlative."[1] This is not, however the way in which these topics have been treated by the legislation in this field.

---

[1] *The Second Report of the Committee dealing with the Law and Practice relating to the Acquisition and Valuation of Land for Public Purposes,* Cd.9229 (1918) para. 32.

What, if anything, should be done about blight is a question which has troubled **16—02** successive governments for many years. On the one hand, it may be argued that blight should be regarded as one of the risks of land ownership and that there is no case for remedial measures.[2] On the other hand, it may be argued that fairness requires that the loss should be shared among the wider community who benefit from the actions and decisions giving rise to blight. There is, indeed, as McAuslan shows, a strong public interest incentive in alleviating the hardship.[3] By way of example, he cites the Minister of Local Government and Development in the context of the debate in 1972 on the Land Compensation Bill which introduced proposals for improving the compensation entitlement where land is depreciated by public works. "I believe," said the Minister, that the proposals will have "the beneficial effect of speeding up the administration of development projects. There will I believe be less incentive for those affected to obstruct good public schemes by using every legal means at their command."[4]

In the discussion in Chapter 15 on "Compensation for Regulation" we suggested that the essence of the compensation problem is whether the cost of compliance should fall upon the landowner or whether it should be shared amongst the wider community who are benefiting from the regulation. We concluded that, although the pattern is by no means consistent, the history of the imposition of regulation has been to push the point at which the wider community are expected to share the burden progressively further away.

The essence of the problem of blight may be presented in similar terms. Should **16—03** the injury fall upon the landowner or should it be shared amongst the wider community who are benefiting from the public works giving rise to the blight? The history of the involvement by the state in alleviating blight suggests that, unlike regulation, the burden on the wider community has steadily increased over the years. In reality, the question has not been whether something should be done but where the line should be drawn; how far the state should go in granting relief from blight.

Blight manifests itself in different ways. Some of these manifestations have already been considered in earlier chapters in this book. In Chapter 9 we discussed the interrelation between section 6 of the Land Compensation Act 1961 and the *Pointe Gourde* principle, both of which require that in assessing compensation for the compulsory acquisition of land no account is to be taken of any decrease in the value of that land due to the scheme. Reference was also made to section 9 of the 1961 Act which requires any depreciation in the value of land due to an

---

[2] See, for example, the discussion of this by the government's inter-departmental working party on blight cited in J.B. Cullingworth, *Environmental Planning*, (HMSO, 1980) Vol. IV, p. 209.

[3] P. McAuslan, *Ideologies of Planning Law* (Pergamon Press, 1980) Chap. 4.

[4] H.C. Deb., vol. 847, col. 39. See, too, the recommendation in the Fifth Report from the Environment Committee, *Planning: Appeals, Call-In and Major Public Inquiries* (HMSO, 1986) that "the Department of the Environment undertake a cost-benefit analysis of paying realistic compensation to those financially disadvantaged by the consequences of proposals which are the subject of major inquiries as against the costs to the national economy of such inquiries" (para. 167).

indication that it is likely to be acquired for public purposes to be ignored when assessing compensation upon its eventual acquisition. And in Chapter 12 the entitlement to compensation for depreciation in the value of land "held together with" land taken for the scheme was examined.[5] These are all forms of blight.

There are, however, other manifestations and these are the subject of this chapter. Its concern is with depreciation in the value of land which has not, or which has not yet, been acquired for or "held together with" land acquired for the scheme.

16—04 The chapter is divided into three parts. In the first part attention focuses on the topic of "planning blight." For more than 30 years now the State has given relief to owners of land blighted by its earmarking for eventual acquisition for public purposes. Subject to certain qualifications, such an owner may serve a "blight notice" requiring the public authority responsible for the blight to purchase the land at a price which ignores the blighting effect of the scheme. It is a form of inverse compulsory purchase.

In a recent discussion paper the Royal Institution of Chartered Surveyors recommended that the right to require a public authority to buy land should be extended to cases where land which is not earmarked for eventual acquisition suffers material detriment from the execution or use of works on neighbouring land.[6] It could be argued that this is the logical extension of section 58(1) of the Land Compensation Act 1973 (to which reference was made in Chapter 4) which provides that in assessing material detriment to a "house, building or manufactory" in the context of a notice of objection to severance, regard may be had to the consequences of the use of the land acquired and of other land for public purposes. In other words, why should one landowner be in a better position to serve what amounts to a "blight notice" (see below) than another when faced with the same form of material detriment simply because of the coincidence that some of his land has been acquired for the public works?

16—05 The question might be extended further by asking why the blight notice provisions are not available to anyone whose land is substantially depreciated in value regardless of whether the land is earmarked for eventual acquisition and regardless of whether the level of depreciation is such as to amount to "material detriment."[7] The answer advanced by the government interdepartmental working party on blight which preceded the 1959 planning legislation[8] was that there is a qualitative distinction between blight arising from the earmarking of land for public purposes and blight caused to neighbouring land by the use of the earmarked land for public purposes. The latter, concluded that committee, may be regarded as one of the risks of ownership; the former is not. Although there is some substance in this distinction, it simply focuses on different aspects of the same problem — the

---

[5] See, too, the provisions for serving a "notice of objection to severance" discussed in Chapter 4.
[6] *Compensation for Compulsory Acquisition* (1989), para. 5.20.
[7] See, for example, P. Cooke-Priest, "Improving Compensation Provisions" [1988] 07 E.G. 66.
[8] See J.B. Cullingworth, *Environmental Planning*, Vol. IV, *supra*, at p. 209.

problem of hardship resulting from depreciation caused by proposed or implemented public works. A more pragmatic answer is that a balance has to be maintained between alleviating hardship to landowners and imposing too great a burden on public authorities. The blight notice provisions discussed in the first section of this chapter are directed towards giving relief in the most serious cases of hardship.

The government, however, has not been allowed to ignore the plight of owners of land adjoining public works. The need to make some provision for compensation for damage to neighbouring land caused by major works carried out under statutory authority was particularly apparent during the railway building era of the nineteenth century. More recently, the urban motorway building programme, proposals for a third London airport and the plan to build a high speed rail link between the Channel Tunnel and Kings Cross have again focused attention on the hardship suffered by neighbouring proprietors. The second part of this chapter examines the complex provisions for compensating such proprietors in respect of this form of blight.

The payment of compensation does not, of course, remove the cause of depre-   **16—06** ciation. The promoter of the scheme effectively buys the right to continue the nuisance indefinitely. Those affected may well prefer the steps should be taken to reduce the nuisance so far as practicable. The third part of this chapter describes the provisions for mitigating the injurious effects of public works.

These three approaches to tackling blight are now considered in turn.

Planning blight

The Planning Advisory Group in their report on *The Future of Development Plans*[9]   **16—07** defined planning blight as "the depressing effect on existing property of proposals which imply public acquisition and disturbance of the existing use." The earmarking of land in a development plan for future public purposes is likely, for example, to have an adverse effect on its marketability. The uncertainty surrounding its future will deter investment and a landowner will only be able to sell, if at all, at a significantly reduced price.

The massive programme of public works planned in the aftermath of the Second World War, coupled with the requirement that development plans should designate as land subject to compulsory acquisition any land allocated for public purposes,[10] gave rise to very considerable planning blight and, to that extent, modified the general scheme of the post-war planning legislation which was to

---

[9] H.M.S.O. 1965.
[10] Town and Country Planning Act 1947, s.3(2).

leave the existing use value of land in the hands of landowners.[11] In some cases of blight, a landowner could implement the purchase notice provisions in section 17 of the Town and Country Planning Act 1947. In such cases, the local authority would be required to purchase the property at a price which ignored the effects of blight. However, the provisions in section 17 could only be implemented where it could be shown that the land had become incapable of reasonably beneficial use. In many cases where property was blighted there was nothing to prevent the existing beneficial use continuing until such time, if ever, as the property was eventually compulsorily acquired for the public works.

16—08   If the owner of blighted property can hold on until it is eventually acquired for public purposes there will be no problem. The price paid upon acquisition will be that which would have been realised on a sale in the open market by a willing seller ignoring the blighting effects of the scheme. However, the lead time for finalising and implementing schemes of public works is commonly a matter of years. An owner, for reasons beyond his control, may have to place the property on the market in the interim. In these circumstances, the blighting effects of a scheme may give rise to very considerable hardship.

Increasing concern about the effects of blight led to the setting up by the government in the mid 1950s of an interdepartmental working party. Its terms of reference were to consider ways of reducing hardship to landowners occasioned by the publication of proposals foreshadowing the public acquisition of their property at some future time.[12] It was apparent to the working party that the blighting effects of a proposal were not necessarily confined solely to land earmarked for eventual acquisition. A proposed scheme of public works might also affect the value of other property in the vicinity. Nonetheless, the working party felt that a distinction could be drawn between blight caused by the prospect of compulsory acquisition and blight caused by the prospect of an alteration by a scheme of public works to the character of an area and that the former justified separate treatment. The solution proposed, which was modelled on the purchase notice provisions, was the introduction of a right to require the advance purchase of blighted property. The solution was given legislative effect in Part IV of the Town and Country Planning Act 1959.

16—09   Subsequently, the requirement that development plans should designate for compulsory acquisition land required at some future time for public purposes was repealed.[13] This has served to alleviate the impact of blight on land which would otherwise have been so designated. Nonetheless, the publicity which attaches to public sector proposals signalled in development and other plans will still have some blighting effect which, in the absence of locational precision, may now be distributed more widely.

---

[11] See, generally, J.B. Cullingworth, *Environmental Planning* (HMSO, 1980) Vol. IV, at p. 207 *et seq.*
[12] *Ibid.*
[13] See the White Paper, "Town and Country Planning", Cmnd. 3333 (1967) para. 26.

The power to serve a blight notice is contained, in amended form, in Part VI (Chapter II) of the Town and Country Planning Act 1990. It arises where a person with an interest in land qualifying for protection has made reasonable endeavours to sell that interest but has been unable to do so except at a much reduced price because the land has been identified as likely to be affected by public works (section 150(1) 1990 Act).[14] A person seeking to take advantage of the provision must, therefore, satisfy three requirements:

1. Qualifying interest

The person serving the blight notice[15] must show that on the date of service of the blight notice he has a "qualifying interest" because he is: **16—10**

(a) the resident owner-occupier of the whole or part of a hereditament;[16]
(b) the owner-occupier of the whole or part of a non-residential hereditament, for example a shop or office, the annual value[17] of which does not exceed an amount prescribed by order made by the Secretary of State;[18]
(c) the owner-occupier of the whole or part of an agricultural unit.[19]

The reference to an "owner's" interest includes the interest of a lessee under a lease, the unexpired portion of which on the date of service of the blight notice has not less than three years remaining unexpired.[20] The term "owner-occupier" bears a somewhat specialised meaning. The "owner-occupier" of a hereditament means a person who occupies the whole or a substantial part of the hereditament as owner and who has done so for the six months preceding the date of service of the blight notice; or a person who has occupied the whole or a substantial part of a hereditament as owner for a period of six months ending not more than 12 months before the service of the notice, the hereditament or part having been **16—11**

---

[14] See, generally, on blight notices, Michael Purdue, Eric Young and Jeremy Rowan-Robinson, *Planning Law and Procedure*, Butterworths (1989), Chap. 17.

[15] As to the power of a mortgagee to serve a blight notice, see s.162.

[16] Defined by s.171(1) of the 1990 Act to mean a "relevant hereditament" within the meaning of s.64(4)(a) to (c) of the Local Government Finance Act 1988, i.e. (a) lands; (b) coal mines; and (c) mines of any other description, other than a mine of which the royalty or dues are for the time being wholly reserved in kind. Incorporeal hereditaments are excluded: *Ley and Ley v. Kent County Council* (1976) 31 P. & C.R. 439.

[17] Defined by s.171(1) as the value which, on the date of service, is shown in the valuation list as the rateable value of that hereditament. Where, however, the hereditament is non-rateable the annual value is 5 per cent. of the compensation that would be payable if the property was acquired compulsorily.

[18] Presently £18,000 (Town and Country Planning (Blight Provisions) Order 1990 S.I. 1990 No. 465).

[19] Defined by s.196(1) as land occupied as a unit for agricultural purposes, including any dwelling-house or other building occupied by the same person for the purpose of farming the land.

[20] See s.168(4).

unoccupied since the end of that period (section 168(1)). "Owner-occupier" in relation to an agricultural unit refers to a person who owns the whole or part of the unit and who either occupies the whole of the unit at the date of service of the notice and has done so during the preceding six months or has occupied the whole of the unit during a period of six months ending not more than 12 months before the service of the blight notice (section 168(2)). And the term "resident owner-occupier" in relation to a hereditament refers to a person who either occupies as owner the whole or a substantial part of the hereditament as a private dwelling and has so occupied it for the six months preceding the date of service of the blight notice; or occupies as owner the whole or a substantial part of their hereditament as a private dwelling for a period of six months ending not more than 12 months before the date of service of the notice, the hereditament or part having been unoccupied since the end of that period (section 168(3)).

These somewhat complex provisions are designed to limit public liability by admitting only certain classes of property owners to the right of advance purchase. In particular, they reflect the belief that large businesses and investment owners are better able to absorb the hardship created by blight. These limitations have not gone unchallenged.[21]

2. Qualifying Land

16—12   Blight may arise from the point in time at which the prospect of land being required for public purposes first becomes public knowledge. That prospect may, however, never become a reality; and, even if it does, it may be some considerable time, perhaps a matter of years, before the prospect takes any concrete form. Determining the point in time at which a right of advance purchase should come into operation which is fair both to the public authority and to the landowner raises issues which JUSTICE acknowledged to be both complex and intractable.[22] The legislation in this area has tended to move cautiously by postponing the right of advance purchase to the point at which compulsory purchase is foreshadowed or has begun. This point is differently defined according to the public purpose for which the land is required. The blight notice provisions may be operated by a person with a qualifying interest from the point in time at which the land can be shown to fall within one of the "specified descriptions" (below). Experience indicated that, in some respects, these descriptions were at first too narrowly drawn. The government responded to pressure for change[23] by enlarging the

---

[21] See Chartered Land Societies Committee, *Compensation of Compulsory Acquisition and Planning Restrictions* (1968) paras. 75–78; also JUSTICE, *Compensation for Compulsory Acquisition and Remedies for Planning Restrictions together with a Supplemental Report* (Stevens, 1973) paras. 74–84 and 126–132; and the Royal Institution of Chartered Surveyors, *Compensation for Compulsory Acquisition* (1989), paras. 6.23–6.25.

[22] *Ibid.* para. 79.

[23] See Chartered Land Societies Committee and JUSTICE, *supra.*

descriptions somewhat in the Land Compensation Act 1973.[24] The relevant provisions have since been consolidated by section 149 of and Schedule 13 to the Town and Country Planning Act 1990. This Schedule, which is headed "Blighted Land" contains 23 categories of land which qualify for these purposes.[25] In summary, they are as follows:

1. Land indicated in an approved structure plan as land which may be required for the purposes of any functions of a government department, local authority, statutory undertaker, or British Coal Corporation or the establishment or running by a public telecommunications operator of a telecommunications system, or as land which may be included in an action area. This provision also applies to land so indicated in proposals submitted to the Secretary of State for the alteration of a structure plan, or in modifications proposed to be made by the Secretary of State to any such submitted plans or proposals. The provision does not, however, apply if a local plan is in force which already allocates or defines land in the area for such purposes.

2. Land indicated for the purposes of any such functions as are mentioned in 1. **16—13** above in an adopted local plan or land defined in such a plan as the site of proposed development for the purposes of any such functions. This provision applies also to land so indicated or defined in a local plan which has been made available for inspection prior to adoption or approval, or in proposals for alterations to a local plan which have similarly been made available for inspection, or in modifications proposed to be made by the local planning authority or the Secretary of State to any such plan prior to adoption or approval.

3. Land indicated in an adopted unitary development plan as land which may be **16—14** required for any such functions as are mentioned in 1. above or as land which may be included in an action area. This provision also extends to land referred to in such a plan, copies of which have been made available for inspection prior to adoption, and to land indicated in proposals for alteration of a unitary development plan or in modifications proposed to be made by the local planning authority or the Secretary of State prior to adoption or approval.

4. Land indicated in an adopted unitary development plan or in the additional circumstances mentioned in 3. above which is allocated for the purposes, or defined as the site, of proposed development for any such functions as are mentioned in 1. above.

---

[24] See the White Paper, *Development and Compensation — Putting People First* (HMSO, 1972) paras. 57–64 and Appendix.
[25] Two descriptions added by s.22(6) and 23(8) of the Community Land Act 1975 were subsequently repealed on the abolition of that Act by s.101(1) of and Sched. 17, para. 2 to the Local Government, Planning and Land Act 1980.

5. Land indicated in any other plan (not being a development plan) which has been approved by a resolution of the local planning authority for development control purposes as land which may be required for any such functions as are mentioned in 1. above.

6. Land which the local planning authority have resolved to safeguard for development for any of the functions mentioned in 1. above, or which is the subject of a direction from the Secretary of State directing them to safeguard the land for such development by restricting the grant of planning permission.

7. Land within the area described in a draft order made under the New Towns act 1981 designating the site of a proposed new town.

8. Land within the area designated as the site of a proposed new town by an operative order under the 1981 Act.

9. Land within an urban development area designated under section 134 of the Local Government, Planning and Land Act 1980 or which is within an area intended to be so designated.

10. Land within an area declared by a local housing authority to be a clearance area by a resolution under section 289 of the Housing Act 1985.

11. Land which is surrounded by or adjoins a clearance area which the local housing authority have determined to purchase under section 290 of the 1985 Act.

12. Land which is indicated by information published by a local housing authority under section 92 of the Local Government and Housing Act 1989 as land which they propose to acquire following declaration of a renewal area under Part VII of that Act.

16—15   13. Land indicated in a development plan for construction, improvement or alteration of a road.

14. Land on or adjacent to the line of a highway proposed to be constructed, improved or altered, as indicated in a proposed or operative order or scheme under Part II of the Highways Act 1980 being land required for the purposes of such construction, improvement or alteration and land required to mitigate[26] the adverse effect which the existence or use of a new or improved highway will have on the local area.

---

[26] See s.246 of the Highways Act 1980.

15. Land shown on plans approved[27] by resolution of the local highway authority as included in the site of a proposed scheme for the construction, improvement or alteration of a highway or as land required to mitigate the adverse effect which the existence or use of a new or improved highway will have on the local area.

16. Land comprised in the site of a highway proposed to be constructed, improved or altered by the Secretary of State if he has given written notice of the proposal to the local planning authority together with maps or plans sufficient to identify the land affected.

17. Land shown on plans approved by a resolution of a local highway authority as land which they propose to acquire for the purposes of mitigating the adverse effect which the existence or use of a new or improved highway has, or will have, on the local area.

18. Land shown in a written notice given by the Secretary of State to the local **16—16** planning authority as land which he proposes to acquire for the purpose of mitigating the adverse effect on the local area of a highway which he proposes to provide.

19. Land which is within the outer lines prescribed by an order specifying the minimum width of new streets[28] or has a frontage to a highway declared to be a new street and lies within its minimum width. This only applies, however, if the land consists of the whole or part of a dwelling erected before the date of the order or consists of the whole or part of the curtilage of a dwelling.

20. Land which is indicated by information published by a local housing authority under section 257 of the Housing Act 1985 as land which they propose to acquire following declaration of a general improvement area under Part VIII of that Act.

21. Land authorised for compulsory acquisition in a special Act or land within the limits of deviation in respect of which such powers can be exercised.

22. Land in respect of which a compulsory purchase order is in force, whether in respect of the land or any right over it, but where no notice to treat has been served by the acquiring authority. This includes land which is the subject of a compulsory purchase order which has been submitted for confirmation or has been prepared in draft by a Minister and he has served a notice[29] stating the effect of the draft order.

---

[27] As to the meaning of "approved" see *Fogg v. Birkenhead County Borough Council* (1971) 22 P. & C.R. 208; *Page v. Borough of Gillingham* (1970) 21 P. & C.R. 973.
[28] See s.188 of the Highways Act 1980 and s.30 of the Public Health Act 1925.
[29] See s.2(3) of and Sched. 1, para. 3(1)(a) to the Acquisition of Land Act 1981.

23. Land which is to be acquired compulsorily by virtue of an order under sections 1 or 3 of the Transport and Works Act 1992, or falls within the limits of deviation within which powers of compulsory acquisition are exercisable.

16—17   It would seem that the onus is upon the person serving the blight notice — the claimant — to show that the land falls clearly within one of the Schedule 13 classes of blighted land. In *Bolton Corporation v. Owen*,[30] where land, including the subject land, had been earmarked in a development plan for clearance and redevelopment for residential purposes, the Court of Appeal declined to speculate on the probability or otherwise of all or part of the redevelopment being carried out by the local authority rather than by private enterprise. The claimant had not discharged the onus of showing that the land was allocated in a development plan for the purposes of any functions of a local authority. However, where in any of the "scheduled classes" reference is made to an "indication" in a plan, it would seem that a diagrammatic representation will be enough. The word "indicated" said the Lands Tribunal in *Bowling v. Leeds County Borough Council*[31] is a word "of simple meaning which does not import any requirement of resolution by the Council or programming by it or allocation of money by it."

There will, inevitably, be cases where land is blighted which does not fall within one of the classes specified in Schedule 13. Local authorities have been given some encouragement to consider alleviating hardship in such cases where eventual acquisition is likely by exercising their powers to acquire land in advance of requirements.[32]

Blight caused by proposed public purpose

16—18   It is not enough for a claimant to show that he has a qualifying interest in land falling within one of the specified descriptions. Subject to two exceptions, he must also show that he has made reasonable endeavours to sell that interest but has been unable to do so except at a substantially lower price because the land has been identified as required or likely to be required for public purposes (section 150(b) and (c). The two exceptions from this requirement are land coming within paragraphs 21 and 22 above, both of which concern compulsory purchase powers.[33] While the claimant will have to give particulars of his claim in the blight

---

[30] [1962] 1 Q.B. 470. See, too, *Ellick v. Sedgemoor District Council* (1976) 32 P. & C.R. 134; *Broderick v. Erewash Borough Council* (1976) 34 P. & C.R. 214.

[31] (1974) 27 P. & C.R. 531; also *Williams v. Cheadle and Gately U.D.C.* (1965) 17 P. & C.R. 153. But see *Comley and Comley v. Kent County Council* (1977) 34 P. & C.R. 218.

[32] Memorandum to M.H.L.G. Circular 48/59, para. 64; Annex to DoE Circular 73/73, para. 74.

[33] The Royal Institution of Chartered Surveyors in 1989 commented "it seems particularly unnecessary, where a compulsory purchase order is in force, to require proof that the owner has made reasonable endeavours to sell his interest" and they recommended that this requirement should be deleted in such circumstances (*Compensation for Compulsory Acquisition* (1989) para. 6.22). This recommendation was accepted and implemented by s.70 of and Sched. 15, para. 13 to the Planning and Compensation Act 1991.

notice, he need not prove his claim unless it is resisted by the authority on which it is served by the issue of a counter-notice under section 151(1).

In some cases the diminution in value of the property may be due to more **16—19** than one factor. Where any additional factors are not within any of paragraphs 1– 23 of Schedule 13 above, the claimant will need to demonstrate (in the event of service of a counternotice) how the Schedule 13 matter has substantially lowered the value independently of any other causes. In *Bowling v. Leeds County Borough Council*[34] the corporation maintained that the clearance of houses in the neighbourhood was the principal reason for the diminution in value of the claimant's shop. In holding that the objection to the blight notice was not well-founded, the Lands Tribunal accepted that the claimant had successfully demonstrated the blighting effect of a road widening scheme. The correct approach is for the claimant to establish what price the property would have realised having regard to the other factors referred to by the corporation but disregarding the effects of the road proposal and then to show that because of the road proposal that price could not be realised. Where a claimant fails to distangle the effects of the relevant Schedule 13 category of blighted land from the other effects, the blight notice will fail.[35]

What is meant by "reasonable endeavours to sell" will turn very much on the **16—20** particular circumstances of each case.[36] It seems, however, that an actual attempt to sell must be made. In *Perkins v. West Wiltshire District Council*[37] the Lands Tribunal held that it was not enough to instruct an estate agent to sell and then accept his advice that a sale would be impossible because any purchaser would lose interest on being informed that the land was allocated for public purposes. In *Lade & Lade v. Brighton Corporation*[38] the Tribunal member, while accepting that in general the normal procedure for sale should be carried out, held that in the particular circumstance (which involved a shop selling antiques and bric-a-brac) it was sufficient to put a notice to the window of the shop and to inform visiting dealers. In *Mancini v. Coventry City Council*[39] a blight notice was served in respect of two dwelling-houses converted for use as one, with office accommodation and a detached workshop at the rear used for the manufacture of ice-cream. In an effort to sell the premises, the claimant had advertised in the press, informed various business acquaintances, and instructed a local estate agent. The council argued that in view of the specialised nature of the property a more forceful selling programme was required involving wide circulation among agents specialising in business transfers and advertisements in nationally distributed trade journals. The Tribunal held that, as the claimant was endeavouring to sell the premises, not the business, and as the principal value of the premises arose from their residential and

---

[34] (1974) 27 P. & C.R. 531.
[35] *Malcolm Campbell v. Glasgow Corporation*, 1972 S.L.T. (Lands Tr.) 8.
[36] *Lade & Lade v. Brighton Corporation* (1971) 22 P. & C.R. 737.
[37] (1975) 31 P. & C.R. 427.
[38] *supra.*
[39] (1982) 44 P. & C.R. 114 L.T.; (1983) 49 P. & C.R. 127 C.A.

not their manufacturing use, putting the premises in the hands of an estate agent was sufficient.

Procedure; blight notice, counter-notice and reference to the Lands Tribunal

16—21 If a person has a qualifying interest in land which falls within one of the categories of blighted land and has been unsuccessful in his endeavour to sell that interest he may serve a blight notice in the prescribed form[40] on the authority responsible for the blight[41] requiring the acquisition of the entirety of his interest.[42]

Within two months, the appropriate authority may serve a counter-notice on the claimant in the prescribed form[43] objecting to the blight notice (section 151(1)). The seven grounds upon which objection may be made are as follows:

1. That no part of the hereditament or agricultural unit to which the notice relates is comprised in blighted land (section 151(4)(a)).

2. That the appropriate authority do not propose to acquire any part of the hereditament or in the case of an agricultural unit any part of the affected area (section 151(4)(b)).[44]

3. That the appropriate authority propose to acquire only that part of the hereditament or of the affected area specified in the counter-notice (section 151(4)(c)).[45]

4. That in the case of land falling within paragraph 1, 3, or 13 (but not 14, 15, or 16 of Schedule 13 to the 1990 Act), the appropriate authority do not propose to acquire any part of the hereditament or of the affected area during the period of 15 years from the date of the counter-notice or such longer period from that date as may be specified (section 151(4)(d)).

5. That on the date of service of the blight notice the claimant did not have a qualifying interest (above) (section 151(4)(e)).

---

[40] See the Town and Country Planning General Regulations 1992, reg. 16 and Sched. 2.

[41] Referred to as the "appropriate authority", a term which is defined in s.169(1) of the 1990 Act. In the event of a dispute as to which is the appropriate authority the matter will be resolved by the Secretary of State.

[42] s.151(1). Such a notice may subsequently be withdrawn within the time specified in s.156.

[43] Town and Country Planning General Regulations 1992, Sched. 2. The Lands Tribunal would appear to have no jurisdiction to entertain an objection not made within the prescribed period (*Essex Incorporated Congregational Church Union v. Essex County Council* [1963] A.C. 808; *Church of Scotland General Trustees v. Helensburgh Town Council*, 1973 S.L.T. (Lands Tr.) 21).

[44] "Affected area" in relation to an agricultural unit, means so much of that unit as consists of any land described in Sched. 13 on the date of service of the blight notice (s.171(1)).

[45] But note the possibility of the service by the claimant of a notice of objection to severance (para. 4–15).

6. That for the reasons specified in the counter-notice, the interest of the claimant is not one which qualifies for protection[46] (section 151(4)(f)).

7. That the claimant has not made reasonable endeavours to sell his interest or cannot show that he has been unable to sell his interest otherwise than at a substantially lower price (section 151(4)(g)).

The counter-notice must specify the grounds on which objection is made **16—22** (section 151(3)).[47] An authority may not, however, object to a blight notice on the ground that they have no intention of acquiring the interest in the next 15 years (section 151(4)(d)) if, in fact, they have no present intention of acquiring it at all. They should in these circumstance employ section 151(4)(b). If a counter-notice cites the ground specified in section 151(4)(c) but proposals for the acquisition of the land are subsequently abandoned, it is not open to the appropriate authority to amend the counter-notice by subsisting section 151(4)(b).[48]

The ability of the appropriate authority to object to a blight notice under section 151(4)(c) on the ground that they intend only to acquire part of a hereditament or, in the case of an agricultural unit, part of an affected area, does not affect the right of a claimant under normal compulsory purchase legislation to object to severance and, in prescribed circumstances, to insist on selling the whole (section 166).[49] With this possibility in mind the Lands Tribunal are required when determining an objection relating to a hereditament under section 151(4)(c) (in addition to the other matters to which they should have regard) to apply the same tests as for a notice of objection to severance. They must consider whether: (a) in the case of a house, building or manufactory, the part may be taken without material detriment to the whole; or (b) in the case of a park or garden belonging to a house, the part can be taken without seriously affecting the amenity or convenience of the house.[50]

Section 158 of the 1990 Act provides that, where a blight notice is served in **16—23** respect of an interest in the whole or part of an agricultural unit and that unit or part contains land which does not fall within one of the categories of blighted land (the unaffected area), the claimant may include in the notice a claim that the unaffected area is not reasonably capable of being farmed, either by itself or in conjunction with other "relevant land"[51] as a separate agricultural unit. Where

---

[46] For example because the (non-domestic) property is exempt from rates: *Essex County Council v. Essex Incorporated Congregational Church Union* [1963] A.C. 808.

[47] It would seem that a new ground of objection may not subsequently be introduced (see *Essex County Council v. Essex Incorporated Congregational Church Union* [1963] A.C. 808; and see, too, *Bins v. Secretary of State for Transport* (1985) 50 P. & C.R. 468).

[48] *Burn v. North Yorkshire County Council* [1992] 29 E.G. 128.

[49] See para. 4–15.

[50] *Randell v. West Glamorgan County Council* (1975) 234 E.G. 999; *Burn v. North Yorkshire County Council* [1992] 29 E.G. 128.

[51] Defined by section 158(3) as any other agricultural unit occupied by the claimant of which he is the owner or has a lease with at least three years unexpired.

such a claim is made the appropriate authority may object to the blight notice on the ground that it is not justified (section 159(1)). Indeed, such an objection must be taken where the authority are also seeking to rely on section 151(4)(c) (section 159(2)). Where such a claim succeeds the authority are required to purchase the claimant's interest in the whole unit (section 160(1)).

16—24   Where a counter-notice has been served, the claimant may, within two months, require the objection to be referred to the Lands Tribunal (section 153(1)). On any such reference, the Tribunal must uphold the objection unless the claimant shows that it is not well-founded (section 153(4)).[52] Exceptionally, where objection is made on the grounds set out in section 151(4)(b), (c), or (d), the onus rests upon the appropriate authority to show that it is well-founded (section 153(4)).[53] In *Sabey and Sabey v. Hartlepool County Borough Council*[54] a blight notice was served in respect of a house included in an area allocated in the development plan for civic, cultural and other special uses. The Lands Tribunal declined to accept that an objection, based on the ground that the local authority of had no intention of acquiring the land, was well-founded. The house was still earmarked in the development plan. As the Tribunal observed: "[i]f all that be required in order to avoid the consequences of a purchase notice (sic) is a statement by the local authority of its intentions, as expressed in this case, it is difficult to see the purpose of [section 153(4)]. It seems to me that in placing the onus on a local authority to show that an objection of this kind is well-founded, Parliament must have intended the Lands Tribunal to look at all the facts of the case and to dismiss the objection unless satisfied that an effective protection against 'blight' is provided."[55]

16—25   In *Mancini v. Coventry City Council*[56] the Court of Appeal held that the material date for determining whether an objection can be established was the date of the counter-notice rather than the date of the blight notice. Purchas L.J. went on to say that nothing in his judgment should be taken to preclude the possibility of contending in an appropriate case that the material date might even by postponed to the date of the hearing by the Tribunal. And in *Charman v. Dorset County Council*[57] the Lands Tribunal considered that, in dealing with the substance of an objection to a blight notice, it could not shut its eyes to events subsequent to the date of the counter-notice.

If an objection on the ground that the authority have no intention of acquiring the interest at all (section 151(4)(b)) or within the next 15 years (section 151(4)(d))

---

[52] The hardship faced by the claimant and the prospect of alleviating that hardship are irrelevant to the question whether objections are well-founded: *Mancini v. Coventry City Council* (1985) 49 P. & C.R. 127).

[53] See *Charman v. Dorset County Council* (1986) 52 P. & C.R. 88.

[54] (1970) 21 P. & C.R. 448.

[55] See, too, *Duke of Wellington Social Club v. Blyth Borough Council* (1964) 15 P. & C.R. 212; *Louiseville Investments Ltd v. Basingstoke District Council* (1976) 32 P. & C.R. 419; *Charman v. Dorset County Council* (1986) 52 P. & C.R. 88.

[56] (1983) 270 E.G. 419 L.T.; (1983) 49 P. & C.R. 127 C.A. See, too, *Cedar Holdings Ltd v. Walsall Metropolitan Borough Council* (1979) 38 P. & C.R. 715.

[57] (1986) 52 P. & C.R. 88.

is upheld, any power compulsorily to acquire that interest will cease to have effect (section 155(1) and (2)). And similar provision operates where objection is successfully made on the ground that the authority intend to acquire only part of an interest in land (section 151(4)(c)). Any power compulsorily to acquire the remainder of the land will cease to have effect (section 155(3) and (4)). Where the Tribunal decides not to uphold an objection it will declare the blight notice valid (section 153(5)).[58]

Where a blight notice has been served and either no counter-notice is served **16—26** or a counter-notice is served but the objection is subsequently withdrawn or is not upheld by the Tribunal, the appropriate authority is deemed to be authorised to acquire the interest compulsorily and to have served a notice to treat[59] (section 154(1)(2)). The power conferred by section 31 of the Land Compensation Act 1961 on authorities to withdraw a notice to treat does not apply in these instances (section 167).

Compensation is assessed as for compulsory acquisition.[60] The effects of blight resulting from the land falling within one of the categories of blighted land are, therefore to be ignored.[61] The provisions relating to "home loss" and "farm loss" payments contained in section 29 and section 34, respectively, of the Land Compensation Act 1973 also apply.[62]

Compensation for injurious affection

There is an alternative way of alleviating hardship resulting from depreciation in **16—27** the value of land arising from public works which imposes less of a burden on public authorities than an obligation to buy the land. Compensation may be paid. In Chapter 12 we suggested that where a body carrying out a scheme of public works is rendered immune by statutory authority from an action at common law in respect of the consequences of the scheme, it is reasonable to expect that Parliament will make provision for compensation in lieu.[63] We went on to explain that that expectation is satisfied as regards injury to land formerly held together with land acquired for the scheme.

---

[58] Where an objection is upheld under section 151(4)(c), the notice will be declared valid as regards the remaining part (s.153(6)).

[59] The date of the notice to treat will be the date specified in a direction given by the Lands Tribunal following the reference of an objection or, in any other case, two months from the date of service of the blight notice (s. 154(3)).

[60] But see the 1990 Act, s. 157(1)(2) as regards two circumstances in which special rules apply.

[61] Land Compensation Act 1961, s.9.

[62] These provisions were formerly excluded by s.29(5) and s.34(6), respectively, until the repeal of those provisions by ss.68(2) and 70 of and Sched. 15 para. 6 to the Planning and Compensation Act 1991.

[63] See para. 12–10.

The blighting effects of a scheme do not, however, discriminate between those who have had some of their land acquired for the scheme and those who have not. The question which is addressed in this part of this chapter is the extent to which this expectation of compensation is satisfied as regards landowners *who have had no land acquired for the scheme.*[64]

In Chapter 5 it was pointed out that the entitlement to compensation for expropriation depends upon statutory authority[65] but that "there is a natural leaning in favour of compensation in the construction of a statute."[66] The entitlement to compensation for injurious affection in the absence of expropriation also depends upon statutory authority and it is now appropriate to consider such authority and the way in which the courts have "leaned" in the construction of such authority.

16—28   Prior to the decision of the House of Lords in *Metropolitan Board of Works v. McCarthy*[67] (below) the courts took the view that the Lands Clauses Acts made no provision for compensating injurious affection except where the land in question had been held together with land acquired for the scheme of works.[68] Owners, none of whose land has been acquired, had to rely on provisions, relating to injurious affection, if any, in other legislation[69] authorising the particular undertaking. As many of the claims for injurious affection during the last century arose from the construction of the railways, particular reliance was placed on sections 6 and 16 of the Railways Clauses Consolidation Act 1845.

Section 6 provides that:

> "The Company shall make to the owners and occupiers of and all other parties interested in any lands taken or used for the purposes of the railway, or injuriously affected by the construction thereof, full compensation for the value of lands so taken or used, and for all damage sustained by such owners, occupiers, and other parties, by reason of the exercise, as regards such lands, of the powers of this, or the Special Act, or any Act incorporated therewith, vested in the Company."

And section 16 requires the Company to make "full satisfaction . . . to all parties interested" for all damage resulting from the carrying out of various works connected with the construction of the railway.

16—29   In *Metropolitan Board of Works v. McCarthy* section 68 of the Lands Clauses

---

[64] The same question also arises with regard to the proprietors of remaining land which was not "held together" with land acquired for the scheme (see *City of Glasgow Union Railway v. Hunter* (1870) 8 M. (H.L.) 156).

[65] See para. 5–01.

[66] *Burmah Oil Company (Burma Trading) Ltd v. Lord Advocate*, 1964 S.C. (H.L.) 117, *per* Lord Hodson at p. 154.

[67] (1874) L.R. (H.L.) 243.

[68] *Hammersmith and City Railway v. Brand* (1869) L.R. 4 H.L. 171; *City of Glasgow Union Railway Co. v. Hunter* (1870) 8 M. (H.L.) 156.

[69] See, for example, the Railways Clauses Consolidation Act 1845, s.6; and the Markets and Fairs Clauses Act 1847, s.6.

Consolidation Act 1845[70] was "benevolently misinterpreted" by the House of Lords so as to enable a person, none of whose land had been acquired for the scheme, to claim compensation for injurious affection. The decision has been described by Davies[71] as a "misinterpretation" because the section appears in that part of the Act concerned with the purchase and taking of land otherwise than by agreement and appears to be directed at laying down a procedure for settling compensation where land has been taken in advance of payment. Davies regards the misinterpretation as "benevolent" because it can be construed as a "lamentably clumsy attempt" to mitigate the consequences of a previous much criticised decision.[72]

Interpretation of section 6 by the courts during the second half of the nineteenth century has given rise to very considerable complexity[73] which unfortunately remains with us today. The following propositions appear to have been established by judicial authority:

1. The injury complained of must arise from the legitimate exercise of statutory powers.
2. The injury must be such that but for the statutory powers, it would have founded an action in tort at law.
3. The injury must be one affecting the value of land.
4. The injury must arise from the construction of the public works and not from their subsequent use.

These propositions[74] are now examined in turn.

1. The injury complained of must arise form the legitimate exercise of statutory powers

In Chapter 12, mention was made, in the context of the entitlement to compensation for injurious affection where land has been acquired, that for anything done in excess of or contrary to statutory powers, the common law remedy remains.[75] Compensation may only be claimed under section 6 of the Railways Clauses Act in respect of losses sustained in consequence of what the promoter may lawfully do under the powers conferred by Parliament. It is well established that "for anything done in excess of these powers, or contrary to what the Legislature, in

16—30

---

[70] See, now, s.10 of the Compulsory Purchase Act 1965.

[71] K. Davies, "Injurious Affection" and the Land Compensation Act 1973" (1974) 90 L.Q.R. 361.

[72] See the discussion at p. 363 of the decision in *Hammersmith and City Railway Co. v. Brand* (1869) L.R. 4 H.L. 171.

[73] See further H. Parrish, *Cripps on Compulsory Acquisition of Land* (Stevens & Sons Ltd, 11th ed.), Chap. 25.

[74] These propositions are often referred to as the "McCarthy Rules" after the decision of the House of Lords in *Metropolitan Board of Works v. McCarthy* (1874) L.R. (H.L.) 243.

[75] See para. 12–09.

conferring these powers, has commanded, the proper remedy is a common law action in the Common Law Courts."[76] Thus in *Samuel v. Edinburgh and Glasgow Railway Company*[77] an action was brought against the railway company in respect of damage to the pursuer's farm alleged to have been caused by the inadequacy of the arrangements for carrying off surface water during the formation of the railway. The defendant argued that the action was incompetent, statute having made provision for determining questions of damage arising from the construction of the railway. It was held that the provisions of the statute applied to the original construction of the railway but not to questions of damage which might subsequently occur arising from the insufficiency of the works.

2. The injury must be such that but for the statutory powers, it would have founded an action in tort at law

16—31 This proposition derives from the decision of the House of Lords in *Caledonian Railway v. Ogilvy*.[78] A proprietor claimed £300 by way of compensation for injurious affection for the "very material injury done to the place as a residence, and deterioration to the amenity and value of the house and policy" resulting from the inconvenience, interruption and delay caused by the placing by the railway company of a level crossing on a public road some 50–60 yards from the entrance to the property. In the course of his judgment Cranworth L.C. stated:

> "the construction that is put upon this expression, 'injuriously affected', in the clauses in an Act of Parliament which gives compensation for injuriously affecting lands, certainly does not entitle the owner of lands which he alleges to be injuriously affected, to any compensation in respect of any act which, if done by the Railway Company without the authority of Parliament, would not have entitled him to bring an action against them."[79]

16—32 An illustration of this test is provided by the decision in *Re Penny and the South-Eastern Railway Co.*[80] where the question arose whether the Lands Clauses Consolidation Act 1845 enabled compensation to be claimed, following the construction of a railway, for annoyance caused by persons standing on the bank of the railway and overlooking the claimant's premises, no land having been acquired from the claimant for the railway. The court held that it did not. Lord Campbell C.J. said:

---

[76] *Imperial Gaslight and Coke Company v. Broadbent* (1859) 7 H.L. Cas. 600.
[77] (1849) 11 D. 968.
[78] (1856) 2 Macq. 229. See, too *Re Penny and South Eastern Railway Co.* (1857) 7 E. and B. 660; *Ricket v. Metropolitan Railway Co.* (1867) L.R. 2 H.L. 175; *Metropolitan Board of Works v. McCarthy* (1874) L.R. (H.L.) 243; and *Caledonian Railway Co. v. Walker's Trustees* (1882) 9 R. (H.L.) 19.
[79] *Ibid.* p. 235.
[80] (1857) 7 E. and B. 660.

"The test is, whether, before the railway Act passed authorising the company to do what has been done here, an action would have lain at common law for what has been done, and for which compensation has been claimed . . . if the land is not taken and nothing is done which would have afforded a cause of action before the Act passed, then although it may produce a deterioration of the property, it does not injuriously affect the land and constitute a ground for compensation."

In this case an action would not have lain in the absence of statutory authority for the construction of the railway for the claimant's grounds being overlooked and his privacy being disturbed.

These decisions indicate that the basis of the claim for compensation for injuri- **16—33** ous affection where no land has been taken is *damnum cum injuria*. The inference drawn from the legislation was that Parliament simply intended to confer on landowners a compensation entitlement coextensive with the right of action removed by statute. This contrasts with cases where the affected land was held together with land taken for the scheme.[81] The entitlement there, following the decisions in *Re Stockport, Timperley and Altrincham Railway Co.*[82] and *Cowper Essex v. Acton Local Board*[83] would appear to rest upon *damnum* alone. Crompton J. in *Re Stockport*, etc explained the distinction in this way:

"Where, however, the mischief is caused by what is done on the land taken, the party seeking compensation has a right to say, 'it is by the Act of Parliament, and the Act of Parliament only, that you have done the acts which have caused damage; without the Act of Parliament, everything you have done, and are about to do, in making and using the railway, would have been illegal and actionable, and is, therefore, matter for compensation according to the rule in question'."[84]

Whilst this may be a ground for awarding some special element in the compensation for the land taken, it would seem to have very little to do with injury to the land retained. While reservations were subsequently expressed about the requirement to establish that the injury would have been actionable but for the statute,[85] it remains a prerequisite for a claim for injurious affection where the affected land was not held together with land taken for the scheme.

3. The injury must be one affecting the value of the land

An owner, says Cripps, is only entitled to compensation "for loss caused by inter- **16—34**

---

[81] See Chap. 12.

[82] (1864) 33 L.J.Q.B. 251.

[83] (1889) 14 App. Cas. 153, H.L. See, too, *Duke of Buccleuch v. Metropolitan Board of Works* (1872) L.R. 5 H.L. 408.

[84] At p. 253. See, too, *Duke of Buccleuch, supra*, per Hannen J. at p. 445.

[85] See, for example, *Ricket v. Metropolitan Railways Co.* (1867) L.R. 2 H.L. 175 per Lord Westbury at p. 202; *Metropolitan Board of Works v. McCarthy* (1874) L.R. 7 H.L. 243, per Cairns L.C. at p. 252 and Lord O'Hagan at p. 266; and *Caledonian Railway Co. v. Walker's Trustees* (1882) 9 R. (H.L.) 19 per Lord Selborne at p. 23.

ference with an interest in lands, and not for damage to his trade or business, or for damages resulting in personal loss or inconvenience, unless such damage is reflected in the depreciation in the value of the land."[86] Thus in *Caledonian Railway v. Ogilvy*[87] (above) the House of Lords considered that the injury suffered by the location of a level crossing on a public road at a distance of some 50–60 yards from the entrance to a property was not an injury to the property but in the nature of personal inconvenience:

> "for all attempts at arguing that this is a damage to the estate is a mere play upon words. It is no damage at all to the estate, except that the owner of that estate would oftener have a right of action from time to time than any other person, inasmuch as he would traverse the spot oftener than other people would traverse it."[88]

16—35 It was in the context of temporary or permanent obstruction of access to premises that this proposition gave rise to particular difficulty. In *Ricket v. Metropolitan Railway Co.*[89] the occupier of a public house experienced temporary loss of trade while the usual (public) access to his premises was obstructed during the construction of the Metropolitan Railway. His claim in respect of this loss under section 16 of the Railways Clauses Consolidation Act 1845 was rejected by the House of Lords, Lord Westbury dissenting. Lord Chelmsford, the Lord Chancellor, after an extensive review of the decisions in this field, considered, *inter alia*, that the injury was too remote from the mischief to which the section was directed. Cranworth L.C. concluded that no damage had been occasioned to the land:

> "Both principle and authority seem to me to show that no case comes within the provisions of the statute, unless where some damage has been occasioned to the land itself, as by loosening the foundation of the buildings on it, obstructing its lights or its drains, making it inaccessible by lowering or raising the ground immediately in front of it, or by some such physical deterioration."

16—36 Cranworth L.C.'s catalogue would seem to be incomplete in so far as it is directed at physical deterioration in the land itself. The decision of the House of Lords in *Metropolitan Board of Works v. McCarthy*[90] established that depreciation resulting from interference with any right, public or private, which owners and occupiers are entitled to use in connection with property and which gives an additional market value to the property, apart from the uses to which any particular owner might put it, could found a claim for compensation. Moreover, though the injury is to the land, it need not be upon the land provided the premises suffer special

---

[86] H. Parrish, Cripps on Compulsory Acquisition of Land (Stevens & Sons Ltd, 11th ed.), para. 5–0322.
[87] (1856) 2 Macq. 229.
[88] *Ibid.*, per Lord Cranworth L.C. at pp. 236–237.
[89] (1867) L.R. 2 H.L. 175.
[90] (1874) L.R. 7 H.L. 243.

damage. This point is well illustrated by the decision in *Caledonian Railway Co. v. Walker's Trustees*[91] The trustees owned a mill and rented buildings located to the west of Eglinton Street, one of the main thoroughfares in Glasgow. Access to Eglinton Street was by either of two road contiguous to and to the north and south of the premises. The operations of the railway company effectively blocked such access. The only alternative access involved a considerable detour and a steeper gradient. The trustees' claim for compensation[92] in respect of the diminution in the value of their premises was upheld in the House of Lords. Lord Watson said:

> "When an access to private property by a public highway is interfered with, the owner can have no action of damages for any personal inconvenience which he may suffer in common with the rest of the lieges. But, should the value of the property, irrespective of any particular uses which may be made of it, be so dependent upon the existence of that access as to be substantially diminished by its obstruction, then I conceive that the owner has, in respect of any works causing such obstruction, a right of action if these works are unauthorised by Act of Parliament, and a title to compensation under the Railway Acts if they are constructed under statutory powers."[93]

4. The injury must arise from the construction of the public works and not from their subsequent use

Sections 6 and 16 of the Railways Clauses Consolidation Act 1845 refer to damage caused by the construction of the works. In *Hammersmith and City Railway Co. v. Brand*[94] the House of Lords concluded that these provisions did not entitle a claimant to compensation for injurious affection arising, not from the *construction* of the works, but from their subsequent *use*. The claimants owned a house adjoining the defendant's railway. No part of their land had been acquired for the construction of the railway. They claimed compensation, *inter alia*, for depreciation in the value of their property resulting from vibration, arising from the proper and ordinary use of the railway by trains. In the House of Lords it was accepted that the use of the railway had, indeed, depreciated the value of the property. Lord Chelmsford said "The plaintiff's remedy by action being taken away, the question remains, whether they are entitled to receive compensation from the company for the injury done to their house — a question which must be decided entirely by the provision of the Acts of Parliament relating to the subject." After an examination of these provisions he concluded "it is not that the Legislature has excluded compensation for injury arising as the necessary con-

16—37

---

[91] (1882) 7 App Cas. 259.
[92] Under s.6 of the Railways Clauses Consolidation (Scotland) Act 1845.
[93] *Ibid.* at p. 278.
[94] (1869) L.R. 4 H.L. 171.

sequence of using the railway, but that it has not, as far as I can discover, given any right to claim compensation for this species of injury."[95]

16—38 The House of Lords reached a similar conclusion the following year in *City of Glasgow Union Railway Co. v. Hunter*[96] A proprietor of a block of tenement houses and shops which were adversely affected by the use by trains of a new railway bridge constructed near the property claimed compensation for injurious affection. The claimant sought to distinguish *Brand* on two grounds. First of all, it was argued, he was entitled to all loss arising from the construction and use of the railway as part of his land had been acquired for its construction.[97] This argument was rejected on the ground that the claim did not arise in connection with anything done on the land taken (see para. 12–18); and, furthermore, that the land taken for the scheme, although adjoining the tenement and held under the same title, had not been "held together" with it.[98] The claimant was, therefore, in the same position as regards a claim for injurious affection as a person who had none of his land acquired for the for the scheme. Secondly, it was evident that if sections 6 and 16 of the Railways Clauses Act governed his claim, his position was indistinguishable from that in *Brand*. Mr Hunter, accordingly founded his claim on sections 17 and 48 of the Lands Clauses Act, particularly the latter. The claim was rejected by their Lordships who considered that the provisions in question were concerned with the respective rights of the promoter of the undertaking and the owners of land acquired in order to carry out the work.

16—39 It would seem from the four propositions described above that the attitude of the courts to claims for injurious affection compensation where no land is taken is somewhat different to their approach to such claims where expropriation has occurred. We referred earlier in the context of expropriation to the "natural leaning in favour of compensation in the construction of a statute." The courts appear to have leaned the other way where no land is taken. "It is not," said Lord Chelmsford in *Brand*, "that the Legislature has excluded compensation for injury arising as the necessary consequence of using the railway, but that it has not, as far as I can discover, given any right to claim compensation for this species of injury."[99] Yet the logic of this distinction is questionable as the injurious effects of public works do not discriminate between those who have had land acquired for the works and those who have not.

---

[95] *Ibid*, at pp. 202–203. In *Allen v. Gulf Oil Refining Ltd* [1979] 3 W.L.R. 523. The Court of Appeal adopted somewhat similar reasoning to very different effect. An examination of the private Act authorising the compulsory acquisition of land at Milford Haven for the construction of an oil refinery revealed that the Act specifically authorised its construction but did not specifically authorise its use. Therefore, said the court, the right of a neighbour to sue the promoters at common law for nuisance caused by the use of the refinery was retained. It was left to the House of Lords ([1981] 1 All E.R. 353) to point out the "remarkable consequences" of such a proposition and to hold that "construction" in the private Act implied "use" as well.

[96] (1870) 8 M. (H.L.) 156.

[97] See Chap. 11.

[98] See para. 12–13.

[99] (1869) L.R. 4 H.L. 171 at p. 203.

Compensation for injury arising from the use of public works

The considerable hardship arising from the decision in *Hammersmith and City*   **16—40**
Railway Co. v. Brand that compensation could only be recovered for injurious
affection arising from the construction and not the use of works was somewhat
alleviated by the decision in *Re Simeon and Isle of Wight Rural District Council*[1] on
the meaning of the words "execution of the works" in section 68 of the Lands
Clauses Consolidation Act 1845. Section 68 had been construed in *McCarthy* as
entitling a person, none of whose land had been acquired for the works, to claim
compensation for injurious affection arising from the "execution of the works".[2]
In *Re Simeon and Isle of Wight Rural District Council*, Luxmoor J. interpreted these
words as having a wider compass than "construction of the works", the term used
in section 6 of the Railways Clauses Consolidation Act 1845. They include, he
said, "the exercise, that is, the carrying out and the execution, of the appropriate
statutory powers."[3] Cripps suggests that, as a result, where the statutory works
include construction and maintenance of user, "then compensation may be
claimed for injury by construction or user but only in respect of injury to land."[4]

The urban motorways programme of the 1960s and the proposal for a third   **16—41**
London Airport served to focus attention on the anomalous distinction drawn by
the courts between injury caused by the construction of the public works and
that resulting from their use. Householders affected by urban motorways might
be exposed to considerable disturbance from a substantial volume of traffic passing
close to their houses, in some places at first floor level, at all hours of the day and
night without compensation unless some part of the land had been acquired for
the road. "We believe it to be a sad commentary on the present law," observed
JUSTICE, "that an owner of land in an area through which a motorway is to be
constructed should prefer that the motorway takes the whole of his property than
go near to it."[5] McAuslan suggests that the JUSTICE report was instrumental in
creating "an informed climate of opinion amongst policy-makers about compensation and its inadequacies."[6] Other reports around the same time[7] culminating
in the report of the Urban Motorways Committee[8] commented on shortcomings
in the compensation arrangements. The Urban Motorways Committee recommended that "compensation for injurious affection should be extended generally

---

[1] [1937] Ch. 525.
[2] See para. 16–29.
[3] *Ibid.* at p. 529.
[4] H. Parrish, Cripps on Compulsory Acquisition of Land, *supra*, para. 5–031.
[5] JUSTICE, *Compensation for Compulsory Acquisition and Remedies for Planning Restrictions* (1969) *together with a Supplemental Report* (Stevens, 1973) para. 55.
[6] P. McAuslan, *The Ideologies of Planning Law* (Pergamon Press, 1980) at p. 107.
[7] Chartered Land Societies Committee, *Compensation for Compulsory Acquisition and Planning Restrictions* (1968); *the Report of the Commission on the Third London Airport* (HMSO, 1971).
[8] *New Roads in Towns* (HMSO, 1972).

to cases where no land is taken but where property suffers loss of value because of the effects of the road."[9]

16—42   In a white paper in 1972[10] the government acknowledged that the time had come to redistribute the burden of cost arising from public developments so that more would be borne by the community at large in the form of improvements in the arrangements for compensating those most affected by such developments.[11] These improvements were introduced in Part I of the Land Compensation Act 1973.[12] The provisions of Part I do not alter the present arrangements described above for compensating loss resulting from the *construction* of public works where no land has been taken. They simply confer an additional entitlement to compensation for depreciation caused by the *use* of the works.[13]

Section 1 of the 1973 Act provides that if the value of a qualifying interest in land is depreciated by physical factors caused by the use of public works, the responsible authority will pay compensation for that depreciation in response to a claim made by the person entitled to that interest. "Qualifying interest," "physical factors," "public works" and "responsible authority" all require definition.

16—43   An interest qualifies for compensation under Part I if it was acquired[14] by the claimant before the "relevant date" (below) and the following requirements are satisfied on the date of service of the notice of claim (section 2(1)): (i) as regards a dwelling-house, the interest is an owner's interest; and if the interest carries the right to occupy the dwelling, the claimant is in occupation in right of that interest as his residence (section 2(2)); (ii) as regards other land, the interest is that of an owner-occupier and the land is or forms part of either an agricultural unit or a hereditament the annual value of which does not exceed an amount prescribed by regulations[15] made by the Secretary of State (section 2(3)).

An "owner's interest"[16] includes the interest of a lessee under a lease, the unexpired period of which on the date of service of the notice of claim is not less than three years (section 2(4)). "Owner-occupier" in relation to land in an agricultural unit means a person who occupies the whole of that unit and is entitled while so occupying it to an owner's interest in the whole or any part of that land. In relation to land in a hereditament, the term refers to a person who occupies the whole or a substantial part of the land in right of an owner's interest therein (section 2(5)).

---

[9] *Ibid.* para. 12.7.
[10] *Development and Compensation — Putting People First*, Cmnd. 5124 (1972).
[11] *Ibid.* paras. 5, 6 and 9.
[12] For a discussion of these provisions see, generally, P. McAuslan, *The Ideologies of Planning Law*, *supra.*, Chap. 4; K. Davies, "'Injurious Affection' and the Land Compensation Act 1973" (1974) 90 L.Q.R. 361; R.N.D. Hamilton, "Land Compensation Act 1973 — I and II" (1973) 117 S.J. 514 and 538; Alec Samuels, "The Land Compensation Act 1973" (1973) 123 N.L.J. 556.
[13] For an explanation of these provisions see DoE Circular 73/73.
[14] For the position where an interest is acquired by inheritance, see the 1973 Act, s.11.
[15] See the Town and Country Planning (Blight Provisions) Order 1990 (S.I. 1990 No. 465) which prescribes a maximum annual value of £18,000.
[16] For the position of mortgagees and trustees for sale, see the 1973 Act, s.10.

The physical factors which may trigger a claim in respect of depreciation are **16—44** defined in section 1(2) of the 1973 Act. They are:

(i) noise;
(ii) vibration;
(iii) smell;
(iv) fumes;
(v) smoke;
(vi) artificial lighting;[17]
(vii) discharge on to the land in respect of which the claim is made of any solid or liquid substance.

The source of the "physical factor" or factors giving rise to the claim must be situated on or in the public works in question. Exceptionally, depreciation resulting from aircraft arriving at or departing from an aerodrome[18] is to be treated as caused by the use of the aerodrome, whether or not the aircraft are within the boundaries of the aerodrome (section 1(5)).

The "public works," the use of which has given rise to physical factors causing depreciation, are defined in section 1(3). They are:

(i) any highway,[19]
(ii) any aerodrome; and
(iii) any works or land (not being a highway or aerodrome) provided or used in the exercise of statutory powers.

The compensation entitlement is not confined solely to depreciation arising from the bringing into use of new public works but extends also to depreciation arising from alterations to existing highways, the reconstruction, extension or alteration of other existing public works or from a change of use of any existing public works[20] other than a highway or aerodrome. Alterations to an existing aerodrome will only give rise to an entitlement if they take the form of alterations to existing runways or aprons (section 9(3)).[21] And the carriageway of a highway may be considered to be altered if, but only if, the location, width or level of existing carriageway is altered (otherwise than by resurfacing), or an additional carriageway is provided for the highway beside, above or below an existing one (section 9(5)); the entitlement will then lie in respect of depreciation arising from physical factors caused by the use of, and the source of which is situated on, the length of carriage-

---

[17] A term which would seem to encompass both street lights and vehicle lights.
[18] For the meaning of "aerodrome", see the Civil Aviation Act 1982, s.105(1).
[19] "Highway" means a highway or part of a highway maintained at the public expense as defined section in s.329(1) of the Highways Act 1980.
[20] References in the 1973 Act, s.9 to "a change of use" do not include references to the intensification of an existing use (s.9(7)).
[21] As defined in the 1973 Act, s.9(6).

way as so altered or the additional carriageway and the corresponding length of the existing one, as the case may be.

The authority responsible for compensating a claimant is, in relation to a highway, the appropriate highway authority,[22] and in relation to other public works, the person managing those works.

16—45   Compensation is not payable under the provisions of Part I in respect of the use of any public works, other than a highway, unless legislation relating to those works confers immunity from actions for nuisance in respect of that use, either expressly or by implication (section 1(6));[23] neither is it payable in respect of aerodromes and physical factors caused by aircraft unless the aerodrome is one to which section 77(2) of the Civil Aviation Act 1982 applies (which confers immunity from actions for nuisance). And no compensation is payable in respect of physical factors caused by accidents involving vehicles on a highway or accidents involving aircraft (section 1(7)).

16—46   The procedure for a claim is set out in section 3. A claim under Part I is made by serving a notice on the responsible authority containing the particulars referred to in section 3(1) of the 1973 Act.[24] Subject to the one exception referred to below, no claim may be made before the expiration of 12 months from the "relevant date" (section 3(2). The day following the expiration of the 12 month period is referred to as "the first claim day." The "relevant date" is defined, as regards a highway, as the date on which it was first opened to public traffic[25] and as regards other public works the date on which they were first used after completion (section 1(9)).[26] With regard to claims arising from alterations to carriageways, the relevant date is the date on which the road was first open to public traffic after completion of the alterations; and with regard to claims arising from alterations to other public works, the relevant date is to be that on which the works were first used after completion of the alterations. The relevant date in respect of a change in the use of any public works, other than a highway or aerodrome, is to be the date of the change of use (section 9(2)). The responsible authority is required to keep a record of the appropriate relevant date and to furnish information about it on request (section 15)(1)). A certificate from the Secretary of State as to the relevant date in respect of runway or apron alterations at an aerodrome is to be taken as conclusive (section 15(2)). The time-limits are "designed to ensure that

---

[22] As defined in s.19(1) of the 1973 Act.
[23] But see the 1973 Act s.16 (reference of questions of disputed compensation to the Lands Tribunal). In *Vickers v. Dover District Council* [1993] 20 E.G. 132 the Lands Tribunal held that where powers are exercised under the Road Traffic Regulation Act 1984, no compensation was payable under the 1973 Act since there is no provision in the 1984 Act conferring immunity from actions in nuisance.
[24] See, too, the 1973 Act, s.9(4).
[25] But see the 1973 Act, s.19(3).
[26] See *Davies v. Mid-Glamorgan County Council* (1979) 38 P. & C.R. 727; and *Shepherd and Shepherd v. Lancashire County Council* (1976) 33 P. & C.R. 296.

land valuations have had time, following first use on the relevant date, to settle down and show the full extent of any depreciation."[27]

The only circumstance in which a claim may be lodged prior to the "first claim day" is where the claimant during the 12 months preceding that day has contracted to dispose of his interest or to grant a tenancy of the land (provided the land does not comprise a dwelling) and the claim is made before the interest is disposed of or the tenancy is granted (section 3(3)). It appears that the words "interest is disposed of" refer to actual disposal and not to a contract for its disposal.[28] Even then, compensation in respect of such a claim is not payable before the "first claim day." **16—47**

A claim must be lodged within six years of the "first claim day" (section 17(2A)).[29] The compensation is to be assessed having regard to the following matters.[30] It is to be assessed by reference to prices current on the "first claim day" (section 4(1)). Depreciation is to be estimated by reference to the level of use of the public works on the "first claim day", but having regard to any intensification that may then reasonably be expected (section 4(2)).[31] Account is to be taken of the benefit of any sound-proofing works which could be or could have been carried out, or in respect of which a grant could be or could have been given, under this or other legislation[32] and of any mitigating works carried out under section 27 of the 1973 Act or section 282 of the Highways Act 1980[33] (section 4(3)). An interest is to be valued by reference to the nature of the interest and the condition of the land as it subsisted at the date of service of notice of the claim (section 4(4)(a)); and in accordance with rules (2) and (4) of section 5 of the Land Compensation Act 1961[34] (section (4)4(b)). In *Inglis v. British Airports Authority (No.2)*[35] the Lands Tribunal for Scotland described the claim as "akin to one for injurious affection on a before and after basis." The proper valuation approach, observed the Tribunal, in respect of a claim for depreciation to a dwelling-house caused by physical factors arising from the bringing into operation of a new runway,[36] "was to assess the open market value of the house as at 7th April 1977 with no runway and, second, the market value taking into account the use of the runway as at that date and any intensification of usage which might then reasonably be expected." No account is to be taken of a mortgage, or to a contract **16—48**

---

[27] *Inglis v. British Airports Authority*, 1978 S.L.T. (Lands Tr.) 30.
[28] *Ibid.*
[29] Added by the Local Government, Planning and Land Act 1980, s.112(6) and (9).
[30] See, generally B. Sparks, "Land Compensation Act 1973: A Practical Approach to Part I Claims" (1986) 278 E.G. 1464. Also P. Cooke-Priest, "Improving Compensation Provisions" (1988) 8807 E.G. 66.
[31] See *Dhenin v. Department of Transport*, unreported, but see [1989] E.G.C.S. 57.
[32] See para. 16–56.
[33] See para. 16–58.
[34] See Chap. 7.
[35] 1979 S.L.T. (Lands Tr.) 10.
[36] See, too, *Stuart v. British Airports Authority*, 1983 S.L.T. (Lands Tr.) 42.

of sale or a contract made after the relevant date for the grant of a tenancy (section 4(4)(c)). Neither is account to be taken of any value attributable to any building, or to any improvement or extension of a building, if it was first occupied after the relevant date; nor of any value attributable to a change in the use of the land made after that date (section 4(5)).

16—49   Certain assumptions may be made in assessing the value of the interest in respect of which a claim is made. First of all, it is to be assumed that planning permission would be granted in respect of the land in which the interest subsists (the "relevant land") or any part of it for development of any class specified in Part I of Schedule 3 to the Town and Country Planning Act 1990[37] (section 5(2)). No permission to be assumed, however, for the rebuilding of a building or the resumption of a use which is required to be removed or discontinued, as the case may be, by virtue of a discontinuance order made under section 102 of the 1990 Act in respect of which compensation has become payable (section 5(3)(c)).

16—50   No further assumptions as to planning permission are to be made; even if planning permission has been granted for the development of the whole or a part of the relevant land which does not fall within one of the categories of development in Part I of Schedule 3, it is to be assumed that no such permission has been granted in so far as the permission relates to development that has not been carried out (section 5(4)).

Betterment arising from the scheme is to be set-off. Any increase in the value of the claimant's interest in the land in respect of which the claim is made,[38] and any increase in the value of any interest in other land contiguous or adjacent to that land to which the claimant is entitled in the same capacity[39] at the relevant date, which is attributable to the existence of or the use or prospective use of the public works to which the claim relates, is to be set-off against any compensation which is payable (section 6(1)). Section 6(3) and (4) prevents the operation of double set-off in the event of the subsequent acquisition of the interest in such other contiguous or adjacent land, the increased value of which has already been taken into account.

16—51   Five other restrictions on a Part I claim deserve mention. First of all, compensation is not payable on any claim unless the compensation exceeds £50 (section 7). Secondly, a claim is to be made once and for all. Where compensation has been paid or is payable under Part I in respect of depreciation in the value of an interest in land caused by the use of any public works, no subsequent claim will be entertained in respect of the same works and the same land (section 8(1)).[40] Thirdly, compensation is not payable under Part I in respect of land retained which constitutes "other land or lands" within the meaning of section 63 of the

---

[37] See Chap. 8.
[38] In assessing any such increase in value, the provisions of ss.4 and 5 of the 1973 Act do not apply (s.6(2)).
[39] For the meaning of this see the 1973 Act, s.6(5).
[40] Although this does not preclude a claim in respect of a dwelling by both the owner of the fee simple and a tenant.

Lands Clauses Consolidation Act 1845 or section 7 of the Compulsory Purchase Act 1965 (which provisions provide for compensation for injurious affection) whether or not compensation for injurious affection in respect of the retained land is paid under either of those provisions (section 8(2)). It is unlikely that such a duplication of claims will arise as the notice to treat in respect of the land to be acquired will generally precede the opportunity to claim under Part I. Furthermore, the compensation entitlement under section 63 of the 1845 Act or section 7 of the 1965 Act may, in some respects, be more generous.[41] Fourthly, where after a claim has been lodged under Part I in respect of depreciation in the value of an interest in land the whole or a part of the land in which that interest subsists is compulsorily acquired, then if the depreciation is established but the compensation for the compulsory acquisition falls to be assessed without regard to the depreciation, the compensation for the acquisition is to be reduced by an amount equal to the compensation paid or payable on the Part I claim (section 8(6)). Finally, where a compensation entitlement under Part I is duplicated in other legislation, compensation will not be payable twice in respect of the same depreciation (section 8(7)).

Any question of disputed compensation under Part I is to be referred to and determined by the Lands Tribunal although no question arising out of a claim may be referred before the "first claim day" (section 16). Compensation will carry interest at the prescribed rate[42] from the date of service of the notice of claim or from the "first claim day," whichever is the later, until payment (section 18). The responsible authority will also pay, in addition to the compensation, any reasonable valuation and legal expenses incurred by the claimant in preparing and prosecuting the claim (section 3(5)).[43]   **16—52**

The provisions of Part I which are described above do not entirely close the gap as regards an injurious affection claim between a person who has had land acquired for the scheme and one who has not. The provisions of Part I appear to be coextensive with and a substitute for an action for nuisance.[44] "We are putting the public authority in the same position of liability," said the Minister for Local Government and Development during the committee stage of the Land Compensation Bill, "as is the private individual so far as permanent depreciation to the property is concerned. There is no justification for placing on the public authority a greater liability than the law places upon the private citizen."[45] Thus, no claim arises under Part I in respect of depreciation caused by loss of a view or loss of privacy. These are not among the factors listed in section 1(5)).[46]

---

[41] See Chap. 12.

[42] Prescribed under s.32 of the Land Compensation Act 1961.

[43] But without prejudice to the power of the Lands Tribunal in respect of the expenses of proceedings before the Tribunal by virtue of s.16 of the 1973 Act.

[44] Contrast the position as regards a claim for injurious affection in respect of land "held together with" land acquired for the public works (see para. 12–13).

[45] Standing Committee A, December 5, 1972, col. 16.

[46] And see *Shepherd and Shepherd v. Lancashire County Council* (1976) 33 P. & C.R. 296; and *Hickmott v. Dorset County Council* (1977) 35 P. & C.R. 195.

16—53   The provisions have also been criticised on other grounds. Denyer-Green,[47] for example, has drawn attention to the "severe limitation on the right to claim" which results from the requirement that the physical factors must be situated on or in the public works thus eliminating claims for depreciation resulting from an intensification in the use of existing roads feeding a new motorway unless an alteration has been made to the road to accommodate the greater intensity of use. As with planning blight the definition of interests qualifying for compensation excludes those with an interest in land, other than a dwelling, comprising a hereditament the annual value of which exceeds a prescribed amount. And the provision for setting-off betterment arising from the works operates, as Davies[48] points out, regardless of the fact that any increase in the value of some other owner's land goes scot-free if he does not happen to suffer depreciation.

There is no doubt that Part I seeks to strike a balance between compensating those who are most seriously affected by public works and containing the burden of compensation imposed on public authorities. Notwithstanding the criticisms voiced above, the provisions go a long way towards remedying the difficulty created by the distinction between injury arising from the construction of works and that from their use drawn by the House of Lords in *Brand* and *Hunter*.

Mitigation

16—54   In the introduction to this chapter we suggested that those likely to be injuriously affected by the bringing into use of a scheme of public works might prefer the injurious effect to be abated rather than receive compensation. The Urban Motorways Committee in their reports *New Roads in Towns*[49] recognised that much could be done during the design and implementation of major roads to alleviate the adverse effects of the use of such roads on neighbouring land. The Committee recommended that highway authorities should be given appropriate powers to mitigate the impact of roads on the environment of adjacent areas and to enable works to be carried out to fit highways more satisfactorily into their surroundings. They further recommended that highway authorities should be required to pay for sound insulation. In the White Paper *Development and Compensation — Putting People First*[50] the government accepted these recommendations, suggested that the same approach could be applied to other public works and announced their intention to introduce the necessary legislation. Provisions for mitigating the injurious

---

[47] B. Denyer-Green, *Compulsory Purchase and Compensation* (Estates Gazette Ltd, 2nd ed.) p. 255.
[48] K. Davies, "Injurious Affection" and the Land Compensation Act 1973" (1974) 90 L.Q.R. 361.
[49] HMSO, 1972.
[50] Cmnd. 5124 (1972).

effects of public works are contained in Part II of the 1973 Act as amended.[51] These are considered under three headings.

1. NOISE INSULATION

Section 20 deals with noise insulation. It enables the Secretary of State to make **16—55** regulations imposing a duty or conferring a power on responsible authorities to insulate buildings against noise caused or expected to be caused by the construction or use of public works.[52] Such regulations may also provide for the making of grants in respect of the cost of insulation. It should be remembered that, in assessing a claim for compensation under Part I of the 1973 Act, it will be assumed that any entitlement under section 20 has been exercised.[53]

The Noise Insulation Regulations 1975,[54] made under section 20, provide for **16—56** the insulation of buildings against noise caused or expected to be caused by traffic using new highways and certain altered highways. Regulation 3 imposes a *duty* on the appropriate highway authority to carry out sound insulation or to make a grant in respect of the cost of such insulation where the use of a highway to which the regulation applies causes or is expected to cause noise at a level not less than the specified level which affects an "eligible building." The regulation applies to new highways and existing highways for which an additional carriageway has been or is to be constructed. To qualify, the noise level, which is to be calculated in accordance with advice and instructions issued by the Minister, must be greater by at least 1dB(a) than the prevailing level immediately before works began and must be not less than the specified level (regulation 6). "Eligible buildings" comprise dwelling-houses and other buildings used for residential purposes which will be not more than 300 metres from the nearest point on the carriageway of the highway after its construction or alteration (regulation 7). The highway authority must prepare and publish a map or list identifying eligible building having a façade in respect of which the noise level is greater than the specified level. Provision is made for offer and acceptance of insulation work or grant, for establishing the nature and extent of the work to be undertaken and for determining the amount of grant (regulation 8).

Regulation 4 also gives the appropriate highway authority a *discretion* to carry **16—57** out insulation works or to make a grant in respect of noise caused or expected to be caused by alterations to an existing road and in other prescribed circumstances.

---

[51] The provisions in ss.22–25 of the 1973 Act were repealed and replaced by ss.246, 253, 272 and 282 of the Highways Act 1980.

[52] "Public works " and "responsible authority" in section 20 bear the same meaning as in s.1 of the 1973 Act except that "public works" does not include an aerodrome, and "responsible authority" in respect of a highway includes an authority empowered to make a traffic regulation order under ss.1 or 6 of the Road Traffic Regulation Act 1984.

[53] See para. 16–48.

[54] S.I. 1975 No. 1763, as amended by S.I. 1988 No. 2000.

The discretion could be exercised, for example, if the appropriate highway authority are subject to a duty under regulation 3 in respect of an eligible building, but not under a duty in respect of another eligible building and the façades of both building are contiguous or form part of a series of contiguous façades.

Similar power to that set out in section 20 of the 1973 Act is conferred on the Secretary of State by section 79 of the Civil Aviation Act 1982. If it appears to the Secretary of State that buildings near to an aerodrome designated by the minister require protection from noise and vibration attributable to the use of the aerodrome, he may make a scheme requiring the person for the time being managing the aerodrome to make grants towards the cost of insulating such buildings against noise. Such a scheme is limited to a particular aerodrome and its locality.

2. MITIGATING WORKS

16—58 Section 246 of the Highways Act 1980[55] enables a highway authority to acquire land, compulsorily or by agreement, for the purpose of mitigating any adverse effect which the existence or use of a road constructed or improved by them[56] (or proposed to be constructed or approved by them) will have on the surroundings of the road (section 246(1)). The authority may also acquire, but only by agreement, land the enjoyment of which is seriously affected by the construction or improvement of a road (section 246(2)(a)) or by the subsequent use of the road (section 246(2)(b)); the interest of the seller of such land must however fall within the definition of a "qualifying interest" for the purposes of the planning blight provisions.[57] The powers under section 246(1) and (2)(a) may not be exercised unless the acquisition is begun before the date on which the road, or the improved road, as the case may be, is opened to public traffic, and the powers conferred by subsection (2)(b) may not be exercised unless the acquisition is begun before the end of one year after the date (section 246(3)).[58] These powers were extended by s.62(2) of the Planning and Compensation Act 1991 to enable the highway authority to acquire land by agreement if the enjoyment of the land will, in their opinion, be seriously affected by the carrying out of works for construction or improvement of a proposed highway on blighted land. This enables voluntary acquisitions to be made from the date of announcement of the scheme.

---

[55] ss.246, 253, 272 and 282 of the Highways Act 1980 replaced ss.22–25 of the 1973 Act (which were repealed by s.343(3) of the Sched. 25 to the 1980 Act.

[56] References to the construction or improvement of a road in sections 246 of the 1980 Act include references to the construction or improvement of a road under an order made under sections 14 or 18 of that Act (s.246(7)).

[57] The reference to the date of service of a notice under section 150 of the 1990 Act is to be taken as a reference to the date on which a purchase agreement is made under s.246(2) of the 1980 Act.

[58] The circumstances in which an acquisition is to be treated as begun for the purposes of s.246(3) are defined in subs. (4).

Section 282 of the 1980 Act empowers a highway authority to carry out on land acquired under section 246 or on other land belonging to them[59] works for mitigating any adverse effect which the construction, improvement, existence or use of any highway has or will have on its surroundings. These works may include the planting of trees, shrubs, or plants and the laying out of any area as grassland (section 282(2)). The authority may also develop or redevelop such land for the purpose of improving the surroundings.

A highway authority may also negotiate an agreement with any person having **16—59** an interest in land adjoining or in the vicinity of a highway or proposed highway, with a view to restricting or regulating the use of the land permanently or for a specified period so as to mitigate the adverse effect generated by the construction, improvement, existence or use of such highway. The agreement may provide for the planting and maintenance of trees, shrubs or plants and for restricting the lopping or removal of trees, shrubs or plants. Any such agreement will be enforceable not only against the person who made it, but also against any person deriving title from him. An agreement under this provision constitutes a local land charge and should therefore be registered in the local land charges register pursuant to the Local Land Charges Act 1975 (section 253(3) and (4)).

Somewhat similar powers to acquire land by agreement and to carry out works for the purpose of mitigating the adverse effects of public works on their surroundings are conferred on the "responsible authority"[60] by sections 26 and 27 of the 1973 Act.

3. EXPENSES OF TEMPORARY REMOVAL

A highway authority, in respect of the construction and improvement of a road, **16—60** and a "responsible authority" in respect of the construction or alteration of other public works, are empowered to pay the reasonable expenses of the occupier of a dwelling adjacent to the works who is required temporarily to find and move to suitable alternative accommodation because the carrying out of the works affects the enjoyment of the dwelling to such an extent that continued occupation is not reasonably practicable (section 28 of the 1973 Act). No payment can be made, however, unless an agreement has been made with the occupier before the expenses are incurred. Expenses can only be paid under this provision to the extent that they exceed the expenses that would have been incurred had the dwelling continued to be occupied.

---

[59] Such works may be carried out by the highway authority on a highway for which they are the highway authority and on a highway which they have been authorised to improve or construct by an order under ss.14 or 18 of the 1980 Act (s.282(1)(c) and (d))

[60] "Public works" and "responsible authority" are defined by s.26(6) by reference to ss.1 of the 1973 Act except that "Public works" does not include a highway or any works forming part of a statutory undertaking as defined in s.336(1) of the 1990 Act.

Index

Acquisition
extinguishment
order, 2–32—2–33
Advance payment
agreed compensation, in excess of,
13–41
amount of, 13–40
entitlement to, 13–40
home loss payment, 13–41
interest on, 13–45
local land charges register, entry in,
13–41
mortgage, land subject to, 13–40
payment of, 13–41
possession, prior to taking of,
13–41
request for, 13–40
supplementary payment, 13–41
Agreement
acquisition, by
farm loss payment on, 13–32
home loss payment on, 13–12
valuation date, 6–10
Agricultural holding
compensation, assessment of, 6–20,
13–04
disturbance, 13–05, 13–35
injurious affection, 13–05, 13–33,
13–35, 13–37
landlord
compensation, entitlement to,
13–33—13–34

Agricultural holding—*cont.*
notice to quit
compensation, effect upon, 13–
04, 13–34
severance 13–05, 13–33, 13–35
short tenancy, 13–04
tenant
compensation, entitlement to
notice of entry, following
allowance by incoming tenant,
13–37
farm loss payment, 13–38
home loss payment, 13–38
injurious affection, 13–37
loss or injury, 13–37
reorganisation payment, 6–
20, 13–37—13–38
severance, 13–37
value of unexpired term or
interest, 13–36
notice to quit, following
disturbance, 13–35
compensation, entitlement to,
notice to quit, following,
election, right of, 13–38—
13–39
compensation, entitlement to
notice to quit, following
injurious affection, 13–35
part of holding, 13–35, 13–
39
rent, abatement of, 13–35

336